D1190800

ALL ABOUT
GREENHOUSES
—with 15 build-your-own plans

DEDICATED
TO
MY SISTERS

Annette Galman Williams
Silvia Galman Bonebrake
Maureen Louise Galman Klein

If we could first know where we are, and wither we are tending we could better judge to do and how to do it

... Abe Lincoln

I pass from relief
from the turning serf
of Cause and Theory to the
firm ground of Result and Fact

... Winston Churchill

No. 1302
$19.95

ALL ABOUT
GREENHOUSES
with 15 build-your-own plans

— BY BETTE GALMAN WAHLFELDT

TAB **TAB BOOKS Inc.**

BLUE RIDGE SUMMIT, PA. 17214

FIRST EDITION

FIRST PRINTING

Copyright © 1981 by TAB BOOKS Inc.

Printed in the United States of America

Library of Congress Cataloging in Publication Data

Wahlfeldt, Bette G. (Bette Galman)
    All about greenhouses.

    Includes index.
    1. Greenhouses—Design and construction. 2. Greenhouse gardening. 3. Garden structures—Design and construction. I. Title.
SB415.W27   690'.892   81-9158
ISBN 0-8306-0033-7   AACR2
ISBN 0-8306-1302-1 (pbk.)

Photos on Covers 1 & 4 Courtesy of Lord & Burnham, Irvington, NY 10533

Contents

Acknowledgments

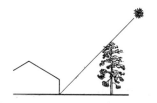

Sincere appreciation is extended to those individuals and organizations who provided information during my research for this work.

Helen M. Sullivan, advertising public relations, Costitch and McConnell, advertising specialists for Lord & Burnham, Irvington, New York: Margaret E. Lee, marketing services coordinator, Lord & Burnham, Irvington, New York. Harold E. Gray, president, National Greenhouse Company, Pana, Illinois. Frank G. Fink, Jr. Greenhouse Specialities Company. Evert R. Thompson, advertising architects for Peter Reimuller and the Peter Reimuller Greenhouse Company, Pacific Grove, California. Anne P. Carney, director communications, Materials Department, Portland Cement Association, Joel Davidson, solar energy supervisor, Albert Skiles, Solcar counselor, William E. Smith, Human Concern, and Barry Weaver, Ed Jeffords and Mary Jo Rose, Ozark Institute without whose help the solar section could not have been included.

To those in the Department of the Florida Extension Service, Gainesville, Florida, especially Benny Tjia who "says it with flowers." Henry A. Fully, Escambia County, Pensacola, Florida, who got me started on my research. Jim Cronley, president, Cronley construction who gave me precious time with interviews helping me understand the facts about building and then allowing me to interview, on the job, Master Mason Andry (Andy) Jackson who attempted to impart 30 years of bricklaying know-how from time from his busy work schedule to answer innumerable questions regarding his trade. Andy Capp, Pensacola Brick Company, Pensacola, Florida, who taught me "a bit" about bricks and blocks

7

and helped me lay out the specific "common designs" for the do-it-yourselfer.

Kathleen Bourke for the beautiful line drawings; and many listings taken from the *Handbook For Greenhouse Gardeners* edited by Elvin McDonald, Published by Lord & Burnham which saved me unaccountable hours of additional work in order to bring to you, the home greenhouser, needed information for the joy of operating and owning a home greenhouse.

To my many friends in Pensacola, Florida who allowed me to visit their home greenhouses, free-standing, lean-tos, add-on's large and small.

Without all of these people this book could not have come to be.

SPECIAL THANKS. The author sincerely thanks the following organizations who have so unselfishly allowed me to use their basic plans and, when needed, literature for adaptation to those who have the desire to "build your own" greenhouse.

Greenhouse Specialties Company, St. Louis, Missouri.

Lord & Burnham, Irvington, New York.

National Greenhouse Company, Pana, Illinois.

Peter Reimuller—The Greenhouseman, Pacific Grove, California.

Ozark Institute and the Office of Human Concern for their help with the solar section.

Foreword

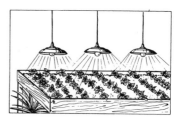

Years ago, older homes had attached glass rooms which were called conservatories. They had glass roofs and sides and drew their heat from the inside of the home.

Today we call them greenhouses. In the past, only the wealthy owned the type home which had a conservatory. Now it is within the financial scope of most to have a home greenhouse. While the cost of energy for the home greenhouse has become a major and understandably grave concern, don't let it deter your decision to get into greenhousing. You can, with a bit of planning and foresight, get your investment back in a relative short time. Consider some of the facts.

The expense of buying plants and table vegetables, even cut flowers, at local nurseries and supermarkets is climbing even more rapidly than energy costs. The retailers must pass their energy costs, plus overhead margins, to their customers—to say nothing of the flavor and nutrition of vegetables raised in the greenhouse.

Plants purchased at a nursery, and planted directly in the garden, are many times more expensive than plants started from seed in the greenhouse and then transplanted to the garden when weather permits.

No, you don't have to use your greenhouse the year around but you can still save on food costs. Many people who live in areas that are extremely cold in winter use their greenhouse only nine or 10 months of the year and still obtain a healthy savings over not owning a greenhouse.

The very special people who are greenhouse enthusiasts with even the smallest model want not only self-sufficiency in growing vegetables for themselves and families, but they also want flowers and plants to brighten homes and gardens. It satisfies your basic need to grow things. It provides you the pleasure of watching your efforts result in bountiful plant life. From miniature cacti to orchids, herbs for drying to truly fresh lettuce and tomatoes, and the many other vegetables which you can raise year around—if you desire—the greenhouse is for fun and profit.

In today's society with more leisure time available, greenhousing is becoming an increasingly popular hobby. It enables the flower enthusiast to create his or her own season and it allows you to create exactly the natural environment of temperature and moisture control—a requirement for all plants. In cold climates, owning a greenhouse has additional advantages because it makes a 12 month growing season possible. Not only does it enable you to store potted plants during the cold months, propagate your favorite ornamentals, raise early garden seedlings for vegetable and flower garden, raise plants without regard to their natural habitat, a home greenhouse provides additional value to your real estate—your home.

For the home gardener, the special needs are to have a greenhouse that can be operated economically; one that can be controlled mechanically—if necessary—to protect plants during the working day or when the family is off on vacation. Flowering ornamental, vegetable, even berries, tropicals and desert loving varieties can be grown in a greenhouse at the same time. Having a home greenhouse for fun and profit should be:

- ☐ Within your financial means.
- ☐ Within your capacity in terms of constructing the unit.
- ☐ Designed to fit the space you have available.
- ☐ Geared for economical operation.
- ☐ Able to be maintained in your time.

No matter what type of greenhouse you build—lean-to, free-standing, glass, fiberglass, plastic covered—just walk into the warmth and beauty of your greenhouse on a cold day and breathe deeply the earthy lifeness of the air and touch the rich foliage. That's when you will know what "greenhousing" is really about.

Whether you prefer to call them conservatories or greenhouses, stating it simply: a greenhouse is any building or a section of a building—such as a lean-to provides—which receives an ample amount of sunlight and/or light hours in order to store or raise plants.

One of the most satisfying things about greenhouse gardening is its therapeutic value. Age has no boundaries inside the greenhouse. Only a few minutes in its environs finds taut nerves loosening as one captures the inner exhilarations as it gives pleasure and contentment that goes with living close to nature.

Bette Galman Wahlfeldt

Chapter 1
Introduction

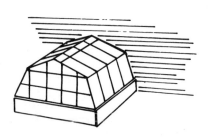

Several greenhouse designs have become standards for the home greenhouseman. These are the window box appearing as a bay window—considered excellent for a miniature solar house—the lean-to—an enclosure attached to the side of the home, garage, or outbuilding (Figs. 1-1A and 1-1B), and the most serviceable—the free-standing model (Fig. 1-2)—which can be accommodated on even the smallest city lot.

For those who plan to "design" and "build" your greenhouse from scratch, there are a few major points to remember.

GREENHOUSE WIDTH

Determine the width of your greenhouse by adding the width of the plant benches and the walks. Allow approximately 6 inches for walls at either side and 2 inches for an air circulation space between the side walls and the benches.

Side benches are serviced from only one side and should be no wider than you can reach across. For some people, this will be 2 feet and for others perhaps as much as 3 feet.

Center benches are services from both sides and can be as wide as 6 feet. They should be no wider than to permit you to work comfortably.

Determine the width of the walks in your greenhouse by how they are to be used. If the walks will be used only as a place to stand while servicing the benches, an 18-inch or 19-inch walk is sufficiently wide. If a wheelbarrow is to be brought into the greenhouse, the width must be greater. Wide walks, 23" to 30" will

Fig. 1-1A. Glass lean-to attached to a garage.

allow easy passage for visitors who might not be used to walking between rows of plants.

GREENHOUSE LENGTH

Determine the length of your greenhouse by multiplying the number of plants you can grow across the benches by the number of plants you want to grow. Then, round off the measurement so that—in the case of glass constructed greenhouses—there will be no need to cut glass to fill odd sash bar spacing. The sash bar is a shaped wooden, or metal, bar used in the construction of a sash or frame, and designed to support and hold the glass structure to it. Standard glass sizes are 16″ × 24″, 18″ × 20″, and 20″ × 20″. Larger glass sizes means fewer sash bars and less shadow inside the greenhouse.

Most plastics are available in 100-foot lengths. When you figure the length of a glass greenhouse, allow for the width of the projecting part of each sash bar plus a fraction of an inch clearance. For plastics, allow an extra 24″ to fasten the plastic properly.

GREENHOUSE HEIGHT

The height of the greenhouse depends on the desired height to the eaves. An eave height of 5 feet is satisfactory for side benches

Fig. 1-1B. Glass lean-to (courtesy of Lord & Burnham).

13

with low growing plants. If you want to grow tall plants, however, you will want an eave height of 6 to 7 feet.

The pitch of the roof should be 6 in 12 (approximately 27 degrees). The eave height is the distance from the side wall to the center of the greenhouse. The roof pitch will determine the height of your greenhouse at the center. The height of the greenhouse should be equal to the eave height plus one-fourth inch of the width of the greenhouse.

For instance, in an even span greenhouse 18 feet wide, the distance from the side wall to the center of the greenhouse is 9 feet. The difference in height between the center of the greenhouse and eaves will be one-half of 9 feet, or 4½ feet. If the eave is 5 feet high, the greenhouse should be 9½ feet at the center.

Prior to construction:

☐ Select a site protected from winter winds by trees, a wall or a building.

☐ The ground should be reasonably level to simplify foundation work.

☐ Summer shade from maples, oaks or other deciduous trees is good; it will minimize the amount of shading and cooling required if you plan to operate your greenhouse through the summer.

☐ Avoid shade from trees that do not shed their leaves in winter.

☐ Try not to install an attached even span or lean-to below a building roof that lets snow accumulate to slide onto the greenhouse. Otherwise you will have to stretch a snow guard of one-fourth inch mesh hardware cloth over the greenhouse roof.

DESIGNS

The various common shapes and advantages or special features of each type are outlined below. All are acceptable if properly designed and erected. The choice is yours.

Quonset. Quonset greenhouses (Fig. 1-3) have the same general shape as the Quonset huts of World War II. They have simple and efficient construction using thin-wall electrical conduit for houses up to 10 to 12 feet wide or galvanized steel pipe commercially formed for wider houses up to 36 or 40 feet. They are primarily constructed using plastic covering which is applied externally. Strong fastening at the ends and edges is very important. Various types of extruded metal bars with rod inserts and screw-down clamps are available. Double-layer plastic is recommended for covering.

Fig. 1-2. Free-standing glass model (courtesy of National Greenhouse Company).

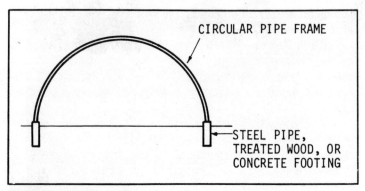

Fig. 1-3. Quonset frame detail.

This type greenhouse provides clear-span interior with minimum shading but has some sidewall height restriction on tall crops unless higher foundations are used. This would also significantly increase the strength required and the potential for wind damage. Usually, this style will require extra wooden construction for ends, doors, fan-shutter-louver framing, etc. The endwall covering can be the same as the rest of the structure.

Gothic. This style (Fig. 1-4) is fabricated by bending pipe or lamenating wood strips in a Gothic shape to provide a most aesthetic appearance. The Gothic style provides excellent height near the sidewalls. It allows more heat loss than other designs because it has a greater exposed surface-to-ground area ratio. Good air circulation in this style is important in order to prevent air and heat stratification in the gable. The extra volume allows

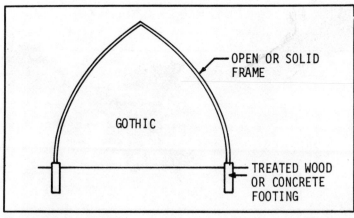

Fig. 1-4. Gothic frame detail.

sufficient space for mixing ventilation or heated air with greenhouse air.

Rigid Frame. This is the most commonly used design for home greenhouses and provides high strength per unit of wood used in widths up to 40 feet (Fig. 1-5). It provides an unobstructed clear-span interior and is easy to cover with film or rigid plastic materials.

The rigid frame construction has excellent strength which permits a relatively small number and size of wood or metal members to be used resulting in minimum shading. While foundations are not always necessary, when needed, the proper foundation piers or concrete wall for adequate support of large lateral loads should be considered in locations which have extra high winds and heavy snows.

SLOPE OF ROOF

The roof slope affects the runoff of condensed water from the ceiling. Slopes of 28 degrees are considered minimal if runoff without severe dripping is to occur. With lower slopes, runoff is restricted and dripping is a serious problem. Drops occur more readily on plastic than on glass and, therefore, even greater slopes are desirable for the most commonly used plastic coverings.

WHICH TO CHOOSE?

Free-standing, lean-to, window box; glass, vinyl plastic, fiberglass, build from scratch or buy a prefab, the type you choose will depend upon your needs. If you want only to enjoy a few potted plants of low growing nature, raise a few annuals—vegetables and flowers—from seed, the miniature window box variety or the small Quonset style will suit your needs well. But for most greenhouse

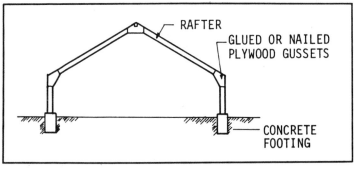

Fig. 1-5. Rigid frame detail.

Fig. 1-6. A 12' Pearl-Mist greenhouse (courtesy of Peter Reimuller).

enthusiasts, the larger lean-to has a greater advantage because it enables you to make the greenhouse a part of your home as a live-in plant area—a conservatory. By far the most efficient, however, is the free standing model.

Some Basic Facts

A free-standing greenhouse (Fig. 1-6) can be installed anywhere that is convenient to provide the most attractive appearance in your garden. A lean-to or attached, even-span greenhouse (Fig. 1-7) requires more care in selecting an appropriate site.

Plant growth takes place most rapidly in the morning. The ideal location should let the greenhouse face morning sun in the winter.

In a greenhouse with roof sash, it isn't necessary to orient the ridge line in any particular direction. However, if you purchase automatic roof vent equipment, install it to operate the sash on the side away from the prevailing winter wind.

In a fan-ventilated greenhouse, it is best to face the structure with the ridge parallel to prevailing summer wind; install the fan in the downwind end.

Fig. 1-7. Glass to ground lean-to (courtesy of National Greenhouse Company).

When planning an attached greenhouse, make sure it doesn't interfere with anything on the face of the building to which it will be attached: doors, windows, a chimney, or the roof line of a one-story building. Cut a stick to the height of the greenhouse ridge and hold the stick up against the building where the greenhouse will be installed. This way you can determine if any obstructions exist and how they can be overcome.

If the ridge is too high, you can lower the greenhouse foundation and excavate inside for headroom. Or you can increase the height of the greenhouse foundation to raise the ridge over existing doors or windows. If a chimney is in the way, the depth of a lean-to can be extended with a "deck" of locally purchased lumber to build around the obstruction (Fig. 1-8 and 1-9).

If a really tricky installation seems likely, it's best to draw the outline of the greenhouse on the building face with chalk or to construct a framework outline of the greenhouse using 1″ × 2″ lumber to hold against the building to determine the exact place the greenhouse can be located. (Fig. 1-10).

In certain instances, it will be necessary to build a frame against a building for your lean-to (Fig. 1-11). Figure 1-12 shows the placement of extrusions for gable extension. If a door is installed in the gable next to the building, use a standard masonry opening. If a door is installed in the center of a gable, provide a 3′ 1″ masonry opening.

If a workroom or potting shed is to be attached to the greenhouse, it should be located at the north or west end to provide protection for the greenhouse from cold winter winds.

Minimum Size

Regardless of which style you choose to build, a good minimum size would be a 7 x 12. A too small greenhouse would be difficult in which to maintain as close as possible natural temperature and salubric atmospheric conditions. Even during the winter when the days are sunny, the temperature in a 5 x 7 can quickly rise in excess of 100 degrees and when the sun goes down the temperature cools equally as rapidly. Plants will not grow under such adverse conditions. The larger the house the greater volume of air is contained and a more even temperature provides simple and good ventilation and it is more easily maintained.

In lean-to greenhouses, you will want to take advantage of all of the limited amount of space, every inch of it can be put to good use by using benches, ledges, shelves and hangers (Fig. 1-13). A

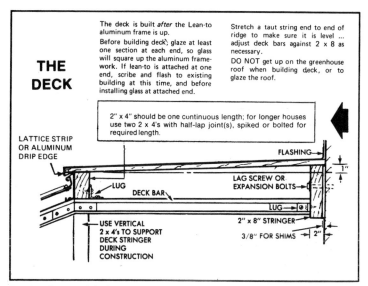

THE DECK

The deck is built *after* the Lean-to aluminum frame is up.

Before building deck, glaze at least one section at each end, so glass will square up the aluminum framework. If lean-to is attached at one end, scribe and flash to existing building at this time, and before installing glass at attached end.

Stretch a taut string end to end of ridge to make sure it is level ... adjust deck bars against 2 x 8 as necessary.

DO NOT get up on the greenhouse roof when building deck, or to glaze the roof.

2" x 4" should be one continuous length; for longer houses use two 2 x 4's with half-lap joint(s), spiked or bolted for required length.

LATTICE STRIP OR ALUMINUM DRIP EDGE

FLASHING

LAG SCREW OR EXPANSION BOLTS

LUG

DECK BAR

LUG

USE VERTICAL 2 x 4's TO SUPPORT DECK STRINGER DURING CONSTRUCTION

2" x 8" STRINGER

3/8" FOR SHIMS

2"

1"

Fig. 1-8. Details of deck extension (courtesy of Lord & Burnham).

straight-sided greenhouse will provide not only additional space, but make it possible for you to use or raise or store taller plants closer to the glass, plastic or fiberglass.

Watch for plant burning even during cold winter months. This is especially true for plants that have been stored. Even during the coldest period, the sun coming in through the covering can reach very high temperatures. Another redeeming factor of the straight-sided greenhouse is the shelves which provide better insulation (thus easier, important temperature control).

There are many greenhouse companies with perfected prefabricated greenhouses—such as the plans which follow in the construction portion of this book—which are ideal for the home greenhouseman. All of the materials are premeasured and precut saving much time and labor. Whether you plan to cut and measure your own lumber or purchase prefabricated materials, construction is the same.

LOCATION OF GREENHOUSE

A window box or lean-to should be constructed against the south side of the house or garage and, wherever possible, at a corner angle to obtain exposure to the southwest unless you live in areas where the temperatures are extremely hot and dry where an eastern (northwest) exposure will provide sufficient cooling.

SECTION THRU DECK AT GABLE RAFTER

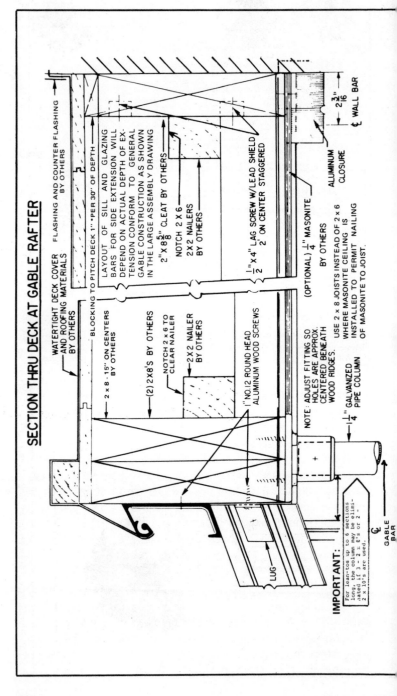

WATERTIGHT DECK COVER AND ROOFING MATERIALS BY OTHERS

FLASHING AND COUNTER FLASHING BY OTHERS

BLOCKING TO PITCH DECK 1" PER 30' OF DEPTH

LAYOUT OF SILL AND GLAZING BARS FOR SIDE EXTENSION WILL DEPEND ON ACTUAL DEPTH OF EXTENSION CONFORM TO GENERAL GABLE CONSTRUCTION AS SHOWN IN THE LARGE ASSEMBLY DRAWING

2" x 8⅝" CLEAT BY OTHERS

NOTCH 2 x 6
2X2 NAILERS BY OTHERS

½" x 4" LAG SCREW W/LEAD SHIELD 2' ON CENTER STAGGERED

2 3/16" WALL BAR

₵ WALL BAR

ALUMINUM CLOSURE

(OPTIONAL) ¼" MASONITE BY OTHERS

2 x 8 - 15" ON CENTERS BY OTHERS

(2) 2x8'S BY OTHERS

NOTCH 2 x 6 TO CLEAR NAILER

2X2 NAILER BY OTHERS

1" NO.12 ROUND HEAD ALUMINUM WOOD SCREWS

NOTE: ADJUST FITTING SO HOLES ARE APPROX. CENTERED BENEATH WOOD RIDGES.

USE 2 x 8 JOISTS INSTEAD OF 2 x 6 WHERE MASONITE CEILING IS INSTALLED TO PERMIT NAILING OF MASONITE TO JOIST.

1¼" GALVANIZED PIPE COLUMN

LUG

₵ GABLE BAR

IMPORTANT: For lean-tos up to 6 sections long, the column may be eliminated if 3 - 2 x 8's or 2 - 2 x 10's are used.

22

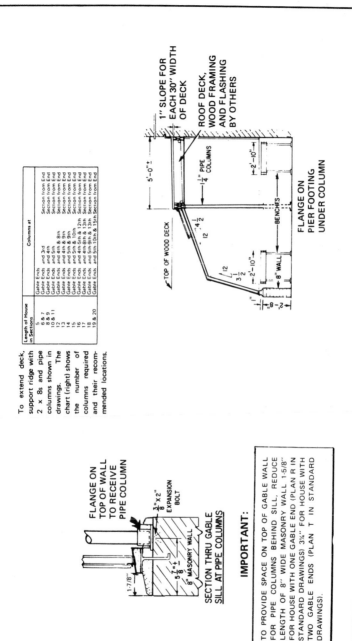

To extend deck, support ridge with 2 x 8s and pipe columns shown in drawings. The chart (right) shows the number of columns required and their recommended locations.

Length of House in Sections	Columns at	
5	Gable Ends	and 3rd Section from End
6 & 7	Gable Ends	and 4th Section from End
8 & 9	Gable Ends	and 5th Section from End
10 & 11	Gable Ends	and 5th Section from End
12	Gable Ends	and 4th & 8th Section from End
13	Gable Ends	and 4th & 9th Section from End
14	Gable Ends	and 5th & 9th Section from End
15	Gable Ends	and 5th & 10th Section from End
16	Gable Ends	and 4th-5th & 12th Section from End
17	Gable Ends	and 4th-8th & 13th Section from End
18	Gable Ends	and 5th-9th & 13th Section from End
19 & 20	Gable Ends	and 5th-10th & 15th Section from End

1" SLOPE FOR EACH 30" WIDTH OF DECK

ROOF DECK, WOOD FRAMING AND FLASHING BY OTHERS

TOP OF WOOD DECK

1" PIPE COLUMNS

5'-0"±

2'-10"

BENCHES

8" WALL

2'-10"

FLANGE ON PIER FOOTING UNDER COLUMN

4 ½ / 12

3 ½ / 12

1"

2'-8"

FLANGE ON TOP OF WALL TO RECEIVE PIPE COLUMN

3/8" x 2" EXPANSION BOLT

5 ⅞"±

8" MASONRY WALL

1-7/8"

SECTION THRU GABLE SILL AT PIPE COLUMNS

IMPORTANT:

TO PROVIDE SPACE ON TOP OF GABLE WALL FOR PIPE COLUMNS BEHIND SILL, REDUCE LENGTH OF 8" WIDE MASONRY WALL 1-5/8" FOR HOUSE WITH ONE GABLE END (PLAN R IN STANDARD DRAWINGS) 3¼" FOR HOUSE WITH TWO GABLE ENDS (PLAN T IN STANDARD DRAWINGS).

Fig. 1-9. Suggested details for lean-to deck (courtesy of Lord & Burnham).

23

The free-standing structure should be built on a line running northeast or southwest if you live in cold climates. Living further south enables you to sit it in any direction and makes an ideal "complementary" structure to the patio area.

Sunlight provides energy for plant growth and is generally the limiting factor in greenhouses. When planning the construction, primary consideration should be given to obtain maximum sunlight exposure during the "short" days of midwinter when the sun is lowest in the sky. Maximum sun altitude occurs at noon and varies from a high in June to a low in December. At noon the sun is located due to south. This means that the building site should, preferably, have an open southern exposure.

Avoid constructing the greenhouse near large trees, buildings or other obstructions which will shade it. Figure 1-14 indicates the ratio of shadow length and height obstruction for selected altitudes. To determine how far an obstruction must be to prevent casting a shadow on the greenhouse, multiply the ratios indicated by the obstruction height. As a general rule, no objects taller than 10 feet should be within 27 feet of the greenhouse in either the east, west or south direction. Even objects of this height cast long shadows in the early morning when the sun is particularly low in the sky.

DRAINAGE

A well drained level site should be selected to reduce problems with salt buildup and insufficient soil aeration. A high water table can result in saturation of the soil and prohibit effective use of the greenhouse. Ground water that might flow into the house might carry soil diseases. If necessary, drain tile should be used in the area of construction (Fig. 1-15).

If you plan ground beds in your greenhouse, they should be almost level because sloping beds in any direction will cause water to concentrate in the low areas and accentuate any problems of poor drainage. Also, slopes inside the greenhouse allow hot air to rise and cold air to settle. This causes environmental difficulties. A greenhouse in a low, damp area could be subject to higher humidities and dampness (causing excessive leaf mold, diseases, etc.).

STRENGTH OF GREENHOUSE

While the home greenhouseman is not usually overly concerned with damage from inclement weather conditions, regard-

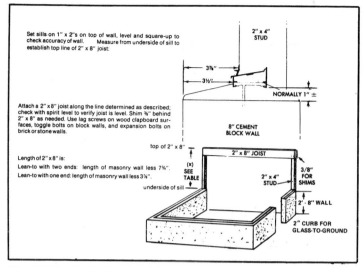

Fig. 1-10. Framing for lean-to details (courtesy of Lord & Burnham).

less of the region in which you live you can suffer from excessive winds or sleet and snow. It is well to understand how wind can affect the greenhouse because it is one of the conditions that most often occurs and it could have a bearing on the construction of the particular greenhouse you select.

For most sections of the United States, high winds from time to time are not uncommon. A wind blowing at 80 mph develops a maximum possible pressure of 16.4 pounds per square feet on a flat surface perpendicular to the wind. However, the actual wind load on buildings are not this severe due to the height adjustment made in construction.

Wind speeds are measured and reported by the U.S. Weather Bureau for heights of 30 feet above the ground. The wind is less intense closer to the ground. The wind velocity reduction from 30 feet above ground to the ground surface is shown in Fig. 1-16. The pressure developed by the wind is related to the square of the wind velocity. The wind pressure reduces more rapidly than the wind velocity as the ground surface is approached.

As indicated in Fig. 1-16, the pressure and wind velocity at 15 feet are approximately 85 percent and 90 percent, respectively, of that at 30 feet. At 10 feet, the values are 73 percent and 85 percent respectively. The height of the building will, therefore, affect the wind load. The effective height of a building is defined as the distance above the ground at which the wind force acts.

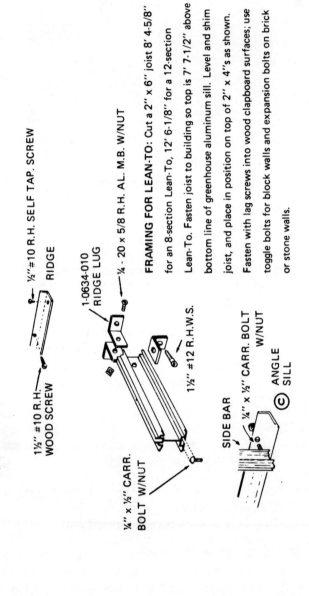

½" #10 R.H. SELF TAP. SCREW

RIDGE

½" #10 R.H. WOOD SCREW

1-0634-010 RIDGE LUG

¼ - 20 x 5/8 R.H. AL. M.B. W/NUT

1½" #12 R.H.W.S.

¼" x ½" CARR. BOLT W/NUT

SIDE BAR

¼" x ½" CARR. BOLT W/NUT

ANGLE SILL

C

FRAMING FOR LEAN-TO: Cut a 2" x 6" joist 8' 4-5/8" for an 8-section Lean-To, 12' 6-1/8" for a 12-section Lean-To. Fasten joist to building so top is 7' 7-1/2" above bottom line of greenhouse aluminum sill. Level and shim joist, and place in position on top of 2" x 4"s as shown. Fasten with lag screws into wood clapboard surfaces; use toggle bolts for block walls and expansion bolts on brick or stone walls.

26

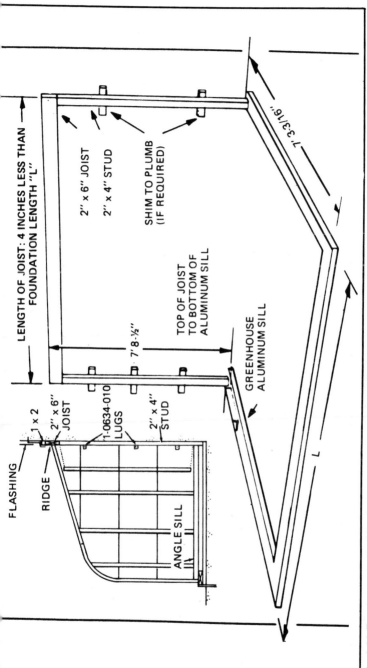

FLASHING

1 x 2

RIDGE

2" x 6" JOIST

1-0634-010 LUGS

2" x 4" STUD

ANGLE SILL

LENGTH OF JOIST: 4 INCHES LESS THAN FOUNDATION LENGTH "L"

2" x 6" JOIST

2" x 4" STUD

SHIM TO PLUMB (IF REQUIRED)

TOP OF JOIST TO BOTTOM OF ALUMINUM SILL

GREENHOUSE ALUMINUM SILL

7' 8-½"

7' 3-1/16"

L

L

Fig. 1-11. Framing against building for lean-to (courtesy of Lord & Burnham).

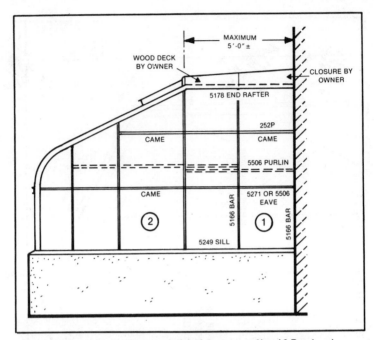

Fig. 1-12. Typical gable with extended deck (courtesy of Lord & Burnham).

MAXIMUM LIGHT TRANSMISSION (COVERINGS)

During much of the off-season production period, light becomes the limiting factor. Therefore, everything that can be

Fig. 1-13. Rods attached to purlins on which to hand plants (courtesy of John Walfeldt).

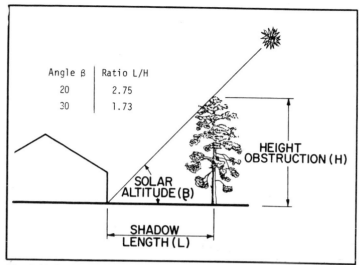

Angle β	Ratio L/H
20	2.75
30	1.73

SOLAR ALTITUDE (β)

HEIGHT OBSTRUCTION (H)

SHADOW LENGTH (L)

Fig. 1-14. Ratio of shadow, length and obstruction height for selected solar altitudes.

done to obtain maximum light intensity within the greenhouse should be accomplished. Therefore, the greenhouse ridge should run north and south in the southern parts of the United States.

Another means of obtaining maximum light transmission is to minimize the number and size of structural members in the roof area plus using highly transparent glazing material. Wide span glass is most permanent, most efficient but also most expensive. For the home greenhouse, the less expensive plastics and fiberglass are most widely used and highly recommended.

Glass is the covering for the small window box and lean-to which becomes a part of the home. Free-standing models provides more of an individual choice: vinyl plastic, polyethelene, fiberglass or glass. Four to six mil ultraviolet vinyl plastic and polyethelene

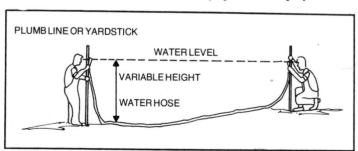

PLUMB LINE OR YARDSTICK

WATER LEVEL

VARIABLE HEIGHT

WATER HOSE

Fig. 1-15. Determining level of drainage.

29

are easy to apply to both metal and wooden framed houses simply by stapling the material to the frame after it has been stretched taut across the structure.

However, while the use of these materials will initially save you money, hot summer sun, heavy rains and other inclement weather conditions will ruin it and necessitate recovering the entire structure at least every two to four years. It is, therefore, recommended that a more permanent covering, such as the popular fiberglass, be used.

For the past 30 years, tests carried out on fiberglass have shown that of all the rigid materials used in greenhouse construction, fiberglass is the most popular not only for its durability but for its ease in storage and its light weight. Available in smooth or corrugated panels, the weight most commonly used to cover greenhouses is 8 ounces per square foot.

Because fiberglass is manufactured in many different colors, only the clear or white should be purchased for use in covering your greenhouse. Materials come in standard sizes; you are able to plan ahead as to cost and size of the sheets with which you will cover the greenhouse. For example, sheets measuring 51½ inches will be installed on rafter spaces of 48 inches on the center while 38-inch sheets will be installed on rafter space of 3′ 9″ on center. Any deviation of width or length is easily corrected by using a sharp handsaw to cut any overage.

The major advantage in using fiberglass, or any other rigid material, is that as light passes through these materials it is diffused. The result is an even light intensity throughout the house.

SUCCESSFUL STRUCTURAL DESIGNS

The ultimate success of a greenhouse will depend upon the ability of the greenhouseman to control the environmental conditions within. Therefore, the structural influence on heating and ventilation needs to be considered. While any shape can be successfully heated and ventilated, some designs greatly increase the difficulty or cost.

In greenhouses used this year around, the solar intensity during the winter will often become sufficiently intense enough to require ventilation even when outside temperatures are near freezing. If this air is brought into the house and directed on the plants without first intermixing with the air within the greenhouse, growth will be hurt. Similarly, if hot air from heating units is allowed to come in direct contact with the plants, rapid drying and poor growth will also occur.

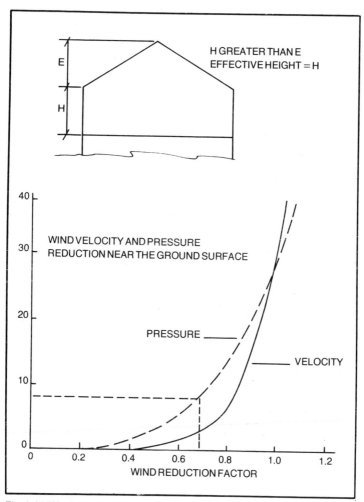

Fig. 1-16. Wind reduction factor diagram.

Attempts must be made to mix ventilation or heating air with the greenhouse air in the space above the plants. In bedding plants and other low crop production, adequate space exists within even low profile houses to effectively achieve this mixing above the plants and crops. However, with tall crops on benches, adequate space might not be available. This is particularly true in narrow houses where the rise from the eaves to the peak is small. An important factor in the cost of heating is the amount of exposed wall or ceiling area. Any heat added to a greenhouse remains in the house until it passes through the covering material.

31

FOUNDATIONS AND SILLS

The earth covering the continental United States consists of loam, sandy loam, sand shale, mud and mud loam with varying degrees of shifting. Your choice of foundation will depend on your geographic location, climatic conditions, and the use of a lean-to, or free-standing structure. A poured concrete foundation can be used, but it is expense and usually not deemed warranted for the home greenhouse. It is, however, recommended that a foundation of from 8 inches to 24 inches be installed regardless of where you live because it will provide a more permanent and solid structure.

Foundation

If post construction is used, where the main sidewall members are set directly into the ground and where the soil around the post is intended to prevent overturning, depths deeper than 18 inches are recommended. The most common failure of greenhouse construction in this manner is the tipping of sidewalls within a subsequent dropping of the ridge line and a weakening of the rafter-to-eave plate joint. The filling of post holes with concrete is helpful, but it is no substitute for placing the posts to an adequate depth (Fig. 1-17).

When building the foundation, if there is a door in the greenhouse wall, leave a 2″ ± drop in the footing for the door buck spreader. If this is not done, you will have to reduce the length of each door buck by cutting the excess off the top.

The normal wall height can be raised or lowered to suit local conditions. If the wall is raised, increase the height of the door "sill" an equal amount and build a sloping ramp or steps as needed. If the wall height is lowered, build an excavated areaway for the door or raise the door and frame and cut the glass lite over the door to fit.

For a greenhouse attached to another building, determine the furtherest projection on the building face in the area where the greenhouse is connected and drop a plumb bob to establish a starting point for the construction of the masonry footing.

Lay out the rough trench dimension for the footing width and length. In solid ground if the footing is dug with a narrow trenching shovel, no concrete pouring forms will be necessary nor are they recommended. Wood boards are required as shown in Fig. 1-18. These are usually 1″ x 6″ lumber; although they can be deeper if necessary to correct for a sloping grade condition. The top boards must be 1″ above grade at the center of the door end of the

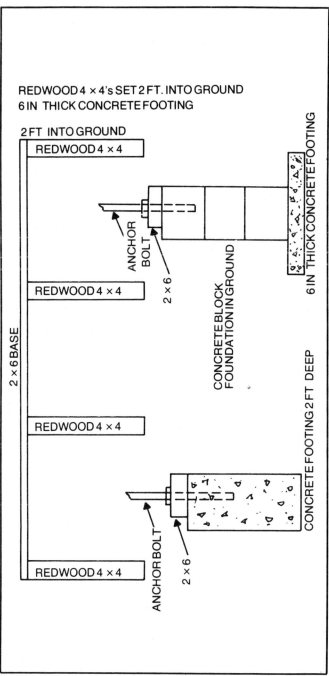

REDWOOD 4 × 4's SET 2 FT. INTO GROUND
6 IN THICK CONCRETE FOOTING

2 FT INTO GROUND

REDWOOD 4 × 4

ANCHOR BOLT

2 × 6

REDWOOD 4 × 4

2 × 6 BASE

CONCRETE BLOCK FOUNDATION IN GROUND

6 IN THICK CONCRETE FOOTING

REDWOOD 4 × 4

CONCRETE FOOTING 2 FT DEEP

REDWOOD 4 × 4

ANCHOR BOLT

2 × 6

Fig. 1-17. Suggested footing for a 14 x 14 fiberglass greenhouse (courtesy of Greenhouse Specialists Company). These are three different types of footings.

33

greenhouse. The pouring boards should be 8″ apart (inside measure). Note that the width and length dimensions of the footing are from inside faces of the outer wood boards.

Wood boards must be level the full length of the house, and to each other. It is extremely important that the foundation be straight and square. Pour the footing and form a continuous slot in the top of the concrete for the anchor bolts (Fig. 1-19).

Foundation and wall details for a lean-to greenhouse are shown in Fig. 1-20. Foundation and wall details for a free-standing greenhouse are shown in Fig. 1-21.

Sill Installation (Glass House)

Place the still on the wall using wood blocks about 1-inch thick plus shingle wedges for accurate leveling. Nail through the 1-inch blocks and on each side of sill, as shown in Fig. 1-22, to prevent movement of sills while the greenhouse frame is being assembled and the glass is being installed. Make sure that the aluminum sill is straight and level with all corners at right angles. *Do not* cement sills until the greenhouse is glazed; the nails through the 1-inch wood blocks will hold the frame in place and allow for any required adjustment while glazing. Verify that the width between sills is the same at the front, center and back of greenhouse.

Cementing the Sills

Glaze the greenhouse before cementing sills as the glass will square up the framework.

☐ Cement in the sill anchors; for a hollow block wall, stuff newspapers below anchors to avoid excess use of cement (Fig. 1-23).

☐ Before cementing sills, check again to make sure they are square and level. Stretch a taut cord along the sills from end to end to make sure they are straight.

☐ Remove wood leveling blocks and cement in sills (Fig. 1-24).

☐ Work the grout well up under the sills; do not finish with a feather edge, but leave a well-rounded thickness of cement to prevent chipping. Do not work the exposed grout higher than the bottom edge of the sill both front and back.

☐ A slate or stone cap can be used instead of grout.

☐ Allow sill anchors to set for 24 hours before removing leveling blocks and proceeding with grouting.

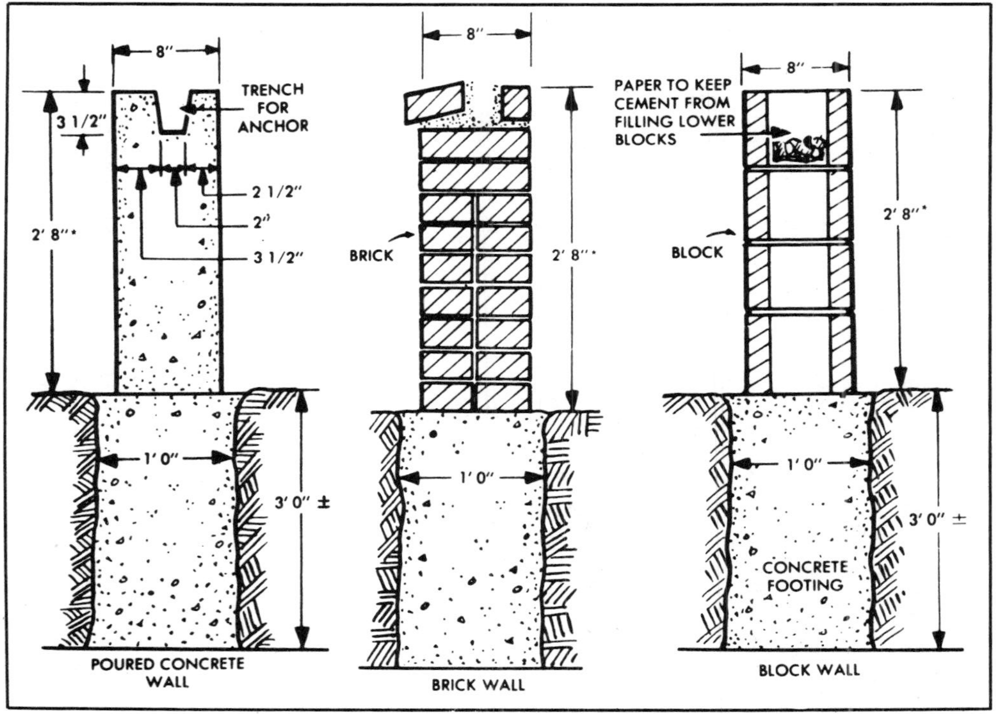

Fig. 1-18. Trench for footing, glass to ground model (courtesy of Lord & Burnham).

GLAZING (GLASS HOUSES)

Until your greenhouse is installed, the framework will not be completely rigid. If the first few panes or "lites" of glass do not fit correctly, rock the framework slightly until the glass squares itself in the openings.

The roof sash is glazed with vinyl "U" plastic channel on the top and both sides. Apply the plastic in one continuous piece to cover all three edges. Cut off the excess "bulge" at the two top corners with sharp scissors.

Vinyl "U" plastic channel is also used on the top edge only of the side glass where it fits into the eave and on the outer edge of gable glass where it fits into the groove in the end rafter (s).

Glass for the sides, roof and gable section is glazed with plastic foam tape to bed the glass, and a top bead of compound. Apply the plastic foam tape to the glazing shoulder of the bars with the paper side up. *Do not* remove the paper or plastic backing; it provides a smooth surface on which the glass can slide to facilitate installation.

General glazing instructions are shown in Fig. 1-25. Install the vent glass first, then the roof, sides and gables, in that order. Barcap as you go to keep the glass in place.

FLASHING

If the greenhouse is to be attached to a building, the glass opening next to the attached end should not be glazed until the flashing work has been completed. A space of approximately 3 inches should be left between the last glazing bar in the greenhouse and the building. Scribing boards and flashing to fill this space and form a support for the flashing materials should be made from 1¼" or 1" x 5" redwood or treated lumber. Cut the scribing boards as closely as possible to conform with the surface of the building and attach to the short lengths of lumber to act as blocking around the curve. Use angle lugs to connect to the building.

Flash and counterflash according to the suggested methods shown in Fig. 1-26. Flashing is attached to the scribing material. Counterflashing must extend up into something on the building and also cover a portion of the flashing. On clapboards or shingles, it can be pushed under the overlap. On brick or stucco buildings, some of the masonry must be cut away and counter-flashing notched into the side of the building. When this is done, a good caulking material should be used to seal the counterflashing in the wall crevice (Fig. 1-27).

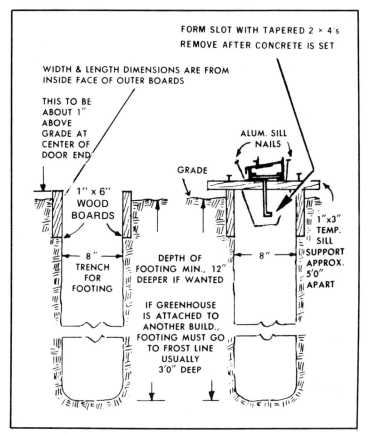

Fig. 1-19. Details of poured footings (courtesy of Lord & Burnham).

DOORS

Regardless of the style greenhouse you construct, you will have the choice of either a standard door or a Dutch door. Be sure to leave a 2-inch drop in the footing at the door location for the door sill spreader, and to permit a sufficient amount of concrete when grouting to provide a solid threshold.

Standard Door

The following steps outline door installation for a glass door. However, they are adaptable to any type material being used (Fig. 1-28).

☐ Attach gable purlin with T-bolts and lockwashers. Leave T-bolts loose for adjustments.

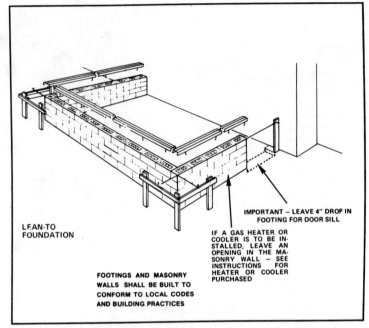

Fig. 1-20. Foundation footing and wall for lean-to (courtesy of Lord & Burnham).

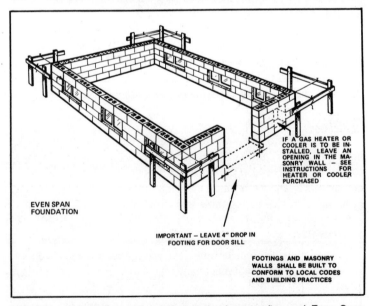

Fig. 1-21. Foundation and wall footing for free-standing and Evan Span greenhouses (courtesy of Lord & Burnham).

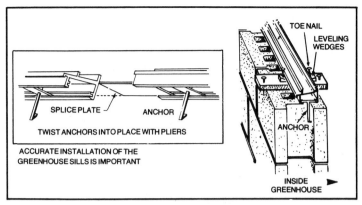

Fig. 1-22. Details for installation of sills (courtesy of Lord & Burnham).

□ Attach door head buck to angle purlin with 3 T-bolts and lock-washers. At the center T-bolt attach the door chain lug for later attachment of the door chain.

□ Adjust the angle purlin and door head buck so that the center line of the screw slot in the buck is 3' to 9 3/32″ from the glass seat on the sill. Tighten T-bolts.

□ Hold door in Z-frame up to bucks; make sure door is plumb and square. Drill 5/32″ holes into door buck where (and if) they appear in the door frame.

□ Remove screws holding door to Z-bar. Some doors have rivets that can be removed after the door and frame are connected to the door bucks. Use a knife or putty blade to cut the rivets.

□ Use #10 round head self-tapping screws to attach door frame to bucks (Figs. 1-29 and 1-30).

Dutch Door

The small, home greenhouse is most conducive to a Dutch door being hung to provide not only an aesthetic appearance, but

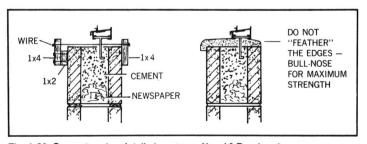

Fig. 1-23. Cement coping details (courtesy of Lord & Burnham).

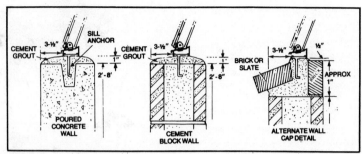

Fig. 1-24. Cementing the sills—to be done after glazing (courtesy of Lord & Burnham).

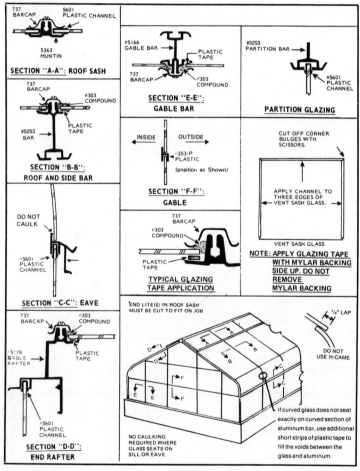

Fig. 1-25. Glazing Details (courtesy of Lord & Burnham).

during the winter months in areas which do not suffer from heavy frosts, the top part of the door can be left open during the day. It is simple to construct and it basically involves using a regular door which is then cut in halves. The following steps will assist you in building a Dutch door.

☐ Put the center braces in the door and then cut down in half.

☐ Make sure the door is square.

☐ Fasten door ends and sides. Drill corner holes. Place bolt heads on the front of the door and the nuts on the rear using a one-fourth inch drill. To make certain the front and rear holes are in alignment, drill front and rear holes simultaneously. If you have a wood clamp, use it to hold the structure steady. If not, bolt as firmly as possible by holding the structure by hand. Tighten bolts securely using a small wrench. Be sure to place a washer under both the head of the bolt and nut.

☐ After door parts are bolted together, measure from the bottom of door to find the center of the door and leave one-eighth of an inch between the two middle.

☐ Screw ledge onto the bottom section of the door using 1½″ screws from the rear.

☐ Attach ledge block underneath ledge for support.

☐ Door will open from either left or right. Screw barrel bolt on front of the door and mount handle.

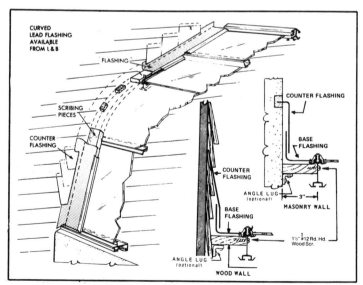

Fig. 1-26. Flashing to building details (courtesy of Lord & Burnham).

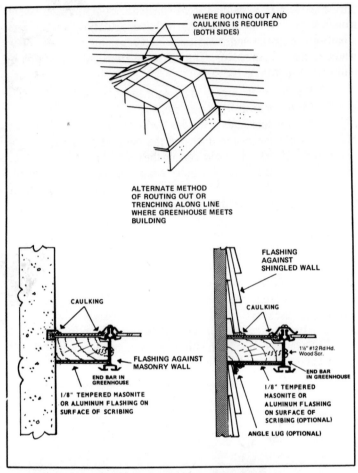

Fig. 1-27. Caulking to building (courtesy of Lord & Burnham).

☐ Attach door to greenhouse by screwing the hinges in a straight line to make sure the door will open easily.

☐ When door is hung, measure half-way to find center of door and cut in halves to produce the finished Dutch door (Fig. 1-31).

BENCHES

Because the home greenhouse must accommodate a variety of plants from seedlings to potted plants, benches offer many advantages over planting directly in the greenhouse soil or setting pots in the soil. And, of course, for the home greenhouse they are a must for getting the maximum use out of a limited amount of space.

Plants set on benches are at a more convenient height to work comfortably; they permit a more effective display of your plotted plants for attractiveness and they provide improved air circulation and better environmental control around the plants. Most importantly, they permit better control of disease and growth control.

Greenhouse benches also aid in air circulation which is very important for good plant growth. While plants might dry more rapidly when grown on benches, this is often an advantage due to the better control of excess watering. With this control, watering and fertilizing can be properly applied with regard to both time and amount. Increased air circulation also assists in minimizing root and foliage diseases because it causes the plant surfaces to dry more rapidly after watering instead of allowing moist areas to persist (which are prime areas where sports can germinate). Also,

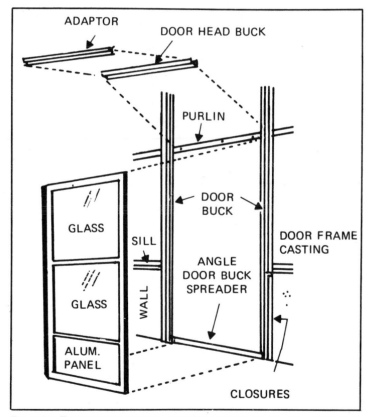

Fig. 1-28. Typical standard glass door for greenhouse (courtesy of Lord & Burnham). Not drawn to scale.

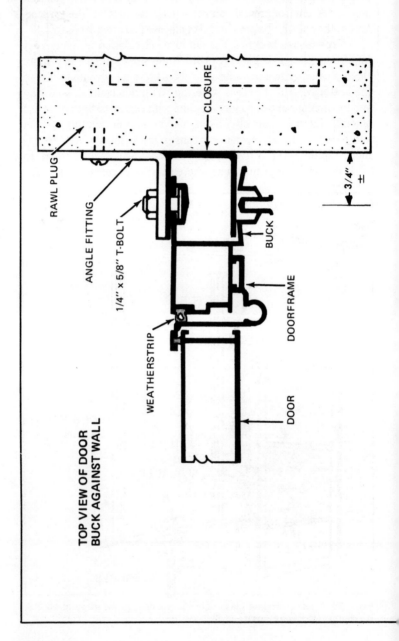

TOP VIEW OF DOOR
BUCK AGAINST WALL

RAWL PLUG

ANGLE FITTING

1/4" x 5/8" T-BOLT

WEATHERSTRIP

CLOSURE

3/4"

BUCK

DOORFRAME

DOOR

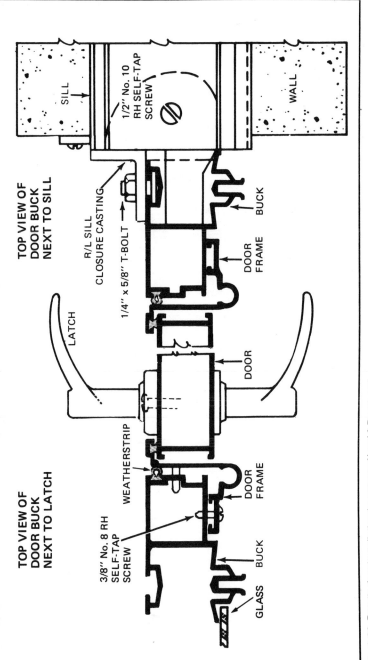

TOP VIEW OF DOOR BUCK NEXT TO SILL

SILL

1/2" No. 10 RH SELF-TAP SCREW

WALL

R/L SILL CLOSURE CASTING

1/4" x 5/8" T-BOLT

BUCK

DOOR FRAME

LATCH

DOOR

TOP VIEW OF DOOR BUCK NEXT TO LATCH

WEATHERSTRIP

3/8" No. 8 RH SELF-TAP SCREW

DOOR FRAME

BUCK

GLASS

Fig. 1-29. Details door installation (courtesy of Lord & Burnham).

45

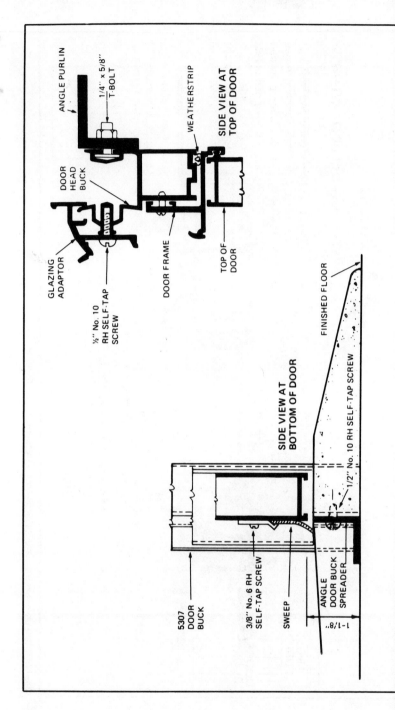

ANGLE PURLIN

1/4" × 5/8" T-BOLT

WEATHERSTRIP

SIDE VIEW AT TOP OF DOOR

DOOR HEAD BUCK

GLAZING ADAPTOR

½" No. 10 RH SELF-TAP SCREW

DOOR FRAME

TOP OF DOOR

FINISHED FLOOR

SIDE VIEW AT BOTTOM OF DOOR

1/2" No. 10 RH SELF-TAP SCREW

5307 DOOR BUCK

3/8" No. 6 RH SELF-TAP SCREW

SWEEP

ANGLE DOOR BUCK SPREADER

1-1/8"

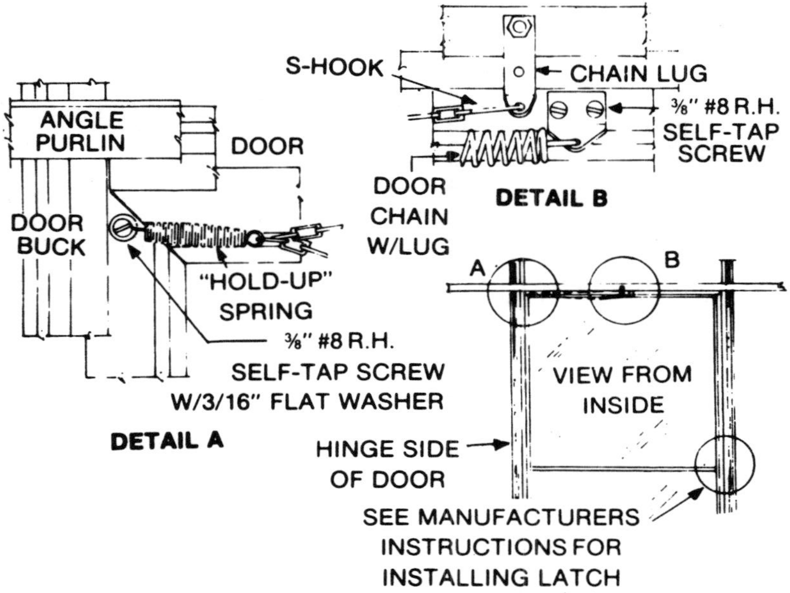

INSTALLING THE DOOR CHAIN

Attach the door chain (spring end with lug) to the door head at the pre-punched holes with self-tapping screws. On door provided with (2) sets of holes for this purpose select the holes furthest from the hinge side.

Hook the other end of the chain to the lug with S-hook already attached to the angle purlin.

Attach the small "hold-up" spring at the door top corner on the hinge side with a self-tapping screw and 3/16" flat washer. Close the door, allowing the chain to hang vertically, thread the chain's lowest link into end of "hold-up" spring.

S-HOOK

CHAIN LUG

⅜" #8 R.H.
SELF-TAP
SCREW

DOOR
CHAIN
W/LUG

DETAIL B

B

A

VIEW FROM
INSIDE

SEE MANUFACTURERS
INSTRUCTIONS FOR
INSTALLING LATCH

ANGLE
PURLIN

DOOR

"HOLD-UP"
SPRING

⅜" #8 R.H.
SELF-TAP SCREW
W/3/16" FLAT WASHER

DETAIL A

DOOR
BUCK

HINGE SIDE
OF DOOR

Fig. 1-30. Door details and chain installation details (courtesy of Lord & Burnham).

47

due to air circulation under benches and around pots, the roots of plants on benches stay warmer. This results in greater growth for the plants.

The size of the benches will depend on several factors. Bench size will vary according to how you intend to use your greenhouse. If the greenhouse is to be devoted entirely to growing, you will want to provide as much bench space as possible. If you plan to share it with plants as a Solarium or sun room—such as your lean-to—the bench size will have to be determined accordingly. If the bench is to run the length of the greenhouse, be sure to allow at lease 2" between the bench sides and the walls. This prevents plants close to the glass—or fiberglass, plastic, etc.—from reacting to the cold outside.

A tall person with a long reach could comfortably work with a higher and wider bench, but for the average person approximately 32 to 36 inch bench weight is a workable height. The width is generally 41 to 48 inches wide if they are going to be used from either side and 30 to 36 inches if they are only accessible from one side.

In most home greenhouses, as well as in commercial houses, much use is made of the space underneath the benches where you can store mature plants of varied heights. In home greenhouses where a great number of different plants having different temperature requirements are grown, the cooler outside bench—a bench attached or running along the wall of the greenhouse—can be utilized to obtain a desirable difference in environmental conditions for particular plants.

There are three types of benches commonly used in the home greenhouses. The *flat bench* is a table upon which the plants are placed. *Step benches* are mainly used for showing off specialty plants. In addition, there are benches with or without side boards.

The step bench is light in construction in order that it provides ease of handling to move from one area of the greenhouse to another. There is one disadvantage, however, to a step bench and that is that plants on them receive more light from one direction. This results in uneven plant growth unless the plants are rotated occasionally.

Open benches might or might not have sides. Where sides are used, they serve primarily to keep plants from being brushed off the benches.

Wooden Step Bench. The wooden step bench, as shown in Fig. 1-32, can be constructed any size, width, angle or height to

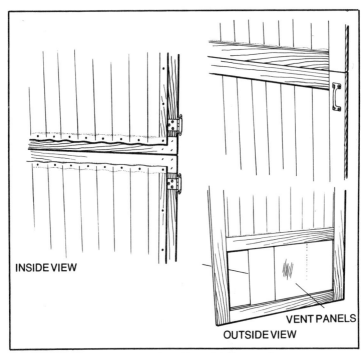

Fig. 1-31. Dutch door (courtesy of Peter Reimuller Company).

INSIDE VIEW

VENT PANELS

OUTSIDE VIEW

accommodate the particular type of plant for which it is being used. Step benches can be set side to side to make them a two-sided step bench, but it should be remembered that plants on the norther side of the bench will receive less sun than those on the southern side. Orientation of the benches is required in order that the morning and afternoon sun will shine on each side equally.

Lath Fence Bench. One of the least expensive wooden benches is the lath fence (Fig. 1-33). It is ideal for small pots and plants being raised in flats or market packs. The lath fence bench allows good air circulation around the pots. This bench, although inexpensive to construct, is not long lived; it is, however, easily replaced when deterioration requires.

Wooden Board Bench. Wood can be used for flat or step benches, but care must be taken to make sure that any preservatives used will not cause harm to the roots of plants that grow in contact with the wood. Only woods treated with waterborne, salt-type preservatives should be used.

The wooden board bench (Figs. 1-34, 1-35 and 1-36) is constructed with 1-inch thick boards. For flat-topped wood

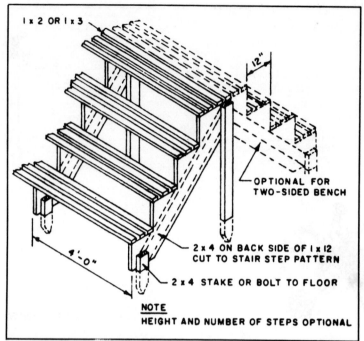

Fig. 1-32. Wooden step bench.

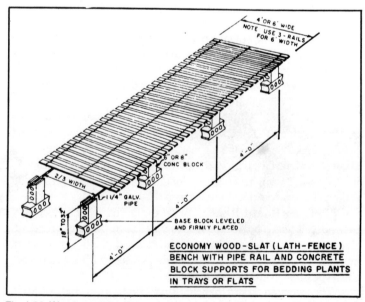

Fig. 1-33. Wood-slat (lathe-face) bench.

benches, a one-eighth inch to one-fourth inch crack should be left between the bottom and side boards to allow water to drain from the bench and to prevent damage to the bench if the wood swells due to moisture absorption. Cross supports should be spaced not more than 4 feet apart.

Wire Mesh Benches. Benches of wire mesh are widely used in pot plant culture and are excellent in providing air drainage and insect control. The construction is simple (Figs. 1-37 and 1-38). The framework can be made of 2-inch to 4-inch wood. The welded wire fabric is then stapled to the framework. A 1″ x 2″ welded mesh 12½ or 14-gauge provides excellent results with the heavier being preferred because sagging could be a problem. To minimize sagging, cross support should be spaced 2 feet apart, but care should be taken to set the pots evenly to avoid sagging. Staples should be 1¼″ to 1½″ long and the use of galvanized wire and

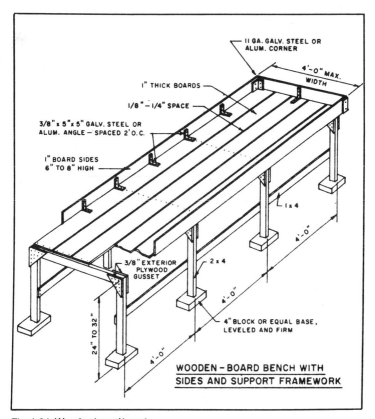

Fig. 1-34. Wooden board bench.

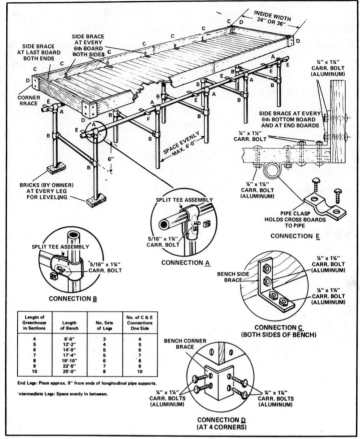

Fig. 1-35. Wooden bench details.

staples will delay, although not prevent, rusting. The cost of this bench is also comparatively low.

Corrugated Asbestos Benches. Though this bench is quite expensive, it can be constructed from flat asbestos (Fig. 1-39) or corrugated asbestos (Fig. 1-40). Its durability might be well worth the additional expense. Asbestos is strong; however it will crack or break if abused. Corrugated asbestos will not rot or deteriorate. Available with corrugations every few inches—usually 2½″ spacing—the 2½″ material is recommended because it is easier to handle.

For small pots, lay wire mesh over the corrugations. If you want to use sides, they should be from 6″ to 8″ high and made from flat cement-asbestos material.

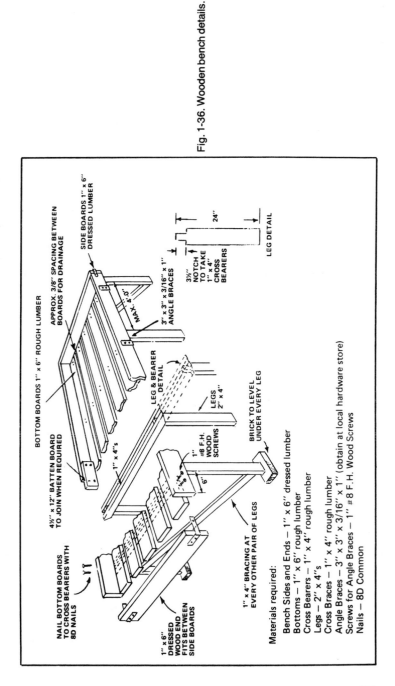

Fig. 1-36. Wooden bench details.

SIDE BOARDS 1" x 6" DRESSED LUMBER

24"

NOTCH TO TAKE 1" x 4" CROSS BEARERS

3½"

LEG DETAIL

BOTTOM BOARDS 1" x 6" ROUGH LUMBER

APPROX. 3/8" SPACING BETWEEN BOARDS FOR DRAINAGE

SIDE BOARDS 1" x 6" DRESSED LUMBER

4½" x 12" BATTEN BOARD TO JOIN WHEN REQUIRED

MAX. 4'-0"

3" x 3" x 3/16" x 1" ANGLE BRACES

LEG & BEARER DETAIL

LEGS — 2" x 4"

NAIL BOTTOM BOARDS TO CROSS BEARERS WITH 8D NAILS

1" x 4"'s

1" #8 F.H. WOOD SCREWS

6"

BRICK TO LEVEL UNDER EVERY LEG

1" x 6" DRESSED WOOD END FITS BETWEEN SIDE BOARDS

1" x 4" BRACING AT EVERY OTHER PAIR OF LEGS

Materials required:

Bench Sides and Ends — 1" x 6" dressed lumber
Bottoms — 1" x 6" rough lumber
Cross Bearers — 1" x 4" rough lumber
Legs — 2" x 4"'s
Cross Braces — 1" x 4" rough lumber
Angle Braces — 3" x 3" x 3/16" x 1" (obtain at local hardware store)
Screws for Angle Braces — 1" #8 F.H. Wood Screws
Nails — 8D Common

53

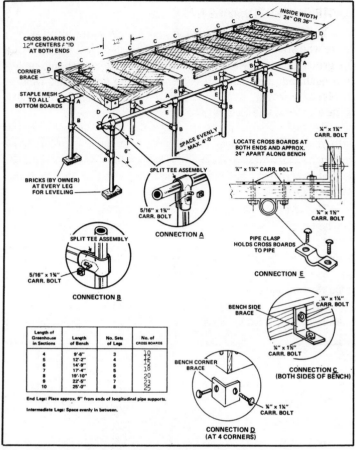

Fig. 1-37. Wooden bench details.

The major factors in determining what type of bench to build are:

□ Shading problems.
□ Work efficiency.
□ Space utilization.
□ Turning pots on step benches will maintain uniformity of plants when the ligh intensity is higher on one side of the bench than the other.
□ For all lumber, use decay resistant species like redwood, or pine and fir, pressure treated with a waterborne salt-type preservative, for long life. Metal angles holding sideboards can be on the outside surface if you preferred.

ELECTRICAL AND PLUMBING TIPS

Your greenhouse will need electricity and water utilities. For those who are not familiar with any type of electrical work, wiring the greenhouse for whatever electricity you require should be left to a qualified electrician. If care is taken to understand what is involved, however, it will not be too difficult for those who have some electrical knowledge to do the wiring themselves.

Before you begin any "home electrical work" be sure to check with your electrical power supplier on your legal status in doing wiring for your state, county and city codes. In most states, you can do your own work, but the law might require that you have the wiring inspected.

The walks of the greenhouse are usually damp or wet; soil in the benches is wet and a hose can be carelessly used. It is, therefore, extremely important that every piece of electrical equipment in the greenhouse be grounded in an approved manner.

Safe wiring depends on good design, proper materials, and good workmanship. Don't go about it casually.

Electrical. Probably the most baffling part of the electrical installation is the fusebox. On the outside of the building, it is

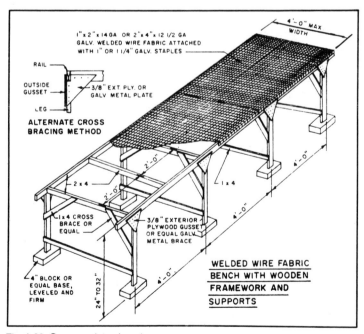

Fig. 1-38. Open mesh top benches.

55

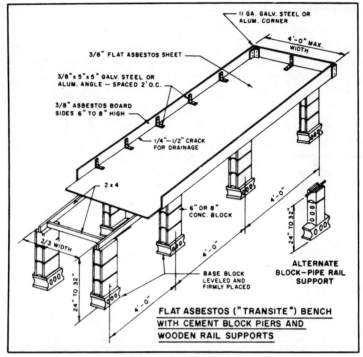

Fig. 1-39. Flat asbestos bench.

required that the fusebox be a weatherproofed receptacle which usually has a spring loaded cover with rubber gaskets to keep moisture out.

Romex, type NM (non-metallic) wire is most commonly used in dry locations. Type NMC is non-metallic cable for corrosive or damp locations.

A three-wire system is used in homes to provide both 120 and 240 volts. For lights and small appliances, 120 volts is used and 240 volts is used for larger appliances.

To install an electrical system in your greenhouse:

☐ Dig a narrow trench from the fusebox—usually affixed to the outside of the main structure, house or garage (often in the garage)—and bury it to a depth determined by the frost line in your area.

☐ Staple the Romex to the framework and set your light switches and receptacles at locations desired (Fig. 1-41).

Switches and plugs wear out eventually. You can replace these switches and receptacles if care is provided to put them back

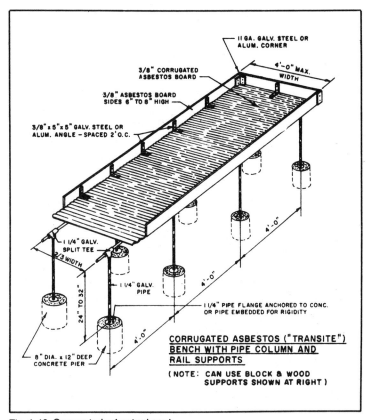

II GA. GALV. STEEL OR ALUM. CORNER

4'-0" MAX. WIDTH

3/8" CORRUGATED ASBESTOS BOARD

3/8" ASBESTOS BOARD SIDES 6" TO 8" HIGH

3/8" x 5" x 5" GALV. STEEL OR ALUM. ANGLE – SPACED 2' O.C.

I 1/4" GALV. SPLIT TEE

2/3 WIDTH

I 1/4" GALV. PIPE

4'-0"

4'-0"

24" TO 32"

I 1/4" PIPE FLANGE ANCHORED TO CONC. OR PIPE EMBEDDED FOR RIGIDITY

8" DIA. x 12" DEEP CONCRETE PIER

4'-0"

CORRUGATED ASBESTOS ("TRANSITE")
BENCH WITH PIPE COLUMN AND
RAIL SUPPORTS
(NOTE: CAN USE BLOCK & WOOD
SUPPORTS SHOWN AT RIGHT)

Fig. 1-40. Corrugated asbestos bench.

Fig. 1-41. Romex stapled to framework (courtesy of John Wahlfeldt).

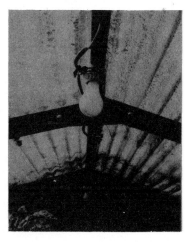

57

as they came apart. (Fig. 1-42). In wiring a plug, the wires should be run around the prongs to the screw. The end of the wire is twisted and run clockwise around the screw. A protective disc (not shown) slips over the prongs and conceals the connections (Fig. 1-43).

Switches are available that have a pilot light so they can be found in the dark and you can get switches that operate silently. Receptacles also wear out even though this is not always realized. Bending the prongs of a loose-fitting plug is only a temporary solution at best. On a heating device, you could cause overheating of the plug.

If the receptacle is the three-prong ground type be sure the bare or green ground wire is connected under the green, hexagon-shaped screw. The white wire goes to the silver screw. The black or red wire goes to the brass-colored screw.

A great variety of light bulbs and fluorescent tubes is available for initial use or replacement. Fluorescent lamps are available in color ranges from "cool-white" to "warm-white." They might be clear, inside-frosted or all white. Most light bulbs ae designed to burn from 750 to 1000 hours.

Plumbing. Many people who are hobby greenhouse en-thusiasts do not bother to install indoor plumbing. Instead they depend on the use of outside hoses and buckets of water. For those building larger greenhouses, it is advisable to install an ample number of hose bibbs—strategically located for convenience. A tub is useful for washing pots and general clean-up. Supply it with hot water if possible and install a misting faucet with hose thread so that you can water plants with tepid water. A typical wiring and plumbing layout is shown in Fig. 1-44.

TOOLS TO GET THE JOB DONE

Along with the usual array of hammer, screwdriver, etc., a number of small tools are necessary to complete your project whether it be only constructing the greenhouse or continuing to additional projects, such as the patio and walls. Prior to beginning, make certain you have all the tools on hand in order to provide as much professionalism as possible to your finished product. A basic knowledge of what each tool is for and how to use it will make your job easier and more pleasurable. A variety of tools is shown in Fig. 1-45.

Trowels. Used for brick work, they come in various sizes and in lengths from 9 to 14 inches and widths from 4 to 7 inches. They

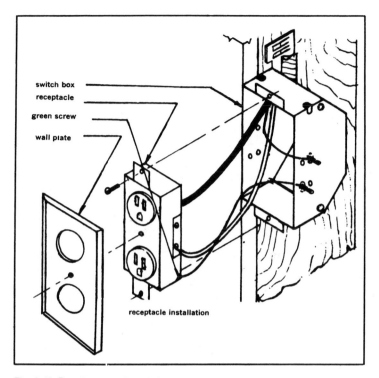

Fig. 1-42. Detail receptacle installation.

can be wide-heeled or round-heeled. The heel is the width of the trowel from the base of the handle.

Handling the trowel properly will not only make your bricklaying more efficient, but it will provide the maximum effectiveness for the ultimate gluing together of brick to brick or block to block. It also assists you from becoming overtired. See Fig. 1-46. Picking up a trowel full of mortar "cleanly" and spreading a sufficient amount to lay 2 to 4 bricks/blocks can be accomplished after a little practice.

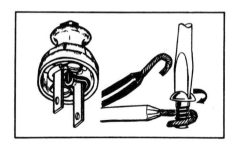

Fig. 1-43. Detail plug wiring.

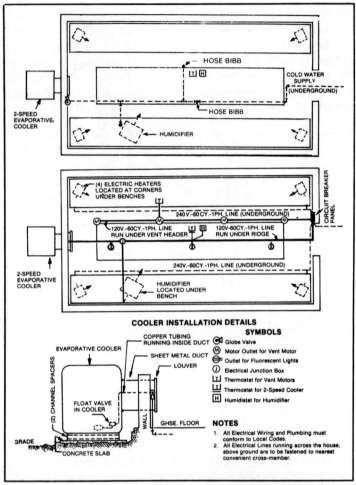

Fig. 1-44. Typical wiring and plumbing layout (courtesy of Lord & Burnham).

Level. Used to assure plumbness of structure, most levels have one or two gauges (bubbles) in the center with one at each end. The level is used consistently as you are building the greenhouse, laying the foundation, laying bricks/blocks and it is one of the most important "small tools" in your toolbox. Because all portions must be level, it is used in all types of construction work, large and small. When the gauges (bubbles) appear in the immediate center of their gauged, the area is "level."

Jointer. A jointer is used to finish the mortar joints in order to make them appear smooth and to tighten the joint made. The jointer is "pulled" down or across the mortar joint cleaning away excess mortar.

Brick Hammer. Used for splitting brick or block, a brick hammer is made of hard tempered steel. It has a square head and the edges must be kept sharp. Splitting the brick/block is accomplished by making light blows in a line completely around the brick/block with the sharp edge of the hammer head. A sharp blow

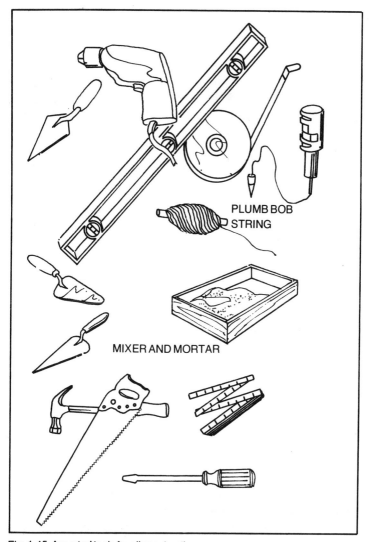

PLUMB BOB
STRING

MIXER AND MORTAR

Fig. 1-45. Assorted tools for all construction.

61

Fig. 1-46. Holding trowel correctly (courtesy of John Wahlfeldt).

of the hammer head at the line made, at approximately the center of the brick/block, will split it. The rought spots are trimmed away with the sharp edge of the hammer.

Line. Made of nylon or other taut material, the line is used to keep each row (course) of bricks/blocks level and free from bulges. Held in places on either end of the row being laid by brick nails around which the line is tied, the line is placed so that the face (front) of the brick/block touches the cordline. Do not allow the brick/block to slacken the line. Otherwise, the next row will be out of plumb. By "flicking" the line, you can see that it is properly strung. If the brick/block get out of the plumb, jiggle the line until the cordline touches it.

Rules and Tape Measures. The common wooden fold-out rule and the metal tape rule which slides out from its enclosures are marked for measuring wood and metal to special masonry scales.

Learning how to read the scale prior to beginning any project will make your construction easier. For example, when laying a 2¼ inch high brick with a three-eighth inch mortar joint, the total height would be 2⅝ inches on the rule. This will correspond to the number 3 on the scale. Instead of measuring 2⅝ inch for each row, simply locate "4" for each successive layer.

Electric Drill. An electric drill can be used for drilling holes in wood, metal and fiberglass. Drill bits are especially useful to ease nailing through metal and fiberglass. Determine the size bit by the screw or nail being used.

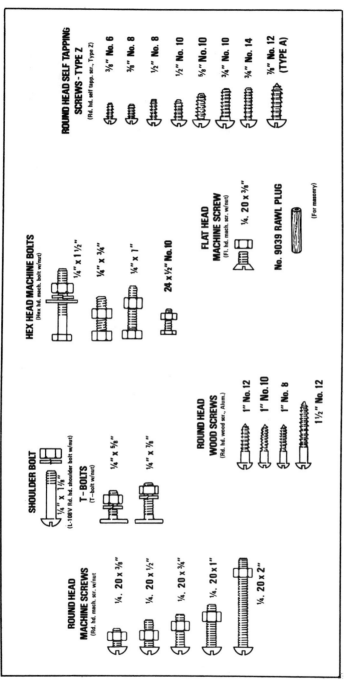

ROUND HEAD MACHINE SCREWS
(Rd. hd. mach. scr. w/nut)

¼ 20 x ⅜"
¼ 20 x ½"
¼ 20 x ¾"
¼ 20 x 1"
¼ 20 x 2"

SHOULDER BOLT
¼" x 1⅛"
(L-108 V. Rd. hd. shoulder bolt w/nut)

T–BOLTS
(T–bolt w/nut)

¼" x ⅝"
¼" x ⅞"

HEX HEAD MACHINE BOLTS
(Hex hd. mach. bolt w/nut)

¼" x 1½"
¼" x ¾"
¼" x 1"
24 x ½" No. 10

ROUND HEAD WOOD SCREWS
(Rd. hd. wood scr., Alum.)

1" No. 12
1" No. 10
1" No. 8
1½" No. 12

FLAT HEAD MACHINE SCREW
(Fl. hd. mach. scr. w/nut)

¼ 20 x ⅜"

No. 9039 RAWL PLUG
(For masonry)

ROUND HEAD SELF TAPPING SCREWS - TYPE Z
(Rd. hd. self tapp. scr., Type Z)

⅜" No. 6
⅜" No. 8
½" No. 8
½" No. 10
⅝" No. 10
¾" No. 10
¾" No. 14
⅞" No. 12 (TYPE A)

Fig. 1-47. Identification chart for nuts, bolts and screws commonly used in construction (courtesy of Lord & Burnham).

63

Table 1-1. Fasteners.

FASTENER TYPE	USE TO FASTEN
1" #8 RH WOOD SCREW	CLOSURES TO BLOCKING LEAN-TO "7" GABLES
1" #10 RH WOOD SCREW	RIDGE END CLOSURE 1365 (L & R) LT "7"
1" #12 RH WOOD SCREW	PURLIN ANGLE FITTING TO BLOCKING "7" GABLES
1½" #12 RH WOOD SCREW	ANGLE FITTING AT LEAN-TO ROOF AND GABLE. BAR, RIDGE, RIDGE SPLICE, CLOSURE TO BLOCKING, BAR TO SCRIBING ALL MODELS
⅜" #6 RH SELF-TAPPING SCREW TYPE A	DOOR SWEEP TO DOOR BOTTOM
⅜" #8 RH SELF-TAPPING SCREW TYPE Z	DOOR CHECK FITTING—GL. CLIP AT HEADER GABLE END CLOSURE
½" #8 RH SELF-TAPPING SCREW TYPE Z	BARCAPS TO BAR
½" #10 RH SELF-TAPPING SCREW TYPE Z	ANGLE FITTING TO SILL, EAVE, RIDGE TO BAR AND BUCK CASTING TO SILL
⅝" #10 RH SELF-TAPPING SCREW TYPE Z	ANGLE FITTING TO HEADER
¾" #10 RH SELF-TAPPING SCREW TYPE Z	SASH JUNCTION CLOSURE TO RIDGE AT PARTITION AND BREAK IN SASH RUN
¾" #14 RH SELF-TAPPING SCREW TYPE Z	ANGLE FITTING PARTITION SILL, FLAT BRACE TO SILL (G TO G MODELS)
⅞" #12 RH SELF-TAPPING SCREW TYPE A	ANGLE FITTING TO MASONRY AT DOOR BUCKS
½ #10 FH SELF-TAPPING SCREW TYPE Z	HINGE TO BUCK AND DOOR
¼ .20 x ⅜ RH MACH. SC. W/NUT	SPLICE AT HEADER, EAVE-ANGLE FITTING AT EAVE END
¼ .20 x ⅝ RH MACH. SC. W/NUT	ANGLE FITTING AT SILL, BUCK SPREADER, DECK BAR, G TO G GABLE CORNER SPLICE AT BOTTOM RAIL RIDGE, SHAFTING AND HEADER END
¼ .20 x ¾ RH MACH. SC. W/NUT	RAFTER SPLICE, SILL CORNER CASTING, SASH, MUNTIN
¼ .20 x 1" RH MACH. SC. W/NUT	BAR SPLICE, SASH MUNTIN AT SPLICE
¼ .20 x 2" RH MACH. SC. W/NUT	BUCK TO BAR AT SIDE ENTRANCE
24 x ½" #10 HEX. HD. MACH. BOLT W/NUT, ALUMINUM	SASH BEARER FITTING TO BOTTOM RAIL
¼" x ¾" HEX. HD. MACH. BOLT W/NUT, ALUMINUM	VENT ROD TO SASH BEARER
¼" x 1" HEX. HD. MACH. BOLT W/NUT, LOCK, WASHER, GALV.	MOTOR BRACKET Z FITTING TO BAR
¼" x 1½" HEX. HD. MACH. BOLT W/NUT, FLAT LOCK WASHER, GALV.	VENT SHAFTING COUPLING
¼" x 1⅛" SHOULDER BOLT W/NUT AND LOCK WASHER, GALV.	VENT SASH ARM AND ROD ASSEMBLY
¼" x ⅝" T-BOLT W/NUT AND LOCK WASHER, GALV.	ANGLE FITTING AT BUCK CLOSURE—LOCK STRIKE BUCK TO SILL FITTING
¼" x ⅞" T-BOLT W/NUT AND LOCK WASHER, GALV.	BUCK AND BAR TO GABLE RAFTER, ANGLE PURLIN TO BUCK AND BAR. ANGLE POST TO G TO G. EXTENSION BAR.
¼ .20 x ⅜ FH. MACH. SC. W/NUT ALUMINUM	SPLICE AT VENT TOP RAIL
¼" x 1" CARR. BOLT W/NUT AND LOCK WASHER, GALV.	MOTOR BRACKET TO Z FITTING
#9039 RAWL PLUG	ANGLE FITTING AT BUCK CLOSURE TO MASONRY

GLOSSARY

MACH. SC. -MACHINE SCREW	RH -ROUND HEAD
CARR. BOLT -CARRIAGE BOLT	FH -FLAT HEAD
GALV. -GALVANIZED	SC -SCREW
GL. -GLAZING	W/NUT -WITH NUT
G TO G -GLASS TO GROUND	HEX. HD. - HEXAGONAL HEAD

Nuts, Bolts And Screws. There are a variety of nuts, bolts and screws which might or might not be needed during the construction of your greenhouse, but which are the most commonly called for in any type of construction. Table 1-1 is an identification chart of those used most often. The glass greenhouse models described in Chapter 2 will require the nuts and bolts as indicated in Table 1-1.

Chapter 2
Constructing
Your Greenhouse

Research has shown that a standard contemplation of people who are planning to construct a greenhouse is to consider purchasing or constructing one as large as the space, finances and working time allows. Plants have a way of expanding to fill all the available space and just a little bit more. Practically everyone who has a greenhouse soon finds there is not enough space to keep all plants that are of interest to them. Owning a greenhouse increases your interest to raise many different varieties of plants. Therefore, the size of the greenhouse depends, initially, upon how it is to be used. For example:

☐ What types of plants and/or vegetables will be grown? Will they be warm temperature or cool temperature plants?

☐ Will plants be grown from seed, purchased as mature plants or a combination of both?

☐ Will the plants be grown in the greenhouse for transplanting to the vegetable garden proper or harvesting for food direct for the table from the greenhouse? Will the plants be for cut flowers, for house plants, for landscaping or combinations of the preceding?

If you are planning to use your greenhouse primarily for growing edibles, an 8' x 12' unit can produce sufficient amounts for a family of four. However, for four people an 8' x 16' would be better. For a two-person family, a greenhouse that is approximately 7' x 12' would be adequate. An 8' x 12' greenhouse would provide ample space for both vegetables and florals.

For instance, a 7' x 12' greenhouse enables you to raise between 15,000 to 20,000 seedlings prior to (1) planting your vegetable garden outside, and (2) selling the excessive seedlings.

Regardless of the type greenhouse you construct, companies such as Greenhouse Specialties, St. Louis, National Greenhouse Company, Panam, Illinois, Lord & Burnham, Irvington, New York and Peter Reimuller of California, to mention just a few, have worked for many years to bring to the hobbyist greenhouser the "built-it-yourself" greenhouse. They can make hours of laborious work much easier; many of their designs are incorporated in this chapter.

Whether you choose the plastic, fiberglass or conventional glass models, there are some general do's and don'ts which will make your work easier and provide you with a professionally finished product. These general areas of information will be cited in the plans and constructions steps.

SOME FACTS ABOUT MATERIALS

The most popular greenhouse framing materials are aluminum, woods—such as redwood, cedar and cypress—steel and various types of plastic materials. There are pros and cons to each.

Aluminum has an excellent strength-to-weight ratio and is considered "maintenance free." Despite its high initial cost, it unquestionably has a very long life. Aluminum transmits heat and cold much more easily than other framing materials. Therefore, the greenhouse structure itself is more costly to heat or cool unless the structural members are somehow insulated from contact with the outside environment.

Aluminum structural framing is usually mill-finish or painted at extra cost. Aluminum oxide forms quickly on mill-finish and can become unsightly. It is difficult to remove and, like rust on iron or steel products, it tends to come right back. Acrylic painted aluminum wears very well unless the finish becomes cracked or is chipped away; then it is difficult to restore or maintain its original appearance. This, of course, would not be conducive to the aesthetic value of the home greenhouse which needs to blend in with the surroundings and provide beauty in itself.

Wood is considered traditional as a framing material. It is still the most easily obtained, the most workable and the most versatile material in the marketplace.

Redwood, western red cedar and cypress make the best framing materials in terms of decay and insect resistance. The strength/bulk ratio is rated as medium compared to high for aluminum and very high for steel. But for the home greenhouse, it is still "ideal" and used with most of the foregoing plans.

Wood is versatile; it can be used with any type of fastener from glue to bolts. Wood is thermally efficient. It is some 1300 times as efficient as aluminum.

While wood does require periodic maintenance, and it might require some replacement over a period of time, usually these replacement members can be purchased at a local lumberyard at minimal cost. When you are considering cost, availability, workability and range of finishes available, plus the thermal desirability, wood is still the number one product for framing the home greenhouse. But again, the choice is yours!

FIBERGLASS AND PLASTIC MODELS

The Extra Purline Model. This "more Purlin model" (Fig. 2-1) is a 14' x 14' model which has a little different effect in its construction in that it has more purlins—horizontal timbers—in its design. It is, therefore, provided much sturdiness due to the additional lumber and would be ideal for the location which is susceptible to high winds and yet where no foundation is necessary.

This greenhouse can be made longer in 2-foot sections by making the base, eave and ridge 2 feet longer for each 2-foot section added, and adding for each 2 foot section the following materials:

Two 6 ft. 2 x 4's cut to 66-¾" for side rafters.

Two 8 ft. 2 x 4's cut to the size shown on the plan. Structural details for this model are shown in Fig. 2-1.

Materials Required

2½" x ½" Corrugated Crystal Clear Fiberglass 5 oz, GH Wt.
Sides—14 sheets - 6 ft x 26 inch.
Front—4 sheets - 8 ft x 26 inch.
        2 sheets - 10 ft x 26 inch.
Back—4 sheets - 8 ft x 26 inch.
        3 sheets - 10 ft x 26 inch.
Roof—14 sheets - 8 ft x 26 inch.
Ridge Cap—7 pieces, 28 in. long.
Caulking (to seal laps) 5 tubes.
Aluminum nails with Neoprene washers: 3 boxes of 525 each box.
Poly-foam closure strips (to close corrugations at ends and sides) 59 pieces. Corrugated, 177 ft. and 32 pieces. Crown, 96 feet.

Lumber Required

Base—4 - 14 ft. 2′ x 6′s

Eave—3 - 14 ft. 2′ x 4′s for both sides and back.

 2 - 6 ft. 2′ x 4′s for front.

Side Rafters—26 - 6 ft. 1′ x 4′s to be cut to 66-3/5″ long.

Roof Rafters

Sixteen 8 ft. 2′ x 4′s to be cut on ends to allow for 2″ additional height on greenhouse sides to make wall 6 ft. high.

Ridge

One 14 ft. 2′ x 6′.

Door Frame

Two 8 ft. 2′ x 4′s to be cut to 6′ 8″ and one 4 ft 2′ x 4′ to be cut to 3′ 3¼″

2′ x 4′s to close space between eaves and rafters on front and back ends.

Two 6 ft 2′ x 4′s and two 8 ft 2′ x 4′s to be cut to sizes needed.

Door

One door—3 ft. wide x 6 ft. 8″ tall. One pair door hinges.

Nails

Approximately 5 pounds of 12-penny common nails and approximately 5 pounds of 16-penny common nails.

Purlins

138 ft. of 2′ x 2′s. Purlins between roof and side rafters and to close space at ends of roof rafters. (Three rows between roof rafters and one row between side rafters.)

Total Lumber Required

5—14 ft 2′ x 6′s

3—14 ft 2′ x 4′s

20—8 ft 2′ x 4′s

1—4 ft 2′ x 4′

138 feet of 2′ x 2′s.

FREE-STANDING GREENHOUSES

These greenhouses can be installed on any level surface if you live in an area where a foundation is unnecessary. If you want to

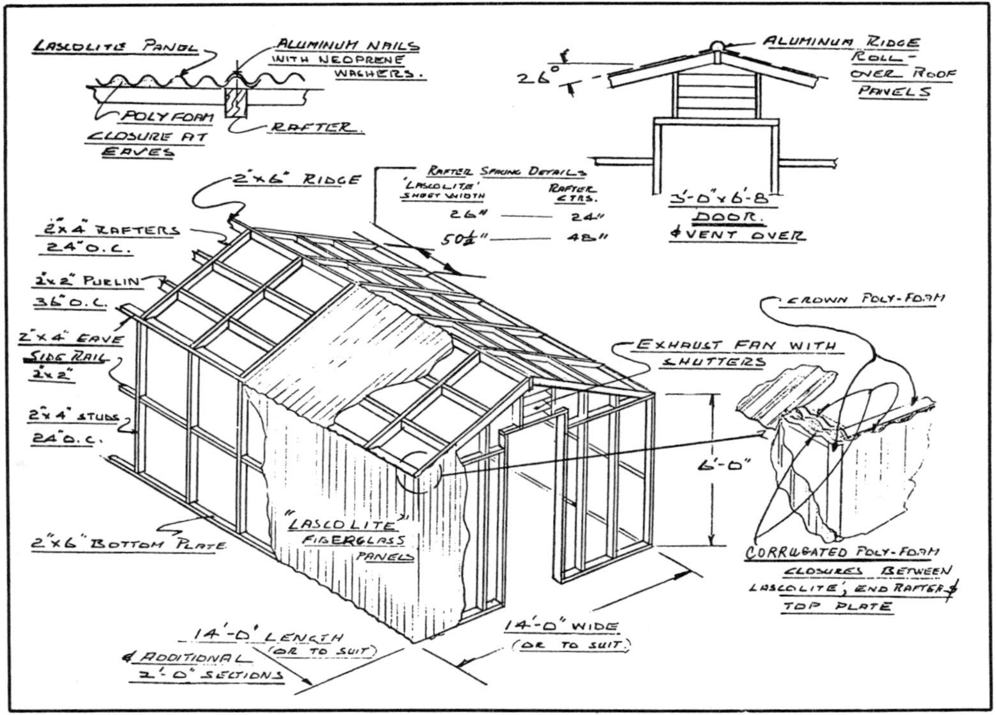

Fig. 2-1. The Extra Purlin model details (courtesy of Greenhouse Specialties Company).

69

install them on a paved area, the method is also very simple. On soft paved areas like asphalt, drive small pipes down about 1 foot through the surface and anchor the greenhouse to them. On brick areas, remove bricks and use your wood stakes. On concrete, it is necessary to drill holes and use anchor bolts available for that purpose.

On any surface, you may use 2' x 4's, 4' x 4's or railroad ties as a base. Either nail, bolt, or use other anchoring devices to secure the greenhouse in place. When using 2' x 4's or 4' x 4's on any hard surface, it is recommended that you lag-bolt the sills into the surface before anchoring the greenhouse to them.

In the construction steps that follow, remember these important points:

☐ *All* bolts use a washer under the nut, not under the head.

☐ *All* boltheads go to the *outside* of the greenhouse. Be sure to *use the correct bolt lengths* as indicated in the instructions. During subassembly—all materials should be layed out prior to starting—tighten all nuts *only finger tight* until that section is completed, then tighten all nuts with an adjustable wrench. For best results, and to avoid splitting, always support the surface you are nailing into.

Although it is not necessary, it is helpful to predrill a 3/32" starter hole at all 6d nail, screw nail and screw points in both the redwood and fiberglass for better results.

Windy conditions can seriously damage an uncompleted greenhouse. Make every attempt to get all of the major construction completed in 24 to 48 hours. With the help of family and friends, this can easily be accomplished.

The following directions and instructions are designed for a framework of an 8-foot model (Fig. 2-2). This model can be constructed in sizes ranging up to 16 feet. If you decide to construct the 16-foot model, pay attention to supplemental instruction at the end of each instruction step.

You will note that each piece of framing is designed by number. This number corresponds to that as outlined in the "Inventory List: Parts Inventory." (Appendix A: 8-foot; Appendix B: 12-foot; Appendix C: 16-foot.)

Step One: Check the Inventory

Prior to beginning, make yourself an inventory list as set forth in the parts inventory schedules in the Appendices. As you proceed, lay out the pieces and check them off the inventory list that corresponds to the size greenhouse you are constructing. It will help you if you write the name on each part. Remember that a 1″ x 3″ actually measures 11/16″ x 2½″. See Fig. 2-3.

Step Two: Assemble Both Side Sections

Place the 47½″ x 78″ corrugated fiberglass panels down ¼″ from the top of a No. 14 side plate (Fig. 2-4). (See note at end of Step Two for 16-foot model.) Place them between boltholes (Fig. 2-4). Drive a 6d nail part way in at each corner as a temporary fastening. Now, as suggested, you may drill starter holes in each valley of the fiberglass panels approximately ½″ from the edge. Slip a 1″ strip of closure foam in place between the side plate and the fiberglass flush with the top of the fiberglass. Now, drive a screw nail into each valley but not into the corners. Remove the temporary 6d nails. Repeat this process until all panels are attached to the top plate.

Position the other No. 14—which becomes the bottom sill—under the lower edge of the fiberglass panels so that the bottom edge of the No. 14 measures exactly 78″ from the top. The fiberglass may extend as much as ½″ below the bottom, and it may

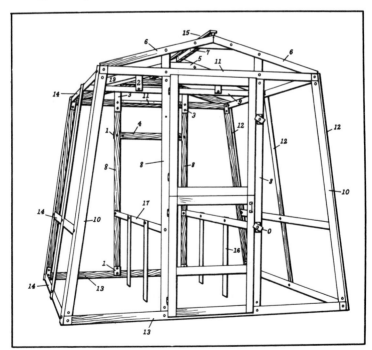

Fig. 2-2. Framework 8′ model (courtesy of Peter Reimuller Co.).

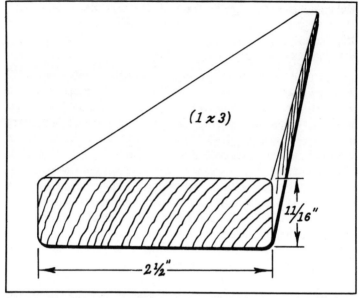

Fig. 2-3. Cutaway of actual measurements of 1 x 3 (courtesy of Peter Reimuller Co.).

vary slightly with each panel. Repeat as you did on the top, insert closure strip and nail.

Stand the unit upright and place the side studs No. 12 against the bottom sill. Make sure that the next bolt hole is 27¾" above. Angle brackets must be sandwiched between Parts No. 14 and No. 12 at all four corners (Fig. 2-5). The unattached ends of the brackets point toward the inside of the greenhouse. Use 2-inch bolts at all locations.

Lay the side unit down with the sill and plate facing up. Nail down fiberglass to each stud with screw nails spaced approximately 6" apart (Fig. 2-6).

To complete the second side, *repeat* all of step two.

For a 16' Model Only. To make side plate and sill for a 16-foot model, proceed as follows.

Place a No. 14 and a No. 140 0 end to end (the ends at which holes are 1¼" from the end) and join together with a metal fastener. This will hold the two parts together until the flat bracket and fiberglass panels are installed. This assembly will be referred to in further instrucitons as a *No. 14.* Now continue with Step Two. Attach the side studs to the top plate and bottom sill. Fasten the plates, end sills, plate and sill extensions together with a 2" x 4" flat metal plate. Use a 2-inch bolt through the stud location and a 1¼"-bolt through the other hole (Fig. 2-7).

Step Three: Construct Rear End Section

Lay out all parts for the rear end section (Fig. 2-8). Note that the end plate assembly No. 11 has a grooved filler strip, which goes to the inside with the groove toward the top. The outside of the end corner stud No. 10 must be in exact alignment with the top corner of the end place No. 11 (Fig. 2-9). Make sure the bolt holes for attaching the rear vent support are down 11⅝" from the top of the rear end posts No. 8. The vent groove in the No. 4 vent support goes toward toward the top (Fig. 2-9). Measure between No. 4 and No. 11 and set the distance to 10⅜" before tightening bolts to insure proper vent fit. Be sure all parts and holes are in proper alignment *before* fastening together!

Fasten each joint with one fastener as shown. Using screw nails, fasten the small angular pieces of flat fiberglass corner panels to the rafters No. 6. Place the 5½" short edge to the inside toward

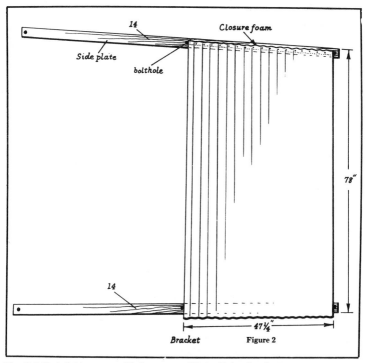

Fig. 2-4. Detail ridge assembly (courtesy of Peter Reimuller Co.).

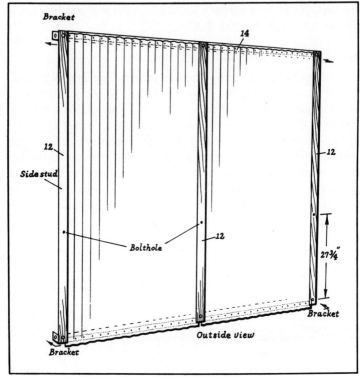

Fig. 2-5. Angle bracket detail (courtesy of Peter Reimuller Co.).

the center of the greenhouse. Align with the edge of the boltholes in the rafter and end plate (Fig. 2-10).

Place one corrugated fiberglass and panel on the frame so that the edge running along the end post will curve up and lap the end posts 1 inch.

The top edge should be flush with the top of the end plate. Square the frame if necessary. Use 6d nails to temporarily fasten the panel. The bottom of this panel will overhang the end sill by about 1 inch. This may be trimmed if necessary to fit on a foundation. Otherwise, the overhang will settle into the ground and act as a seal. Insert closure foam to fit the top, bottom and diagonal side. Lift the panel and slip foam in place. Nail in each valley as you proceed. Nail twice in each valley down the diagonal side, but do *not* nail the outside corner valleys at either the top or bottom edges (Fig. 2-11). Remove the temporary 6d nails.

Repeat this procedure for the opposite side. Be sure that the edge of the panel curves *up* along the end post. Attach the center

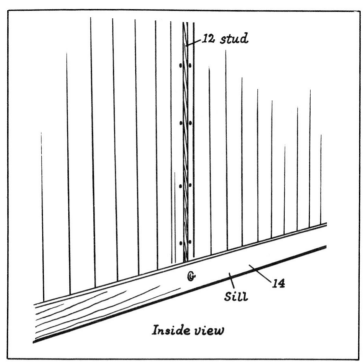

Fig. 2-6. Inside details of sill and plate facing up (courtesy of Peter Reimuller Co.).

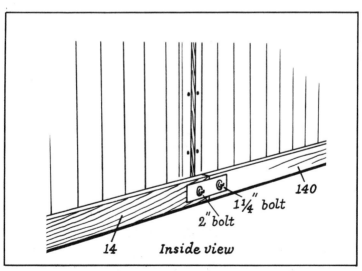

Fig. 2-7. Inside details of levels (courtesy of Peter Reimuller Co.).

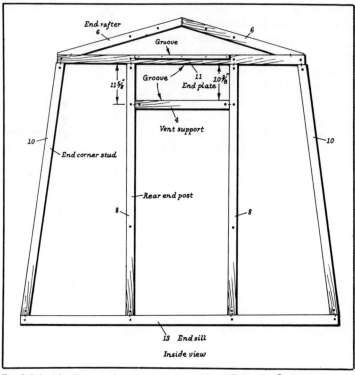

Fig. 2-8. Inside of rear end section (courtesy of Peter Reimuller Co.).

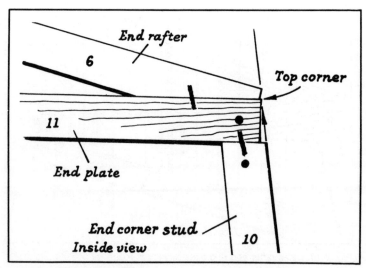

Fig. 2-9. Exact alignment of top corner (courtesy of Peter Reimuller Co.).

76

fiberglass section to the frame in a similar manner. Use closure foam at the top and bottom.

Rafter supports, rafter tie assembly and lower end post backing blocks belong on the inside. Backing blocks for the vent support No. 4 belong on the outside. All use 2″ bolts and all boltheads go to the outside (Fig. 2-12).

Stand the end unit upright and bolt the backing blocks No. 1, the rafter supports, No. 3, and the rafter tie assembly No. 4, into position. Be sure the grooves in the No. 3 supports face each other so the vent panels will fit into these grooves. Flat metal brackets go on all four corners to the inside of the greenhouse and use 1¼″-bolts. Flex two 15″ x 6¾″ flat fiberglass vent panels and place them in the tracks of the upper vent openings. Flex two 15″ x 10¾″ vent panels and place them into the lower vent opening (Fig. 2-13).

Step Four: Construct the Door End Section

The procedure is exactly the same as Step Three except that no vent support is used. There is no center fiberglass panel (Fig. 2-14).

Step Five: Complete the Inside Rafter Frames

Attach two No. 19 inside rafters to a No. 5 rafter tie assembly with 2-inch bolts. Attach the two roof braces to the inside rafters.

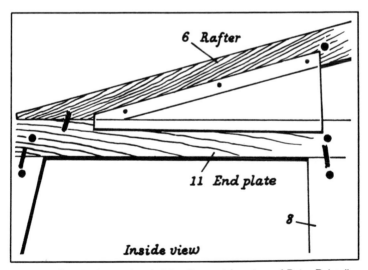

Fig. 2-10. Detail rafter and end plate alignment (courtesy of Peter Reimuller Co.).

Attach a No. 9 side plate cross tie by joining the two roof braces with 2-inch bolts. Adjust the assembly so that the No. 19 inside rafters are flush with, or extend equal distances beyond, the ends of the No. 9 side plate cross tie.

Secure with four metal fasteners (Fig. 2-15). Complete two of these frames for the 12-foot model and three for the 16-foot model.

Step Six: Attach All Frame Sections Together

Additional helping hands during this erection phase will make the job easier and simpler. Please remember, once you attach the frame sections into the upright position, you should completely finish the erection process. High winds might damage a section left partially completed and this could cause extensive damage to the greenhouse framing.

Position one side section to an end section. Remove the 1¼″ corner bolt from each corner of the end unit. Put the unattached end of the corner bracket on the side unit on the outside of the end section (Fig. 2-16). Replace the bolts and tighten the corners together at the top and bottom. Use a large nail or a screwdriver to align the holes.

When all four corners of the greenhouse have been bolted together, align the top of the side studs with the top of the end plates. Nail through the side studs into the corner end studs with three 6d nails each (Fig. 2-17).

Raise the completed inside rafter frames into position and bolt to No. 14 plates. Use angle brackets and 1½″ bolts (Fig. 2-18).

Step Seven: Install Roof

Lift the No. 15 ridge assembly into place. The ends will fit into the slots against the rafters at each end. Drive one 6d nail through the end rafters into each end of the ridge assembly (Fig. 2-19).

For the 16′ model, place the two ridge assemblies together with the ends overlapping and drive a 6d nail down through the ridge cap into the ridge (Fig. 2-20). Fasten the two ridge sections together with a 2″ x 4″ flat metal plate. Use two 2″ bolts.

Place a No. 7 roof support with the narrowest side down on a solid surface. Place a 52½″ x 40″ corrugated roof panel in the proper position on the roof support (Fig. 2-20). The panel should be flush with the edge of the rough, sawcut side of the roof support, and should extend 3″ beyond the end of the roof support. There will be about 4½″ of overhang at the other end. Nail the panel to the support in each valley with a screw nail. Predrilling of nail holes is recommended.

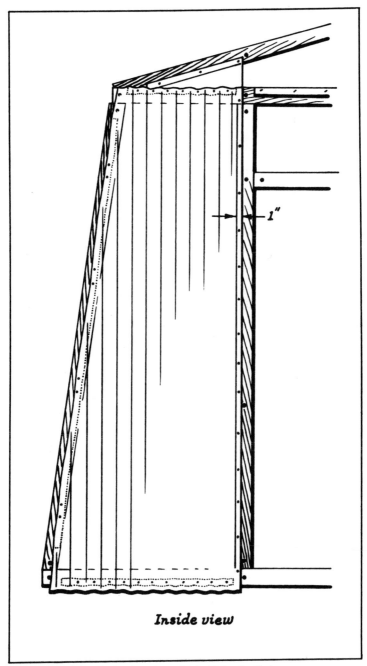

Inside view

Fig. 2-11. Detail inside view (courtesy of Peter Reimuller Co.).

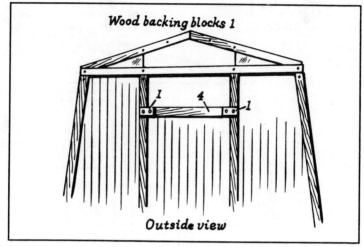

Fig. 2-12. Detail outside view (courtesy of Peter Reimuller Co.).

Lift the roof support and attached panel into position on top of the greenhouse with the 3″ overhang toward the outside end of the greenhouse. Align bolt holes and place two bolts temporarily through the holes. Finger-tighten the nuts. These panels will be removed later before final assembly.

If you are assembling the 16′ model, make sure you use the two No. 70, 41½″ roof supports on each side of the ridge assembly that has the top cap extending 1¼″ beyond the 1″ x 3″ below it (Fig. 2-21).

Working on the same side of the greenhouse, temporarily attach another roof support to the No. 15 ridge assembly. Be sure the rough cut side is against the ridge assembly and that the narrow side is down. Slide another roof panel into position on top of the roof support. Overlap the other panel two or three corrugations with approximately 3″ or more extending to the other end of the roof support.

Working inside the greenhouse and holding the panel in this position, make an alignment mark on the roof support and an exact matching position mark on the underside of the roof panel. Remove this roof support and panel and place the pieces together so that the two marks are lined up exactly. Nail in each valley as before.

Important. Be sure to number or mark each panel so that it can be replaced later in the same roof position. When you have completed one side, remove panels and repeat the same assembly procedure for the other side of the roof.

Using short pieces of tape, attach foam strips to the entire length, and both sides, of the underside of the cap on the ridge assembly (Fig. 2-22). The narrow side of the foam goes toward the top.

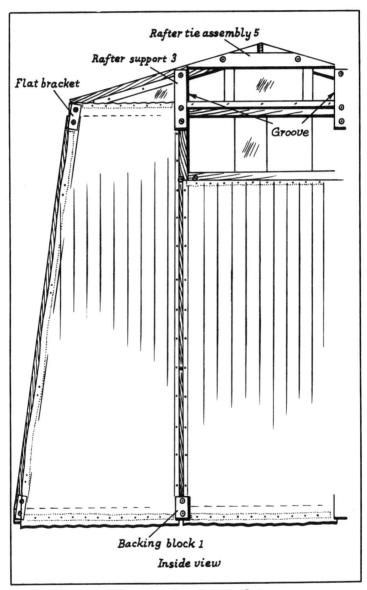

Fig. 2-13. Detail end unit (courtesy of Peter Reimuller Co.).

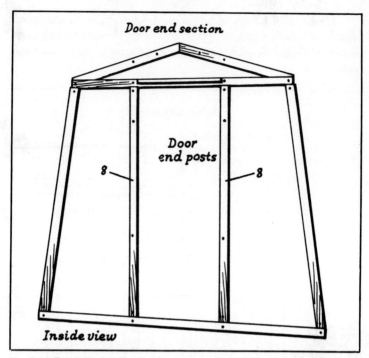

Fig. 2-14. Detail door section, inside view (courtesy of Peter Reimuller Co.).

Starting at one end of the greenhouse, place a pair of opposite roof panels in their original positions and bolt together through the ridge, using 3½" bolts.

Repeat this procedure until all panels are replaced in their proper positions. Tighten all bolts, until foam is completely compressed.

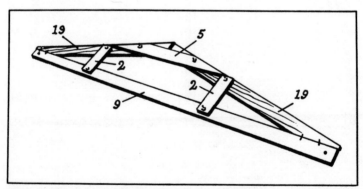

Fig. 2-15. Detail rafter frame (courtesy of Peter Reimuller Co.).

Gently lift the edge of the panels just enough to insert a foam strip on the entire length of the No. 14 top plates. Nail in each valley along the plates. Also nail every 6 inches along the end and inside rafters (Fig. 2-22).

If you have decided that your door will be a Dutch door, the following steps are necessary.

Step Eight: Hang the Dutch Door

Hold the upper half of the Dutch door into position so that it overlaps the door and posts and the door end plate ½" evenly all around. Attach hinges to the door end post. Place the lower half of the door section evenly spaced on the door end posts and about ⅛" so that it clears the upper half of the door down and attach hinges as shown (Fig. 2-2). Use a 3½" bolt through the two latch blocks 0, in both locations 0, See Fig. 2-2 (upper and lower part of door). Nail the first block to the door post to prevent it from turning. Use two nuts on this bolt. Tighten one nut against the other to prevent the latch from loosening (Fig. 2-2).

Step Nine: Assemble Two Benches

Lay a No. 14 rear bench rail on edge and nail a No. 18 bench top board at each end and at the center. The two end boards should

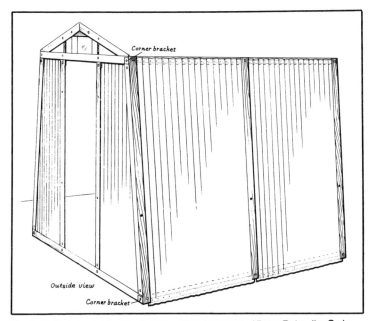

Fig. 2-16. Detail outside view; frame section (courtesy of Peter Reimuller Co.).

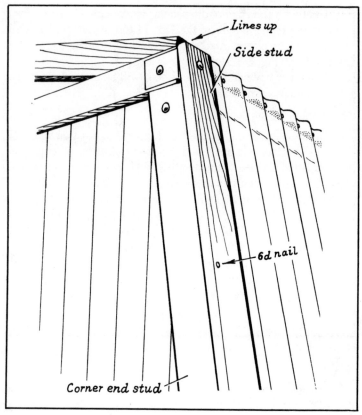

Fig. 2-17. Detail side studs (courtesy of Peter Reimuller Co.).

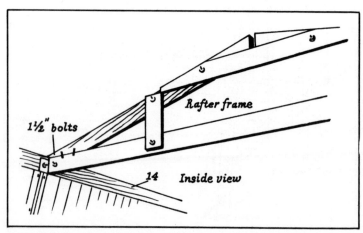

Fig. 2-18. Inside view of rafter frames (courtesy of Peter Reimuller Co.).

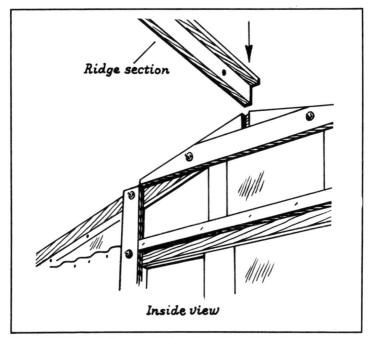

Fig. 2-19. Detail roof rafter assembly (courtesy of Peter Reimuller Co.).

line up flush with the end and the outside of the bench rail. Place a No. 17 front bench rail on edge under the three bench top boards and space parallel with the real bench rail. This spacing must be 28″ from outside to outside (Fig. 2-23). Place the bench top boards across the bench rails, space approximately 1½″ apart. Use two

Fig. 2-20. Detail roof support 16′ model (courtesy of Peter Reimuller Co.)

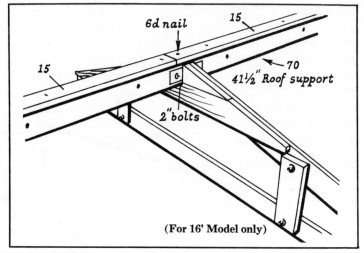

Fig. 2-21. Detail roof support 16' model (courtesy of Peter Reimuller Co.).

nails at each end of the boards. If you want to grow from the ground to top of the greenhouse, leave off the appropriate number of bench top boards.

Fasten a bracket at each end of the rails with a 1¼″ bolt. These brackets go on the back side between the nut and washer and the bench rail. The unattached ends of the brackets go on the same side as the bolt heads (Fig. 2-24). Place the completed bench top assembly into position on the door latchblock side of the greenhouse. Attach the rear bench rail to the side studs with 2″

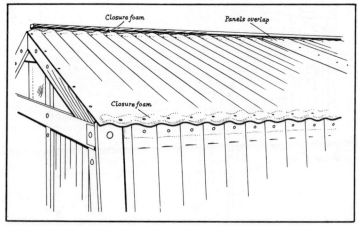

Fig. 2-22. Detail setting closure foam (courtesy of Peter Reimuller Co.).

bolts. Attach the front bench rail to end post and the door post. Use a 1¼" bolt at the end post. Remove the 3½" bolt now holding the door latch blocks. Replace through all parts and retighten. When you attach the opposite bench top assembly, attach the front bench rail at both ends with 1¼" bolts. Using 2" bolts, fasten the legs, Part No. 16, to the front bench rail.

Complete the hinge-side bench top in the same manner. To connect bench rails, refer to Fig. 2-7. Be sure the bolt heads on the front bench rail are on the aisle side of the assembly.

Step Ten: Install Anchoring Stakes

If you did not build a foundation, or any other type of permanent anchoring (such as concrete blocks) for your greenhouse, drive foundation anchoring stakes into the ground as follows.

☐ Two go on each side near the ends and one goes at the center of each end inside the greenhouse.

☐ Keep the stakes vertical and tap them securely into the ground. If you soak the earth a day or two earlier, the stakes will drive in much easier.

☐ Drive stakes far enough into the ground to secure your greenhouse. Leave enough of the stakes above ground so that you can now nail them to the sills.

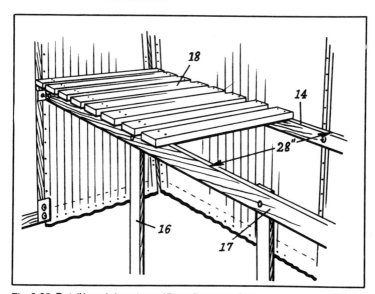

Fig. 2-23. Detail bench (courtesy of Peter Reimuller Co.).

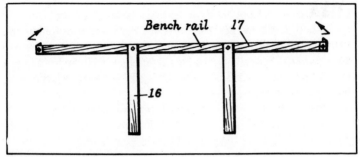

Fig. 2-24. Detail bench rail (courtesy of Peter Reimuller Co.).

Installing Accessories. If you have purchased a vent fan, shutter and other accessories you may install them now.

LEAN-TO GREENHOUSE

This plan is for a 16′ model made of corrugated fiberglass (Fig. 2-24). Its ideal placement is against a wall that has a southern or southeastern exposure so that it will capture the most November through February sunlight.

You might want to place your lean-to over a sliding door, window or standard door. In doing so, you will have access to your greenhouse from within your home, as well as from the Dutch door in this model. This type of placement can provide *some* of the necessary heat to maintain a proper greenhouse temperature.

Unlike the free standing models, lean-to's do require a foundation: concrete, concrete block or wood. The foundation should extend below the frost line and have outside dimensions of 98″ x 86″ for an 8′ model or 86″ x 146″ for a 12′ model and 86″ x 193″ for a 16′ model.

As indicated in Fig. 2-25A, all numbers of materials used correlate to the number in the "Parts Inventory List" (Appendix C).

Many prefabricated models (Fig. 2-25B) are not only precut lumber and fiberglass, but also predrilled. This makes them especially conducive for do-it-yourself greenhouse construction.

Prior to beginning, check your inventory against the Parts Inventory List and mark each piece of lumber with the number and name of the part to correspond to the number in the list. Remember that a 1″ x 3″ actually measures 11/16″ x 2½″ (Fig. 2-3). In the steps to follow be sure that:

☐ *All* bolts use a washer under the nut, not under the head.

88

☐ *All* boltheads go to the *outside* of the greenhouse. Be sure to use *the correct bolt lengths* as indicated in the instructions. During subassembly, tighten all nuts *only finger tight* until that section is completed; then tighten all nuts with an adjustable wrench. For best results, and to avoid splitting, always support the surface you are nailing into.

Although not necessary, you will find it helpful to predrill a 3/32″ starter hole at all 6d nail, screw nail and screw points in both the redwood and fiberglass for better results. This will be recommended in each of the steps to follow.

Step One: Assemble Side Section

Place the 47¼″ x 78″ corrugated fiberglass panels flush with the top of a No. 14 side plate. Place them between boltholes (Fig. 2-26). Drive a 6d nail part way in at each corner as a temporary fastening. Now, as suggested, you may drill starter holes in each valley of the fiberglass panels approximately ½″ from the edge.

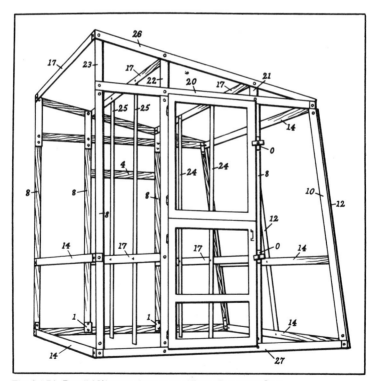

Fig. 2-25A. Detail 16′ lean-to (courtesy of Peter Reimuller Co.).

Slip a 1" strip of closure foam in place between the side plate and the fiberglass flush with the top. Now, drive a ⅝" screw nail into each valley but not onto the corners. Remove the temporary 6d nails. Repeat this process until all panels are attached to the top plate.

Position the other No. 14—which becomes the bottom sill—under the lower edge of the fiberglass panels so that the bottom edge of the No. 4 measures exactly 78" from the top. The fiberglass may extend about ¼" below the bottom, and it may vary slightly with each panel. Repeat as you did on the top; insert closure top and nail with ⅝" screw nails.

Place the side studs No. 12 against the bottom sill. Make sure that the next bolt hole is 27¾" above. Angle brackets must be sandwiched between parts No. 14 and No. 12 at all four corners (Fig. 2-27). The unattached ends of the brackets point toward the inside of the greenhouse. Use 2" bolts at all locations.

For 16' Model Only. To make side plate, sill and rear bench rail for the 16 foot model, proceed as follows.

Place a No. 14 and a No. 140 end to end (both end holes of completed part to be ⅝" from ends) and join together with a corrugated metal fastener. This will hold the two parts together until the flat bracket and fiberglass panels are installed. This assembly will be referred to in further instructions as a No. 14. Attach the side studs to the top plate, side bench rail and bottom sill. Fasten the plates, end sills, plate and sill extensions together with a 2" x 4" flat metal plate. Use a 2" bolt through the stud location and a 1¼" bolt through the stud location and a 1¼" bolt through the other hole (Fig. 2-28).

Bolt a rear bench rail No. 14 on the same side as the sill and plate. Turn the side until over with the sill, plate and bench rail facing up. Nail down fiberglass to each stud with ⅝" screw nails spaced approximately 6 inches apart (Fig. 2-29).

Step Two: Assemble the Two End Sections

Lay out all parts for both the right and left end sections. Note that grooves should be on the No. 20 which must go on the lower edge (Fig. 2-30).

The outside of the end corner stud No. 10 must be in exact alignment with the top corner of the end plate No. 20. See Fig. 2-31. Use a piece of 1 x 3 to obtain correct alignment as shown. All six No. 8 pieces must be placed with the end that has the bolt holes 10⅜" apart toward the top. Be sure all parts and holes are in proper

Fig. 2-25B. A 12' lean-to.

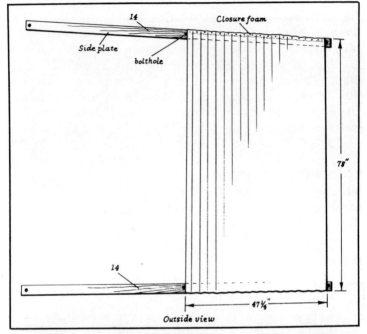

Fig. 2-26. Detail outside view, side section (courtesy of Peter Reimuller Co.).

alignment before fastening together. Now fasten each joint with one corrugated fastener where shown.

Be sure framework is square. Measure diagonally between inside of framing as indicated (Fig. 2-32). Make the measurements equal 86¾".

Position rafter No. 26 as indicated in Fig. 2-33. Attach the angled end with two corrugated fasteners. Use a No. 23 to position the distance between the No. 20 and the No. 26 by aligning the bolt holes. Place bolts through holes temporarily to insure proper spacing until the flat plastic panel is nailed in place.

Using ⅝" screw nails spaced as in Fig. 2-8, fasten one of the angular pieces of flat plastic to the rafter No. 26 and top plate No. 20. Align the plastic panel with the edges of the bolt holes in the rafter and end plates, and slipped under the No. 23. After nailing the panel, remove No. 23 and the temporary bolts.

Place one angular corrugated acrylic end panel on the frame so that the edge laps the end post 1" and is flush with the bottom of the sill. Using ⅝" screw nails spaced 12" apart, attach the panel to the No. 8 end post. Insert closure foam at top, bottom and along the corner stud No. 10. No closure foam is required along the end post.

Nail in each valley along top and bottom. Nail twice in each valley down the diagonal corner stud (Fig. 2-34). Nail the 21″ x 76″ piece of corrugated fiberglass flush with the bottom of the sill.

Bolt the two No. 1 blocks and the three 2″ x 4″ flat metal brackets loosely into position (Fig. 2-34). It will be necessary, in Step Three, to slide the acrylic panel beneath the two No. 1 blocks. Use 2″ bolts for the two No. 1 blocks and 1¼″ bolts for the flat metal brackets.

Insert 2″ bolts through the holes to attach the No. 21, 22, and 23 pieces. Place the three 2″ x 4″ corner brackets as shown (Fig. 2-35). Note that the brackets under No. 21 and No. 22 face each other and the bracket under No. 23 faces the outside of the assembled unit. Use washers and nuts to attach the No. 21, 22 and 23 rafter supports into position.

Turn the two assembled end units over. Block up the units so that you do not bend the three metal corner brackets. Drive to ⅝″

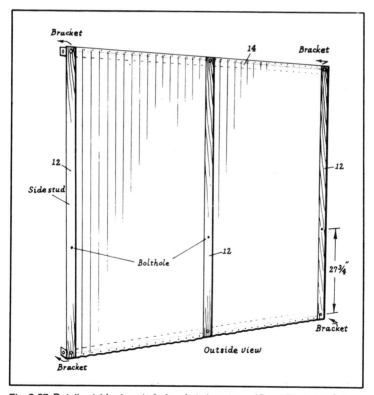

Fig. 2-27. Detail outside view studs; brackets (courtesy of Peter Reimuller Co.).

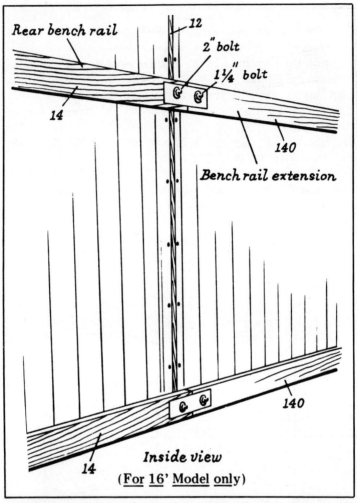

Fig. 2-28. Detail side plate, sill and rear bench rail for 16' model only (courtesy of Peter Reimuller Co.).

screw nails through the first plastic panel into the back of the No. 23 rafter support (Fig. 2-36).

Step Three: Complete Door End and Back End

Decide now on which end of the greenhouse you want the door; you will hang it later.

To complete the other end, turn this unit back over and place the No. 4 rear vent support into position with the grooved edge end

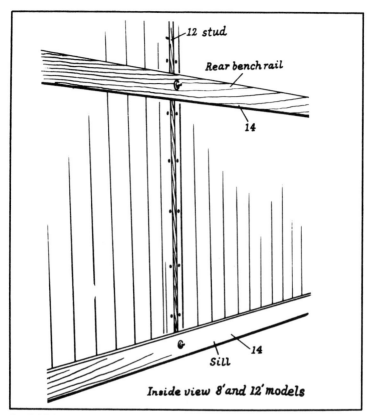

Fig. 2-29. Inside View 8' and 12' models (courtesy of Peter Reimuller Co.).

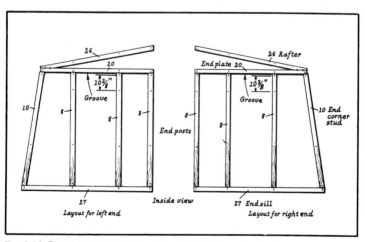

Fig. 2-30. Detail end sections (courtesy of Peter Reimuller Co.).

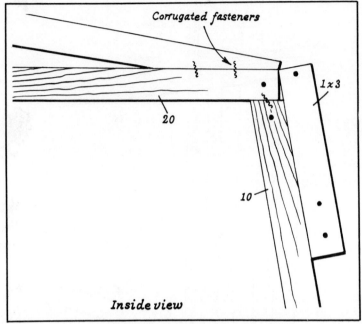

Fig. 2-31. Inside view end plate (courtesy of Peter Reimuller Co.).

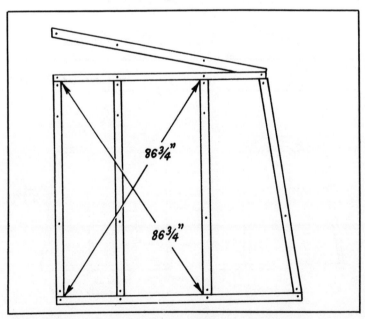

Fig. 2-32. Squared framework detail (courtesy Peter Reimuller Co.).

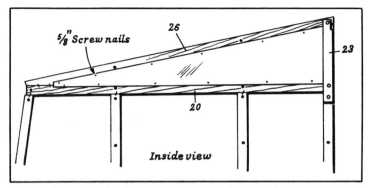

Fig. 2-33. Detail rafter inside view (courtesy Peter Reimuller Co.).

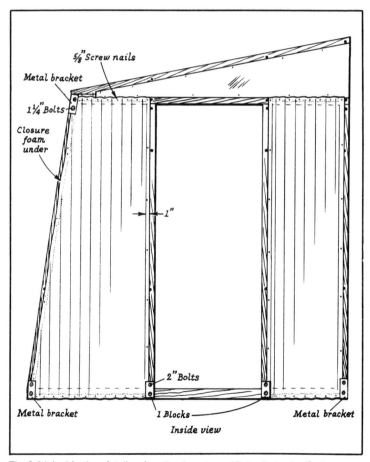

Fig. 2-34. Inside view detail end section (courtesy of Peter Reimuller Co.).

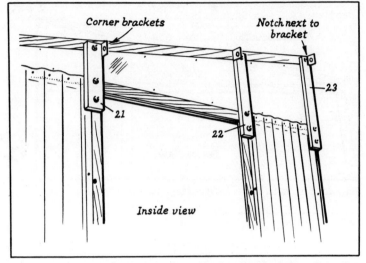

Fig. 2-35. Inside view bracket placement detail (courtesy of Peter Reimuller Co.).

toward the top. Make sure the distance between the No. 4 vent support and the No. 20 is exactly 10⅜″ (Fig. 2-37). Place the 30¾″ x 63″ rear center acrylic panel into position. Insert closure foam strips under the panel along the top and bottom. Nail the panel to the frame with a ⅝″ screw nails spaced as shown. Stand the unit upright and bolt the No. 4 to the two No. 8 end posts. Use a No. 1 backing block at each end (Fig. 2-38).

Flex two of the 10⅔″ flat plastic vent panels and insert into the grooved tracks on No. 4 and No. 20. This completes the end units.

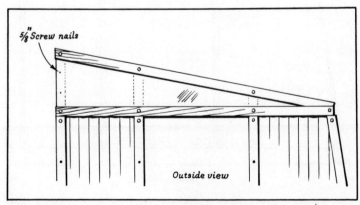

Fig. 2-36. Outside view of a rafter support (courtesy of Peter Reimuller Co.).

Step Four: Attach End Sections to Side Section

Position side section to end section.

Remove the 1¼" corner bolt from each corner of the end unit. Put the unattached end of the corner bracket on the side unit on the outside of the end section (Fig. 2-39). Replace the bolts and tighten the corners together top and bottom. Use a screwdriver to align holes.

When the two corners of the greenhouse have been bolted together, align the top of the side studs with the top of the end plates. Nail through the side studs with the top of the end plates. Nail through the side studs with the top of the end plates. Nail through the side studs into the corner end studs with three 6d nails each (Fig. 2-40).

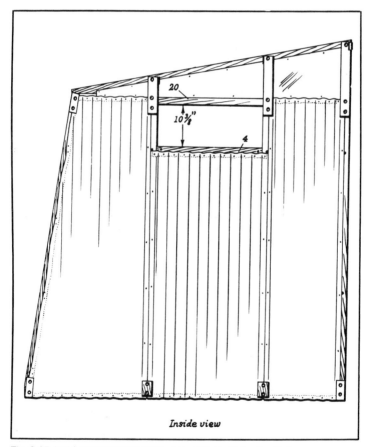

Inside view

Fig. 2-37. Inside view end detail (courtesy of Peter Reimuller Co.).

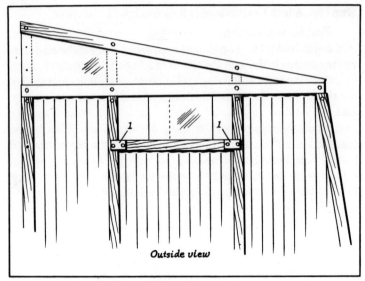

Fig. 2-38. Detail outside view end posts (courtesy of Peter Reimuller Co.).

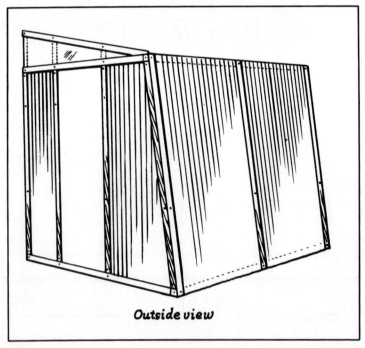

Fig. 2-39. Outside view attached end section to side section (courtesy of Peter Reimuller Co.).

Step Five: Attach Cross Ties, Bench Rails and Roof Supports

Bolt three No. 17 cross ties to the angle brackets on the two ends with 1¼″ bolts (Fig. 2-41). Bolt an angle bracket at each end of the remaining No. 17's with 1¼″ bolts.

Remove the nuts from the lower open end of both end sections. Place the brackets on a No. 17 onto the end section bolts and replace nuts. For benches, install two No. 17's to the proper No. 8 end posts.

Fig. 2-40. Detail end stud alignment (courtesy of Peter Reimuller Co.).

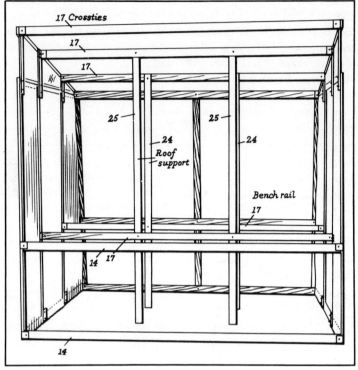

Fig. 2-41. Detail square framing (courtesy of Peter Reimuller Co.).

Using 2″ bolts, attach the two No. 24 and the two No. 25 roof supports to the cross ties and bench rails. The two No. 25 roof supports are longer and go toward the higher side of the greenhouse (Fig. 2-41). Note that the four roof supports must be installed on the aisle side of the bench rails.

Step Six: Install Roof Panels

First, square the greenhouse by taking inside diagonal measurements (Fig. 2-42). These two measurements must be equal.

Slide a 52½″ x 76″ roof panel with curved edge down at the outside of the panel onto the top of the greenhouse. Keep the top edge of the panel even with the outside edge of the top crosstie. Use 6d nails to temporarily fasten the panel to the rafter and the top sill. Drill starter holes through each wall along the top and bottom edges. Carefully lift the panel and place a strip of closure foam under the top and bottom of the panel. Nail the ¾″ screw nails in each valley (Fig. 2-43). Remove the temporary 6d nails. Lap the fiberglass panels over each other by three corrugations so that the roof is evenly covered and nail all into position along the top and bottom crossties. Nail along both end rafters every 6 inches.

Step Seven: Attach Greenhouse To Structure

Your greenhouse may be attached directly to your structure, but it is recommended that you first attach a frame to the structure. The framing should measure 98" x 92" for an 8' model, 146" x 92" for a 12' model, 193" x 92" for a 16' model; 2 x 3's are recommended for this purpose. The framing should be secured with a suitable fastener: 10d to 16d nails for a wood frame structure, expansion bolts for brick, stone or stucco type structures. The framing should be fully caulked between the frame and the structure. The greenhouse may then be attached to this frame with 6d nails driven through the No. 17 top and bottom crossties at 10" intervals. If required, it is also recommended that the top and sides now be flashed or caulked to complete the seal.

Step Eight: Install Bench Tops

Place the 30" long redwood boards and, if two benches are being installed, the 23" long redwood boards, across the bench rails should be spaced approximately 1½" apart. Do not nail the bench boards into place until the uniform distance between the

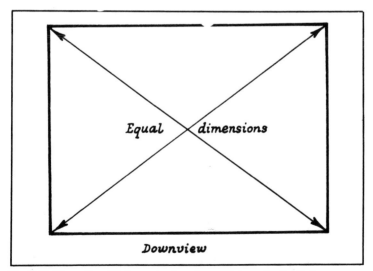

Fig. 2-42. Down view, detail squaring (courtesy of Peter Reimuller Co.).

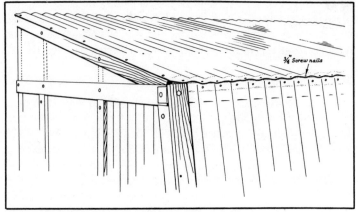

Fig. 2-43. Detail roof panels (courtesy of Peter Reimuller Co.).

boards has been established. Use two 6d nails at each end of each board (Fig. 2-44).

Step Nine: Install Anchoring Stakes

If you live in a climate where it is unnecessary to build any type of permanent foundation, drive the anchoring stakes into the ground as follows. Two go on each side near the ends and one goes at the inside center of the greenhouse.

Keep the stakes vertical and tap them securely into the ground. Soaking the earth a day or two earlier will help you to drive the stakes in more easily.

Drive the stakes far enough into the ground to secure the greenhouse, but leave enough of the stakes above the ground so that you can nail them to the sills.

Step Ten: Install Dutch Door

If you have built a Dutch door for your lean-to, attach two hinges to each door section 4 inches in from the top and bottom of each door section. Install the door handle on the lower door section (Fig. 2-45).

Hold the upper half of the Dutch door into position so that it overlaps the door end posts and the door end plate ½" evenly all around. Attach hinges to the door end post. Place the lower half of the door section evenly spaced on the door end posts and down about ⅛" so that it clears the upper half of the door and attach hinges. Use a 3-inch bolt through the two latch blocks 0, in both locations—upper and lower door. Nail the first block to the door post to prevent it from turning. Use two nuts on this bolt; tighten one nut against the other to prevent the latch from loosening.

Step Eleven: Installing Accessories

A vent fan, shutters and other accessories may be installed now.

Exhaust Fan. Place the fan in the rear vent opening, flush to one side. Fasten the fan in this position with screws (Fig. 2-46). Cut both the fiberglass vents to 9″ wide (scribe with a sharp knife and fold) to allow ventilation when the fan is not in use.

Vent Shutters. See Fig. 2-47. Slide the fiberglass vents to the latch side of the Dutch door. Mount the vent shutters inside the vent panel opening on the hinge side using screws. The shutters open automatically to the inside when the fan is turned on.

Electric Heater. They require no special installation; just plug them in. They may be moved for best heat adjustment, but are most efficient when placed at the back end of the greenhouse. Use a heavy-duty extension cord.

FREE-STANDING POLYETHYLENE GREENHOUSE

A greenhouse of polyethylene can face in any direction; the same goes for fiberglass and glass covered houses. The "arched"

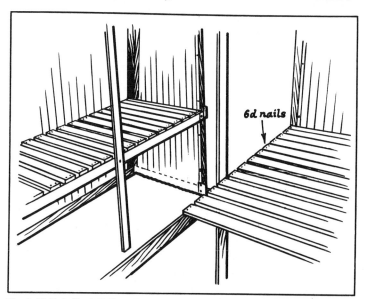

Fig. 2-44. Detail installation of bench tops (courtesy of Peter Reimuller Co.).

Fig. 2-45. Handle installation, dutch door (courtesy of Peter Reimuller Co.).

model (Figs. 2-48A and 2-48B) provides a delightfully aesthetic appearance that will enhance any location. It should, however, receive at least three hours of winter sunlight daily. To keep plants cooler in summer, choose a spot shared by trees that are deciduous.

If you want to provide a foundation, concrete blocks laid in a neat row with outside dimensions of 78″ x 98″ for the 8′ model makes an ideal foundation. Additions must be made if you construct a 12′ model.

Be sure the blocks are level on top and that the diagonal measurements—from corner to corner—are equal. If you are in an excessively windy location, you might want to cement in bolts to secure your polyethylene greenhouse to its foundation.

If you plan to install your greenhouse on a paved area such as asphalt, drive small pipes down about one foot through the surface and anchor the greenhouse to them. On concrete, it is necessary to drill holes and use anchor bolts available for that purpose.

On any surface 2 x 4′s, 4 x 4′s, or railroad ties make an excellent base. Either nail, bolt, or use other anchoring devices to secure the greenhouse in place. When using 2 x 4′s or 4 x 4′s on any hard surface, it is recommended that you lag bolt the sills into the surface before anchoring the greenhouse to them.

The following instructions are for an 8′ model and 12′ model house. If you construct a 12′ structure, note the supplemental instructions included where necessary.

Note that the diagram of the greenhouse (Fig. 2-48) indicates each piece of numbered material. Prepare your inventory sheet and indicate the number along with the name of the piece of material for ease in referring to them during construction assembly. Parts inventory lists are in Appendices E and F.

Remember that a 1 x 3 actually measures 11/16″ x 2½″. It is also important to remember that:

☐ *All* bolts use a washer under the nut, not under the head.

☐ *All* bolt heads go to the *outside* of the greenhouse. Be sure to use the *correct bolt lengths* as indicated in the directions. During assembly, tighten all nuts *only finger tight* until the model is completed; then tighten all nuts with an adjustable wrench. For best results, and to avoid splitting, always support the surface you are nailing to.

☐ It is helpful to predrill a 3/32″ starter hole at all 6d nail, screw nail and screw points for better results.

☐ Do not leave your unit partially assembled, i.e., with the sides and no ends.

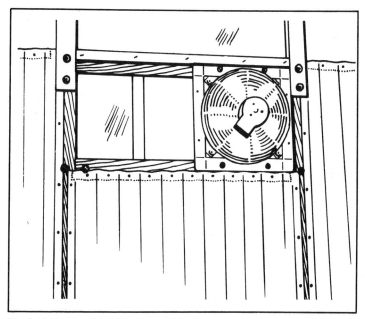

Fig. 2-46. Vent fan detail (courtesy of Peter Reimuller Co.).

Fig. 2-47. Vent shutter inside Dutch door (courtesy of Peter Reimuller Co.).

☐ Mark or paint arches so that you will place the colored end down and the smooth side out when instructed in the steps which follow.

Step One: Assemble Both Sides

Using carriage bolts of the size shown in Fig. 2-49, bolt parts No. 04 and No. 014 together as indicated. For the 12′ model, an additional part No. 04 will be needed for each side, as indicated in the inventory parts list, with a corner bracket between parts No. 04 and No. 014 at each corner with the unattached end of brackets facing up, (Fig. 2-50).

Step Two: Assemble Two Bench Rails

Using 2″ carriage bolts, fasten the two legs, part No. 015, to bench rail, part No. 016, as in Fig. 2-51. For the 12′ model, there will be three legs for each bench rail as indicated in the inventory parts list. Fasten a bracket at each end of the rails with a 1¼″ carriage bolt. These brackets go on the front side between the bolt head and the bench rail. The unattached ends of the brackets go on the same side as the carriage bolt nuts.

Step Three: Assemble Support for Arches

Fasten the two parts No. 05 to the two parts No. 013. For the 12' model, there are three parts No. 05—with two 6d nails at each joint (Fig. 2-52). Parts No. 05 are nailed exactly 32¼" in from the ends.

Step Four: Assemble Ridge Section

Nail part No. 011 to part No. 012 with nails spaced about 1' apart (Fig. 2-53). Attach parts No. 02 to each end of ridge with two nails each. These parts are spaced ¾" *down* from the bottom of the ridge cap.

Step Five: Assemble Door End

Fasten end posts No. 08 to end sill No. 010 using backing blocks No. 1 and 2" carriage bolts (Fig. 2-54). Note that bolt holes in No. 08's that are 14¾" from the end go toward the No. 06. Attach the door header No. 06 across top of posts using the 2" bolts. Insert

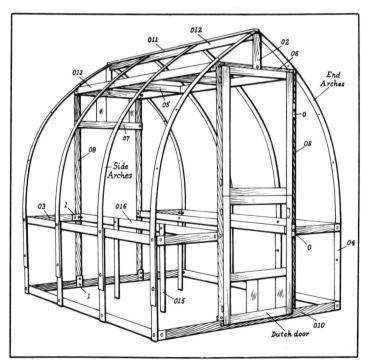

Fig. 2-48A. Arched free-standing polyethelyne model (courtesy Peter Reimuller Co.).

corner angle brackets between the posts and header on both sides with the unattached ends of the brackets facing the inside of the greenhouse. Note that the filler strip that is attached to the door header goes to the outside—flush with and between the door posts.

Step Six: Assemble Back End

Fasten end posts No. 08 to sill No. 010 using backing blocks No. 1 and two 2″ carriage bolts. Attach header No. 06 and vent support No. 07 across end posts using 2″ carriage bolts, inserting brackets between end posts using 2″ carriage bolts, inserting brackets between end posts and header on both sides with the unattached ends of the brackets facing to the inside of the greenhouse (Fig. 2-55). Be sure that grooved filler strips face the *outside*, with the groove on the header facing *down*, and the groove on the vent support facing *up*.

Install the flat fiberglass sliding vent panels now by bending slightly and inserting into the grooved filler strips.

Step Seven: Attach Ends to Side Units

Stand the assembled side units about 6½′ apart and bolt both end units at the sill No. 010 to the lower corner brackets of the side units with 1¼″ carriage bolts. If you are installing benches, place a bench assembly on each side between door end posts and insert a 2-inch bolt through each hole from the outside of the door and rear end posts. Do *not* attach the washer and nut yet.

Bolt the end cross supports No. 03 between the top of the side assemblies and the end posts (Fig. 2-56). Use a 1¼″ bolts at the side unit brackets. Use the backing blocks No. 1 and two 2-inch bolts—one of which is already holding the bench rail into position if you have benches—at the post end of each cross brace.

Step Eight: Install Arch Support Unit

Lift the arch support assembly into position and fasten with 1¼″ carriage bolts with the bolt heads to the outside of the greenhouse (Fig. 2-57).

Step Nine: Attach Ridge Assembly

Place the ridge assembly into position on the headers (Fig. 2-57) and fasten with 2″ bolts.

Step Ten: Install Arches

In Fig. 2-48, you will find that the arches go into position with the colored end down and the smooth side out as indicated in the

Fig. 2-48B. Arched free-standing polyethelyne model (courtesy of Peter Reimuller Co.).

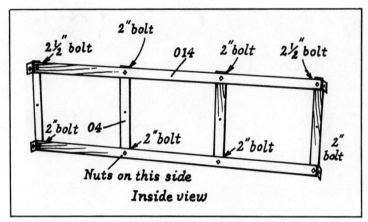

Fig. 2-49. Detail of carriage bolts (courtesy of Peter Reimuller Co.).

parts inventory list. Arches with six bolt holes must be used at the four corners. Arches with two bolt holes must be used as the side arches. There are four side arches and eight end arches for the 8′ model and six side arches and eight end arches for the 12′ model.

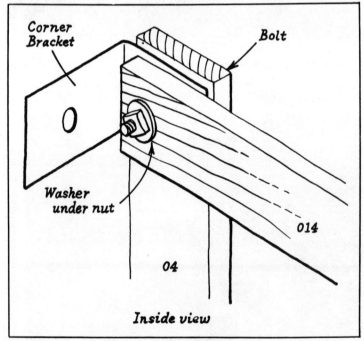

Fig. 2-50. Bracket detail (courtesy of Peter Reimuller Co.).

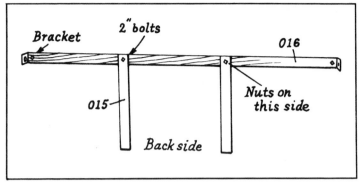

Fig. 2-51. Details of Bench rails (courtesy of Peter Reimuller Co.).

Attach arches one at a time. Remove the bolt at the top rail of the side assembly. With the pointed end *down*—again on parts inventory list—place the proper arch in position and then replace the bolt to hold the arch to side unit.

Bolt the bottom end of the arch into position. Bottoms of corner arches require a 2-inch bolt and side arches use a 1¼" bolt. When all arches are bolted to side assemblies, square up the entire greenhouse framework and tighten all nuts except the 2½" bolts at the upper corners of the side assemblies. Fit the upper ends of the arches under the ridge cap. Be sure that the tops of the corner arches are flush with the outside of No. 02 ridge supports (Fig. 2-58). Nail all arches to the arch support members No. 013. Use one nail at each location.

Step Eleven: Cut Covering

Cut all covering to approximate sizes (Fig. 2-59). Check carefully to be sure all of your dimensions are measured correctly before proceeding. Fig. 2-60 shows a cutting pattern for a 12′ model.

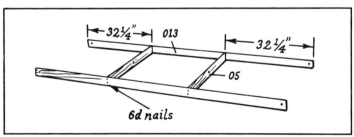

Fig. 2-52. Detail arch assembly support (courtesy of Peter Reimuller Co.).

113

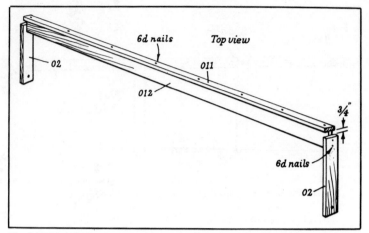

Fig. 2-53. Detail ridge section assembly (courtesy of Peter Reimuller Co.).

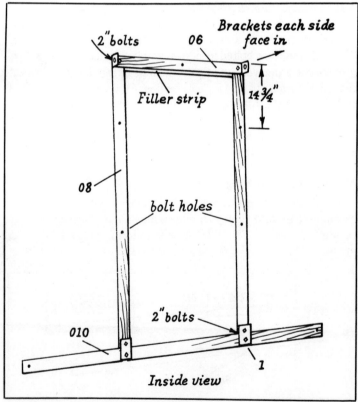

Fig. 2-54. Door end assembly details (courtesy of Peter Reimuller Co.).

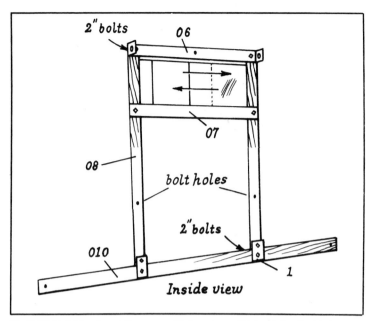

Fig. 2-55. Detail back end door assembly (courtesy of Peter Reimuller Co.).

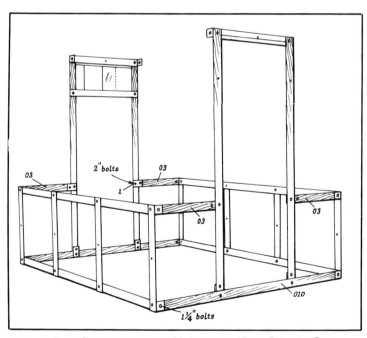

Fig. 2-56. Detail Cross support assembly (courtesy of Peter Reimuller Co.).

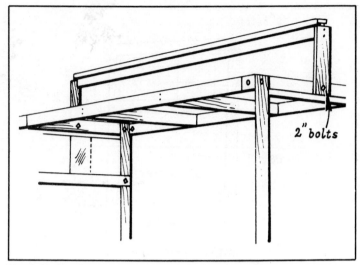

Fig. 2-57. Detail arch support unit and ridge assembly (courtesy of Peter Reimuller Co.).

Step Twelve: Attach Covering to Door and Door Installation

Trim the polyethelene covering to the outside dimensions of each door section. Fasten the hinges to each door section (Fig. 2-61). Now place the covering on the same side as the hinges. This will be the inside of the door when completed.

Fold the material under about 1¼″ to the inside of the door frame. Place the nailing strip along the folded edge. Nail through the strip about every 4 inches with the ⅝″ screw nails. Complete both sections of the Dutch door and mount to the door post. Hold the upper half of the Dutch door into position so that it overlaps the door end posts and the door end plate ½″ evenly all around. Attach hinges to the door end post. Place the lower half of the door section evenly spaced on the door end posts and down about ⅛″ so that it clears the upper half of the door and attach hinges as above (Fig. 2-61). Install the door handle on the lower door section. Flex the two flat fiberglass vent panels and place them into the tracks at bottom of Dutch door.

Step Thirteen: Install U.V.I (Polyethelene) on End Sections

Push on the greenhouse framing until the end is square with the door. This will re-square the entire end section and ready it for the U.V.I (polyethelene) installation. Take one of the pieces of U.V.I. you have cut for the door end and tack it to the sill and door

116

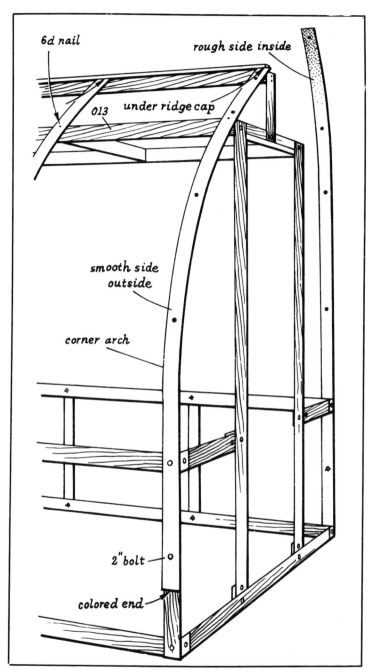

Fig. 2-58. Detail insulation arches (courtesy of Peter Reimuller Co.).

117

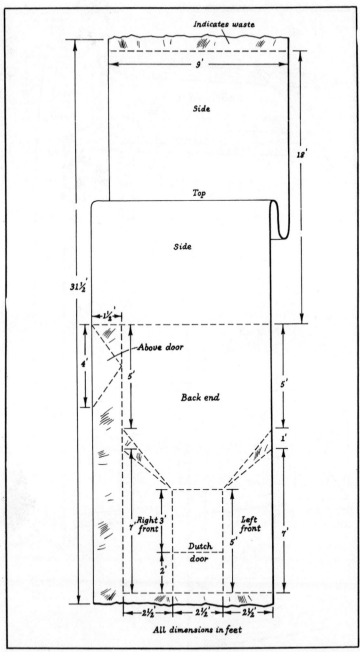

Fig. 2-59. Pattern to cut the cover for an 8' model (courtesy of Peter Reimuller Co.).

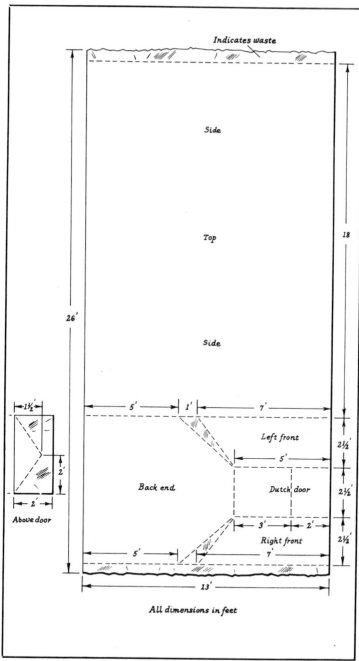

Indicates waste

Side

Top

Side

26'

18

1½'

5'   1'   7'

Left front

5'

2½'

2'

Back end

Dutch door

2½'

2'

3'   2'

Above door

Right front

2½'

5'   7'

13'

All dimensions in feet

Fig. 2-60. Cutting pattern for a 12' model (courtesy of Peter Reimuller Co.).

119

post. Use the nailing strip and fold the edge of the covering as you did in covering the door (Fig. 2-62). Pull the covering across the arch. Make a cut and overlap where necessary to prevent wrinkling. Tape the U.V.I. temporarily, with short pieces of tape, to the underside of the arch. Do the other panel and the area above the door the same way. Be sure to fold the lower edge and use the nailing strip. Square the back end. The rear U.V.I. panel is one large section and it is installed in the same manner. Place in position, wrap around the arches and tape temporarily to the underside (Fig. 2-62). Cut out the area for the vent, slit the corners at a 45-degree angle, fold under the tack into place using the nailing strip (Fig. 2-63). Continue the nailing strip down each end post and across the width of the sill.

Both ends of the greenhouse are now complete. The turn latches can now be installed to secure the door. Remove the 2-inch bolt from the door post. Replace this bolt with a 3½″ bolt through the two latch blocks No. 0. Cut the nailing strip away from under the latch block. Nail the first block to the door post to prevent it from turning. Use two nuts on this bolt; tighten one nut against the other to prevent the latch from loosening. Repeat this procedure for the upper half of the Dutch door (Fig. 2-64).

Step Fourteen: Install U.V.I. on Sides

Take the large piece of U.V.I. and drape it over the greenhouse frame so that the edges are evenly spaced. The extra arches are to be used, one at each corner, to hold all the covering firmly and permanently in position.

Slip one of the arches under the covering at one back end corner with the *colored* end up (Fig. 2-65). Wrap the U.V.I. under this loose arch toward the inside of the greenhouse. Repeat this step on the other back end corner arch. The U.V.I. should be as even as possible under the loose arches. Position the arches so that the bolt holes line up. Use a sharp pencil to make a hole through the covering. Place one 1¼″ bolt through the bolt hole nearest the top of each arch and finger tighten the nut.

Repeat this at the two door end-corner arches. Be sure that the U.V.I. is as tight as possible. Have a helper stretch the covering from the inside. This will remove wrinkles and will make a smooth appearance and a stronger greenhouse. As your helper stretches the U.V.I., punch a hole through the cover at the second bolt hole from the top and insert a bolt. Tighten the nut only finger tight. Repeat at the other three corners.

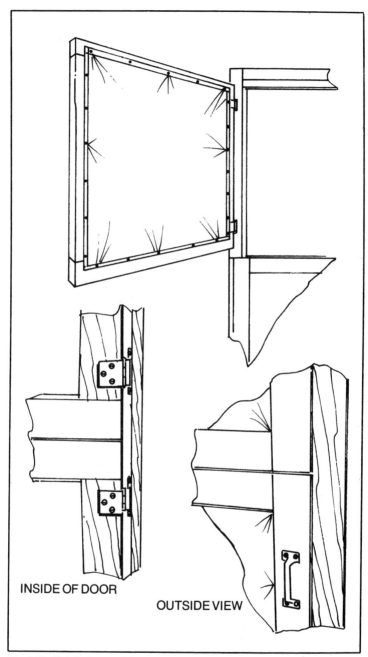

INSIDE OF DOOR

OUTSIDE VIEW

Fig. 2-61. Details for attaching a covering to door insulation (courtesy of Peter Reimuller Co.).

121

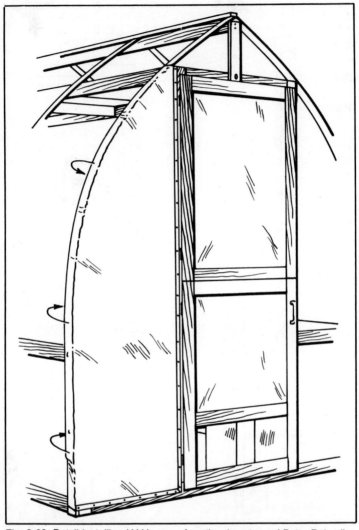

Fig. 2-62. Detail installing U.V.I. on end section (courtesy of Peter Reimuller Co.).

Repeat this process until all bolts are in place and the covering is tight. The bolt that holds the arch to the upper side rail must be removed and run through all parts. Likewise for the 2-inch bolt at the bottom of the corner arches. When all arches and bolts are in place, have your helper stretch the U.V.I by pulling from the inside and down while you tighten the nuts, working from the top to the bottom of the greenhouse.

When finished with the sides, complete the bottom edges by folding under the excess covering and tacking to the outside of the bottom rail. Use the tacking strip. Use a sharp knife or razor blade to trim off excess U.V.I. inside the greenhouse for a neat appearance.

Step Fifteen: Install Bench Tops

Place 24-inch long redwood boards across the bench rails. Space them approximately 1½ inches apart. Do not nail the bench slats into place until uniform distance between the slats has been determined. Use two nails at each end of each slat. Be sure to support the bench rails when nailing the bench boards (Fig. 2-66).

Step Sixteen: Install Anchoring Stakes

If you did not build a permanent foundation for your plastic covered greenhouse, drive the foundation anchoring stakes into

Fig. 2-63. Installing U.V.I. around vent (courtesy of Peter Reimuller Co.).

Fig. 2-64. Detail door bolts (courtesy of Peter Reimuller Co.).

the ground as follows. Two go on each side near the ends and one goes at the center of each end inside the greenhouse.

Keep the stakes vertical and tap them securely into the ground. Drive the stakes far enough into the ground to secure the greenhouse. Leave enough of the stakes above ground so that you can nail them to the sills.

THE DOME GREENHOUSE

This greenhouse offers much for the small city lot and makes an ideal addition to the patio area. Constructed from fiberglass, it will provide many years of carefree maintenance.

A dome greenhouse, although smaller than most, gives the advantage of raising plants directly in the soil itself. The dome's shape and height allow sufficient area to raise taller plants than in many of the conventional houses (Fig. 2-67).

It does not require a separate foundation. Staking it to the ground with redwood stakes is sufficient. However, in areas where high winds (over 40 mph) are common, a simple brick or cement block foundation is recommended.

The foundation for the Sun Dome is a decagon—10 sided polygon—and should measure as shown in Fig. 2-68. Be sure the blocks are level on top. Cement in bolts to secure the greenhouse to its foundation.

If you have decided to install your dome on a paved area such as asphalt, drive small pipes about 1 foot through the surface and

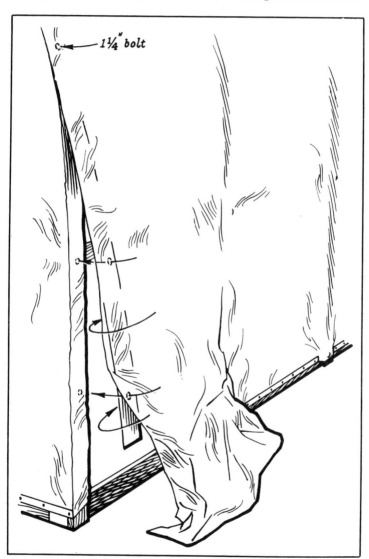

Fig. 2-65. Installing U.V.I. on sides (courtesy of Peter Reimuller Co.).

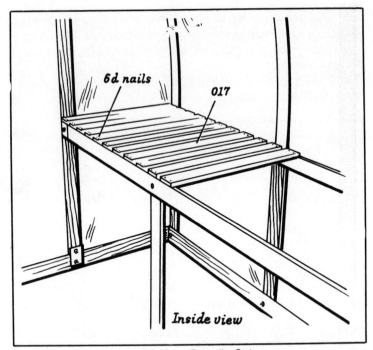

Fig. 2-66. Bench tops (courtesy of Peter Reimuller Co.).

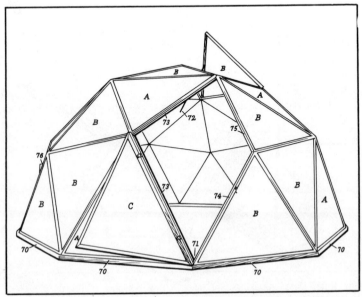

Fig. 2-67A. Details of a dome greenhouse (courtesy of Peter Reimuller Co.).

126

Fig. 2-67B. A dome greenhouse (courtesy of Peter Reimuller Co.).

anchor the greenhouse to them. On brick areas, remove bricks and use redwood stakes. On concrete, it is necessary to drill holes and use anchor bolts available for that purpose.

In the construction steps which follow, remember for *all* bolts use a washer under both the nut and under the head of the bolt. During assembly, tighten all nuts *only finger tight* until the model is completed; then tighten all nuts with an adjustable wrench. For best results and to avoid splitting, always support the surface you are nailing into.

Each part indicated in the illustrations has been provided a code number to correspond to the parts inventory list. Prior to

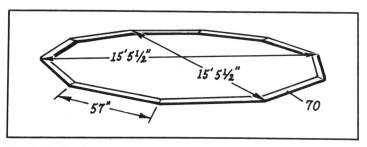

Fig. 2-68. Detail measurement for 10-sided polygon (courtesy of Peter Reimuller Co.).

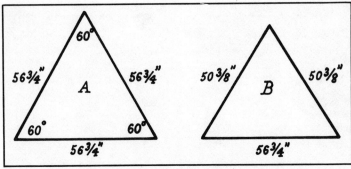

Fig. 2-69. Inside view of triangles (courtesy of Peter Reimuller Co.).

beginning construction, make sure that you have marked each section with a number and the name of the part to make your work flow easier. The parts inventory list for the dome greenhouse is given in Appendix G. There are two shapes of triangles included in the Dome greenhouse (Figs. 2-69 and 2-70).

Step One: Assemble Decagon Base

Lay out the 10 #70 base segments as shown in Fig. 2-68. Measurements should be 15 feet 5½″ from point to point as indicated. Nail the 10 base pieces together with two 6d nails at each joint (Fig. 2-71). Determine now at which joint you want your door to be. Nail the #71 base tie to the inside of the frame at the door position (Fig. 2-72).

Step Two: Assemble "B" Triangles Into Five Pentagons

Although caulking between the triangles is not necessary, you could use architectural caulking compound if you prefer. Using five "B" triangles, assembly into a pentagon as follows.

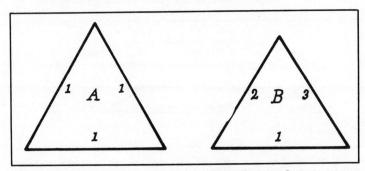

Fig. 2-70. Looking inside triangles (courtesy of Peter Reimuller Co.).

128

☐ Lean one of the triangles against a wall with side one *down*.

☐ Attach another "B" triangle to your left. Use #8-32 machine bolts through the three holes in the side of the triangle. Bolt holes in all triangles go to the inside of the greenhouse.

☐ Carefully line up the corners of the triangles. Use washers under each bolt head and nut. Tighten finger tight. Be sure to join side three to side two. This combination of side three to side two will be followed throughout the assembly of "B" triangles into pentagons.

☐ Attach another "B" triangle to your right by joining side three and side two. Join the other two triangles above in a like manner.

This completes one basic pentagon unit (Fig. 2-73). Using "B" triangles, assemble three more regular pentagons. Assemble the fifth (top) pentagon, as previously outlined, using your regular "B" triangles and the "B" triangle without fiberglass.

Step Three: Basic Assembly

Working from the *inside* place a regular "A" triangle to the immediate right of the #71 base tie piece. Hold upright and bolt one of the completed "B" pentagon units on the right-hand side of this "A" triangle (Fig. 2-74). Do not attach any portion of the greenhouse to the base until you reach instructions in Step Six.

Hold an "A" triangle, with accessories frame, to the right of the pentagon and bolt into position. Working to your right around the base, bolt a second "B" pentagon into position (Fig. 2-75).

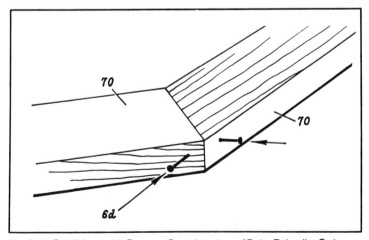

Fig. 2-71. Detail Assembly Decagon Base (courtesy of Peter Reimuller Co.).

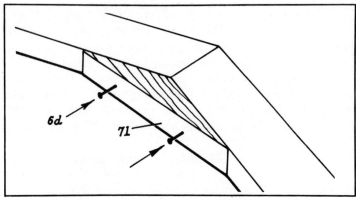

Fig. 2-72. Base tie attachment (courtesy of Peter Reimuller Co.).

☐ Bolt a regular "A" triangle to the second pentagon.

☐ Bolt a third pentagon into position.

☐ Bolt the other "A" triangle, with accessories frame, to the third pentagon (Fig. 2-76).

☐ Bolt a fourth pentagon into position.

☐ Bolt a regular "A" triangle to the fourth pentagon.

☐ Bolt side one of a "B" triangle to this "A" triangle.

☐ Attach another "B" triangle to this "B" triangle with side one resting on the base and with the right corner of the triangle next to the #71 base tie piece (Fig. 2-77).

Step Four: Install Top Pentagon with Vent

Lift the top pentagon unit into place and bolt it into position. The venting opening should be placed facing the prevailing wind in your area (Fig. 2-79).

Attach the cabinet hinges to one side of the remaining "B" triangle about 10 inches from each end (Fig. 2-80).

Lift this triangle into position and slip the butts of the two hinges between the frames of the supporting triangles. Use four 1½" wood screws through both frame pieces next to the edges of the hinge butts (Fig. 2-81).

Attach a #72 vent positioner to the middle hole on the number two side of the vent triangle with a nut and bolt so that the positioner swings freely. Use two nuts on this bolt and lock together for a permanent fastening. The end of the vent positioner with the drilled holes goes toward the top of the greenhouse.

Insert a 1½" wood screw into the vent support frame, 2" down from the center nut and bolt. Place this screw through one of the

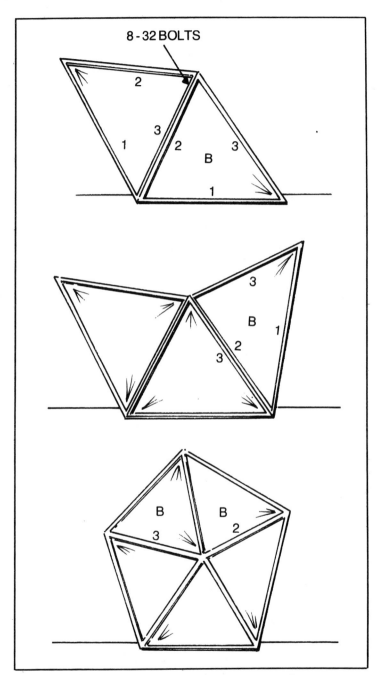

Fig. 2-73. Detail triangle assembly (courtesy of Peter Reimuller Co.).

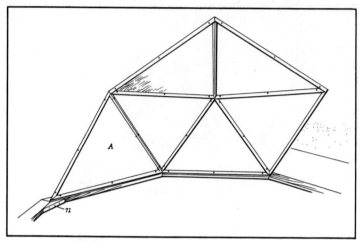

Fig. 2-74. Assembly detail, inside (courtesy of Peter Reimuller Co.).

holes in the positioner. Use the other holes to adjust the vent opening for more ventilation or less ventilation. Install a hook and eye to keep the vent securely closed (Fig. 2-82).

Step Five: Assemble and Attach Door

Take the two "C" door triangles and position side three to side two with the stapled side up (Fig. 2-83). Space the two triangles exactly ¼" apart so that the door will fit snugly when closed. Attach

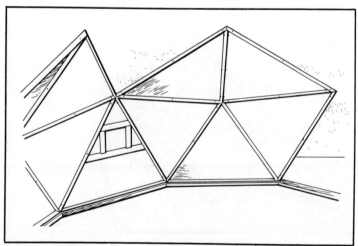

Fig. 2-75. Detail for bolting second unit in place (courtesy of Peter Reimuller Co.).

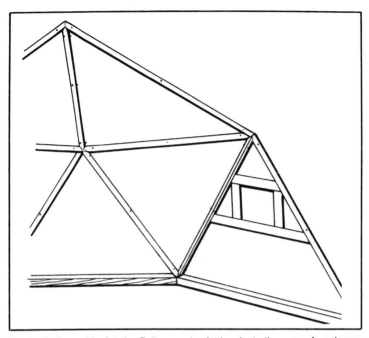

Fig. 2-76. Assembly details. Bolt a regular A triangle to the second pentagon (courtesy of Peter Reimuller Co.).

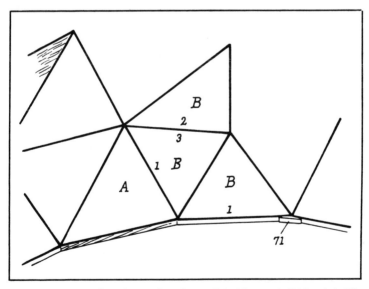

Fig. 2-77. Attaching B sections to A sections. Bolt side one of a B triangle to this A triangle (courtesy of Peter Reimuller Co.).

133

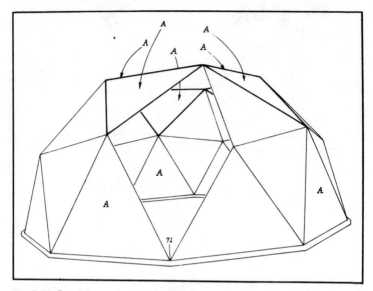

Fig. 2-78. Detail Assembly. Fill in A triangles. (courtesy of Peter Reimuller Co.).

the two triangles with the butt hinges about 10 inches from each end.

Fold the two triangles together and attach the offset door hinges to side one of the top triangle, about 10 inches from each end (Fig. 2-84).

Place the offset door hinges over the door frame (Fig. 2-85) but do not attach. Bolt two #73 door jambs against the two "A"

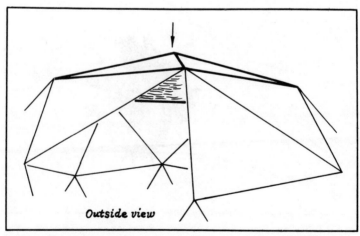

Fig. 2-79. Details for installing a top pentagon (courtesy of Peter Reimuller Co.).

Fig. 2-80. Attaching hinges (courtesy of Peter Reimuller Co.).

triangles. Bolt a #74 to the lower right-hand door frame and a #75 to the upper right-hand section (Fig. 2-86).

Close the door into the folded position and align the corners of lower half of the door with the center of the joints at both edges of the door triangle (Fig. 2-87). From inside of the greenhouse, attach

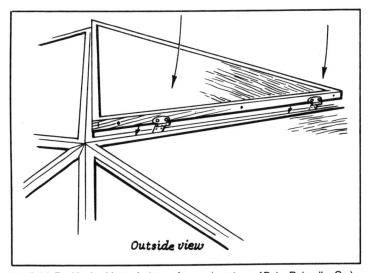

Outside view

Fig. 2-81. Positioning hinges between frames (courtesy of Peter Reimuller Co.).

135

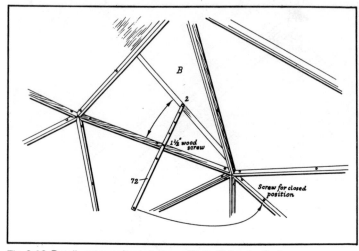

Fig. 2-82. Detail vent opening (courtesy of Peter Reimuller Co.).

the exposed end of both hinges with screws. Use four 1½″ wood screws through both door jamb pieces next to the edges of the hinge butts to hold the door firmly in position (Fig. 2-88).

Attach hooks and eyes to secure both sections of the door (Fig. 2-89).

Step Six: Attach Greenhouse to Decagon Base

Center the greenhouse on the base and attach it with #10 screws through each of the 30 holes in the triangles. Line up all

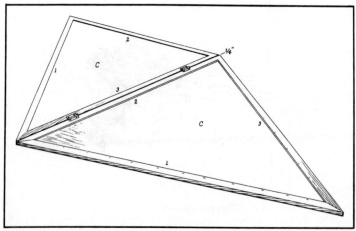

Fig. 2-83. Door Assembly (courtesy of Peter Reimuller Co.).

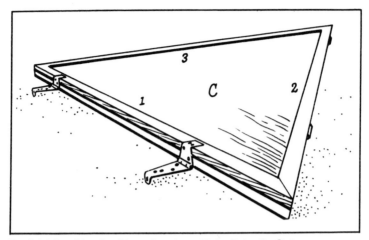

Fig. 2-84. Attaching door hinges (courtesy of Peter Reimuller Co.).

joints of triangles and firmly tighten all nuts throughout the greenhouse with an adjustable wrench.

Step Seven: Install Anchoring Stakes

If you did not build a permanent foundation for your dome greenhouse, drive the anchoring stakes into the ground with one at the corner of each of the five "A" triangles of the greenhouse.

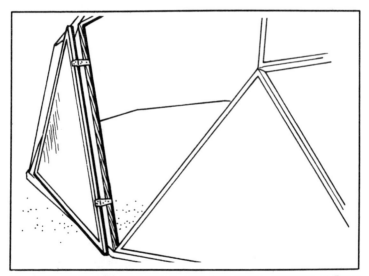

Fig. 2-85. Unattached door hinges over door frame. (courtesy of Peter Reimuller Co.).

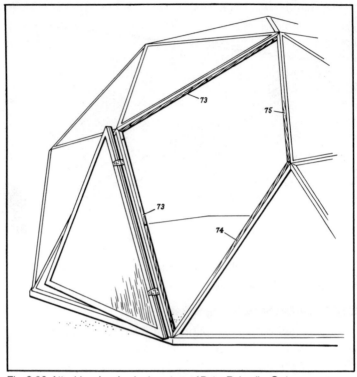

Fig. 2-86. Attaching door jambs (courtesy of Peter Reimuller Co.).

Keep the stakes vertical and tap securely into the ground. Drive stakes far enough into the ground to secure your Dome greenhouse leaving enough of the stakes above ground so that you can now nail them to the #70 base segments.

INSTALLING ACCESSORIES IN A DOME GREENHOUSE

Vent Shutters. With a sharp knife, and working from the outside, cut out fiberglass flush with inside opening of the accessory frame in the triangle. From the outside of the greenhouse, place the inlet shutters through this opening. Use the #76 spacer block to space the shutters away from the opening at the top of the framework with the wide side of the block placed on the top of the inlet frame (Fig. 2-90). Attach the shutters at the top with two 3½″ round head screws over the top of the spacer block. Use two ½″ screws to secure the shutter frame at the bottom. The shutters open automatically to the inside when the fan is running.

Exhaust Fan. Cut the fiberglass away as you did for the inlet shutters. From the inside of the greenhouse, place the fan in the opening and attach with four ½″ screws into the framework (Fig. 2-91).

Electric Heaters. They require no special installation. Just plug them in. They can be moved for best heat adjustment, but they are more efficient when placed opposite from the door and raised about 12 to 18″ above the floor level. Use a heavy-duty extension cord to minimize power loss.

Thermostat/Thermometer. Mount this unit away from the heater and shield it from the heater and also from direct sun. This will keep the sun or heater from overheating it. Keep it free to the air so that it will measure the correct temperature in your greenhouse.

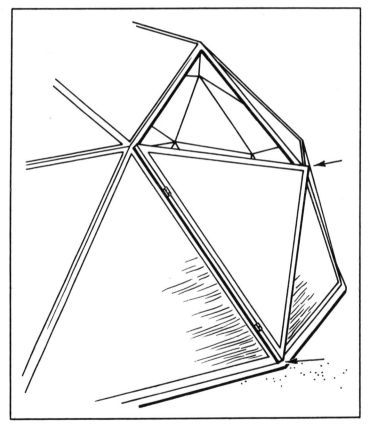

Fig. 2-87. Corner alignment of door (courtesy of Peter Reimuller Co.).

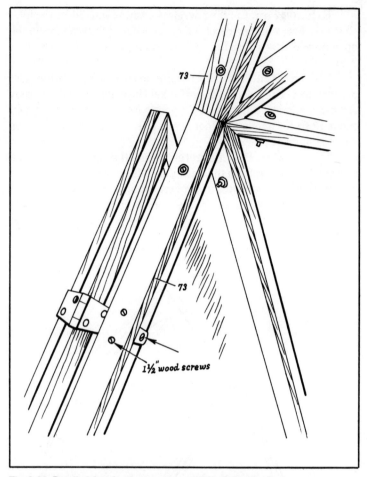

73

73

1½" wood screws

Fig. 2-88. Detail of door jambs (courtesy of Peter Reimuller Co.).

Attach the thermostat directly in one side of the power line that runs the fan. Break one-half of the power line and attach the two leads to the thermostat at screws #3 and #2 on the back (Fig. 2-92).

Humidifier. Place your humidifier under a bench or at one side of the greenhouse. If you can place it higher, this is good because the cool air will drop down low when it comes from the humidifier. Hook the humidifier to a garden hose and it will keep the moisture up constantly (Fig. 3-93).

Humidistat. Mount this like the thermostat, but keep it at the opposite side of the greenhouse from the humidifier (Fig.

140

3-93). The humidistat then will keep the humidity up to whatever level you desire. It is a good idea to shield the humidistat from direct sunlight or excessive heat.

Addition Helpful Hints. In windy areas, you might want to add additional gate hooks to hold your door securely when you are inside. Use one hook on the upper and lower parts of the door, on the inside, to keep the door solidly closed while you are working in the greenhouse.

After assembly, wash the sides of the fiberglass with water to remove any dust particles left on the fiberglass to allow more sunlight for plant growth.

In very cold areas, you might want to use two heaters at opposite ends of the dome to maintain proper temperature.

THE HANDI-GRO GREENHOUSE

This 4 x 8 model is ideal for the hobbyist who doesn't want to spend a lot of time raising many different plants, has a small area, yet wants a place in which to "putter." The ideal placement for this model is against a wall that has a southern or southeastern exposure. Or you might want to place it over a sliding door, window or standard door. In doing so, you will have access to your

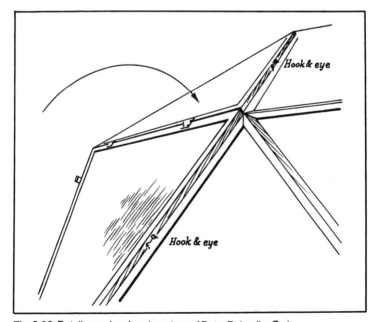

Fig. 2-89. Detail securing door (courtesy of Peter Reimuller Co.).

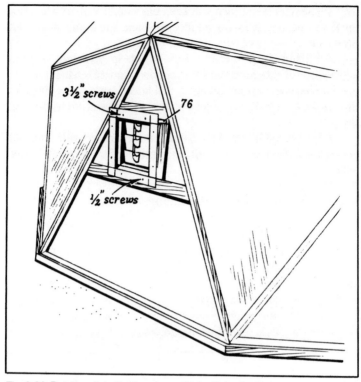

Fig. 2-90. Detail vent shutter (courtesy of Peter Reimuller Co.).

greenhouse from the home as well as the exterior Dutch door. Also, this type of placement can provide *some* of the necessary heat to maintain proper greenhouse temperature.

Unlike free standing models which will move with the ground during temperature extremes, your Handi-Gro will be attached securely to your house. In other words, it is a miniature lean-to.

You will need a foundation if you live in areas where winter frost and ground upheaval normally occur; this means a concrete slab, concrete block or wood foundation in accordance with local building codes. This foundation should extend below the frost line and have outside dimensions of 5″ x 98″.

Before you begin, make yourself a materials list as outlined in the parts inventory list. You will note that each number in Fig. 2-94A corresponds to the number in the parts inventory list (Appendix H-1). It is a good idea to name the part and number on each piece of material to make your construction simpler (Fig. 2-94B).

Remember that a 1 x 3 actually measures 11/16″ x 2½″. Also, all bolts use a washer under the nut, not under the head. All boltheads go to the outside of the greenhouse. Be sure to use the correct bolt lengths as indicated in the instructions. During subassembly, tighten all nuts *only finger tight* until that section is completed; then tighten all nuts with an adjustable wrench. For best results, and to avoid splitting, always support the surface you are nailing into.

Predrilling a 3/32″ starter hole at all 6d nail, screw nail and screw points in both the redwood and fiberglass provides better results.

Step One: Assemble Both Side Sections

Place a 47¼″ x 78″ corrugated fiberglass panel flush with the top of a No. 14 side plate. Place it between bolt holes (Fig. 2-95). Drive a 6d nail part way in at each corner as a temporary fastening. Now, as suggested, you could drill starter holes in each valley of the fiberglass panels approximately ½″ from the edge. Slip a 1″

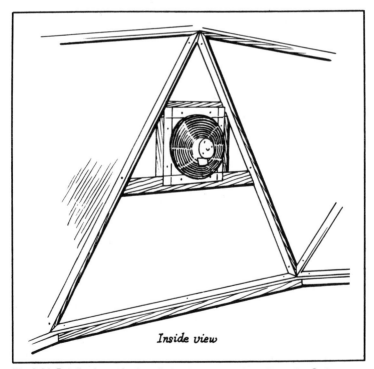

Fig. 2-91. Detail exhaust fan installation (courtesy of Peter Reimuller Co.).

143

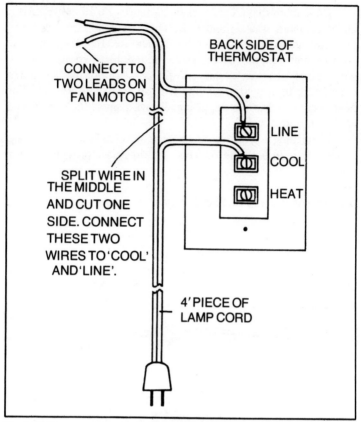

CONNECT TO
TWO LEADS ON
FAN MOTOR

BACK SIDE OF
THERMOSTAT

LINE

COOL

HEAT

SPLIT WIRE IN
THE MIDDLE
AND CUT ONE
SIDE. CONNECT
THESE TWO
WIRES TO 'COOL'
AND 'LINE'.

4' PIECE OF
LAMP CORD

Fig. 2-92. Thermostat installation (courtesy of Peter Reimuller Co.).

strip of closure foam in place between the side plate and the fiberglass flush with the top. Drive a screw nail into each valley but not into the corners. Remove the temporary 6d nails. Repeat this process until the panel is attached to the top plate.

Position the other No. 14 (which becomes the bottom sill) under the lower edge of the fiberglass panel so that the bottom edge of the No. 14 measures exactly 78″ from the top. The fiberglass may extend about ¼″ below the bottom and it may vary slightly with each panel. Repeat as you did on the top, insert closure strip and nail.

Stand the unit upright and place the side studs No. 12 against the bottom sill. Make sure that the next bolt hole is 27¾″ above. Angle brackets must be sandwiched between parts No. 14 and No. 12 at the three corners as shown in Fig. 2-96. The unattached ends

144

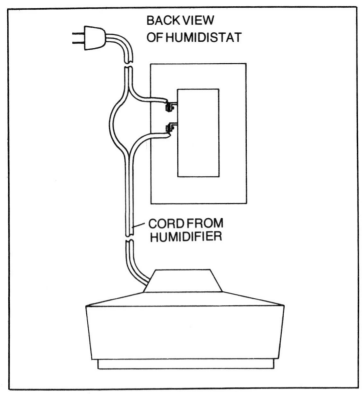

Fig. 2-93. Humidistat; humidifier detail (courtesy of Peter Reimuller Co.).

of the brackets point toward the inside of the greenhouse. Use 2-inch bolts at all locations.

If you are using benches, bolt a rear bench rail No. 14 on the same side as the sill and plate. Lay the side unit down with the sill, plate and bench rail facing up. Nail down fiberglass to each stud with screw nails spaced approximately 6″ apart (Fig. 2-97).

Repeat all of Step One to complete the *second side*.

Step Two: Finish Dutch Door

Build your Dutch door so that it will be ready for hanging when you have completed the remainder of the construction.

Step Three: Assemble Rear End Roof Support

Lay out all parts for the rear roof support section. The filler strip on the end plate assembly No. 11 should be grooved. It goes to the inside with the grooves toward the top.

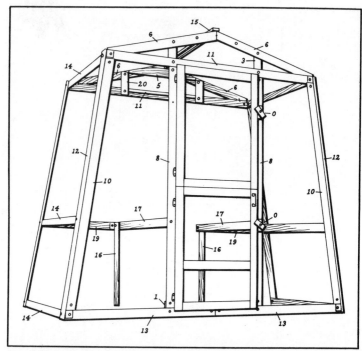

Fig. 2-94A. Details of the frame for 4 x 8 Handi-grow (courtesy of Peter Reimuller Co.).

Fig. 2-94B. Finished Handi-grow (courtesy of Peter Reimuller Co.).

146

Be sure that all parts are in proper alignment before you fasten them together. Fasten each joint with one metal fastener (Fig. 2-98).

Step Four: Construct the Door End Section

Lay out all parts for the door end section (Fig. 2-99). The outside of the end corner stud No. 10 must be in exact alignment

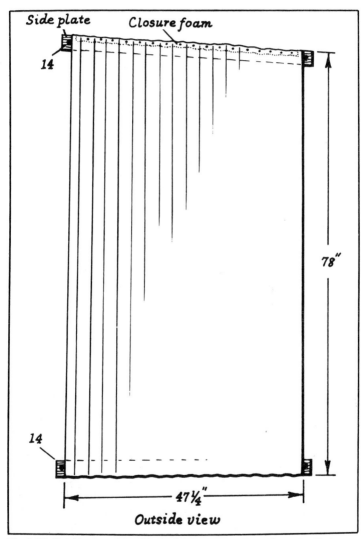

Fig. 2-95. Outside view of the side section (courtesy of Peter Reimuller Co.).

with the top corner of the end plate No. 11. Make sure the bolt holes for attaching the bench rails are up 27¾" from the bottom. Attach the two No. 13 end sills together with a No. 1 backing block and two 2-inch bolts. The backing block goes on the inside of the door end section. Be sure that all parts and holes are in proper alignment before you fasten them together. Fasten each joint with one metal fastener as shown. Using screw nails, fasten the small angular pieces of flat fiberglass corner panels to the rafters No. 6. Place the 5½" short edge to the inside toward the center of the greenhouse. Align them with the edge of the bolt holes in the rafter and end plate (Fig. 2-99).

Place one corrugated fiberglass front end panel on the frame so that the edge running along the end post will curve up and lap the end posts 1".

The top edge should be flush with the top of the end plate. Use 6d nails to temporarily fasten the panel.

The bottom of this panel will overhang the end sill by about 1". This can be trimmed if necessary to fit on a foundation. Otherwise, the overhang will settle into the ground and act as a seal. Use closure foam to fit the top, bottom and diagonal side. Lift the panel and slip foam in place. Nail in each valley as you go. Nail twice in each valley down the diagonal side, but do not nail the outside corner valleys at either the top or bottom edges (Fig. 2-100). Remove the temporary 6d nail.

Repeat this procedure for the opposite side. Be sure that the edge of the panel curves up along the end posts.

Rafter supports, rafter tie assembly and lower door post backing blocks belong on the inside. All use 2-inch bolts and all boltheads go to the outside.

Stand the end unit upright and bolt the backing blocks No. 1, the rafter supports No. 3, and the rafter tie assembly No. 5 into position. Flat metal brackets go on all four corners to the inside of the greenhouse and use 1¼" bolts. Flex two 15" x 6¾" flat fiberglass vent panels and place in the tracks of the upper vent opening (Fig. 2-101).

Step Five: Attach All Frame Sections Together

Position one side section to the front section. Remove the 1¼" corner bolt from each corner of the front unit. Put the unattached end of the corner bracket on the side unit on the outside of the front section (Fig. 2-102). Replace the bolts and tighten the corners together at the top and bottom. Use a large nail or a

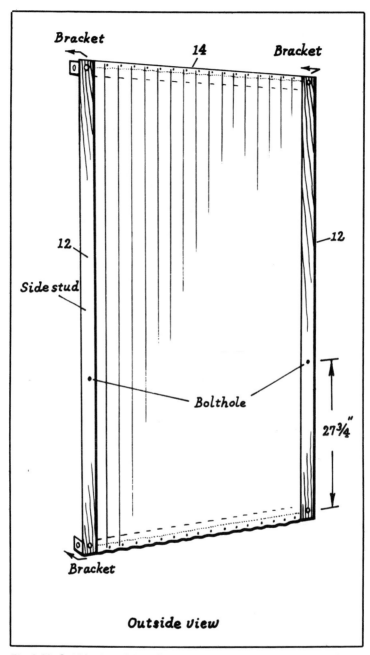

Fig. 2-96. Outside view of the side section stud placement (courtesy of Peter Reimuller Co.).

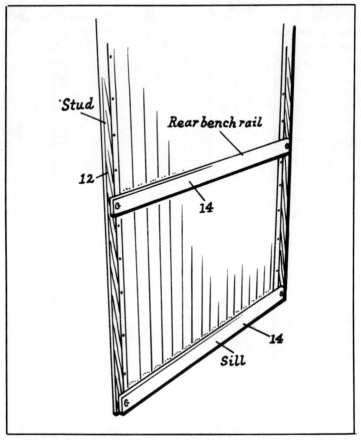

Fig. 2-97. Inside view of bench rail placement (courtesy of Peter Reimuller Co.).

screwdriver to align holes. Attach the second side assembly the same way.

When both sides of the greenhouse have been bolted together at the top and bottom, align the top of the side studs with the top of the end plates. Nail through the side studs into the front corner end studs with three 6d nails each (Fig. 2-103).

Attach the rear end roof support unit. Use 1¼″ bolts through the corner brackets on the top of the two side panels (Fig. 2-104).

Step Six: Install Roof

Lift the ridge section into place. The ends will fit into the slots against the rafters at each end. Drive one 6d nail through the end rafters into each end of the ridge assembly (Fig. 2-105).

Cut one strip of closure foam lengthwise and insert the pieces into the space directly under the ridge cap (Fig. 2-106). Leave the lower edge loose.

When both panels are in place and nailed at the ridge, align to the side plate. Carefully lift the panel and place a strip of closure foam along the top of the plate. Nail with screw nails in each valley (Fig. 2-106). Nail along both end rafters every 6″.

Step Seven: Hang the Dutch Door

Hole the upper half of the Dutch door into position so that it overlaps the door end posts and the door end plate ½″ evenly all around. Attach hinges to the door end post. Place the lower half of the door about ⅛″ so that it clears the upper half of the door and attach hinges. Use a 3″ bolt through the two latch blocks 0 in both locations—upper and lower door. Nail the first block to the door post to prevent it from turning. Use two nuts on this bolt; tighten one nut against the other to prevent the latch from loosening (Fig. 2-94).

Step Eight: Assemble Two Benches

Attach a No. 17 front bench rail to the door post with a metal angle bracket. Remember, the latch side will have a 3-inch bolt.

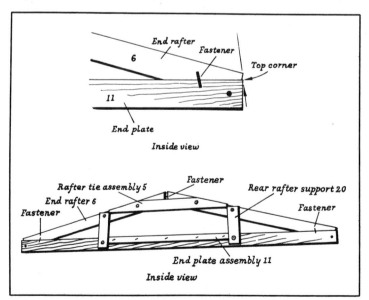

Fig. 2-98. Roof rear end roof support detail (courtesy of Peter Reimuller Co.).

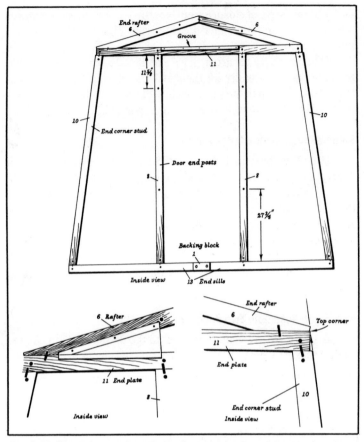

Fig. 2-99. Detail door end section and attached rafter sill (courtesy of Peter Reimuller Co.).

Using a metal bracket, attach a No. 21 leg to the inside of the No. 17 front bench rail. A metal bracket fits between the leg and the bench rail (Fig. 2-107). Using a metal bracket and a 1¼″ bolt, attach the bench end rail No. 19 to the No. 12 side stud. The metal bracket goes to the outside of the No. 19 bench end rail. Attach the other end of No. 19 bench end rail to the outside of the No. 17 bench rail with a 1¼″ bolt (Fig. 2-107). Make the same assembly for the opposite side.

Place the 30″ long redwood boards across the bench rails. Space them approximately 1½″ apart. Do not nail the bench boards into place until a uniform distance between the boards has been determined. Use two nails at each end of each board (Fig. 2-107).

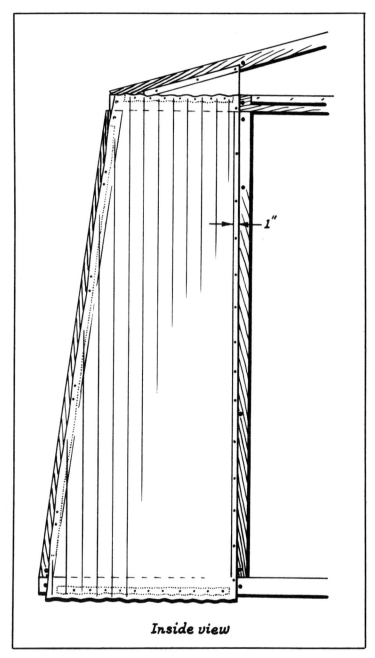

1"

Inside view

Fig. 2-100. Inside view detail overhang bottom of panel (courtesy of Peter Reimuller Co.).

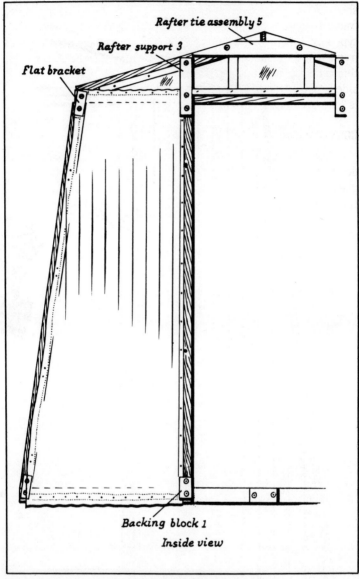

Fig. 2-101. Inside view detail (courtesy of Peter Reimuller Co.).

Step Nine: Attach Greenhouse to Structure

The greenhouse may be attached directly to your structure. However, it is recommended that you first attach a frame to the structure; 2 x 3's are recommended for this purpose. The framing should be secure with a suitable fastener: 10d - 16d nails for a wood frame structure, expansion bolts for brick, stone, stucco or metal type structures. This framing should be fully caulked between the frame and the structure. The greenhouse may then be attached to this frame with 6d nails. To complete the sealing of the top and sides, they may now be flashed or caulked. Be sure the greenhouse is "squared" in relationship to the building.

CONVENTIONAL GLASS MODEL GREENHOUSES

Basic designs for lean-to and free standing glass greenhouses do not differ much in respect to construction except, of course, that glass "lites" are used in lieu of other materials. Figure 2-108 is a curved eave design and Fig. 2-109 is a free standing model. Both

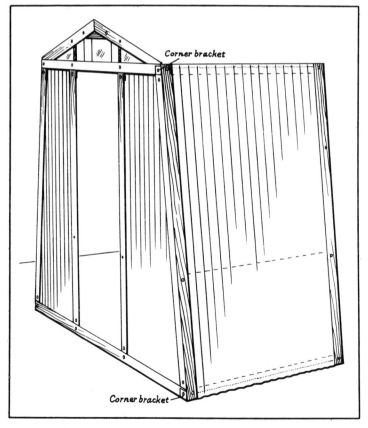

Fig. 2-102. Outside view details side section to front section (courtesy of Peter Reimuller Co.).

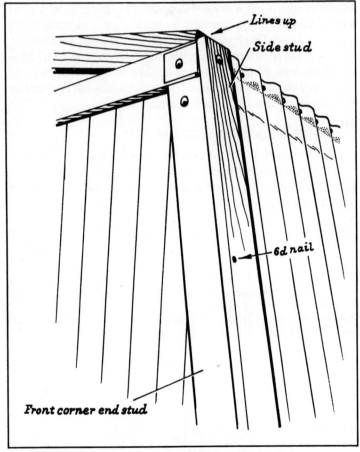

Fig. 2-103. Stud alignment detail (courtesy of Peter Reimuller Co.).

are designed by the National Greenhouse Company of Pana, Illinois. In constructing either model, the following steps should be adhered to in sequence.

☐ Check the foundation for dimension and square for a glass-to-ground or a wall model.

☐ Attach the sill.

☐ Assemble the gable end bars to the corner bars.

☐ Assemble the intermediate bars.

☐ If it is a lean-to model, attach the ridge to the wall against which the greenhouse leans.

☐ Set up the gable end bars.

☐ Set up the intermediate bars.

☐ On free standing models now attach the ridge.
☐ Attach the eave plate.
☐ Attach the vent header.
☐ Install the gable end bars.
☐ Install the door frame in the gable.
☐ Install vents and vent operating equipment.
☐ Glaze the greenhouse in the following order: vents, roof glazing, side glazing, and gable glazing.
☐ Hanging the door.
☐ Caulking.

Horizontal members go up in sections and parts should be marked right hand (RH), left hand (LH), and intermediate (INT). Standing outside of the greenhouse facing the sidewall, the RH or LH applies. Similarly, gable wall sills should be labeled as right or left hand. The same general identification procedure would apply to materials used at the gable end. Facing the gable end, pick right-side or left-side materials.

In these two models, generally all glass in the roof on the side in which there is a vent will be a single lite extending from the vent header to the eave. On the side without a vent, the glass can be in two lites lapped in the roof. All side wall glass in wall models will be single lites extending from the eave to the sill. In glass-to-ground models, the sidewall glass will be in two lites lapped to extend from the eave to the sill. All gable glass is installed as individual sheets.

Roman numerals are shown on the two basic plans Figs. 2-108 and 2-109. The following steps of instructions for construction, therefore, will be keyed to the use of Roman numerals to correspond to the Roman numeral on the details plans.

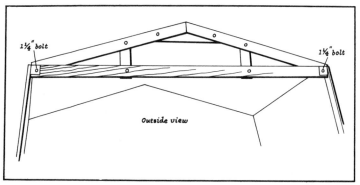

Fig. 2-104. Rear end roof support detail (courtesy of Peter Reimuller Co.).

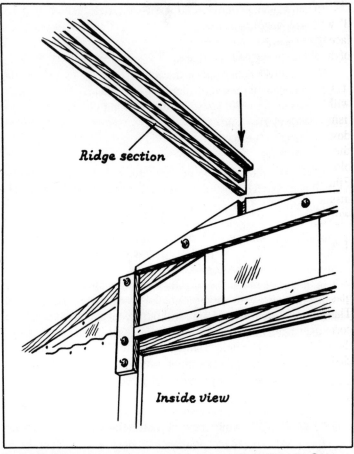

Fig. 2-105. Detail ridge section placement (courtesy of Peter Reimuller Co.).

I. Check the Foundation

For a wall model, the wall height should be 2 feet 5½ inches. This measurement should be held and is based on four standard 8″ concrete blocks starting from 2½″ below ground level. The glass-to-ground model has an 8″ wide footing brought up to grade for attachment of the greenhouse. In either case, an 8″ wall is shown as a standard and is the basis for determining other dimensions.

Be sure that the foundation or masonry wall is level and plumb. The door opening in the wall must be exact. Some tolerance has been considered in the overall width and length dimensions, but these have to be adjusted in setting the sill.

158

In determining dimensions, the house is designed to set on an 8″ wall with the inside face of the sill being 5″ in from the outside face of the wall based on the standard dimensions. The inside face of the sill is chosen as a reference point because it is a flat surface.

When a block masonry wall is used for the wall of a wall model, it is recommended that the cores in the top row of the block be filled with concrete. To fill the top row of block with concrete without using excess concrete, crumpled up newspaper can be stuffed down in the core to the level of the bottom of the first block to retain the concrete without filling the entire core of the wall. A sold cap block would alleviate the need for filling the cores with concrete. Filling the cores of the entire wall with vermiculite or other insulating material up to the level of the top coarse (row) of block will add insulation to the wall and conserve in energy.

II. Attaching the Sill

The sill is an especially extruded aluminum member designed to attach directly on top of the wall or foundation in the case of the glass-to-ground models and support the structure members above. The sill is fabricated to extend the length of the greenhouse and the corners are mitred for a close fit of the gable sill and the sill along the side. It is held in place with expandable anchor bolts. Lay a chalk line on top of the foundation marking the *inside* of the sill.

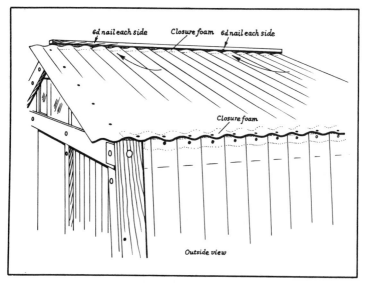

Fig. 2-106. Detail roof panel (courtesy of Peter Reimuller Co.).

Subsequently, the dimensions should be carefully checked using a chalk line. Use the inside dimensions of the sill (which is 5″ less than the out-to-out wall dimension on each side. If there are two sidewalls involved, it is the standard out-to-out dimension less 10″). Check for squareness by measuring across diagonals of the foundation. Lay out the sill loosely on this line and recheck the dimensions. Once these dimensions are checked, holes should be drilled into the masonry wall—using a ¼″ diameter masonry drill—to a depth of 2½″. Sills are predrilled to indicate location of these holes for anchor bolts.

The sill should be placed on the wall and expandable anchor bolts dropped in the holes so drilled. Taking up on the nut of the anchor bolt will expand the bolt in the hole and furnish a firm hold.

The top of the sill should be level all of the way around the foundation. If there are variations in the level of the top of the foundation, thin metal shims should be used under the sill to make sure the sill itself is level.

III. Assembling Gable End Bars

In straight eave models, the gable end roof bar and the corner bar are two different pieces. They should be assembled together on the ground using the end bar connecting plate, which is 3/16″ thick and the necessary ¼″ x ⅝″ round head stove bolts, on the inside face. In curved eave models, this connection is not required because the gable end roof bar and gable end side bar are one continuous piece.

For free-standing greenhouses, the two half arches connected together are as indicated above and should now be connected into a complete arch using the 3/16″ ridge plate as indicated on the drawings. A similar procedure will follow with the curved eave model.

IV. Assembling Intermediate Bars

The intermediate roof bars for the straight eave model should now be assembled to the intermediate side bars with the 3/16″ eave plate as shown on the drawing. Again, curved eave models do not need assembling because the roof bar and the side bar are a continuous piece.

In a free-standing model, the two half arches as assembled above can be then connected to form a complete arch using the 3/16″ ridge plate as shown on the drawings.

V. Attached Ridge for Lean-To Models

The ridge ends of the outside of the bar are ¼″ in from outside of sill. If the wall against which the greenhouse attaches leans over at the top toward the greenhouse, the sill will have to be moved out at the bottom and a filler used. A plumb bob will determine the actual setting. If the wall leans in at the top away from the greenhouse, the ridge can be shimmed out.

Once the location of the ridge is determined, place it against the existing wall and hold temporarily with screws or nails while you determine the final exact position. The ridge position must be the dimension above the wall or floor level as shown by the cross section drawing.

After the correct position has been determined, remove the ridge and apply butyl (cartridge) putty to the upper and lower sections of the ridge. The ridge may be connected by using anchors if the existing wall is of masonry construction. If the existing wall is of wood, use 1½″ #12 round head screws.

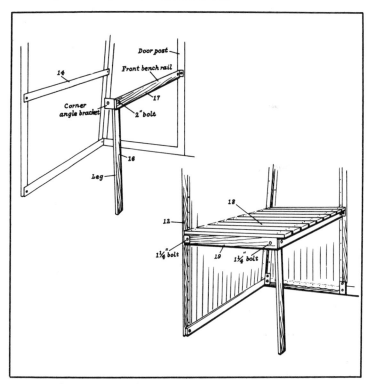

Fig. 2-107. Bench assembly detail (courtesy of Peter Reimuller Co.).

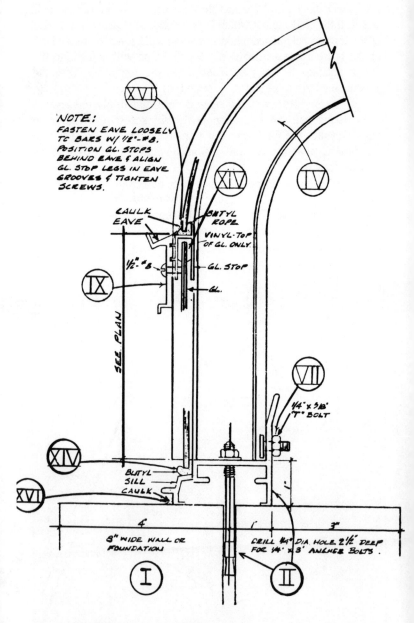

NOTE:
FASTEN EAVE LOOSELY
TO BARS W/ 1/2"-#8.
POSITION GL. STOPS
BEHIND EAVE & ALIGN
GL. STOP LEGS IN EAVE
GROOVES & TIGHTEN
SCREWS.

CAULK EAVE

BUTYL ROPE

VINYL-TOP OF GL. ONLY.

1/2"-#8

GL. STOP

GL.

SEE PLAN

1/4" X 3/8" "T" BOLT

BUTYL

SILL

CAULK

8" WIDE WALL OR FOUNDATION

DRILL 1/4" DIA. HOLE 2 1/2" DEEP FOR 1/4" X 3" ANCHOR BOLTS.

Fig. 2-108. Detailed drawings lean-to (courtesy of National Greenhouse Company).

162

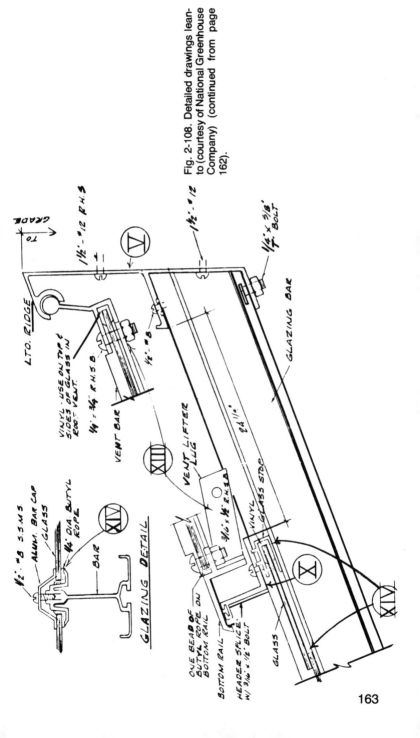

Fig. 2-108. Detailed drawings lean-to (courtesy of National Greenhouse Company) (continued from page 162).

163

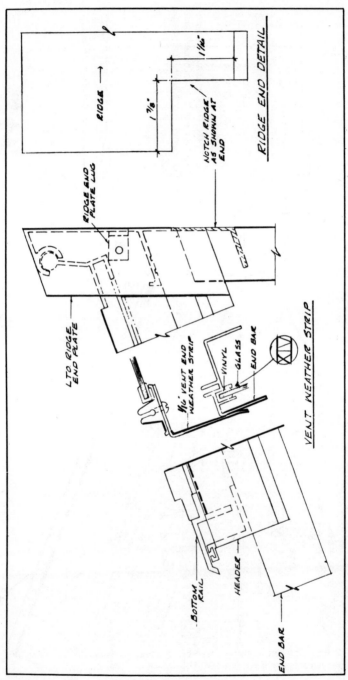

RIDGE END DETAIL

RIDGE

1⅛"

1¹/₁₆"

NOTCH RIDGE AS SHOWN AT END

RIDGE END PLATE LUG

LTO RIDGE END PLATE

³/₁₆" VENT END WEATHER STRIP

VINYL

GLASS

END BAR

VENT. WEATHER STRIP

BOTTOM RAIL

HEADER

END BAR

Fig. 2-108. Detailed drawings lean-to (courtesy of National Greenhouse Company) (continued from page 163).

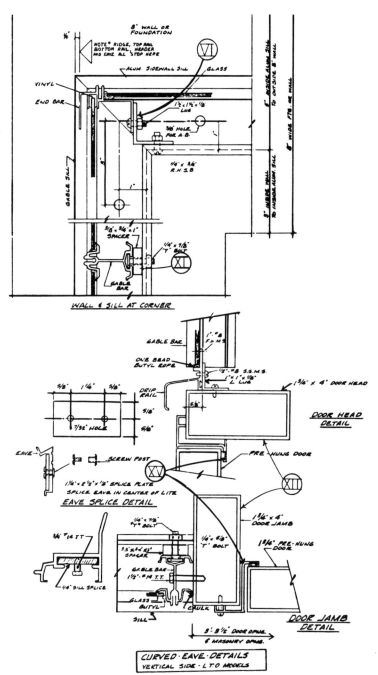

Fig. 2-108. Detailed drawings lean-to (courtesy of National Greenhouse Company) (continued from page 164).

165

VI. Set Up Gable End Bars

Connect the gable end bar at the sill with the 1½″ x 1½″ x ⅛″ angle lug as shown on the drawing, Make the connection loosely at this time.

In the case of the free-standing model, the entire gable arch should be mounted connecting at the sill with the gable end bar lug as shown on the drawing.

VII. Set Up the Intermediate Bars

The intermediate bars are set up in a similar manner to the gable end bars. The attachment at the sill is with a ¼″ x ⅝″ "T" bolt as shown on the drawings. The attachment at the ridge of a lean to is with a ¼″ x ⅝″ "T" bolt through the bottom flange as shown on the drawings. For free-standing models, the attachment is made at both sill lines for the complete arch.

VIII. Attachment of the Ridge on Free-Standing Models

After all of the arches are in place, including gable end bars and intermediate bars, the ridge is placed on top of the bars as shown in the drawings. The ridge is predrilled to take ½″ #8 self tapping screws down into the extruded slot in the tongue of the bar. Leave the ridge loose until the extruded aluminum glass stop on the side with no vent is set underneath and interlocked with the bottom of the ridge in the slots provided. At that time the ridge can be tightened down.

IV. Attach the Eave Plate

The eave plate should be drilled for ½″ #8 self-tapping screws to lock into the bar tongue. The eave should be attached loosely until the glass stop with its extruded locking device is securely positioned in the slots in the back side of the eave. The eave is properly positioned by measuring the dimension from the point on the sill to the point on the eave as shown in the drawing. Once the eave is properly positioned, the screws can be tightened.

X. Attach Vent Header

The vent header is positioned on top of the roof bar and attached by self-tapping screws as shown in the drawing. The header should be attached loosely until the glass stop is positioned and snapped into place in the extruded grooves as provided on the underside of the vent header. The position of the vent header is determined by measuring from the edge of the bottom flange of the ridge to the top edge of the vent header as shown in the drawing.

It is important, before you tighten fastenings, that you make a final check of the greenhouse frame to be sure that it is square and true. I suggest that diagonal measurements be taken of the side to assure the squareness. All bar spacing on the sides and roof should be checked at top and bottom for 24¾" center to center spacing. Once the greenhouse is checked for "square," all fastenings can then be tightened.

XI. Install Gable Bars

The gable bars are installed by attaching them to the vertical leg of the sill with a "T" head bolt and a ⅜" x ¾" x 1" spacer which is used between the bottom of the bar and the vertical leg of the sill to space the bar out properly to meet the glass line. The top end of the bar is bolted to the inner leg of the gable end bar with a "T" head bolt. Before tightening the bolts, make sure that the bars are plumb and spaced to the center to center dimension shown on the plans. The gable bars over the door are fastened at the gable end bar leaving the bottom end loose to serve as a gauge to insure proper height of header and jamb.

XII. Install the Door Frame

The door frame is made up of 1¾" x 4" rectangular aluminum tubing and consists of two longer pieces for the jambs at the side and a shorter piece for the header. The header should be attached to the two jambs with angle lugs. These are mounted to the underside of the header and the inside face of the jamb toward the edge which mounts inside the greenhouse. After the frame is assembled it is set in place. In the free-standing model, it is fastened to the adjacent bar by means of the 1½" #14 tuff-tites inserted through the bar first, and into the jamb.

Be sure to check the jamb for proper dimension and squareness. For the door in a lean-to, one of the jambs has large holes in the door face which are used for socket wrenches to tighten up the anchor bolts or lag bolts that fasten the jamb to the existing solid wall. These holes are set in 1" from the outside face of the jamb so that they will be set into the jambs covered when the door and frame is set into place. In fastening this jamb to the wall, it is important to assure that the wall is vertical. If not, spacers will have to be used so that the door jamb sets plumb.

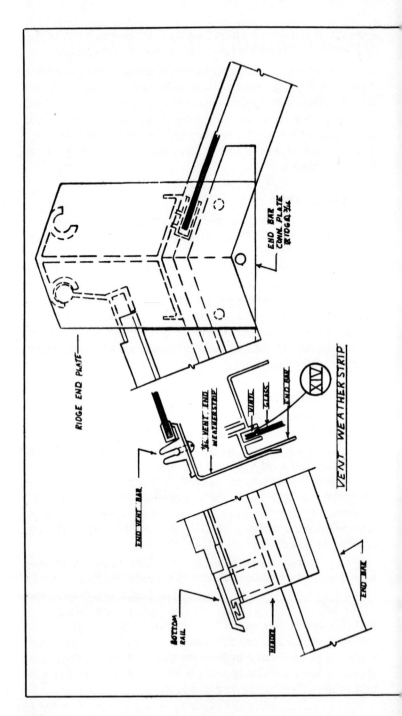

RIDGE END PLATE

END BAR
CONN. PLATE
RIDG & ¾

END VENT BAR

¾ VENT END
WEATHERSTRIP

VINYL

GLASS

END BAR

XIV

VENT WEATHER STRIP

BOTTOM
RAIL

END BAR

HEADER

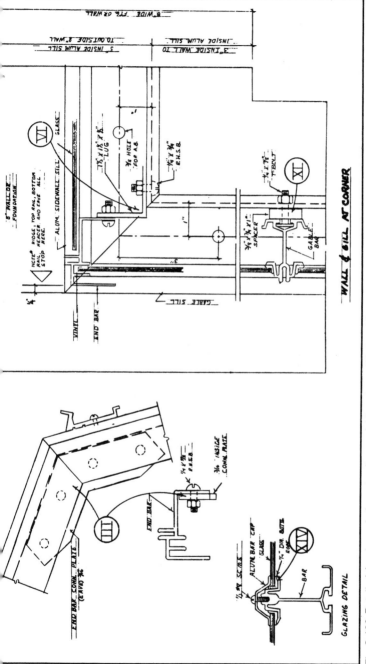

Fig. 2-109. Detailed drawings of a free-standing model (courtesy of National Greenhouse Company.).

169

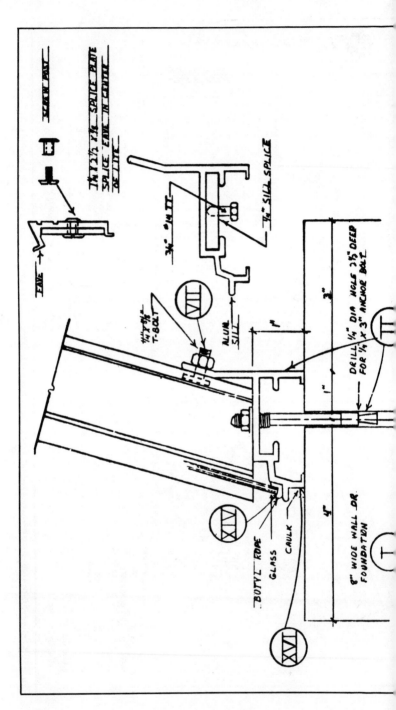

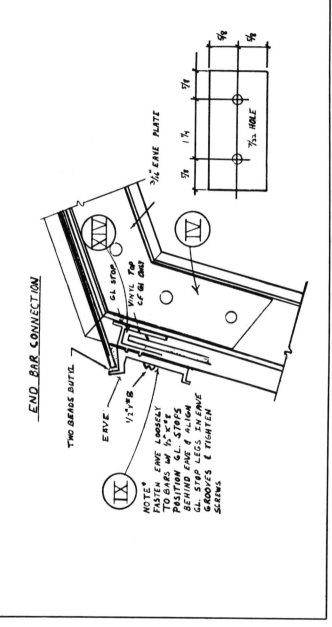

END BAR CONNECTION

TWO BEADS BUTYL

EAVE

1/2"×8

GL STOP

VINYL TOP
GL GH ONLY

XIV

IX

3/16" EAVE PLATE

IV

NOTE*
FASTEN EAVE LOOSELY
TO BARS W/ 1/2"×1"g
POSITION GL. STOPS
BEHIND EAVE & ALIGN
GL STOP LEGS IN EAVE
GROOVES & TIGHTEN
SCREWS

5/8
5/8

5/8

7/32 HOLE

5/8   1 1/4

Fig. 2-109. Detailed drawings of a free-standing model (courtesy of National Greenhouse Company) (continued from page 169).

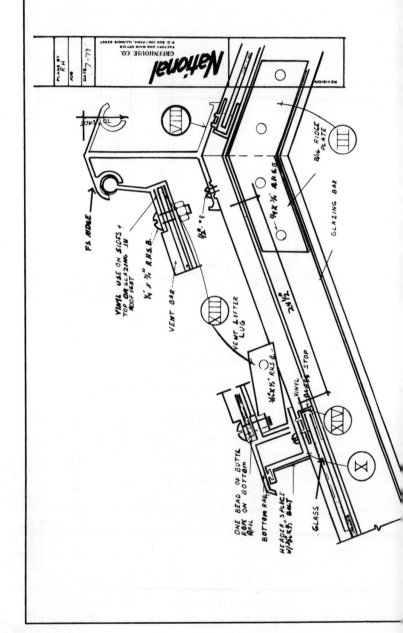

172

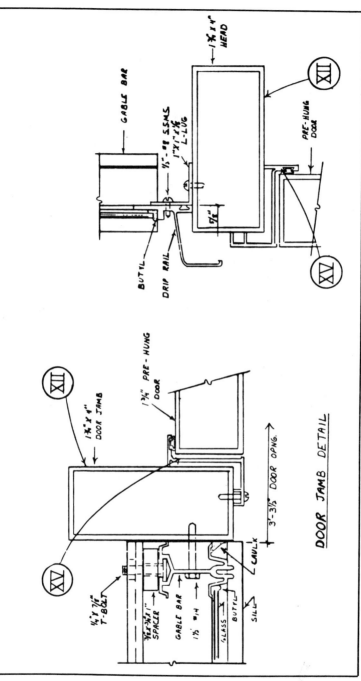

Fig. 2-109. Detailed drawings of a free-standing model (courtesy of National Greenhouse Company) (continued from page 171).

173

The door header has a drip rail mounted on top. Once this header and drip rail is in place, the gable bars over the door should be fastened to the drip rail.

XIII. Install Vents and Vent Operating Equipment

Assemble the vent on the ground. Attach the vent bars to the bottom and top rails by using round headstove bolts. Use 3/6" and ½" bolts at the bottom rail and ¼" and ¾" bolts at the top rail. Vent assembly details show how this is done. The two end bars for the sash have mounted a vent weather strip. This strip is a metal leg that drops down and closes the opening at the end of the sash.

After assembly, slide the vent into the top socket of the ridge. Vaseline, liquid soap or other lubricant will facilitate this. On free-standing models, the vent may be placed on either side of the ridge, but preferably opposite the winter prevailing wind. After the vent is slid into place, the ridge closure plate is mounted to the ridge at both ends and held in place with the ridge and plate lug as shown in the drawing.

In the assembly of the vents, the vent lifter lugs should be mounted to the bottom rail at the same time. After the vents are in place, the shaft hangers and shafting are to be mounted. The mounting bracket is installed with "T" head bolts a distance of 14" from the bottom end of the roof bar to the center of the upper bolt of the shaft hanger. Be sure that the shaft hanger legs are parallel to the roof bar so the shafting will be perpendicular. Next, install the shafting and the roof vent lifting machine. Line up so the shafting will run straight through.

Install the shafting and shaft collars on each end. Place the shaft collars just inside the end hangers. Bolt on the lifter arms at this time and make sure they are perpendicular in operation to the sash. Run the vents up and down several times to make sure operation is easy without binding and check the sash end closures for operation without binding.

XIV. Glazing the Greenhouse

In general, the glass in the sash are full, single *lites* that extend from the top rail to the bottom rail. The glass in the roof is a single piece from the vent header down to the eave plate on the sash side of straight eave models. On the curved eave model, the roof lite laps over the curved lite. On the roof side, without sash in both curved eave and straight eave models two or more lites of lapped glass are used up the roof. In wall models, the side lites are single lites both in curved eave and straight eave models. Glass-to-ground models require two lites lapped in the sidewall. All gable lites are butted and separated with a plastic strip called a *came*.

Two distinct types of bar cap are used: a crimped cap with one end crimped and a non-crimped cap. The crimped cap is used where the glass is lapped so that the crimp hangs down over the lower edge of the upper lite and holds it in place without excessive pressure. The cap below the upper lite butts to the bottom edge of the lite to keep it from slipping. All lites except the sash lites rest on butyl rope which is used for beading the glass. This butyl rope is paper backed and it is layed on the bar with the paper up; then the paper is peeled back.

In glazing the sash, a line of the butyl rope should be mounted along the bottom rail of the sash for the lower end of the lite of glass to rest on. The top and sides of the sash lites should be covered by a vinyl channel which goes around the three sides. When bending it around the top corners, make a small "V" shaped notch in the two legs of the channel so that the channel will not bunch. In placing the sash lites, line the sash; the top end with its vinyl channel cover is pushed up into the glass stop and the lite of glass is pressed down on the butyl rope at the bottom. The bar caps are then mounted on top of the sash bars and screwed in place with self-tapping screws.

In glazing the roof of a curved eave model, the curved eave lite is put in place first. A line of butyl rope is applied to the top of the eavy plate where the glass rests and layed along the glass shoulder continuously up the roof bars. When the curved lite is in place, the bar cap can be applied and fastened down by tightening the middle screw first. On the sash side, the next lite will be a lite that laps over the curved lite. A vinyl strip is placed across the top edge and the glass pushed up into the glass stop and pressed into the butyl rope firmly so that there is a lap over the curved lite of approximately three-eighths of an inch. Crimped caps are then used to hold this glass in place. The crimp of the cap hangs over the bottom edge of the upper lite and the lower cap is butted against the bottom of the lower edge of the upper lite.

In straight eave models with one lite in the roof, a line of butyl rope is layed along the top of the eave and a vinyl channel is placed over the top edge of the glass. The top edge is pushed into the glass stop and pressed firmly into the butyl rope on the bars and one the eave. If more than one non-crimped cap is used to hold this glass in place, fasten the lower cap first and then the upper cap with a slight overlap.

Where more than one lite is used up the roof and lapping takes place, the bottom lite next to the eave is installed first and followed by the upper lite placed in a manner similar to the lite over the curved eave. Side lites in a single piece are installed in the same manner as single lites in the roof. Applying a vinyl channel across the top of the lite and laying butyl rope along the sill and up the glass seats of the bar, where two lites are used and lapped, the bottom lite should be installed first followed by the upper lite with a crimped cap similar to that described in the roof. After caps are in place, seal the upper ends of caps at the eave with caulking.

Gable lites are installed by applying butyl rope on the sill and on the gable bars. Where the two lites butt, a plastic glazing came is pushed over the top edge of the lower lite and the next upper lite seats on it. Glass is held in place by non-crimpled caps which are overlapped with the upper one lapping over the lower one by approximately three-eighths of an inch. All edges of glass that go into the roof end bar and side end bar should be covered with the vinyl glazing channel.

XV. Hanging the Door

Your door fits into the framed opening you provided with the rectangular jambs. Mount the door using self-tapping screws. After the door is hung, the door, closer, wind chain, and lockset are mounted.

XVI. Caulking

The final step for providing a finished look to your greenhouse and sealing up air leaks is caulking. Run a bead of caulk continuously around the outside of the sill under the protruding lip. On greenhouses which attach to other buildings, apply a bead of caulking at the juncture. Seal around the door jamb next to the building in the same way. On curved eave models, caulk between the bottom of the lite and the top of the eave.

Extrusions, Screws, Bolts

Unlike fiberglass greenhouses, glass houses—which are built with wood or aluminum—require metal extrusions and a variety of screws and bolts. Figures 2-110 and 2-111 show the various types of extrusion bars and screws and bolts used for the greenhouse plans described above.

Lord & Burnham, Irvington on Hudson, New York, a major do-it-yourself greenhouse company have designed glass greenhouses which make it easy for the handyman, do-it-yourselfer to construct. All material is prefabricated, prenumbered and precut where necessary. Some of their most popular models are among the plans which follow this chapter.

STRAIGHT-EAVE MODELS

There are some basic rules which are presented in the following steps.

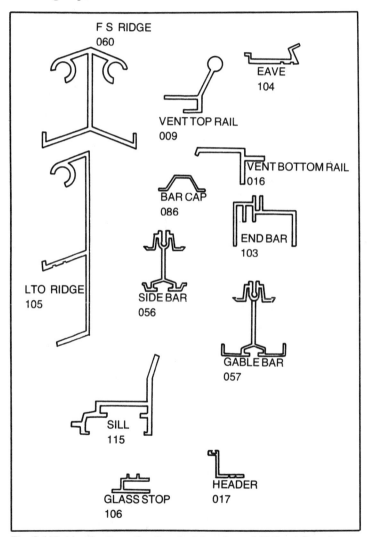

Fig. 2-110. Identification extrustion chart (courtesy of National Greenhouse Company).

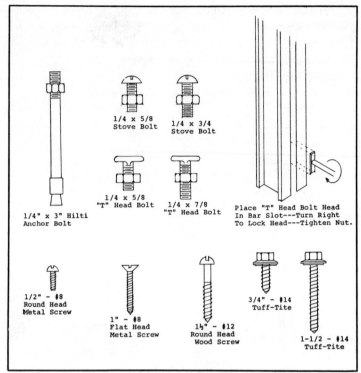

Fig. 2-111. Screw and bolt identification chart (courtesy of National Greenhouse Company).

Assembling the Framework

Before connecting the roof and side bars, note where carriage bolts are required. Slide bolt heads into the back of the bar; hold them in place with plastic tape (Fig. 2-112).

Assemble the roof and side bars with splice fittings. Use two per intermediate connection and one per end (Fig. 2-113).

Even Span Models. Attach assembled frames to the sills; intermediate side bars bolt directly to the back of the sill. Corner side bars are connected to the sill with an angle lug.

Attach the ridge with self-tapping screws; overlap at the joints. Ridge sections are the same shape as eave purlins, but approximately 1″ longer.

Lean-To. Attach the ridge lug to the end of each intermediate roof bar, but not on the end bar. Place the upper edge of the aluminum ridge ¼″ below the top of the 2″ x 6″ joist. Check for level along roof bars using a taut string end to end of ridge joist. To

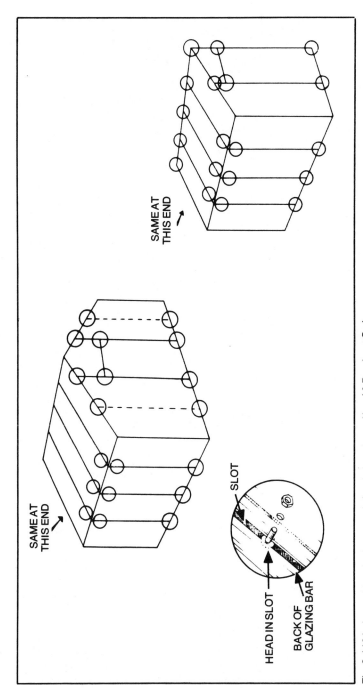

SAME AT THIS END

SAME AT THIS END

SLOT

HEAD IN SLOT

BACK OF GLAZING BAR

Fig. 2-112A. Assembling the framework details (courtesy of Lord & Burnham Co.).

179

Fig. 2-112B. Straight eave model (courtesy of Lord & Burnham Co.).

Fig. 2-112C. Straight eave model (courtesy of Lord & Burnham Co.).

181

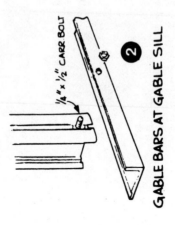

¼" x ½" CARR BOLT

② GABLE BARS AT GABLE SILL

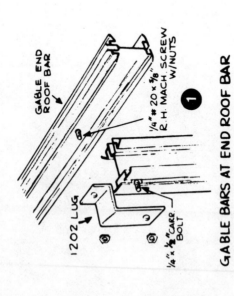

GABLE END ROOF BAR

¼" #20 x ⅝" R.H. MACH. SCREW W/NUTS

1202 LUG

¼" x ½" CARR. BOLT

① GABLE BARS AT END ROOF BAR

182

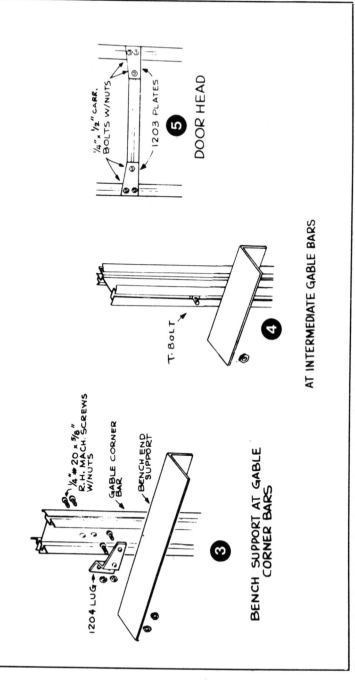

Fig. 2-113. Details gable end framing (courtesy of Lord & Burnham Co.).

183

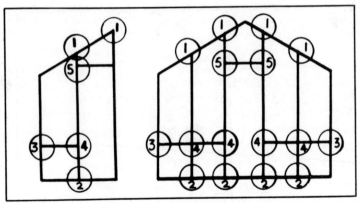

Fig. 2-113. Details gable end framing (courtesy of Lord & Burnham Co.) (continued from page 183).

attach the ridge, drill the lead holes into 2″ x 6″ through holes in ridges; fasten them with wood screws.

All Models. Install eave purlin using two carriage bolts at intermediate bars; secure them to corner bars with two eave purlin clamps. In 12′ and 18′ long greenhouses, also use clamps at purlin joints (Fig. 2-114).

Gable End Bars. Slide vinyl weatherstrip into the groove in both door bucks and door head buck. Insert vinyl into the groove and pull into place with pliers. Secure bars to the sill with carriage bolts. Connect the tops of bars to the roof bar with offset lugs (Figs. 2-115 and 2-116).

Install Door

The doors are outswinging and hinged on the left or the right at your option during installation (Figs. 2-117 and 2-118). Figure 2-117 is for a lean-to with the hinge on the *right jamb*. Installation of the door in an Evan Span greenhouse is the same except that no angle lugs or framing lumber are required.

Cut the expander and piano hinge 5/16″ less than the door opening height. Drill the piano hinge with a ⅛″ drill bit. The first hole should be 1″ from the top of the hinge. The second hole should be ½″ from the first and the rest spaced every 12 inches. Make sure that the holes will not interfere with the rivets on the hinge.

Decide on which jamb you want to install the hinge. Hold the expander against this jamb (open so the rear leaf of the hinge is tight against and snug into the inside corner of the door buck) with equal clearance at both top and bottom.

184

Drill through the holes in the piano hinge into the greenhouse door buck; use a No. 31 bit. Attach the hinge to the buck with 1″ screws so that the hinge and expander hang and swing freely.

Slip the door into the expander. Allow one-eighth of an inch at the top and at the latch side of the frame for clearance. Drill five holes through the face of the expander into the door frame with a No. 31 drill bit and install with ⅜″ screws. Drill holes 4″ from the top and bottom, and one in the center, with two others evenly spaced between. The door should swing freely and be clear at the top, bottom and latch side.

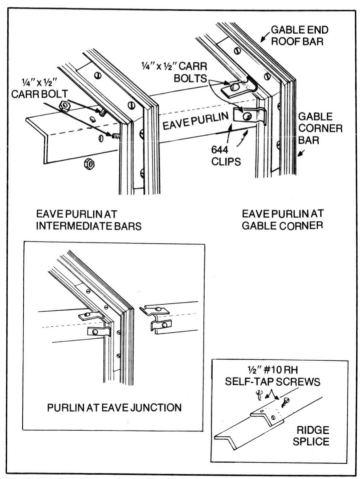

Fig. 2-114. Details eave purlin at gable corners (courtesy of Lord & Burnham Co.).

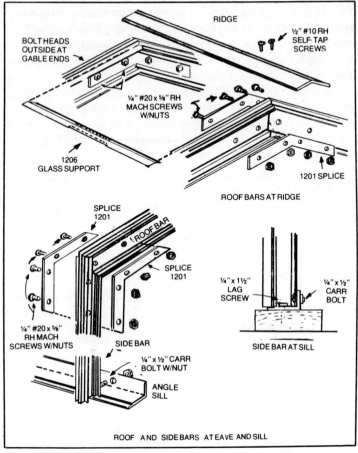

RIDGE

½" #10 RH
SELF-TAP
SCREWS

BOLT HEADS
OUTSIDE AT
GABLE ENDS

¼" #20 x ⅝" RH
MACH SCREWS
W/NUTS

1206
GLASS SUPPORT

1201 SPLICE

ROOF BARS AT RIDGE

SPLICE
1201

ROOF BAR

SPLICE
1201

¼" x 1½"
LAG
SCREW

¼" x ½"
CARR
BOLT

¼" #20 x ⅝"
RH MACH
SCREWS W/NUTS

SIDE BAR

¼" x ½" CARR
BOLT W/NUT

ANGLE
SILL

SIDE BAR AT SILL

ROOF AND SIDE BARS AT EAVE AND SILL

Fig. 2-115. Detail roof bar at ridge connection (courtesy of Lord & Burnham Co.).

Cut the door sweep provided so that it will cover the bottom of the door from the hinge to the frame of the bottom of the door from the hinge to the frame of the greenhouse. Place the door sweep onto the door and drill with a No. 31 drill bit into the bottom rail. Install the ⅜" screws provided and adjust so that the rubber touches the ground. Install the latch and then install the protector chain.

Ends

Glass is butted, as in the sides, with plastic cams at horizontal intersections. Cut and apply U-shaped flexible gray vinyl glazing channel to the outer edges of gable lites only where glass adjoins roof and side. Apply one layer of K-wik-on tape to all vertical bars. Starting with the lowest lite, slide the edge of the pane containing vinyl channel into the groove in back of the gable and bars. Lay the opposite edge of the lite on the bar shoulder and apply glazing clip (Fig. 2-119).

If you have difficulty installing the angular corner lites in the gable (the top lite nearest the eave), disconnect the adjacent vertical gable glazing bar at the top and swing it in (just slightly toward the center of the house). The angular lite should then fit in place and the bar can be moved back and secured.

Fasten Sills to Foundation

After the greenhouse is assembled and glazed, check sills for square; stretch string along each sill to make sure that it is level and straight. Then connect the sills to the foundation:

☐ If built on wood sills, drill lead holes and attach sills with lag screws. Leave shims in place and cut them so pieces under sill remain in place as supports.

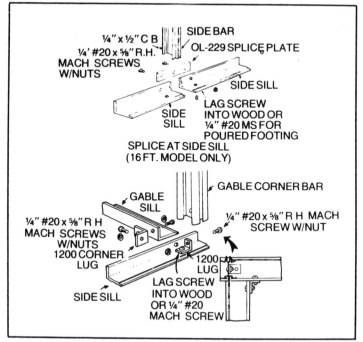

Fig. 2-116. Detail connection side sill, gable sill, and gable corner bar (courtesy of Lord & Burnham Co.).

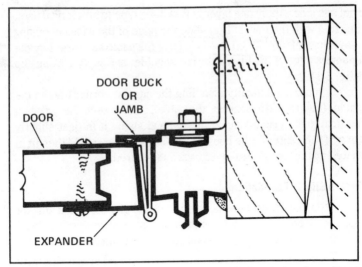

Fig. 2-117. Top view shown at building connection for lean-to (courtesy of Lord & Burnham Co.).

☐ If the greenhouse is on a masonry foundation, cement in anchor bolts; the following day remove 1 x 2's and batter boards. Trowel cement on top of footings and work the cement well under the aluminum sill. Level grout for a neat finish.

Figures 2-120 and 2-121 show glazing clip locations for Lean-to and Evan Span greenhouses.

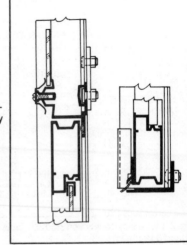

Fig. 2-118. Details side view showing door head and sweep (courtesy of Lord & Burnham Co.).

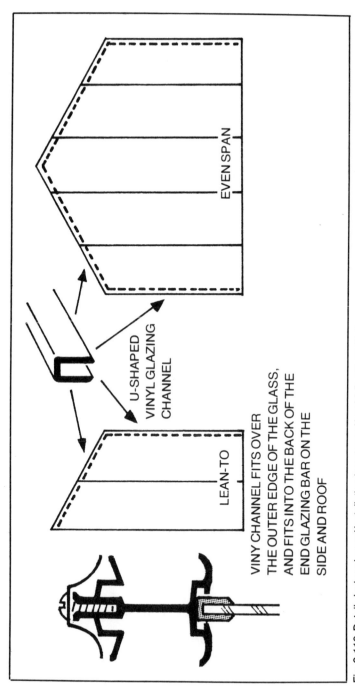

EVEN SPAN

U-SHAPED
VINYL GLAZING
CHANNEL

LEAN-TO

VINYL CHANNEL FITS OVER
THE OUTER EDGE OF THE GLASS,
AND FITS INTO THE BACK OF THE
END GLAZING BAR ON THE
SIDE AND ROOF

Fig. 2-119. Detail glazing channel installation (courtesy of Lord & Burnham Co.).

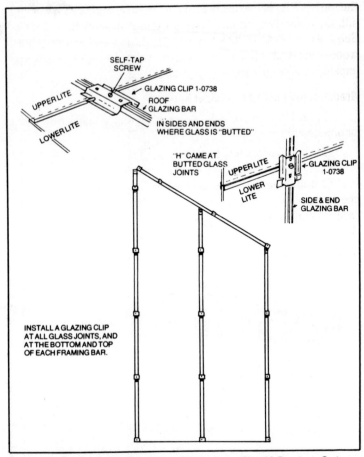

Fig. 2-120. Glazing clip location for lean-to (courtesy of Lord & Burnham Co.).

To form a weather-tight seal at the ridge, cut a piece of Tesafoam 24″ long, remove the backing and lay the sticky side down on the upper edge of the glass lite that fits under the ridge. Place the Tesafoam with ½″ on the glass and ¼″ extending over the edge (Fig. 2-122).

CURVED-EAVE MODELS

The following steps are for building curved-eave models.

Framing Against Building For Lean-To

Cut a 2″ x 6″ joint 8′ 4⅝″ for an eight-section lean-to or 12′ 6⅛″ for a 12-section lean-to. Fasten the joist to the building so that the top is 7' 7½" above the bottom line of the greenhouse aluminum sill. Level and shim the joist and place it in position on top of 2 x 4's. See Figs. 2-123A, 2-123B and 2-124. Fasten with lag screws into wood clapboard surface; use toggle bolts for block walls and expansion bolts on brick or stone walls.

Greenhouse Attached to Another Building

If your Evan Span greenhouse is to be attached to a workroom or other building:

- ☐ Use Standard length dimensions for side foundation.
- ☐ Eliminate footing adjacent to the building.
- ☐ Fill in between the building and the last aluminum bar of the greenhouse with 1 x 4 boards. "Scribe" these to fit neatly to face of building; then caulk or install flashing to keep out rain (Fig. 2-125).

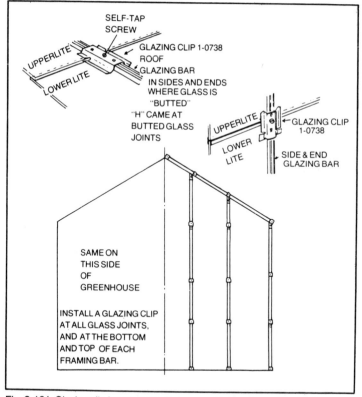

Fig. 2-121. Glazing clip locations for Evan span 9" (courtesy of Lord & Burnham Co.).

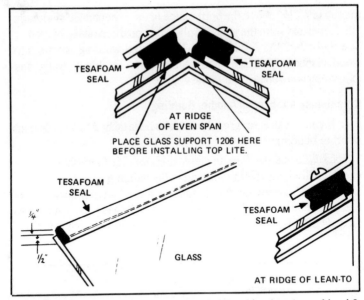

TESAFOAM SEAL

TESAFOAM SEAL

AT RIDGE
OF EVEN SPAN

PLACE GLASS SUPPORT 1206 HERE
BEFORE INSTALLING TOP LITE.

TESAFOAM
SEAL

TESAFOAM
SEAL

¼"

½"

GLASS

AT RIDGE OF LEAN-TO

Fig. 2-122. Placement of weather-tight seal at the ridge (courtesy of Lord & Burnham Co.).

Assembling the Framework

Where ¼" x ½" carriage bolts are required, slide bolt heads into the slot in back of bar; hold them in place with plastic tape.

Evan Span Model. Connect framing bars at the ridge with splice fittings; use two per intermediate connection (Fig. 2-126). Attach frames to sills; intermediate side bars bolt directly to the back of the sill. Corner side bars connect to the sill with an angle lug (Fig. 2-127).

Lean-To. Figure 2-128 illustrates the extension of a lean-to model of 7' up to an extension of 5' on the horizontal dimension. Figure 2-129 indicates the connection of a side sill, gable sill and gable corner bar. Attach two ridge lugs to the end of each intermediate roof bar (one on inner side of end bars). Check for level along the roof bars with a taut string end-to-end of ridge joist. To attach the ridge, drill lead holes into a 2 x 6 through holes in ridge and fasten with wood screws.

All Models. Install side and roof angle purlins using T-bolts at intermediate bars; secure them to corner bars with Z-brackets (Fig. 2-130).

General. Figure 2-131 shows the details for drilling 5/16" diameter holes in order that parts fasten square and in alignment.

Fig. 2-123A. Curved Eave Model (courtesy of Lord & Burnham Co.).

193

Fig. 2-123B. Curved eave model (courtesy of Lord & Burnham Co.).

Figure 2-132 shows details of gable and framing. Figure 2-133 shows details of side end roof angle purlin connection to side and gable bars.

Glazing clip locations for Evan Span and lean-to greenhouses are shown in Figs. 2-134 and 2-135 respectively.

SOLAR GREENHOUSES

The most widely used form of solar heating is sunlight entering a building through windows. Most of the light that enters a building becomes heat. Therefore, greenhouses in themselves are "solar buildings" because they "naturally" soak up the heat during the day.

Nearly everywhere in the continental United States, facing windows admit more heat energy than they lose. In cold climates to effectively reduce heat loss through windows, it is recommended that two layers of glass be used.

Some Generalities About Solar

Studies have shown that the cost and uncertainty of fuel supply continue to be serious concerns for the nation's greenhouse industry. While the hobbyist greenhouser will not need to be overly concerned with regard to fuel shortages, it is interesting to note that, according to the 1969 U.S. Census of Agriculture, there are about 7500 acres of greenhouses in the United States. These, of course, would include the hobby greenhouser.

Assuming the average annual heat input of 4×10^9 BTU per acre of greenhouse, 3×10^{13} BTU are consumed in heating greenhouses. This is equivalent to 300 million gallons of oil annually. For those living in extremely cold climates where winter heating of even the small home greenhouse is necessary, some thought need be given not only the increasing cost of fuel, but more so its unpredictable shortages.

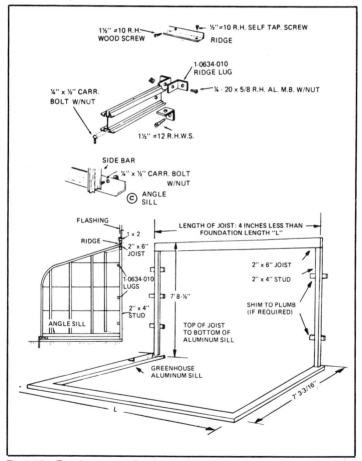

Fig. 2-124. Framing against Building for Lean-to (courtesy of Lord & Burnham Co.).

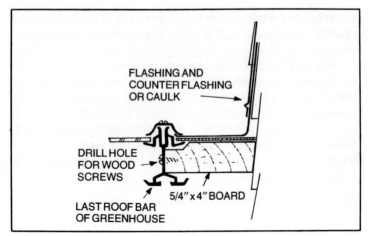

Fig. 2-125. Detail flashing for greenhouse attached to another building (courtesy of Lord & Burnham Co.).

There are two types of solar heating. One is *active* and the other *passive*. There are questions regarding solar heating which the newcomer to this fast-growing heating phase will need answers to.

What is Active Solar? Active solar systems require fans, pumps, and other mechanical equipment to provide and move heat.

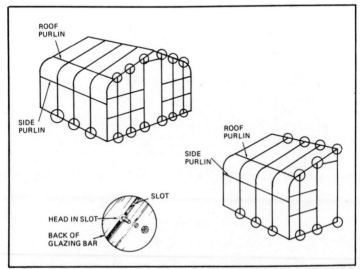

Fig. 2-126. Assembling framework for Evan Span connecting bars at ridges (courtesy of Lord & Burnham Co.).

What is Passive Solar? A passive system radiates the sun naturally (non-mechanically). A greenhouse is a "pure natural" passive solar system.

What is Solar Heat? Direct Gain: when the sun heats air, the warmed air becomes buoyant. Hot air rises and cooler air moves in to replace it. This phenomenon is called *convective air movement*.

What Kind of Solar Heating Systems Are There? Active systems are divided into liquid and air systems. They use pumps and pipes—or fans and ducts—to carry heat from the collectors to storage and from storage to the living place of the building. Therefore, a greenhouse is a passive solar structure.

How Do Solar Energy Systems Work? Radiation is absorbed by a collector placed in storage—with or without the assistance of a transfer medium—and distributed to the point of use. The performance of each operation is maintained and monitored either automatically or with manual controls. An auxiliary heater provides back-up for times when the sun

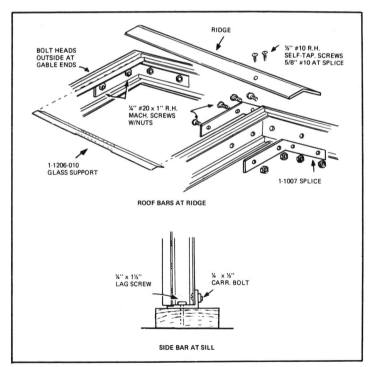

Fig. 2-127. Detail attaching frames to sides (courtesy of Lord & Burnham Co.).

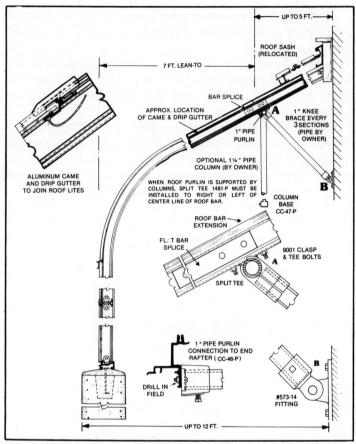

Fig. 2-128. Typical details for extending a 7' lean-to up to 5' on the horizontal dimension (courtesy of Lord & Burnham Co.).

activated-system is not working, An example would be during the winter in extremely cold sections of the country. However, even during the coldest times of the year there is solar heat from the sun. A well designed greenhouse a porch atrium or a window greenhouse unit (lean-to) are solar heated systems.

How A Solar Heater Works

The *solar air heater* is a device for catching some of the sun's abundant energy to help heat a structure, a home, a commercial building or a greenhouse during the winter. It is a simple device. A shallow box covered with some kind of glazing can be used to let the sun's radiant energy in and keep heat from leaving quickly.

Inside the box is an *absorber* for changing the sun's radiant energy into heat energy. The absorber is a piece of metal painted black. Instead of reflecting the sunlight, it absorbs it. Between the glazing and the absorber is a *dead air space* which helps retard any heat captured from escaping to the outside air. Behind the absorber is the *air chamber* through which air from the structure is circulated. The cool air from the structure comes in contact with the absorber and is heated by conduction. Once the air passes through an opening behind the panel, it is heated and it is returned to the structure, such as your greenhouse, through another opening in the panel. These openings are the cool air opening and the hot air opening (Fig. 2-136).

The panel is mounted in a vertical or horizontal position on the south wall. This vertical installation is simple. The panel will catch most of the winter sunlight because the sun is lower in the sky during the winter. In summer, the sun is high in the sky and most of its energy will bounce off the glazing at an angle which will help

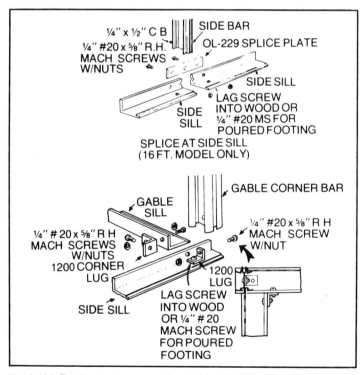

Fig. 2-129. Details showing connection of side sill, gable, sill and gable corner bar (courtesy of Lord & Burnham Co.).

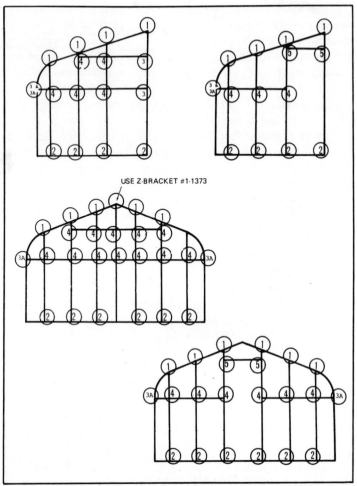

Fig. 2-130. Z-Brackets used at gable end framing (courtesy of Lord & Burnham Co.).

prevent overheating. The only change needed in the construction of a solar-heated greenhouse is for two openings into the panel. Although the panel can be shaded by greenhouse coverings of the many varieties available in the summer, it should receive full sunlight during the heating season (mainly, the winter, especially in heavy frost areas).

The solar heating system described as follows uses some electricity for moveable electric heaters or any other type of electrical system installed for the particular type and size greenhouse you are operating. The cost of electricity is greatly offset by the amount of increased heat brought into the greenhouse. The blower and automatic thermostat make this solar air heater very efficient and easy to live with. It will provide 40 percent to 50 percent effective heating in the home greenhouse.

Constructing Your Solar Heating System

The following is a step-by-step plan to erect the solar heating system as discussed above. The parts inventory list is found in Appendix I.

Step One. Assemble all materials before starting. Read all of the following instructions and be sure you understand each step.

Step Two. Cut 1 x 4 lumber to length (Fig. 2-137).

Step Three. Notch center the baffle and attach the metal ledger to the notch with 1-inch roofing nails.

Step Four. Cut out a 2-inch diameter hot air vent into dead air space on the upper side panel. Install screens and "Temp-Vents"

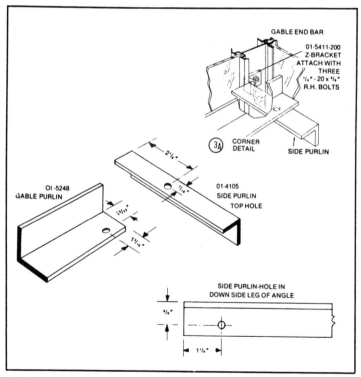

Fig. 2-131. Gable end framing 5/16" (courtesy of Lord & Burnham Co).

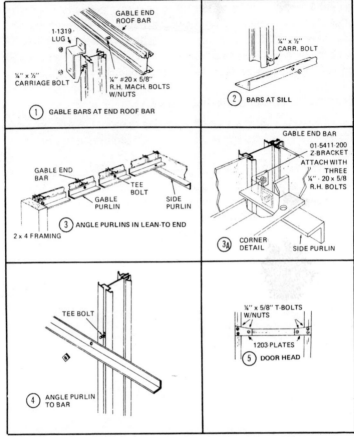

Fig. 2-132. Gable end framing details (courtesy of Lord & Burnham Co.).

over the holes on the inside of the frames. This vent opens automatically to ventilate the dead air space when the temperature reaches 150 F. They open to prevent overheating in summer and will remain closed during winter operation. As a substitute for "Temp-Vents," you can cover the holes with corks or wood during winter and remove them during the summer (Fig. 2-138).

Step Five. Glue and nail the 1 x 4 frame and baffle to the plywood back. Be sure baffle is centered properly. Caulk with latex caulk where the 1 x 4 meets the plywood on the inside to form a weathertight joint.

Step Six. Cut the absorber metal to size. Clean any grease or oil from the metal with detergent or solvent and wash thoroughly. Etch the metal with vinegar or muriatic acid so that paint can

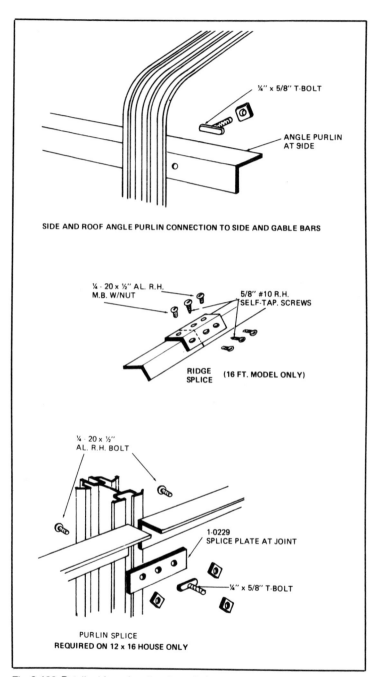

¼" x 5/8" T-BOLT

ANGLE PURLIN
AT SIDE

SIDE AND ROOF ANGLE PURLIN CONNECTION TO SIDE AND GABLE BARS

¼ - 20 x ½" AL. R.H.
M.B. W/NUT

5/8" #10 R.H.
SELF-TAP. SCREWS

RIDGE
SPLICE   (16 FT. MODEL ONLY)

¼ - 20 x ½"
AL. R.H. BOLT

1-0229
SPLICE PLATE AT JOINT

¼" x 5/8" T-BOLT

PURLIN SPLICE
REQUIRED ON 12 x 16 HOUSE ONLY

Fig. 2-133. Details side and roof angle purlin (courtesy of Lord & Burnham Co.).

203

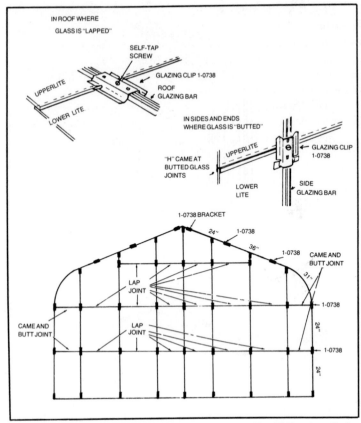

Fig. 2-134. Glazing clip locations Evan Span (courtesy of Lord & Burnham Co.).

adhere to metal. Again, wash the metal to remove the etching solution (Fig. 2-139).

Step Seven. Paint the dry metal absorber evenly with one coat flat black and let dry thoroughly.

Step Eight. Fasten the absorber to the 1 x 2 lip with 1-inch galvanized roofing nails every 3 inches. Apply a thick bead of silicone caulk onto the metal ledger *before* laying down the absorber. This is a "formed-in-place" gasket between the metal ledger and absorber. To keep the absorber embedded in the caulk, drive small nails into the air baffle 1 x 4 to hold the absorber down to the ledger (Fig. 2-138).

Step Nine. Carefully silicone-caulk the entire edge of the absorber where it meets the wood to form an airtight seal between wood and metal.

Step Ten. Touch up the flat black paint at nail heads and any scratches. Paint the inside of the 1 x 4 frame black. Turn the frame over and paint the back of the plywood and outside of 1 x 4's with exterior house paint to seal the lumber (Fig. 2-140).

Step Eleven. Cut fiberglass glazing to size, run a bead of caulk on panel 1 x 4's and lay glazing onto panel.

Step Twelve. Cut the edging (wood or metal) to length and predrill screw holes.

Step Thirteen. Lay the edging onto the glazing and drill through screw holes into the glazing and fasten the edging and glazing to the frame with screws.

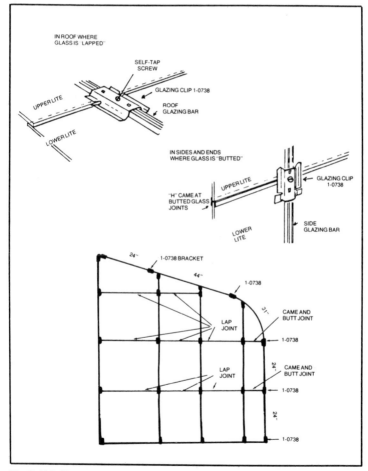

Fig. 2-135. Glazing clip locations lean-to (courtesy of Lord & Burnham Co.).

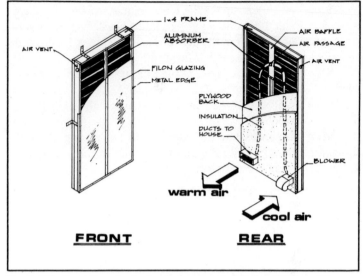

Fig. 2-136. Operation of solar heating system (courtesy of Office of Human Concern written by Joel Davidson and plans by Albert Skiles).

Installation of Collector

Step One. Mark the location of panel and duct openings onto outside of the greenhouse.

Step Two. Cut duct openings into the building.

Step Three. Cut duct openings into the plywood panel back. Remember that air space in the panel is only ¾″ deep. Use a short saw and short drill blade and bit.

Step Four. Fasten the panel to the building. Use eight 3″ x 3″ angles and screw the panel to the building.

Step Five. From inside the building, tape and seal the air ducts.

Step Six. Mount blower on cool-air-in opening.

Step Seven. Wire the thermostat into the hot-air-in opening. Secure the thermostat to the metal absorber with silicone caulk and duct tape.

Step Eight. Cover hot air opening with register or screen.

Step Nine. Plug in the thermostat. It will turn on the blower at 100 F and turn it off at 90 F. See Fig. 2-141.

Maintenance

Once your solar air heater is installed and working, it requires very little maintenance. Because the blower is automatically

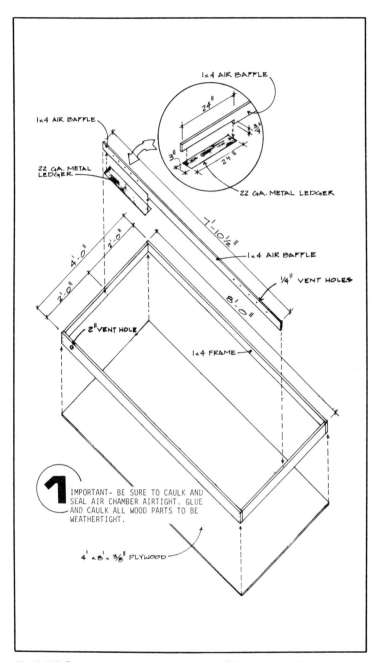

Fig. 2-137. Details of solar system (courtesy of Office of Human Concern written by Joel Davidson and plans by Albert Skiles).

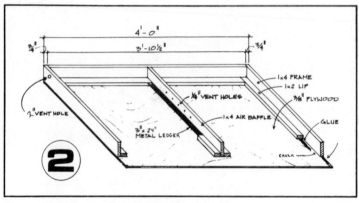

Fig. 2-138. Section, vent openings in dead-air space only. Cut, glue and nail the 1 x 2 lip into frame (courtesy of Office of Human Concern written by Joel Davidson and plans by Albert Skiles).

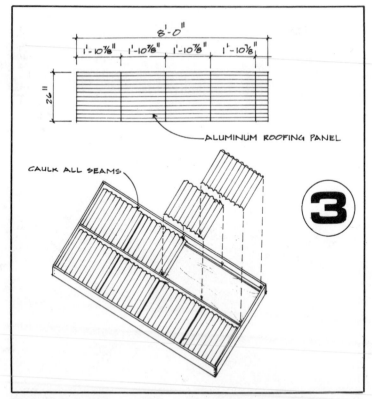

Fig. 2-139. Solar System (courtesy of Office of Human Concern written by Joel Davidson and plans by Albert Skiles).

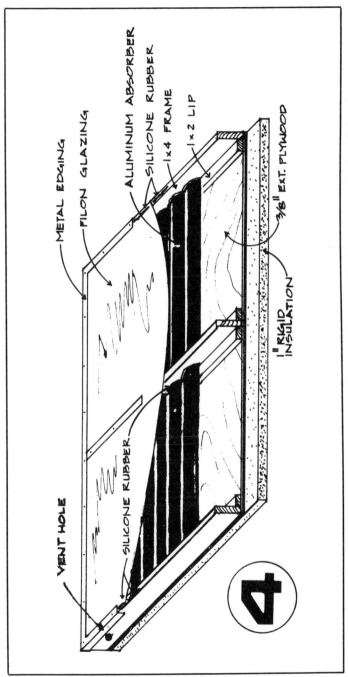

Fig. 2-140. Section of solar system (courtesy of Office of Human Concern written by Joel Davidson and plans by Albert Skiles).

controlled in winter and the heat vents are automatic in summer, your job will be to keep things clean and clear of obstructions.

Because the sun is a natural source of energy, you must understand that there will be days you would like the panel to work but clouds will block the sun's energy. Also, in late spring and early fall the sun will be low enough in the sky to switch on the solar air heater. On those days, be sure to keep the blower unplugged unless you want your greenhouse heated by the solar unit.

Figure 2-142 shows that the air gap behind the absorber for 8 x 8 or 4 x 16 panels should be 1½" deep and the blower should be 192 CFM at .5 static pressure. A larger blower will be needed for long duct runs.

Kitchen Window Greenhouse: A Solar Source

A typical window greenhouse assembly—not scaled to size— is shown in Fig. 2-143. It can be utilized in any size window.

Step One. Assemble the front and side panels with the flange on the lower edge facing in and the slide bottom front panel facing into the side panels. Then slide the upper panel (with vinyl on top) into the sides. Push firmly to interlock the top and bottom panels at the center meeting rail.

Step Two. Slide the roof sash into the extruded hinge. Place the sash assembly in position on the greenhouse and fasten it at each end with No. 6 x ⅝" self-tapping screws.

Step Three. Attach the angle across piece at the bottom using two self-tapping screws.

Step Four. Insert screen clips in the front edge of the top panel and position them about 6" in from each side. Slide in screens from the front. Use a screw driver or putty knife to lift up on the front of the screen. Push the screen in and down to fit snug against the clips.

Step Five. Fasten the curved push arms to the roof sash with the shoulder screws. Lift the greenhouse onto the window sill. Overlap the frame equally on both sides of the window frame.

Step Six. Push the greenhouse in at the bottom, to fit snug against frame, and hold secure while fastening with No. 12 x 1" screws. Fasten the screws at top first. Then fasten the sides from inside the house. Predrill holes for easiest fastening. Back off No. 6 x ⅝" screws at the ends of the roof hinge and refasten into frame. With the greenhouse in place, caulk inside and out to insure a watertight fit.

Around the Window Installation

To install a solar unit that is larger than the window frame, fasten 1 x 4 boards to the building face. Use nails or screws if you are working with a frame construction with plywood or lumber sheating. Use toggle bolts and nails if the sheating is insulating board. Use expansion shields and lag bolts if the house is masonry.

The overall measurements of the frame should be 4″ wider and higher than the greenhouse size you are installing. For a 33″ x 52″ solar unit, frame the 1 x 4's to 37″ x 56″ outside dimensions.

Nail or screw a 1 x 2 cleat across the bottom 1 x 4, flush with the lower edge. Cut the cleat to the actual greenhouse width so that the cleat ends do not project beyond greenhouse sides.

If the face of the building is fairly smooth, run a bead of caulking compound around the outer edge of the 1 x 4's, on top, and on both sides to seal from the weather.

If the face of the building is irregular (as with shingles, clapboard or rough masonry), it will be necessary to add a weather

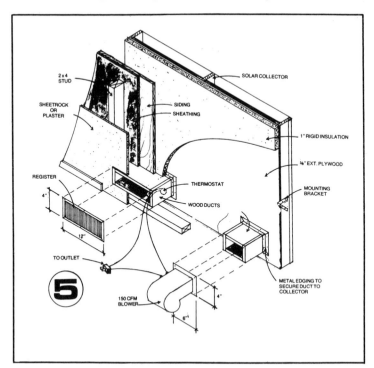

Fig. 2-141. Installation of solar system (courtesy of Office of Human Concern written by Joel Davidson and plans by Albert Skiles).

211

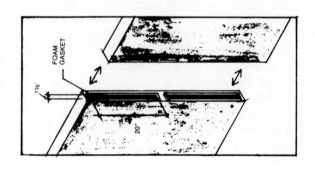

FOAM GASKET

1½"

20"

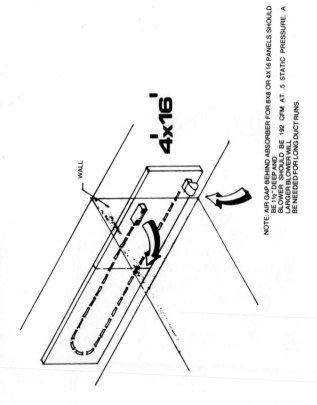

WALL

4'x16'

NOTE: AIR GAP BEHIND ABSORBER FOR 8X8 OR 4X16 PANELS SHOULD BE 1½" DEEP AND BLOWER SHOULD BE 192 CFM AT .5 STATIC PRESSURE. A LARGER BLOWER WILL BE NEEDED FOR LONG DUCT RUNS.

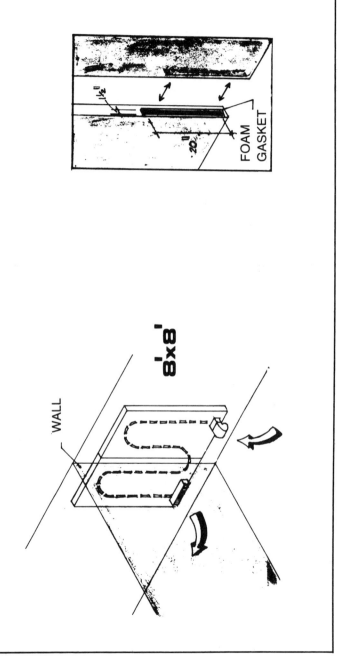

WALL

8'x8'

1½"

20"

FOAM
GASKET

Fig. 2-142. Details of air gap behind absorber (courtesy of Office of Human Concern written by Joel Davidson and plans by Albert Skiles).

213

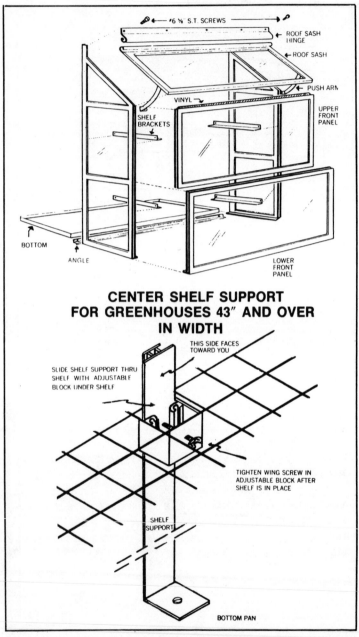

Fig. 2-143. Typical window greenhouse solar assembly, not scaled (courtesy of Lord & Burnham Co.). Note: Be sure shelf bracket screws are tight before installing shelves.

214

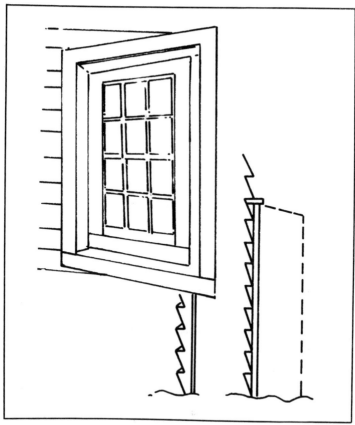

Fig. 2-144. Scribing Board (courtesy of Lord & Burnham Co.).

cap and scribing boards on each side. Use two thin, clear lumber boards 2" x 3" wide, by height of greenhouse plus 6" (Fig. 2-144).

Hold vertically against a 1 x 4 on the 1" dimension. With dividers, mark the irregular shape of building onto side of scribing board. Cut with a coping saw and nail the scribing to the 1 x 4. Caulk on all four edges. Prime and paint the 1 x 4's before assembling and installing the solar greenhouse.

Chapter 3
What To Raise

What is the best use for your greenhouse? What should you raise? How much time does it take? The answers are varied and many. Perhaps the best answer is to grow what you want that will give the most satisfaction in terms of enjoyment and economic savings and spend the time that you feel you can use without it becoming a chore.

One of the most rewarding experiences is the raising of seedlings for your flower and vegetable garden along with the propagation of your favorite plants. By raising your own seedlings, you can choose just the right colors and varieties for your annual garden and you have an earlier flower and vegetable garden. Cut flowers for the house in mid-winter is an added bonus.

While it would be impossible to discuss all of the hundreds of varieties, some of the most popular plants are discussed here. With a little planning, when one variety has finished blooming another kind will begin. For instance, when chrysanthemums are through blooming they can be removed and the bench can be filled with schizanthus or stock.

Unless you plan to specialize and raise only one species such as orchids—keeping a "cool" greenhouse in which winter night temperatures range from 40 F to 60 F is an excellent type greenhouse to operate for the person who wants to grow a wide range of plants that require considerable variance in night temperature. Keeping an inexpensive indoor/outdoor thermometer will assist you in a quick visual aid for temperature readings (Fig. 3-1).

There is much in the beauty of flowers in store for the newcomer to greenhousing. Fall is represented by the queen of fall perennials—chrysanthemums—followed by snapdragon, pansies, schizanthus, stocks—just to mention a few.

The huge array of cacti hold hours of fascination for the experienced and novice alike. And ferns thrive on the humid conditions afforded them in a greenhouse. The grace of hanging baskets too is unsurpassed. All of this will delight and provide a place of peace and tranquility.

For those who want to specialize in bromeliads, camellia or orchids, the challenges are never ending. All of these come together as a whole in the home greenhouse. Experimenting with some or all of these plants provides a constant on-going education to introduce you to new and different species of plants.

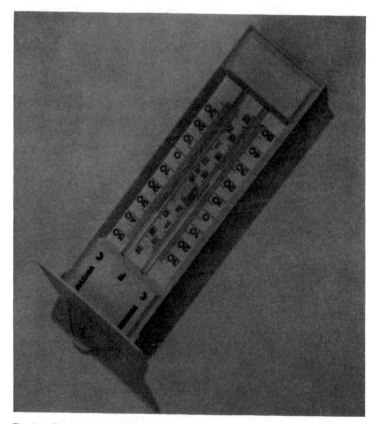

Fig. 3-1. Temperature control is easily located on this mini-maxi thermometer (courtesy of Costitch and McConnell, Inc.).

Some of the plants mentioned above are listed as tropicals. Many newcomers to home greenhousing get "up tight" when told that "tropicals need specific attention." What is all too often overlooked is that most species can be duplicated in even the smallest home greenhouse.

Climate and topography in the tropics are as diverse as the plants themselves. There are desert regions and there are areas of low elevation where it is hot and damp. There are also the mountains where temperatures are cool due to an increase in altitude.

Temperatures at 9000 feet average 54 degrees. Above that, the temperature decreases to freezing in some areas. Even in the tropics, there are snow belts. Plants in the 3000 to 6000 feet range produce flowers and plants which, when taken out of their natural environment, enjoy greenhouse night temperatures in the 60s. Plants that in the tropics grow in cooler temperatures do well in 50-degree temperatures in the greenhouse. And the sea level species, although grown naturally under "warmer" conditions, are content with an average 65 degrees.

HANGING BASKETS

With a little taste and imagination, you can emulate and duplicate the fabled Hanging Gardens of Babylon and the greenhouse is the ideal place to do it. Not only do hanging baskets dress up the greenhouse, you will have their beauty readily available to enhance your patio and porch. They can also be used for a landscaping and housescaping program to blend the house in with the outdoors through the use of floral ornamentation. It is also a challenge to your creativity.

Frequent and thorough watering and fertilizing are of prime importance to the success of hanging baskets. The constant loss of water dripping through not only depletes the moisture, but also carries fertilizers with it.

Baskets can be made up of a variety of materials such as chicken wire, old fashioned fence wire, plastic containers with holes pierced in them, and compressed cardboard are just a few possibilities.

Step One. Use a layer of sphagnum moss which has been soaked in water for several hours (preferably overnight for it to fully expand) and line the basket with an ample supply.

Step Two. Add a lining of fine screen wire to hold the moss in place.

Step Three. Add a good growing medium of humus along with some vermiculite.

Step Four. Insert the plants. Have some directly in the top and others coming out of the sides. In this manner, the ultimate growth of your plants will give you a fully uniform basketful (Fig. 3-2).

It is very important to keep the soil firm. Yet it must be loose enough to allow good drainage in order to prevent the soil from becoming sour which, in turn, helps in protection from insects and disease. Plants whose habits and needs recommend them for successful basket cultivation include the following.

Flowering. Hedera (Ivy), viving geraniums, bougainvillea, nephrolephis and other ferns; coleus, vinca, fuchsia, begonias, cascade chrysanthemums, achimenes, impatiens, lantana, cascade petunia.

Cacti and Succulents. Stapelia (carionflower), hoyas, Christmas cactus, ice plant. Because most cacti bloom, they are delightful in baskets and might even be classified and included in the flowering section.

These are just a few of the many plants conducive to hanging baskets because their pendulous stems display their foliage to better advantage than in a standard container. For best results, fertilize with Nutri-sol every four to six weeks.

CUT FLOWERS

For the average size home greenhouse (10' to 60'), space always seems to be at a minimum. No matter how large a house you begin with and how few plants you have at the onset, your initial stock—once you begin the joy and fascination that comes with greenhousing—quickly produces an abundance of plants being housed and raised. While a smaller house will not allow you enough space to grow innumerable varieties of flowers, even the smallest greenhouse can provide cut flowers that thrive under cool—50 degrees at night and 60 to 65 degrees during the day—greenhouse conditions.

If your greenhouse is large enough, divide sections of benches solely to accommodate cut flower cultivation. You will then be able to have cut flowers year around.

To begin your cut flower cultivation, the following planting guide supplies you with a list of the most popular greenhouse varieties along with the botanical and the common name, whether it is flower or foliage, whether it is considered an ornamental, colors, and other information relative to the variety. Unless otherwise stated, the growing media consists of equal parts (by volume) of garden loam, peatmoss and sand—plus the addition of vermiculite, as needed.

Acacia. A small shrub or tree which should be kept to 5' or less, Acacias mature in approximately one year and produce yellow flowers. Sow seeds in the spring and take clippings during the summer. *Requirements:* Starting temperature 60 F. Growing temperature 40-45 F. Summer light—full sun. Some require cold temperatures in fall and early winter to flower.

Acalypha Hispida (Red-hot Cat-tal/Chenille Plant). Maturing from 1 to 3' in a year, Acalypha Hispida is grown especially for its unusualy red, very showy flowers. Cuttings may be taken during the summer. *Requirements:* Starting temperature 60 F. Growing temperature 60 F. Summer light—full sun, partial shade. Flowering Season is fall to spring.

Achimenes (Nut Orchid, Hot Water Plant). Achimenes grow between 1' to 2' and produce beautiful flowers of crimson, rose, orange, blue, purple and white. They can be cultivated by taking divisions of Scaly Phizones in the spring. They flower from summer to early autumn. *Requirements:* Starting temperature 80 F. Growing temperature 60 F. Summer light—they prefer a shaded area. They also excellent for use in hanging baskets. After flowering, dry and store at 45 to 55 F.

Aeschynanthus (Formerly Trichosporum). Maturing in 12 months, this beautiful plant produces scarlet, green-yellow flowers from spring to fall. Cuttings can be taken in early spring and they are excellent for hanging basket culture. *Requirements:* Starting temperature 65 F. Growing temperature 65 F. Summer light—shade. They enjoy high humidity and even moisture in a good growing medium at all times.

Agapanthus (Lily of the Nile). Maturing in 4 to 6 months to the miniatures of 1½' with giant varieties of up to 4 feet, they produce blue, and white flowers which bloom in the spring and summer. The leaves offer excellent contrast to plants with rounded form. *Requirements:* Starting temperature 50 F. Growing temperature 45-55 F. Summer light—full sun or partial shade. Container—tub for giant; pots for dwarf.

Ageratum (Floss Flower). Maturing in 3 to 4 months from the dwarf varieties of 6-8" to the large of 1 to 2 feet, they produce blue, white and pink flowers which bloom continuously. Cuttings should be taken in the spring or summer. Seeds are sown in spring and summer. *Requirements:* Temperature 65 to 76 F. Growing temperature 50 F. Summer light—full sun. Cut back old plants to 3″ to promote compact new growth or discard after long flowering season and start new cuttings or seeds.

Allamanda. A vining plant, Allamanda produces yellow and purple flowers. Cuttings can be taken in the spring and these plants can be raised in tubs. *Requirements:* Starting temperature 75 to 80 F. Growing temperature 60 F. Plants should be cut back and repotted in January.

Allyssum Maritmum (Sweet Alyssum). Maturing in 3 to 5 months, their size ranges from 3 to 4″ and 5 to 6″ with a continuous flowering season. Their fragrant flowers of white, violet and pink are their special attraction and they are ideal for hanging baskets. *Requirements:* Temperature 65 to 70 F. Growing temperature 55 F. Summer light—full sun. After a long flowering season, shear back to 2 or 3″ to promote compact, new growth.

Amarcrinum. Growing from 3 to 4 feet, Amarcrinum produces fragrant pin flowers with evergreen foliage. Bulbs should be set in the spring or seeds should be sown in the spring.

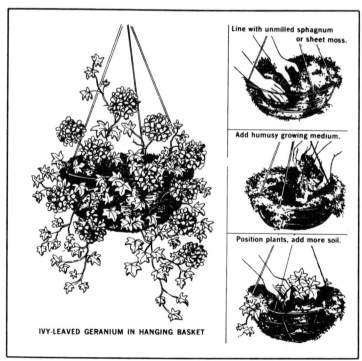

Line with unmilled sphagnum or sheet moss.

Add humusy growing medium.

Position plants, add more soil.

IVY-LEAVED GERANIUM IN HANGING BASKET

Fig. 3-2. Constructing a hanging basket (courtesy of Kathleen Bourke).

Requirements: Temperature 55 to 60 F and 65 to 76 F respectively according to season. Summer light—full sun to partial shade. Container—large pots or tub.

Amaryllis. Maturing in 2 to 4 months (seeds mature in 2 to 4 years), they range in size from 2 to 3′ producing red, pink and white flowers which are their special attraction. Bulbs or seed can be sown in early spring in large pots. *Requirements:* Starting temperature 65 to 75 F. Growing temperature 65 to 76 F. Summer light—full sun, partial shade. They flower in winter and spring and require a cool rest period between September and January. Allow them to grow throughout the summer and then store them in a cool dry area until signs of growth show in the winter.

Anemone. Maturing in 3 to 5 months (seeds 1 year), they produce 6 to 8″ white, pink, lavender, red, magenta and blue flowers. Divisions should be taken in the fall when the temperature is approximately 40 F. Seeds should be sown in the summer. *Requirements:* Temperature 65 to 70 F. Growing temperature 40 F. Summer light—full sun. After flowers stop coming, withhold water. Store dry and cool through summer. Repot in autumn.

Anthurium. Maturing to 1 to 3′ in two years, Anthurium blooms continuously with red, yellow, rose and white flowers. It is also prized for its beautiful foliage. They can be cultivated by air-layering and suckers taken in early spring. Seeds should be sown in the spring. *Requirements:* Starting temperature 65 to 80 F respectively—suckets and/or seeds. Growing temperature 65 F. Summer light—shade. They enjoy high humidity and should be grown in tubs in a media of Osmunda fiber Sphagnum and highly organic medium. The elongated stem should be covered with sphagnum.

Antirrhinum (Snapdragon). The several varieties of this most popular greenhouse flowering plant matures in approximately 5 months from the 6-12″ dwarf to the larger varieties of 1½ to 3 feet. Flowering in winter through spring, they produce flowers of many colors; pink, white, orange, lavender, yellow, red bronze, and mixed. Seeds should be sown in the summer, but they can be raised year around by choosing different groups or utilizing photoperiod. *Requirements:* Starting temperature 65 to 75 F. Growing temperature 65 F for one month, then 50 to 60 F to finish. Summer light—full sun. Photoperiod—long days hasten flowering, but reduces the quality. Short days slow flowering but improve the quality.

Aphelandra. Maturing in 6 months to 12 to 18 inches, cuttings should be taken in the spring. Young plants started annually from cuttings make the best appearance with the handsome foliage and showy flowers of golden yellow. *Requirements:* Starting temperature 70 to 80 F. Growing temperature 55 to 65 F.

Ardisia Crispa. The Ardisia takes a long time to mature, 2 to 3 years, and it grows from 2 to 4 feet. The beautiful long-lasting red berries, with white or reddish flowers, makes it a favorite for a greenhouse specialty. Cuttings can be taken in the late spring. *Requirements:* Starting temperature from seeds sown in spring is 65 F. Growing temperature 60 F from February to October. Summer light—shade. They should be pruned back in March.

Asparagus Fern (Ornamental). No greenhouse should be without some type of fern. See Fig. 3-3. The Sprengeri and Plumosus have rich green coloring and can be divided in spring with temperatures of 60 F or seeds can be sown in spring with

Fig. 3-3. Tomatoes in 2 x 2 x 2 containers (courtesy of John Wahlfeldt).

temperature of 70 to 80 F. They can be raised in pots, tubs or hanging baskets and range from dwarfs of 18″ to 6′ and up. *Requirements:* Growing temperature 60 F. Summer light—shade.

Astilbe Japonica (Spirea). Maturing in four months in the greenhouse, most people think Spirea belongs only on the outside. It makes a delightful greenhouse addition. Producing white, pink flowers in the spring, they prefer to be kept cool in the fall and early winter. Beginning in January, provide them warmth to induce their showy flowers within 12 weeks. *Requirements:* Starting temperature 60 F. Growing temperature store between 32 and 35 F. Force at 60 F. Summer light—full sun.

Azalea. Maturing in 2 to 3 years, cuttings can be taken in late winter for the greenhouse culture of this beautiful plant. The plant can range in size from 1 to 3′ or 3 to 8′ and above. The beautiful showy flowers are short-lived, but worth the effort in colors of red, pink, salmon, fuchsia, and orange. *Requirements:* Starting temperature 80 F. Growing temperature 60 F, but above 60 F for bud invitation. For bud development, below 60 F. They should be stored from 4 to 6 weeks in 40 F and can be forced at the 60 F temperature within 4 to 6 weeks. Summer light—full sun, but shade when they are being stored.

Begonia Fibrous-Rooted (Wax Begonia, Semperflorens). Maturing in 4 to 6 months from 6″ to 9 to 11″ in several varieties, the produce continuous flowering with attractive foliage in red, rose, pink and white. Seeds are sown in late winter for bedding at a temperature of 65 to 75 F or cuttings can be taken anytime. This is especially true during spring at a temperature of 70 F. They may be raised in pots, tubs or hanging baskets. *Requirements:* Growing temperature 65 F. Summer light—full sun for best foliage color. Photoperiod—long days if over 70 F temperature to flower; less than 70 F flowers anyway. They also do well in a shaded area.

Begonia, Semi-Tuberous (Christmas Begonia). Maturing in 10 to 13 months and flowering from December to February with red, rose, pink, orange and white flowers, the foliage is also handsome. Leaf/petiole cuttings and terminal cuttings can be taken in late Winter and Spring. *Requirements:* Temperature 70 F. Growing temperature 60 to 65 F. Summer light—Light shade. Photoperiod—short days bring on the flowers.

Begonia, Tuberous. Maturing in 6 months to sizes of up to 18 inches, the beautiful crimson, red, orange, white, pink, yellow flowers can be sown by seed in winter in pots or tubs. *Require-*

ments: Temperature 65 to 75 F. Growing temperature 65 F. They should be raised in a media of highly organic material to produce flowering in spring, summer and fall. Tubers may be stored in a dry area at 50 F from late fall until winter.

Beloperone (Shrimp Plant). Maturing in 6 to 12 months from 12 to 18 inches, they have a continuous flowering in reddish salmon or chartreuse bracts and white flowers with unusual, colorful shrimp-like bracts surrounded by the white flowers. Cuttings can be taken at any time. *Requirements:* Starting temperature 65 to 75 F. Growing temperature 55 to 65 F. Summer light—full to partial sun.

Bessera Elegans (Mexican Coral Drops). This plant ranges from 1 to 2 feet. Bulbs can be set in the spring to produce red or white flowers during the summer. *Requirements:* Temperature 60 F. Growing temperature 60 F. Summer light—Full sun.

Boston Daisy Marguerite (Chrysanthemum Frutescens). Maturing in 6 months at 1 to 3 feet, this queen of the home greenhouse produces white, yellow and pink flowers that bloom in mid-winter to early fall. Cuttings can be taken in the spring. *Requirements:* Starting temperature 70 F. Growing temperature 50 to 60 F. Summer light—full sun. Photoperiod—long days induce budding for flowers; short days promote vegetation growth. Young plants, 1 to 2 years old, yield larger flowers than old, woody plants.

Bougainvillea. Ideal for hanging baskets with flower bracts of magenta, red, pink or bronze, cuttings can be taken in the spring and are ideal for hanging baskets. *Requirements:* Temperature 70 to 80 F. Growing temperature 55 to 60 F. Summer light—partial shade. Photoperiod—shade before September 20 to increase flower buds. Bougainvillea flowers intermittently from early fall to late spring. Prune back to desired size after each flowering.

Bouvardia. Growing from 2 to 6 feet, the pink, red and white flowers of the Bouvardia are highly attractive; the white is quite fragrant. Terminal cuttings can be taken in late winter or early spring. *Requirements:* Temperature 65 F; if they are taken from divisions in late spring, temperatures should be 60 to 75 F. Growing temperature 60 to 70 F. Summer light—full sun. Photoperiod—long days cause budding and short days hasten bud development at 70 to 75 F. They prefer highly organic, slightly alkaline, pH 6:00 to 7:5 growing medium. Their flowering season is fall-winter and they will not flower at 55 F. Cut back after flowering.

Bromeliads (Member of Pineapple Family). Maturing from 1 to 2 years, Bromeliads can be started from seeds or divisions taken at any time. They flower seasonally, depending on the variety, and their main attraction is the beautiful foliage. *Requirements:* Starting temperature 75 to 80 F. Growing temperature 65 F. They like a highly organic growing medium with Osmunda, sphagnum and peat moss. Many die after flowering. Remove and plant new offsets that form. Recommended genera for a home greenhouse include: Aechmea, Ananas, Billbergia, Cryptanthus, Guzmania, Neoregelia, Tillandsia and Vriesea.

Browallia. Maturing in 5 to 6 months from 10 to 12 inches, they flower during the winter in blue, purple and white. Seeds and cuttings can be taken in the spring and summer. *Requirements:* Starting temperature 65 to 75 F. Growing temperature 65 F. Summer light—full sun. After a season of flowering, cut plants back to encourage new growth. The "orange browallia," Streptosolen jamesoni, requires similar treatment.

Brunsvigia (Cape Belladonna or Beladonna Lily). Matures in 6 to 8 weeks to 2 to 3 feet, bulbs can be set in the winter. They flower during winter and spring with highly fragrant pink and red flowers. *Requirements:* Starting temperature 65 to 80 F. Growing temperature 60 F. Dry off in autumn as for the related Amoryllis.

Buddleia or Beddleia (Butterfly Bush). Buddleia can grow very large and most people don't think of them as greenhouse plants; but grown in large pots they are simply beautiful. They mature in eight to nine months and can be pruned to 4 to 6 feet. Flowering in the winter, their special attraction is their white, lilac, pink, orange or yellow flowers. Terminal cuttings can be taken in the spring. *Requirements:* Starting temperature 60 to 70 F. Growing temperature 60 F or 60 to 65 F for budding. Summer light—shade. Cut back sharply after flowering to induce new growth for another season.

Cacti and Other Succulents. This is a huge family. Two of the most common plants in this category are the Christmas cacti and similar types Schlumbergera and Zygocactus. These are known to set buds during short days. They mature from 1 year and range from miniatures to giants. There is a vast variation. Most cacti flower at any time; this depends upon the kind. They have beautiful, unusual flowers and unusual habits.

Cuttings can be taken in spring and early summer for most, but those making cacti a "special hobby" find that with care and learning they are able to take cacti clippings at any time. *Requirements:* Starting temperature 65 to 75 F. Growing temperature 60 to 70 F. They may be raised in pots, tubs and even hanging baskets. They are desert plants and should be raised in a media of 1:1:1. They should be kept on the dry side with part leaf mold for the jungle varieties. Summer light—full sun to partial sun. Photoperiod—the varieties mentioned set buds on short days. There are even types small enough to make splendid shelf plants for "those little spots" in the home greenhouse. To force all cacti into bloom, let them dry out completely and then water heavily.

Caladium. Maturing in 2 to 3 months, the show foliage of pink, rose, crimson, chartreuse, white or green. They also have a variety of different shaped leaves from soft to curly. They can be divided from large clumps taken in the spring. *Requirements:* Starting temperature 60 to 70 F. Growing temperature 65 to 70 F. Summer light—sun to shade. They do flower in the summer, but most are planted for their beautiful foliage. Dry them off in the fall and store through the winter at 50 F.

Caclceolaria (Pocketbook Plant). Maturing to 1 to 3′ in 8 to 10 months, the flower of the Calceolaria is white, yellow, bronze, red and purple. Seeds can be sown in summer. *Requirements:* Starting temperature 65 to 75 F. Growing temperature 45 to 50 F. For budding 45 to 65 F. Photoperiod—long days hasten buds. They like high moisture, but keep excess water off the foliage.

Calendula Officinalis (Port Marigold). Maturing in 3-4 months from 1-2′ they produce light lemon to rich orange flowers which bloom continuously from Winter through Spring. Seeds may be sown at any time. Starting temperature 65 to 75 F. Growing temperature 40 to 50 F. Summer light: Full sun. Discard this annual after flowering stops and sow new seeds.

Callistephus Chinensis (China Asters). Maturing in 5 months from 2 to 3 feet, the Callistephus Chinensis produces yellow, blue, purple, red, pink, salmon, lilac, and many other colored flowers which bloom continuously. Seeds can be sown continuously. *Requirements:* Starting temperature 65 to 70 F. Growing temperature 50 F. Summer light—full sun. Photoperiod—long days to flower when temperatures are below 70 F. When temperatures are above 75 F, any length of day produces good blooming. To aid in blooming, they are ideal raised from seedlings under lights. Discard plants after flowering.

Camellia. Maturing in two years (3 to 4 years for seedlings), Camellias should be raised in large tubs because they will have to be pruned to keep them in the greenhouse. Most Camellia grow to 40 feet. Terminals or leaf bud cuttings can be taken during summer and fall. Seeds can be sown in spring. *Requirements:* Starting temperature 70 to 75 F respectively. Growing temperature 40 to 50 F. Summer light—continuous shade. Photoperiod—long days hasten flower bud formation. They flower during the winter and spring and have glossy, evergreen foliage. They like high humidity and a highly organic acid pH growing medium.

Campanula Isophylla (Star of Bethlehem). Maturing in one year, the Star of Bethlehem is well known for its Biblical connotation and does beautifully in hanging baskets or in pots where they grow to 12-inch cascades. Cuttings should be taken during the spring. *Requirements:* Starting temperature 65 to 76 F. Growing temperature 45 to 55 F. Summer light—shade. They flower during the summer.

Centaurea Cyanus (Cornflower, Bachelor's Button). Maturing in five to six months from 1 to 2 feet, Centaurea Cyanus has blue, red, maroon, white, pink, and purple flowers which flower continuously or, if kept cut back, during spring and summer. *Requirements:* Starting temperature for seeds 65 to 70 F. Growing temperature 55 F. Summer light—full sun. Photoperiod—long days induce buds; short days delay buds. Discard plants after flowering. Continuous sowings are recommended for continuous blooming because these plants are showy and keep the greenhouse pretty.

Capsicum (Christmas Pepper). Maturing in six to eight months to 6 to 12 feet, Capsicum produces colorful fruits of scarlet or purple with small, white, star-shaped flowers that bloom in the summer. The fruits mature from fall to spring. The seeds should be sown during spring in large pots. *Requirements:* Starting temperature 60 to 70 F. Growing temperature 50 to 55 F. Summer light—sun. They should be treated as a perennial and cut back in spring to encourage new growth. Otherwise, discard and start anew with seed.

Centropogon. Divisions or cutting should be taken in the spring and placed in hanging baskets where they grow from 1 to 2 feet. They produce violet, red, purple and orange flowers. *Requirements:* Starting temperature 60 to 65 F. Growing temperature 60 to 65F. Summer light-shade.

Choisya (Mexican Orange). Maturing in one year from 4 to 8 feet, cuttings should be taken in the spring and summer for the beautiful white fragrant flowers. *Requirements:* Starting temperature 55 to 65 F. Growing temperature 45 to 55 F. Summer light—full sun.

Chrysanthemums. Chrysanthemums are rated as one of the greenhouse favorites whether they are raised commercially or in the home hobby greenhouse. Commercially raised Chrysanthemums are produced year around by regulating the day length to encourage vegetative growth or flowers as needed. Many cultivars are available for greenhouse culture.

Flower types vary from single to full doubles, incurved, thread or spider types, or anenome forms. Flower size varies from less than 1″ in diameter to exhibition types of 8 to 10″ or more. Plant habit varies from dwarf compact forms to tall ones suitable for cut flowers. All can be grown in the home greenhouse.

The natural dates of flowering for Chrysanthemums range from late August and early September to late December. Cultivars are grouped into response groups based on the number of weeks of short days needed to produce flowering. Response groups range from seven to 14 weeks long.

The best "mums" for cut flowers and potted plants are in the nine- to 11-week response group. The crop takes about 16 to 20 weeks from planting to harvest. This varies due to the season of the response groups. Chrysanthemums grow best in porous, well drained soil with a moderate level of fertility. They are happy with a 60 F nighttime temperature.

Single stem flowers are planted on 4 x 6 to 5 x 6 spacings. Multistemmed cut flowers should be planted on 7 x 7 to 8 x 8 spacings. Cut the plants when it is 4 to 6″ tall and allow two or three stems to develop. Potted plants usually have three or four cuttings in a 6″ pot and should be topped once shortly after they become established.

Chrysanthemum Carinatum (Annual). Maturing in three months from 2 to 3 feet, they flower in the spring in white, cream, yellow, red, rose, and purple. Seeds can be sown in the fall. *Requirements:* Starting temperature 60 to 65 F. Growing temperature 45 to 65 F. Summer light—full sun. Photoperiod—long days induce budding; short days prevent budding. Discard plants after flowering or take slips and root them in a hot frame.

Chrysanthemum Morigolium. Maturing in two to five months, depending upon the variety, they range in size from 2 to 3′ with flowers of yellow, white, bronze, pink, red, lavender Cuttings can be taken anytime. *Requirements:* Starting temperature 60 to 65 F. Growing temperature 60 F. Summer light—full sun. Photoperiod—short days induce bud development; long days induce vegetative growth. These are classified as six- to 15-week varieties depending on how long after the beginning of the short-day treatment the plant blooms. Time from propagation to short-day treatment depends on the size of the plant desired. From September 20 to March 20, apply artificial light as a day-extender to promote vegetative growth; otherwise buds will form. After blooming, slips can be taken to raise new plants in a hot frame.

Chrysanthemum Parthenium (Feverfew). Maturing in six months from 1 to 3 feet, they produce white flowers in early summer. Cuttings can be taken in the fall. Seeds are sown in the fall. The large, 1 to 3' flowers bloom in the summer. *Requirements:* Starting temperature 65 to 70 F. Growing temperature 50 to 60 F. Summer light—full sun. Photoperiod—long days induce budding; short days prevent buds.

Clarkia Elegans. Maturing in five months, Clarkia produce 1 to 6' flowers of orange, purple, rose and white. Seeds should be sown in early winter. *Requirements:* Starting temperature 65 to 75 F. Growing temperature 60 to 75 F. Summer light—full sun. Photoperiod—long days hasten maturity and reduce production; short days delay maturity and increase production. They can be grown at any time by starting the seeds at 50 F and raising the temperature to 50 to 60 F for flowering. Discard plants after flowering.

Clematis. Maturing in one year, Clematis is a beautiful vine that can be raised in pots or hanging baskets. The blue, crimson, rose, and white flowers are its main attraction. They flower in spring and summer. Cuttings of partially ripened wood should be taken in the summer. *Requirements:* Starting temperature 75 F. Growing temperature 55 to 65 F.

Clerodendrum. Maturing in one year, cuttings should be taken in late winter and spring to produce white, violet and red flowers on this vining plant. It is large and should be raised in a tub. *Requirements:* Starting temperature 75 to 80 F. Growing temperature 60 to 75 F. Summer light—full sun.

Clivia. Clivia seedlings take from six to seven years to reach full maturity. They are long lasting and divisions can be taken in late winter. Seeds are sown in spring to keep yourself a constant supply. Producing apricot, salmon, scarlet or yellow flowers, it is an evergreen on strap-shaded leaves. *Requirements:* Starting temperature 55 to 65 F. Growing temperature 55 to 65 F.

Seedlings require 75 F to start. Do not let Clivia dry out during a rest period; keep it moist.

Codiaeum (Croton). Maturing in one year to sizes of 2 to 6 feet, the special attraction of Crotons are their unusual leaves. They come in flat and curled leaves with pink, brown, red, yellow and mixed colored foliage. Cuttings should be taken in later winter and early spring. *Requirements:* Starting temperature 70 to 80 F. Growing temperature 60 to 75 F. Summer light—shade. They should be raised in pots, or if you plan to let them get large, in tubs. They prefer high humidity.

Coleus. Maturing from seedlings within weeks to 5 months, there is a large variety of Coleus prized for their variagated, yellow, purple, red and green, flat and curled foliage. Seeds and cuttings can be sown and taken anytime. *Requirements:* Starting temperature 70 F and 60 to 65 F respectively. Growing temperature 60 F. Summer light—partial shade. Coleus requires high moisture content in the soil and slips can be rooted in water or sand anytime for a continuous supply.

Columnea. Maturing in three to six months, the Columnea produces orange, red, and yellow flowers. Cuttings should be taken in the spring. *Requirements:* Starting temperature 75 to 85 F. Growing temperature 60 to 70 F. They should be raised in pots for the upper shelves in the greenhouse or in hanging baskets. They like a media of 1:1:1 with the addition of one part leaf mold. Summer light should be shade. Columnea flower continuously and can also be grown in unmilled sphagnum moss combined with biweekly feedings of fertilizer diluted in water.

Crassula (Jade Plant) C. Argentea. A must for all greenhouses, Crassula has several species (C. Lactea). They range in size from 1 to 10 feet. It takes several years, but they do produce white, rose or yellow flowers. However, their main attraction is their heavy rubbery stems. Cuttings can be taken at any time. *Requirements:* Starting temperature 60 to 75 F. Growing temperature 65 F. Summer light—partial shade. Keep them damp, not wet, and stake the heavy stems. When leaves drop off, let them self-root. They enjoy being "slipped" to keep the leaves large and glossy green. They start easily in a hot frame or in a container with plain sand.

Crocus. Maturing in three months to 3 to 5 inches, the yellow, white, blue, lilac, or purple Crocus is your first sign of spring. Corms should be planted in August or spring for forcing. *Requirements:* Starting temperature 45 to 55 F. Growing temperature 50 F. Plant corms outdoors after forcing them in the greenhouse for winter blooming (one time).

Crossandra. Maturing in three months, cuttings can be taken in spring or summer. Crossandra produces salmon-colored flowers continuously on glossy green foliage. *Requirements:* Starting temperature 65 to 75 F. Growing temperature 55 to 65 F. Summer light—shade. The flowers grow from 6 to 12″ and should be raised in pots for extra show.

Cyclamen. Slow to mature at 1½ years, they produce white, pink, red and purple flowers from 6 to 12″ that flower in the fall and spring. *Requirements:* Starting temperature 60 to 65 F. Growing temperature of seedlings 60 to 65 F and they bloom best at 50 to 55 F. Summer light—shade. Withhold water when flowering ceases and keep nearly dry through the summer. Repot by August 1 and start into new growth.

Cytisus (Broom "Carnariensis Genista" of Florists). Maturing in one year, the yellow blooms appear 4½ months after the start of cool treatment and produce huge 4 to 6′ blooms. *Requirements:* Starting temperature from terminal cuttings taken in the spring is 70 F. Growing temperature 60 F for flowering and more for heavy vegetative growth. Summer light—full sun. Cytisus flowers in the spring. Provide cool, moist atmosphere with ample moisture at the roots.

Daphne Cnerum. Maturing in one to two years, terminal cuttings should be taken in spring to produce pink flowers that bloom in the spring. *Requirements:* Starting temperature 65 F. Growing temperature cool; store at 40 F from September to February then force at 50 to 55 F. They can be forced within 8 weeks to produce 1 to 3′ flowers which are highly fragrant.

Delphinium Afjacis (Larspur). Maturing in eight months, seeds should be sown in the fall. They produce white, blue, lavendar, pink, rose and scarlet flowers in the spring. *Requirements:* Starting temperature 55 to 65 F. Growing temperature 40 to 50 F for two months and when mature 55 to 65 F. Summer light—full sun. The flowers range from 1 to 3 feet. Discard plants after flowering.

Dianthus Caryophyllus (Carnations). Maturing in six months from dwarf 10″ blooms to large 15 to 20″ blooms, they flower continuously. Cuttings can be taken in the winter. Seeds are sown in early spring to produce red, pink, rose, maroon, white, violet, salmon and yellow flowers. *Requirements:* Starting temperature 60 to 65 F. Growing temperature 50 F. Summer light—high intensity. Stake the varieties that grow tall.

Episcia. Episcia is definitely a hanging basket variety. The beautiful cascade of white, lavender, scarlet and yellow blooms flower on attractive foliage. Cuttings should be taken in spring and summer. Starting temperature 65 to 75 F. Growing temperature 65 F. Summer light: shade. They can be raised in pots if desired to 6″ but are most showy if allowed to cascade in hanging baskets. They are highly sensitive to chilling and light frosts. Apply only room temperature water and keep away from drafts such as open vents and door of greenhouse.

Erica (Heath/Heather). Maturing in 2 years to produce white, rose and red flowers from 4″ to 6″ plants they flower in early spring and winter. Cuttings may be taken in the spring, fall and winter. *Requirements:* Starting temperature 60 F. Growing temperature 40 to 50 F. Summer light—shade. Photoperiod—Long days for flower bud initiation.

Eucharis Grandiflora (Amazon Lily). Maturing in three to four months to 2½ feet, the special attraction is the white flower which blooms intermittently year around. Bulbs should be divided in summer. *Requirements:* Starting temperature 65 F. Growing temperature 65 to 70 F. They like a highly organic soil kept moist.

Eucomis (Pineapple/Flower). Maturing in three to four months producing green/white flowers, bulbs should be planted in the spring. *Requirements:* Starting temperature 65 F. Summer light—shade. They flower in spring and summer. Keep them nearly dry in winter.

Eupatorium. There are several species—ligustrinum, micranthum, riparium, atrorubens, sordium, macrophyllum—producing white, violet, pink and purple flowers. They grow from 1 to 3′ and flower in the fall and winter. Cuttings should be taken in late spring. *Requirements:* Starting temperature 65 to 70 F. Growing temperature 60 to 70 F. Summer light—shade. Photoperiod—Long days prevent budding; short days induce budding.

Euphorbia Fulgens (Scarlet Plume). Maturing in six to eight months to 3 feet, the special attraction is the scarlet flower which blooms in the winter. Cuttings should be taken in spring. *Requirements:* Starting temperature 65 to 70 F. Growing temperature 60 F. Summer light—full sun. Photoperiod—long days promote vegetative growth; short days promote budding.

Euphorbia Pulcherrima (Poinsettias). Poinsettias are grown primarily for Christmas plants. They are propagated by stem cuttings from June through mid-September. Rooting under a mist system, in sand or perlite, requires 21 to 24 days. Some growers root directly in pots in a soil mixture. In summer, they can be grown under glass that is slightly shaded to reduce temperatures. They should have full sun starting in mid-September. Poinsettias will flower by mid-December if they receive only normal daylight and temperatures of 60 to 62 F.

If growth is satisfactory and the bracts have developed good color by early December, the temperature may be lowered to 55 F. However, light of any kind at night, even a nearby streetlight, can delay flowering. Growing media should be porous, well drained and slightly acid with a pH of 6:0 to 6:5 soluble liquid or slow releasing fertilizers should be used with the different cultivars.

Poinsettia cultivars are standard or self-branching types. Colors are the familiar red. They are also white, pink or varigated. They are quite difficult to root, but clippings can be slipped while soft and rooted in a hot frame. They mature in three to six months.

Exacum. Maturing in six to eight months to 6 to 12 inches, they produce fragrant star-shaped lavendar, blue and white flowers. Seeds should be sown in the spring. *Requirements:* Starting temperature 60 to 70 F. Growing temperature 50 to 65 F. Summer light—partial shade. Exacum is a biennial. Discard the plant after flowering.

Felicia Amelloides (Agathea, Blue Daisy). Maturing from seedlings in 10 months (five to seven months from cuttings), they grow to 2' and produce blue and white flowers which bloom in the winter and spring. *Requirements:* Starting temperature 60 to 65 F and for seeds sown in late spring 55 to 60 F. Growing temperature 50 to 55 F. Summer light—full sun; partial shade.

Freesia. Maturing in three to four months, corms can be planted in the fall. Seeds should be sown in the spring. Seeds mature in one year. Freesia grows to 1½' and produces blue, yellow and white flowers which are very fragrant. They bloom in late winter. *Requirements:* Starting temperature for corms 45 to 55 F; seeds 65F. Growing temperature 45 to 55 F. Summer light—full sun for seedlings. Photoperiod—long days reduce flowers; short days increase flowering. Do not dry off seedlings until after the first flowering season. Mature freesias should be dried off annually after flowering and kept cool and dry until replanting time in autumn.

Fuchsia. Maturing in eight months, this is another ideal plant for hanging baskets. Terminal cuttings can be taken in late summer. It produces pink, red, purple/red and white flowers. *Requirements:* Starting temperature 65 F. Growing temperature 60 F.

Gardenia. Maturing in one to two years, terminal cuttings should be taken in the winter to produce their beautiful highly fragrant white and sometimes pale yellow blossoms. Growing to 6' if not kept pruned, they should be raised in tubs and prefer a highly organic, acid growing medium. *Requirements:* Starting temperature 75 F. Growing temperature 65 F. Summer light—partial shade. Photoperiod—long days stimulate bud maturity; short days reduce top growth. They bloom in early spring. Maintain a soil pH of 6:00 to 5:5 and keep them moist at all times.

Gazania. Maturing in 10 months, the Gazania's flowers open during the day and close at night. Seeds should be sown in the spring. They produce white, orange, yellow, brown, red and salmon flowers. *Requirements:* Starting temperature 65 to 70 F. Summer light—full sun.

Geranium. Pelargonium/Hortorum matures in three to seven months to produce red, pink, white, orange and lilac blooms. Cuttings can be taken any time and started in a hot frame or pots of sand. *Requirements:* Starting temperature 60 F. Growing temperature 55 to 60 F. Summer light—full sun. There are many varieties of this plant. Some leaves are tinted at the edges.

Gerbera Jaesoni (Transvaal Daisy). Maturing in one year, seeds can be sown in winter and divisions taken in late spring. They produce yellow, orange, pink, red and white blooms on long stems (to 1½'). *Requirements:* Starting temperature 65 to 75 F and 55 to 58 F respectively. Growing temperature 55 to 60 F. They flower in winter through spring and should be staked because they tend to get top-heavy. They prefer a slightly acid soil. Summer light—partial to full shade.

Gladiolus. Maturing in two to three months, to force corms should be planted in winter for flowering in the spring. They produce red, pink, yellow, white, purple, lilac, scarlet blooms and are prized as "cut flowers." *Requirements:* Starting temperature 65 to 70 F. Growing temperature 65 to 70 F. Summer light—full sun. Photoperiod—long days prevent bug blast. They grow up to 3 feet. Cure corms for two weeks at 80 to 85 F. After digging, store at 40 to 45 F until planting. You can force them for greenhouse winter blooming and then plant some outside.

Gloxinia. Sown from seeds or bulbs purchased through seed houses and nurseries, they produce, white, blue, rose, purple, reds that bloom in spring and summer. *Requirements:* Temperature 55 to 65 F. Summer light—sun. They grow to 10 inches.

Godetia. Maturing in four months to 2 feet, seeds should be sown in the fall or winter. They flower in winter and spring with rose, purple, and white blossoms. Raise them in shallow flats because they only reach 1 to 2 feet. *Requirements:* Starting temperature 65 to 75 F. Growing temperature 50 to 55 F. They can flower at any time of the year, but coolness is necessary for complete success. Discard plants after flowering.

Gypsophila (Baby's Breath). Maturing in two to three months to 18 inches, seeds should be sown in winter and spring to produce white or pink flowers that bloom in summer and fall. *Requirements:* Starting temperature 64 to 75 F. Growing temperature 60 F. Summer light—full sun. Discard plants after flowering.

Haemanthus (Blood Lily). Bulbs should be planted in the fall. *Requirements:* Starting temperature 45 to 55 F. Growing temperature 55 to 65 F summer; 45 to 55 F winter. Summer light—full sun. They grow from 1 to 3' and flower in spring, summer and fall (depending upon the variety). Keep them nearly dry in winter.

Heliotrope. Maturing in 6 months to 3 feet, the fragrant flowers are purple, lavender, white or blue. Seeds or cuttings can be taken and seeds should be sown in the spring or summer. *Requirements:* Starting temperature 60 to 70 F. Growing temperature 60 F. They should be raised in pots or hanging baskets. They grow from 1 to 3' and can be trained as a standard. They flower continuously. Cut back to encourage new growth.

Hibiscus Rosa Sinensis (Chinese Hibiscus). Maturing from 3-8' and producing orange, red, yellow, magenta, variously colored flowers on dark green foliage, cuttings are taken in spring and summer. *Requirements:* Starting temperature 75 F. Growing temperature 65 to 70 F. Summer light—shade. Trim back as necessary to keep a convenient size. Chinese hibiscus blooms on current growth.

Hoya Carnosa (Wax Plant). Maturing from a leaf cutting in three years and from slips rooted in sand in six to eight months, the Hoya produces a vining plant that can be raised in pots or baskets. See Fig. 3-4. The fascinating flower of the Hoya is its main attraction and one plant will have as many as 25 at one time. When fully opened, they have pink centers in a dense cluster. Cuttings can be taken at any time. *Requirements:* Starting temperature 75 to 80 F. Growing temperature 60 F. Summer light—sun or partial shade. They flower in the summer.

Hycinthus (Hyacinth). These plants mature in two to six weeks for forcing from 6 to 8″ blooms of blue, pink, white, rose and yellow. Bulbs can be planted in the fall and early winter. *Requirements:* Temperature 54 to 55 F for storage. Growing temperature store six weeks at 53 to 55 F. Force at 65 to 70 F. Summer light—full sun but shade for a few days after bringing them out of storage. They flower in late winter and early spring. Do not begin forcing until 1″ of foliage shows.

Hydrangea. This plant matures to 3′ in three months when forced. Cuttings are taken from terminal, stub, leaf buds during the spring and summer. *Requirements:* Starting temperature 65 to 70 F. Growing temperature 55 to 60 F. Forcing requires acid soil of pH 4:5 to 5:0. To grow, use a pH of 5:5. Buds begin to form at 65 F for six weeks. Force at 60 F. Summer light—full sun, but will need

Fig. 3-4. A 35-year-old Ponderosa Lemon tree (courtesy of John Wahlfeldt)

237

some shading during flowering. For blue color, use no fertilizers. Use acid nitrogen fertilizers. However, in many parts of the country where the soil is naturally acid, the Hydrangea is "naturally blue."

Pink and White Hydrangea. Pink and white Hydrangea can be taken from cuttings, terminal, stub, leaf buds taken in the spring and summer. *Requirements:* Starting temperature 65 to 70 F. Media is pH 6:2 to 6:5 and growing in media of 5:5. Growing temperature 55 to 65 F. Buds initiate below 65 F for six weeks. Buds develop 33 to 40 F in six weeks. Force 60 F for three months. Summer light—full sun but will need shade during flowering. They grow to 6′ and flower in spring and summer. For pink use a high P fertilizer and alkaline nitrogen fertilizer.

Iberis Amara and Umbellata (Candytuft). These plants mature in five to six months 8 to 12″ with some varieties growing to 2 feet. They are pink, red, rose, lavender, white. Seeds should be sown in the fall through winter. *Requirements:* Starting temperature 65 to 75 F. Growing temperature 50 F. Summer light—full sun. Photoperiod—short days vegetative; long days flower. The white flowers are fragrant. Discard the plants after flowering.

Impatiens (Sultana, Patience Plant). Maturing in three months to 6 to 18 feet, Impatiens flower continuously in pink, red, orange, salmon and white. Seeds or cuttings should be taken and planted in the spring through the summer. They are ideal for pots or hanging baskets. *Requirements:* Starting temperature 65 to 70 F. Growing temperature 50 to 60 F. Start new plants annually, for best results, either from tip cuttings or fresh seed.

Incarvillea (Hardy Gloxinia). Yellow, red, rose and purple and maturing to 2 to 3 feet, these plants should be started from seeds in the spring. They are excellent to transplant outdoors in mild climates. *Requirements:* Temperature 60 to 65 F. They flower during the summer. They should be divided as they grow and taken into the greenhouse for the upcoming season of flowering.

Iris, Dutch. Maturing from storage in six weeks, they produce white, yellow and blue flowers. Bulbs are planted in the fall. *Requirements:* Plant and store at 48 to 50 F until foliage is 2″ tall. Move to 6″ bulb pan. Growing temperature to force 40 to 60 F. Summer light—full sun. Photoperiod—long days hasten maturity. They bloom in winter and spring. Temperatures higher than 60 F cause blasting. Root injury (excessive movement) causes failure to flower. Pre-cooled bulbs need no storage. For warm climates, keep the bulbs in refrigerator for six weeks prior to planting.

Ixia. These plants mature to 2′ with white, yellow, orange, lilac, pink, crimson, red, purple and green flowers. Corms should be planted in October through December. *Requirements:* Starting temperature 60 F. Store at 40 F for two months. Force at 50 to 55 F. Mature at 55 to 60 F. They flower winter through spring. Flowers close at night and last for two weeks if left on the plant. After flowering, let foliage mature and die. Then dry off for storage through summer and use again in the autumn.

Ixora. These plants mature in one year to 24 inches. They have a glossy foliage with yellow, white, pink and red flowers. Cuttings are taken in the spring. *Requirements:* Starting temperature 70 to 75 F. Growing temperature 55 to 65 F. Summer light—partial shade. Media 1:1:1 with extra portion of acid peat moss. Prune to shape in spring.

Jacobinia (King's Crown). Maturing to 1 to 3′ in one year, they produce pink, orange, red and yellow flowers which bloom intermittently all year. Cuttings can be taken any time. *Requirements:* Starting temperature 65 to 75 F. Growing temperature 55 to 65 F. Plant in pots. Summer light—sun.

Jasminum (Jasmine). These shrubs or vines should be raised in large tubs. They are highly fragrant and have bright green, glossy leaves with beautiful white flowers. when in bloom in spring and summer. Cuttings can be taken March through Setptember. *Requirements:* Starting temperature 65 to 75 F. Growing temperature 55 F. Summer light—partial shade in the summer. Prune lightly in spring after flowering.

Kaemferia. Maturing in two to three months to 24 inches, the yellow or lavender/blue flowers bloom in summer. Root division is done in the spring. *Requirements:* Starting temperature 65 to 75 F. Growing temperature 60 to 70 F. Summer light—partial shade or sun. Dry off in autumn. Store dormant until spring at 55 to 60 F.

Kalanchoe. Maturing in eight to 12 months to 6 to 12 inches, the scarlet, yellow, purple, salmon pink flowers are a special attraction. Cuttings and seeds should be taken and sown from January through July. *Requirements:* Starting temperature 65 to 75 F. Growing temperature 50 to 75 F. Summer light—partial shade. Photoperiod—start short days about four months before bloom at 60 F and five months before bloom at 50 F. Shade for about four weeks. They flower in January at 60 F and in October with shading. Long days induce vegetative growth and short days induce budding. If you want Valentine's Day blooms, keep the temperature at 50 F.

Lachenalia (Cape Cowslip). Maturing in six to eight months from 9 to 12 inches, they produce red and yellow flowers and can be raised in pots or hanging baskets. Bulbs are planted in late summer and early fall. *Requirements:* Starting temperature 45 F. Growing temperature 45 to 55 F. Summer light—full sun. They flower in winter and spring. Dry off after flowering and keep dormant through summer.

Lathrys Odoratus (Sweet Pea). These plants mature in two to four months from dwarf varieties of 8 to 12" to climbing varieties to several feet. Seeds are sown in late summer or early fall. *Requirements:* Starting temperature 65 to 75 F. Growing temperature 50 to 55 F. Summer light—full sun. Photoperiod— long days stimulate bloom. They can be grown in pots, flats or on a greenhouse bench which must be at least 6" deep. They bloom in winter and spring with fragrant flowers. Discard plants after flowering.

Lilium (Lily). These plants mature in four to five months from 1 to 4' with white, pink or coral blooms. Bulbs are planted in spring or fall. They flower in the summer for spring planting or winter or spring for fall planting. *Requirements:* Starting temperature is pre-cooled 60 to 65 F or store them cool for 6 to 8 weeks at 35 to 40 F. Growing temperature is stored six to eight weeks at 35 to 40 F. Force at 60 to 65 F. Summer light—full sun. Photoperiod—day length controls height. Long days increase stem length. Flowering can be speeded up by raising the forcing temperature to 80 F.

Lobelia. This plant matures in four months. Seeds should be sown on top of flat or in market packs in January to produce showy blue, rosy red, and white flowers which bloom in spring through summer. *Requirements:* Starting temperature 65 to 75 F. Growing temperature 45 to 55 F. May be raised in pots or ideal for hanging baskets. Summer light—full sun, partial shade. Grows to 6 inches.

Mathiola Incana (Stock). Maturing in 4 to 6 months to 3' with dwarf varieties of up to 20 inches, they produce very fragrant white, ivory, pink, red, yellow, blue or lavender flowers. Seeds should be sown in the summer and fall. *Requirements:* Starting temperature 65 to 75 F. Growing temperature 45 to 60 F. Buds at 60 F. Summer light—full sun. Photoperiod—long days hasten bud development at 50 to 60 F, but weakens growth. Discard plants after flowering.

Milla Biflora (Mexican Star). This plant matures in three months to 6 to 18" with fragrant white flowers. Corms may be planted in the fall. *Requirements:* Starting temperature 40 F. Growing temperature 50 F. Summer light—full sun. Dry off during summer dormancy.

Myosotis (Forget-Me-Not). This plant will mature in 6 to 8 months to 6 to 18″ with blue flowers that bloom in the winter. Seeds should be sown in June and August. *Requirements:* Starting temperature 65 to 75 F. Growing temperature 50 F. Summer light—partial shade. Discard plants after flowering.

Narcissus (Daffodils). Maturing in 3 to 6 weeks from 12 to 18 inches, they flower in spring or winter with fragrant white, yellow or bicolored flowers. Bulbs are planted in the fall. *Requirements:* Starting temperature cool. Growing temperature store 10 weeks at 45 to 48 F. Force at 55 to 60 F. Summer light—full sun but shade for several days after cold storage. Precooled bulbs need no cool-storage prior to forcing. Discard after flowering or plant to garden outside.

Nemesia. Sow seeds in the fall and winter to produce 6 to 24″ blue, orange, pink, red, white, and yellow flowers that bloom in the winter and spring. *Requirements:* Starting temperature 65 to 75 F. Growing temperature 45 to 55 F. Summer light—full sun. Photoperiod—long days cause spindling; short days promote compact growth. Discard after flowering.

Nephrolepis Bostoniensis (Boston Fern). These plants mature to full spread at six months at up to 7 feet. As with all ferns, they are most showy in hanging baskets. However, they can be put in large containers and set on "fern stands." Division and runners taken in the spring are most successful; however, they may be taken any time. *Requirements:* Starting temperature 60 F. Growing temperature as low as 50 F but not too particular. Summer light—shade. For propagation, plants are usually benched and new plants form from runners in three to six months.

Nerine. These plants mature in three to four months to 3′ with red, pink and white flowers. Bulbs are planted in the summer and the fall. *Requirements:* Starting temperature 50 F. Summer light—full sun. They flower in fall and early winter. Leaves appear after flowering and last through the winter. Keep dry through summer dormancy.

Nerium Oleander. Maturing in two years to 7 to 15 feet, they should be raised in large pots or tubs to produce rose, red and white blossoms. Cuttings are taken in the summer. *Requirements:* Starting temperature 65 to 75 F. Growing temperature 50 to 60 F. Summer light—full sun. All parts of the plant are poisonous. Prune back after flowering.

Nicotiana (Flowering Tobacco). Maturing in four months from 2 to 4 feet, seeds can be sown in spring to produce white, chartreuse or wine-colored flowers. Only the white flowers are fragrant. *Requirements:* Starting temperature 65 to 75 F. Growing temperature 50 to 60 F. Summer light—sun. Cut back to 1″ or 2″ after flowering. New growth forms from the base.

Nierembergia Frutescens (Cup-Flower). Taking four months to reach full maturity of up to 24″ and more, this is another perfect plant for hanging baskets. They produce violet/blue and white flowers. It is a tender perennial that is often cultivated outdoors as an annual. *Requirements:* Starting temperature 65 to 75 F. Growing temperature 55 to 60 F. Summer light—full sun. They can be raised from seeds or cuttings taken in March. Cut back old plants in August or September and use these cuttings to start new plants in your greenhouse bench.

Orchids. Maturing in one to three years, there are many varieties with varied colors. The division or removal of side shoots is done in the spring. *Requirements:* Starting temperature 60 to 70 F. Growing temperature 50 to 75 F. They like a media of firbark, redwood chips, and osmunda. Summer light—partial sun to shade. They grow from 6 to 36 inches. They flower all year. This is a very large family and usually an orchid grower is a "specialist" in only the Orchid culture because there are so many varieties. However, this does not mean that any greenhouse cannot handle even a few of these interesting and beautiful plants. Many can be grown in an "all-around, cool greenhouse." But for the most part if you become a "true orchid grower," you will not be raising too great a variety of other plants.

Ornithogalum. Maturing in five to six months at 6 to 18 inches, they produce white and yellow flowers that bloom in the spring and are quite fragrant. Bulbs should be planted in the fall. *Requirements:* Starting temperature 40 to 50 F for eight weeks and then 50 to 60 F. Summer light—full sun. Deep dry through summer dormancy.

Osmanthus Fragrans (Sweet Olive). These plants mature in one year to 2′ when kept in large pots or tubs (outside they grow into huge bushes). Cuttings are taken in spring and summer. They produce highly fragrant white flowers in the spring and winter on beautiful glossy leaves. *Requirements:* Starting temperature 65 to 70 F. Growing temperature 50 F. Summer light—partial shade.

Oxalis. Maturing in five to six months to 12 inches, they produce pink, white and yellow flowers in winter and spring. Bulbs should be planted in the fall. *Requirements:* Starting temperature 50 to 60 F. Summer light—full sun.

Passiflora Alato-Caerulea (Passion Flower). Maturing in six months with beautifully unusual purple-upon-white-blue flowers, cuttings should be taken in spring. They should be raised in large pots or tubs with a trellis because the vines are very heavy and you can assure the placement of the showy flowers in this manner. *Requirements:* Starting temperature 65 to 75 F. Growing temperature 50 F. Summer light—full sun or partial shade. They flower in spring and summer and should be cut back in late winter.

Pentas (Egyptian Star-Cluster). Maturing in six months to 1 to 2 feet, Pentas have white, pink, and rose flowers that bloom continuously. Cuttings should be taken in the spring. *Requirements:* Starting temperature 70 F. Growing temperature 50 to 65 F. They need to be raised in large pots or hanging baskets.

Petunia. Maturing in two to three months to 1' and more, they produce rose, scarlet, pink, white, violet, purple, burgundy, blue and yellow flowers. Seeds should be sown in January and February and clippings can be taken from the vining ends and placed in a hot frame for continuous propagation. *Requirements:* Starting temperature 65 to 75 F. Growing temperature 55 F. Summer light—full sun. Photoperiod—in temperatures of 60 to 75 degrees, long days are needed to induce budding. Cut back old, straggly plants to induce new growth.

Philodendron. These plants provide a large variety of green vining foliage. Cuttings can be taken any time. They should be raised in large pots or tubs with bark or fern support. *Requirements:* Growing temperature 65 F. Summer light—heavy shade. High humidity is needed for excellent growth; Philodendron is a tropical plant.

Piqueria Trinervia (Stevia). Maturing in four to eight months to 4 feet, Piqueria produces highly fragrant white flowers that bloom in the winter. Cuttings or seeds are taken and sown in March. *Requirements:* Starting temperature 65 F. Growing temperature 40 to 65 F. Summer light—full sun. Photoperiod—short days; March 20 through September 25 induce bloom. Stake and tie as necessary to keep upright. Start new from cuttings every March.

Plumbago (Leadwort). This plant matures in three to five months and produces pink, red, blue and white flowers in winter and summer. Cuttings are taken in summer. *Requirements:* Starting temperature 65 F. Growing temperature 50 F. Summer light—full sun to parital shade. Cut back after flowering to induce another flowering in the summer.

Primula Malacoides (Baby Primrose). This plant matures in eight to 12 months at 8 to 20″ with rose, lilac, and white flowers. Seeds are sown in March and August. *Requirements:* Starting temperature 65 to 76 F. Growing temperature 50 to 60 F, during short days. Summer light—shade up to October 1. Photoperiod— short days bring on flowers. Discard at the end of the flowering season.

Primula Obconica (Primrose). This plant matures in eight to 12 months from 4 to 10″ and produces dark red, crimson, salmon, pink, blue, violet/blue flowers in the spring. Seeds should be sown in the spring. *Requirements:* Starting temperature 65 to 75 F. Growing temperature 45 to 50 F. Summer light—shade up to October 1. Treat as an annual. Discard after flowering.

Primula Sinensis (Chinese Primrose). This plant matures in eight to 12 months at up to 10 inches. Pink, blue, red and white flowers bloom in the late fall and winter. Sow the seeds in the spring. *Requirements:* Starting temperature 65 to 76 F. Growing temperature 45 to 50 F. Summer light—shade up to October 1. Treat as an annual and discard after flowering.

Ranunculus (Buttercup, Crowfoot). Matures from four to six months for roots and 12 months for seeds with white, yellow, red, pink and orange flowers that bloom from January through March. Roots should be planted in September and seeds are sown in the spring. *Requirements:* Starting temperature 65 to 75 F. Growing temperature 45 to 50 F. Summer light—full sun. After flowering, let the plants mature; then dry off and store dormant through the summer.

Rechsteineria (Gesneria Cardinalis). This plant matures from eight to 12 months at 6 to 12″ with scarlet, and white flowers. Sow the seeds in spring. *Requirements:* Starting temperature 65 to 75 F. Growing temperature 60 to 70 F. Summer light—partial shade. Blooms in winter and spring. Dry off after flowering. Keep tubers in dormancy until new growth appears. Treat like the related Sinningia (gloxinia).

Reinwardtia. This plant matures in three to five months to 1′ with yellow flowers that bloom in the fall and winter. *Requirements:* Starting temperature 65 to 75 F. Growing temperature 55 F. Summer light—shade, but sunny in winter. Pinch frequently to induce branching. Start new plants each summer.

Saintpaulia (African Violet). This plant matures in seven to eight months, at 4 to 6″ with beautiful velvety foliage and lavender, purple, blue, pink, white, rose/red flowers. Single and double and triple flowers bloom continuously. Seeds and cuttings can be sown and taken anytime. *Requirements:* Starting temperature 65 to 70 F. Summer light—partial shade. Photoperiod—long days increase growth. Water the plants from the bottom. Water spilled on foliage causes spots. Use water that is warm or at room temperature water. These plants are ideal for cultivating under fluorescent lights which aid in profuse blooming.

Salpiglossis (Painted Tongue). Maturing in five to six months to 2½ feet, they flower in summer in shades of red, blue, yellow, purple, and violet. Seeds are sown in the fall and winter. *Requirements:* Starting temperature 65 to 75 F. Growing temperature 55 to 60 F. Summer light—sun. Photoperiod—long days hasten bud development. This plant is an annual. Discard plants after flowering.

Schizanthus (Poor Man's Orchid). Maturing in five to eight months at heights of 2′ and up, they flower in spring and winter in white, yellow, lilac, rose, purple/red, carmine. They are ideal as cut flowers. Seeds are sown in the fall. *Requirements:* Starting temperature 65 to 75 F. Growing temperature 45 to 65 F and they withstand a light frost. Summer light—full sun. Photoperiod—long days induce budding but weaken growth. Discard the plants after blooming. But if they are sown in the winter, cut them back after they have bloomed and they will bloom again in the spring.

Senecio Cruentus (Cineraria). These plants mature in seven months from 8 to 24″ with blue, purple, pink, red and white flowers. Seeds are sown in summer and fall. *Requirements:* Starting temperature 65 to 75 F. Growing temperature 45 to 60 F. Summer light—full sun. Photoperiod—long days and temperature below 65 F hasten bud development. For best bud formation six weeks of less than 60 F is required. Treat this plant as an annual; discard it after blooming.

Sedum. A perfect hanging basket plant, Sedum comes in yellow, rose and white flowers growing 2 to 6″ with some varieties up to 2′ and longer. Cuttings are taken in the spring. *Requirements:* Starting temperature 65 F. Growing temperature 55 to 65 F. This plant flowers in season but the attractive foliage is constant.

Sinningia Speciosa (Gloxinia). This plant matures in five to seven months at 6 to 10 feet. It flowers in the summer and fall with blue, purple, pink to red, and white flowers. Seeds are sown in the late winter; tubers are planted in the late winter. *Requirements:* Starting temperature 65 to 70 F. Growing temperature 65 F. Dry off and keep at 50 F for a short resting period after flowering.

Smithiantha (Temple Bells). Scaly rhizomes planted in winter and spring produce yellow, rose, and scarlet flowers with velvety foliage. *Requirements:* Starting temperature 76 F. Growing temperature 55 to 75 F. Summer light—partial shade. Dry off after flowering and store at 50 to 60 F for three months prior to replanting.

Solanum (Christmas Cherry). This plant matures in eight to 10 months at 12 to 19″ with red fruit on glossy green leaves. Seeds are sown in spring. *Requirements:* Starting temperature 65 to 75 F. Growing temperature 60 F from September to Christmas. Summer light—full sun. The bright red fruit appears in winter and makes an ideal potted plant to bring in the house as a Christmas decoration. Trim back and repot in spring to keep the old plants in vigorous growth.

Sparmannia. Maturing in eight months, it is a small tree that can be trimmed to any size you desire during February. Cuttings are taken in the spring. *Requirements:* Starting temperature 65 F. Growing temperature 45 to 50 F. Summer light—full sun. Sparmannia flowers bloom in the spring, summer and fall with its special attraction being white spathes.

Stephanotis Floribunda (Madagascar Jasmine). This plant matures in six months at 8 to 15′ and produces white flowers that are quite fragrant. This vining plant can be grown in large pots or hanging baskets. Cuttings or seeds are sown or taken in spring. *Requirements:* Starting temperature 65 F. Growing temperature 65 F. A trellis is needed for support if it is potted. It blooms from May through October and needs a minimum temperature above 65 F for profuse flowering.

Strelitzia (Bird of Paradise). Maturing in two to three years at 2 to 6 feet, this beautiful specimen should be raised in large tubs. They produce orange, white and blue flowers in the spring, summer, and fall and the flowers are long-lasting. Division is made in the spring. *Requirements:* Starting temperature 65 to 70 F. Growing temperature 55 to 65 F. Summer light—sun. Avoid disturbing established plants. They enjoy being pot bound.

Swainsona (Winter Sweet Pea). Maturing in six to eight months to 3 feet, they flower continuously in blue/violet, purple, red, and white. Cuttings are taken in January. *Requirements:* Starting temperature 45 to 60 F. Growing temperature 45 to 60 F. Summer light—full sun. Photoperiod—long days increase growth and stimulate maturity. Swainsona is a vining plant and if it is raised in pots a trellis should be used for support. Cut back from time to time when growth becomes too large or is not vigorous.

Tagetes Erecta (African Marigold, Marigold). Maturing in three months from 2 to 3 feet, the African Marigold has cream, yellow and orange flowers that bloom in the spring. Seeds can be sown in the fall. *Requirements:* Starting temperature 65 to 75 F. Growing temperature 55 to 65 F. Summer light—full sun. Photoperiod—artificial light in later fall and winter will stimulate vegetative growth. Shade hastens flower development. Plants started in the winter need long days to stimulate stem growth.

Tecomaria Capensis (Cape Honeysuckle). Growing from 6 to 8 feet, this vining plant produces yellow, orange, and scarlet flowers and should be raised in large pots or tubs or hanging baskets. Seeds or cuttings can be sown or taken in the spring. *Requirements:* Starting temperature 65 to 75 F. Growing temperature 55 to 65 F. The flowers bloom in the fall and winter. A trellis is required for support.

Trachymene Caerulea (Didiscus, Blue Lace Flower). This plant matures in seven to eight months at up to 2 feet. Blue and white flowers bloom in the winter and spring. Seeds should be sown in the fall. *Requirements:* Starting temperature 65 to 70 F. Growing temperature; flowers above 60 F and vegetative growth below 55 F. Photoperiod—long days stimulate bloom.

Tropaeolum (Nasturtium). This plant matures in two to four months. Dwarf varieties reach 12 to 15″ and climbers reach 3′ and more. These plants are ideal for hanging baskets. Flowers are yellow, orange, scarlet, rose. Seeds are sown in the fall, winter and spring. *Requirements:* Starting temperature 65 to 75 F. Growing temperature 45 to 70 F or 50 to 60 F for heavy budding and profuse blooming. Summer light—full sun. Photoperiod—artificial light October through April with 63 to 65 F temperatures to induce budding. Short days prevent budding. Flowers bloom in the winter, spring and summer. The hybrids are best for winter bloom. Pick them daily to induce continuous blooming.

Tulip. Tulips mature in 10 to 15 weeks at 1 to 3 feet. There are white, yellow, orange, red, crimson, violet, purple flowers and hybrids of various shapes (singles and doubles). Bulbs are planted in the fall. In warm climates, they are refrigerated for six weeks prior to planting into pots in the greenhouse. *Requirements:* Starting temperature 60 F. Growing temperature—store six to eight weeks at 48 F. Force at 60 F. Summer light—partial shade for one week following removal from storage and then full sun. They flower in the winter and the single and double are the easiest for forcing. After flowering, plant outside and then discard.

Vallota (Scarborough Lily). Bulbs planted in summer mature to two to three feet for flowering in the fall in red and white. *Requirements:* Temperature 50 F. Summer light—full sun. The evergreen star-shaped leaves are most interesting. After flowering, do not water as much; keep the soil moist.

Veltheimia. Maturing in six months at 12 inches, they flower in spring in pink, yellow or white. Remove offshoots in the fall for new starts. *Requirements:* Temperature 50 F. Summer light—darkness. Dry off in summer.

Viola Tricolor (Pansy). Maturing in three to nine months, seeds are taken in the summer. Flowers bloom in the winter or spring in red, orange, purple, lilac, yellow, white, blue, mahogany and bronze. *Requirements:* Starting temperature 65 to 75 F. Growing temperature 45 to 55 F. Summer light—full sun. Photoperiod—long days reduce flower size and increase production. Common pansies grown outside in the summer can be taken into the greenhouse and potted to bloom in the winter through February.

Zantedeschia (Canna-Lily). This plant matures in three to four months at 1 to 3′ with white, yellow and pink flowers that bloom at various times. White flowers bloom in winter and spring and yellow and pink flowers bloom in the spring and summer. In the fall, divide the plants with white flowers. Divide the other plants in the winter or spring. *Requirements:* Starting temperature 60 to 65 F. Growing temperature 55 F. Summer light—shade. These plants should be raised in large pots or tubs. For nearly continuous blooming, do not allow them to dry out and become dormant.

Zephranthes (Zephy-Flower, Fairy-Lily, Rain-Lily). This plant matures in two to four months at 6 to 12 inches. White, pink and yellow flowers bloom in the summer. Bulbs are planted in the spring. *Requirements:* Starting temperature 65 F. Growing temperature 65 F. Summer light—full sun. Alternate periods of moisture and dryness bring on the flowers.

Zinnia Elegans. These plants mature in four to six weeks. Dwarfs grow 3 to 12 inches. Medium size plants grow 12 to 20″ and tall plants grow 20 to 30 inches. Seeds sown in the winter produce flowering in the spring, summer and fall. *Requirements:* Starting temperature 65 to 75 F. Growing temperature 60 F. Summer light—full sun. Photoperiod—long days delay bud development.

Zygocactus (Christmas Cactus.) These plants are appropriate for hanging baskets or pots in reds (most popular) and white. Cuttings are taken in spring. *Requirements:* Starting temperature 60 to 65 F. Growing temperature 55 to 75 F. For budding 55 to 60 F. Summer light—partial shade. Photoperiod—short days in autumn induce budding at 60 to 65 F. The plants mature in six to 12 months and flower in the fall, winter and spring. Do not let the plant completely dry out; keep it moist.

VEGETABLES IN THE GREENHOUSE

The use of a home greenhouse is not confined to producing cut flowers and ornamentals. The trend has changed. Now practically every greenhouse owner grows some herbs and vegetables. There's both beauty and food value to these plants and they answer the desire for something "fresh off the vine" during summer or winter.

The most popular greenhouse vegetables and fruits are tomatoes, bell peppers, carrots, radish, lettuce, lemon, lime, orange. The list is endless when it comes to starting seedlings for later planting in the garden plot. You can be a "jump ahead" of climatic conditions.

A 7 x 12 greenhouse can comfortably accommodate up to 20,000 seedlings. While most people will not want to raise that many for their own use, the excess could be sold for spring, summer and fall gardens. You could enjoy raising and eating your own fresh produce and growing your own fresh flowers while providing a service to your friends, neighbors and the community. In addition, the greenhouse could pay its own way.

Starting Plants

Seeds can be sown in hot frames, flats, market packs or individual containers and then transferred to the counter of your choice when the seedlings have put on the first true set of leaves. Germination time must be considered for different vegetables. Be sure to carefully read the directions on your seed packages. Tomatoes, cabbage and broccoli, for instance, reach the transplanting stage approximately three weeks after germination. However, okra, beets and carrots are slower germinators.

If the winter is unusually warm, with excessive sunshine, "damping off" problems occur. Slower germination time has to be considered. Soil is the key to successful seedlings. Soil should consist of equal parts garden loam, peat moss and sand along with vermiculite and generous amounts of compost added. If the vegetables are to be raised in off-season gardening—for greenhouse to table eating—the container to be used will depend on the vegetable. Flats are excellent for radish, baby carrots and lettuce. Containers for tomatoes can range from 12 to 18″ pots to 2 x 2 x 2 wooden boxes (Fig. 3-3).

The following descriptions offer some suggestions, but don't be afraid to experiment with other methods.

Tomatoes. The kind of tomato you select makes no difference. However, do stay with hybrids. Pixie, early salad and patio are ideal for small containers. Pixie is fast-growing and it ripens early. It grows 14 to 18″ high and bears heavy crops of bright fruit approximately the size of golf ball in approximately 55 days from transplanting. Early salad and the cherry tomatoes, approximately 1½″ to 2″ in diameter, are very sweet and mature rapidly once the fruit sets on. For the larger varieties requiring the large box type container, Burpee's Big Boy and other standard varieties do very well. Seeds can be started any time during the year. Temperatures should be 72 to 80 F for germination and there should be a growing temperature of 60 F. Plants should receive full light. For special cultures, ventilate on hot days and avoid splashing water on foliage. Water in the morning and fertilize with liquid plant food every three to four weeks during the summer. Cut back on feedings when the days are dark in the winter. Use *blossom set* to aid in fruit setting on. To assist in this, you can also spread pollen with your fingers or a brush.

Cucumber. Any variety of cucumber will work for an indoor culture. Highly recommended is the English Telegraph and Burpee Burpless. Seeds can be sown any time of the year in larger containers and set on shelves where the vines will have the chance to hangdown or be trained around the shelf. Plant one or two seeds to a pot. They require full light during the winter with full sun and a little shade on the hottest days during the summer. Use a blossom set to aid in pollination.

Onions. Yellow Sweet Spanish or Ebenezer, which can be eaten as a "green" or for the bulb, are both excellent greenhouse onions. Sets should be purchased at your local nursery or through the seed company and planted any time in flats, or, space permitting, directly into the bench. Growing temperature required are 60 F to start and 70 F to 75 F for maturity. They enjoy full light. Onions grow quickly. Keep them well watered to maintain a sweet flavor.

Mushrooms. Mushroom culture spawns can be purchased through the seed companies. Requiring a minimum 60 F temperature with a growing temperature of between 60 F to 65 F, mushrooms require dark, damp, cool conditions. This can be accomplished by screening off a section under the benches in the greenhouse. The spawn should be spread on dried manure. Do not allow it to dry out. As soon as the white buttons appear, be ready to pick.

Mustard Greens. Green Wave is a well fruited strain which grows quickly and produces tender, inner leaves with a beautiful tight curl. Spicey, pungent and high in vitamin content, they can be started from seed any time in pots or in the bench. Temperatures for starting are 72 F and growing temperatures can be as low as 50 F. They require full light to semishade and like lots of water with ample ventilation.

Carrots. There are many varieties of carrots, but the small baby carrots such as Burpee's Little Finger, Goldenhart (3½" to 4") and Nantes (5") are all sweet and ideal for greenhouse culture. Seeds sown in pots and tubs can be started any time at a temperature of 68 F to 75 F. If sown into the bench, the bench must be built up at least 8" in order to facilitate the carrots growth to full maturity. Make sure that the soil used does not compact; they need light, fluffy textured soil.

Growing temperatures between 45 F to 50 F in full light is required. Seeds should be sown three or four per inch and covered with light soil. Plants can be thinned to 1½" apart. Successive sowings can be made every three weeks for a continuous supply of tender, young carrots throughout the year. Avoid sowing too thick because this would deter the carrots from putting on their "buttoms."

Bush Beans. Any variety of bush beans can be grown. However, they do take up considerable room and they work best if they are planted into ground beds in an area where they can be strung or staked. Seeds can be sown any time at a 72 F to 75 F temperature with a growing temperature of 60 F. If space is available, bush beans are an excellent greenhouse crop because they do not germinate when the soil is cold. Plant seeds 1" apart and cover 1" deep. Thin to 2" apart. Fertilize every six weeks.

Endive. Green Curled, Salad King or Deep Heart (Escarole) are all excellent greenhouse varieties. They can be started from seed any time at a temperature of 50 F to 55 F in pots or directly into a bench. They require full light at all times. Seeds should be sown three per inch and thinned to 8 to 10 inches. For the best flavor, when nearly mature, gather the outer leaves over the center (heart) and tie loosely with string. This balances the center.

Watercress. Improved broad-leaved watercress and pepper-grass are both easy to grow from seed started any time at 50 F in pots or shallow pans or trays in full light during the winter. Watercress, as its name implies, needs lots of water and it thrives in very moist soil. Seeds should be sown three or four per inch and covered with one-half inch of soil and then thinned to 1 or 2 inches apart. Be sure to check daily to be sure that they are kept continuously wet.

Bell Peppers. California Wonder bell peppers make an excellent greenhouse pepper. Sow seeds directly into large containers during September at 60 F to 65F (no more than two per container). Do not overfertilize because too much feeding will attain heavy growth and less fruiting. When pepper begin to form be sure to stake the foliage. They produce large, thick-skinned peppers and the plants can be saved and planted directly into the garden during the summer. They enjoy full light and the soil should be kept damp.

Hot and Sweet Peppers. Vinedale (a dwarf, sturdy vine) and Bell Boy yield heavy crops with thick flesh. Canape produces heavy yields of mild sweet fruit. Hot Portugal has large hot red peppers. Rumanian Wax is the true heavy-yielding dwarf variety hot pepper with large yellow fruit. Seeds can be sown any time at a temperature of between 72 F to 85 F. They prefer very warm temperatures for germination. Add vermiculite and peat moss to your regular potting soil and grow at a 60 F to 65 F temperature. Pepper plants are self-pollinating. They enjoy a uniform moisture. Avoid heavy fertilizing.

Herbs. Not to be outdone by flowers and vegetables, herbs too have their place in the greenhouse. They are easy to raise in pots or benches and do not require a rich soil. Soil should be friable. An ideal nighttime temperature for herbs is 50 F. Herbs like lots of water and good drainage. Don't let the roots stand in water for long periods of time. Most herbs require full sun to insure good flavor.

Chives. Bring chives in from the garden in the fall. Fresh tender shoots will grow through the winter and the onion-flavored leaves are good in omelets, cheese spread, salads and fried eggs. Clusters of small bulbs with pompons of lavender flowers are attractive and the tiny bulbs produced can be pickled as baby onion.

Basil. Sow basil seeds in pots or on a bench. Grow the purple-leaved ornamental basil for a real show. It has a pleasant, sweet flavor and it is useful with tomatoes and other dishes. Both leaves and flowers are used fresh or dried in salads. A few leaves in vinegar adds an interesting color.

Borage. Sow borage seeds in pots. Young leaves are useful in salads and to flavor cool drinks.

Parsley. Start parsley seeds in pots of sand and peat. It is slow to germinate (Six weeks). If you are starting out and have a clump in the garden, bring it in and pot it. Keep it cut back to promote new growth. Do not overwater; that will cause the fleshy tap root to rot.

Sage. Sow sage seeds in pots any time. Sage is a slow grower and several pots should be kept going at all times throughout the year for getting the vest out of this herb.

Specialties. A tremendous advantage to the home greenhouseman in cold climates, especially, is the raising and cultivating of citrus potted plants.

Ponderosa lemons plants produce an abundance of fruit on a small, short plant which is mature at 3 feet. A 20-year-old plant requires potting only twice during that long period. Intermittent refreshing of the top soil is required during each year. The fruit is as big as a grapefruit at times, thick-skinned, and ideal for making pies. The plant has bright green leaves and the thorny stems become soft when raised in the greenhouse (Fig. 3-4).

Lemon Japonica has a narrower leaf than the Ponderosa. It grows taller rather than compact and it matures by the time it has grown to 3 feet. The lemons are small but superior in flavor. There are no seeds to the thin-skinned juicy lemon with an abundance of meat.

The Margot orange matures at 4' to 6' and produces small (approximately 3" to 6" in diameter) fruit with a skin similar to that of the tangerine. The fruit has a pure, sweet orange flavor.

The Otaheite, commonly known as the dwarf orange, is an enigma. It is really not an orange or a lemon, it has pretty, small glossy leaves and it has pinkish/white fragrant blossoms. Although the small fruits are perfectly round and bright orange, they are not .

as useful as the dwarf lemon. They are somewhat bitter and they stay on the tree for an extended period. They provide much aesthetic value and many people use the fruits to flavor tea.

HYDROPONICS

With soil surrounding the beginning home greenhouser, other phases of greenhousing can easily be bypassed or even permanently overlooked. The beauty of a home greenhouse goes beyond all the beautiful things grown, it is also the beauty of knowledge and learning and experimenting—so try hydroponics. Hydroponics is art and science of raising plants in water. It is a science and it might not be for everyone. In order to expand your greenhouse "know-how", you might want to give it a try.

Use none but the best varieties and plants produced in disease-free soil, sand or vermiculite. They should be 6 inches or more high—as in the case of tomatoes—before planting. Thoroughly work the media in the seedling flat with water so that there will be as little injury as possible to the root systems during transplanting. Before planting in the gravel, rinse off the soil or other material that clings to the roots when the plants are dug. You could start plants right in the bed if you want and in thinning you could transplant the plants that are removed. The water level should be kept very high until seedlings germinate and begin to grow.

One type of small home unit suitable for use by amateurs is shown in Fig. 3-5. If space is not available or if you do not want to invest in tanks for hydroponic gardens, plants such as tomatoes, eggplant and pepper can be grown in bushel baskets or 5-gallon cans. Smaller plants can be grown in still smaller containers. See Fig. 3-6. Punch holes in the bottoms to allow adequate drainage. Fill the container with sand, soil, sawdust, shavings, or well-rotted plant materials.

You can use the standard hydroponic fertilizer solution. If only a few plants are involved, you can make a small quantity of solution by reducing all ingredients proportionately. Apply enough of the solution to saturate the growing medium to the bottom of the container at each application. The frequency of application will depend upon the temperature, growing medium, and size of plants. However, an application once every three days should be adequate.

Vining and tall-growing varieties, such as tomatoes, pole beans and cucumbers, will require some type of support such as a trellis.

Nutrient Solutions

No one nutrient solution is superior to all others. Several can be used with much the same degree of success. Growers often prefer to buy the ready-mixed chemical ingredients for the solution. This is recommended for the beginner. However, the solutions are not difficult to mix and they will cost considerably less than ready-mixed salts. Table 3-1 is an example of one nutrient solution mixture. It will provide excellent results.

Table 3-1 represents the chemicals for only the *major* elements. A solution of *micro* or *minor* elements is needed. These can be provided by the combination shown in Table 3-2 when added to the list given in Table 3-1.

Quantities of the solution should be mixed ahead of time so that it can be added to the solution tank when a fresh mixture is prepared.

The primary requisite of any nutrient solution is to secure and maintain a proper balance between total concentrations and proportions of the various chemicals in the solution. Requirements for potassium, calcium, magnesium, nitrogen, phosphorus, and sulfur are relatively large for all plants. They need smaller quantities of iron and only traces of manganese, boron, copper, zinc, and other elements.

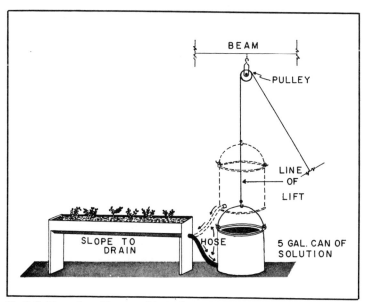

Fig. 3-5. A type of small home unit for hydroponics.

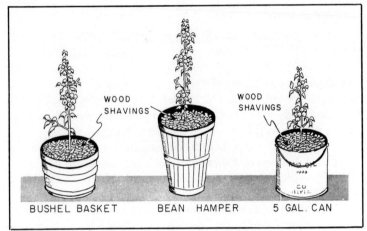

Fig. 3-6. Individual containers in which to raise hydroponic vegetables.

Medium for Growing

Gravel or cinders for the bed should be fairly uniform in texture, about one-half inch to one-fourth inch in diameter, and washed. If you use sand, it should be coarse and it also should be washed. Beds should be filled to within 1″ of the top. Pipes or any metal fittings used in the construction of the beds should be of plain iron or plastic. Do not use galvanized pipe because dissolved zinc from the galvanizing will cause trouble in the nutrient solution.

Cinders or gravel in the beds as a growing medium might contain a wide variety of minerals and the micro or minor elements might not be necessary. If you use commercial fertilizers in place of the pure chemicals in making the solution, impurities might be adequate in some cases to supply the same minor elements. In other cases, impurities might be present in sufficient concentration to cause injury to the plant.

Fertilizers

Commercial fertilizers might contain insoluble material. Possibly one-fourth of the fertilizer might not dissolve. Always use the highest analysis fertilizers available or the most soluble fertilizer salts when making up the solution. The higher grades of magnesium sulfate, potassium sulfate, potassium nitrate, and ammonium sulfate appear to contain fewer impurities and generally none that are harmful. Fertilizer grades of phosphate salts might contain fluorine in amounts higher than 1 percent. Do not use any fertilizers with more than 1 percent fluorine.

256

Table 3-1. A Nutrient Solution.

	Pounds Per 100 Gallons of Water
Magnesium sulfate (Epsom Salts)	3.2
Monocalcium phosphate (good grade)	3.2
Potassium nitrate	6.4
Ammonium sulfate	1.6
Calcium sulfate (agricultural gypsum)	1.3

General

Prepare solutions by dissolving the ingredients in smaller quantities of water and then adding these to the solution tanks. Some of the elements will be absorbed out of the solution by plants. At the same time, there is considerable loss of water through transpiration and evaporation. These processes tend to change the concentration of elements in the water and make the solution stronger or more concentrated. The chief danger is that of creating an imbalance. Water, of course, must be added frequently to replace that which is lost. The tendency, therefore, is for the nutrient solution to gradually become less concentrated or weaker.

The acidity or alkalinity, usually measured by pH of the nutrient solution, affects the availability of some of the nutrient elements. For best results, this should be kept between pH 5:5 and about 6:5.

If the weather is warm and plants are growing rapidly, it might be necessary to empty the solution tanks and substitute new solutions as often as once a month, (sometimes more often). In the small, home greenhouse, in most cases it is cheaper and safer to dump a solution tank than to attempt to adjust to the correct proportion of nutrients. The used solution is still relatively high in some nutrient elements and it can be used on nearby gardens, lawns or plantings. The nutrient solution previously described is relatively low in nitrogen.

Table 3-2. A Nutrient Solution.

	Pounds per 100 Gallons of Water
Iron sulfate (copperas)	.4
Manganese sulfate	.025
Copper sulfate (blue vitrol)	.025
Zinch sulfate (zinc vitrol)	.025
Sodium tetraborate (borax)	.3

Plants might be able to use somewhat more potassium nitrate and ammonium sulfate in warm weather because of more rapid growth. Doubling the amounts of these compounds is often desirable. The same can be said for the other chemicals under those conditions. An increase of 40 percent to 50 percent in concentration of all materials in the solution is often justifiable.

Operating the System

The entire hydroponics system is relatively simple to operate. The quantity of solution in the tank should be just sufficient to bring the water level up to within one-half inch to 1" of the top of the gravel in the beds.

Diseases and Insects

Soil-borne maladies affect nearly all vegetable crops and the fact that soil is not used does not eliminate these troubles. In reality, the problem is magnified because of the danger of carrying disease organisms through the nutrient solution and spreading it quickly to all other plants in the system. There are no known materials that can be dissolved in the nutrient solution to control diseases while the crop is being grown. Therefore, much of the difficulty in hydroponic culture comes from the ease by which disease is spread and the inadequacies of the control methods used.

As in all plant production, the best system is to prevent the introduction of diseases that can spread widely after the initial infection. This calls for a rigorous campaign of sanitation and utmost care in production of plants, handling and treating plants, spraying, and other practices to make certain that diseases are kept away from the production area.

Often it is impossible to ascertain how diseases are carried and consequently it is impossible to forestall their introduction. Once soil-borne diseases have been discovered in the planting area, there might be little that can be done other than to fertilize the plants to the maximum and get the most out of the crop in spite of the disease.

Leaf diseases, such as mildews, blights and leafspots, attack plants under hydroponic culture conditions much as they do when those crops are grown in the open. Also various insect pests must be rigidly controlled.

INSECTS AND DISEASES IN THE GREENHOUSE

Raising plants in a greenhouse does not make them immune to insects. They can fly in, crawl in through cracks—no matter how tight you feel your house is—and even enter by clinging to gardening tools or in the soil you bring in for potting. Regardless of the method they will get in.

While you cannot prevent the pests from getting into your greenhouse, with efficient and good greenhouse management by working in an expeditious manner to alleviate any problems that arise from a "pest attack" you will be able to prevent serious damage to your plants.

Familiarizing yourself with some of the more popular—or unpopular—pests and diseases and how to handle them will enable you to stop infestations before they become severe.

Many insects are not readily visible to the naked eye. There are those which practice concealment by changing color and blending in with the plants. Camouflaging is natural to the insect world. Don't rely on visual inspection. That is often too late for you to correct the problem.

What to look for can be an endless question and answer series. There are, however, some very specific "happenings" to alert even the newcomer to greenhousing that a problem is evident.

To combat insect pests successfully, something should be known about the manner in which they develop and feed. Insects normally hatch from eggs deposited on or near the food supply. In some cases, they hatch within the female's body and the active young emerge from the female. Adults are usually individuals with fully developed wings. A few species of insects never have wings.

Groups of Insects

Pests can be divided into five groups by the way they damage plants.

☐ Insects with piercing-sucking mouthparts. These insects have beak-like mouthparts used for piercing the plant tissue and sucking the plant juices—the plant's life blood. Scales, aphids, whiteflies, mealybugs are examples. See Fig. 3-7.

☐ Insects with chewing mouthparts. They might feed on the leaves, flowers or attack the roots. Caterpillars, beetles, grasshoppers, katydids are examples.

☐ Spider mites. These pests are not insects. They are closely related to spiders and scorpions. They suck plant juices with their piercing-sucking mouthparts. See Fig. 3-8.

☐ Leafminers. These are very small larvae of flies or moths that tunnel between the upper and lower leaf surfaces.

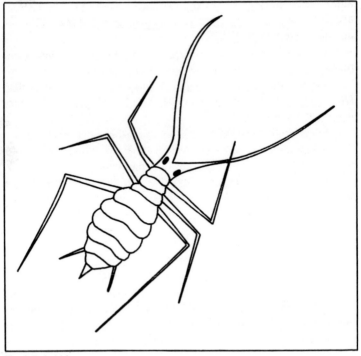

Fig. 3-7. Aphid.

☐ Borers. These are many species of insects. They bore into the twigs or trunks of plants and trees. These are usually the larvae of moths or beetles.

Some Signs of Trouble

Jagged holes in leaves, decay, leaves turning yellow or brown, and slow or stunted growth are trouble signs. Many species of insects leave a residue that attracts ants who, in turn, carry the substance and spread disease from plant to plant.

What to Do

What can you do if you find that any of these problems are occurring in your greenhouse? If the insects are discernible—such as caterpillars, snails, slugs and larger varieties—pick them off and destroy them outside. Spraying plants with a strong stream of water can dislodge some insects. A careful scrubbing with warm, mild soapy water might be necessary to rid the plant of other pests. While mild chemicals, such as Rotenone and Malathion, are adequate for safe use on the insects that attack persistently there are times that a stronger pesticide must be used. *Never* reach for any pesticide before determining, at least to some extent, what is wrong with the plant and what species of insect is causing the problem.

Mechanical Control. Pick or knock the insects off the plant. Destroy them by dropping them into kerosene or cutting them in half with scissors.

Chemical Control. Insecticides are necessary to control insects and related pests on many ornamentals. Most of the newer insecticides kill by contact with the insect or as a stomach poison. The following rules for the use of insecticides should be followed carefully.

☐ Select the right material for the specific pest with which you are dealing.

☐ Apply it at the right time. Insects are easier to control when small in size and few in number. Inspect your plants for insect infestation frequently. Don't let them build up to large populations.

☐ Use the right amount. Read the container label *Carefully* for correct dosage rate. Too little insecticide won't control the pest and too much might injure the plant.

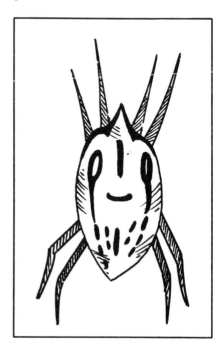

Fig. 3-8. Spider Mite.

☐ Apply it in the right manner. Complete saturation and coverage of the leaves, especially the underside where minute insects are hard to see with the naked eye, is essential. This is especially true for certain scales.

Safety Precautions

☐ All insecticides are poisons and the safety precautions on the container labels should be followed.

☐ Read the entire label, including the small print, before you open the container.

☐ Store pesticides in their original labeled containers out of reach of children, irresponsible people and pets. Preferably, you should keep them under lock and key.

☐ Store pesticides in a dry place. If the label gets blurred and worn, be sure to attach a new label so that you will know which mixture is different.

Most Common Greenhouse Pests

Ants. While not a great threat to plants' health, ants in a greenhouse can be troublesome because they are carriers for other species—aphids, mealybugs, and scale—by transporting such destructive pests from place to place. While busy at work, ants introduce problems such as bacterial and fungus infections. Their burrowing habits disturb and often damage roots. Ants are capable of "carrying" off newly planted seeds. They are attracted to decaying organic matter and they are concealed in unsterilized soil. When an ant mound appears pour Malathion on the mound. If you find ants on plants dissolve Malathion in water and drench the plants.

Caterpillars. These wormlike pests are the immature form of moths and butterflies. They are voracious eaters and devour huge amounts of buds and flowers. They can defoliate a plant quickly. Many species are nocturnal. The ragged holes torn in leaves overnight, along with the black specks of excrement are sure signs that caterpillars are present. If your plants show any of these symptoms, cut the infested leaves and destroy them. Isolate the damaged plants until they are rejuvenated. Caterpillars enjoy dark spots such as the underside of pots and piles of decaying organic matter. Cleaning around pots aids in keeping these pests away.

Crickets. They can be especially harmful in the greenhouse. Moving about freely at night, they feed on the leaves and flowers of plants, vegetables and seedlings. Although nocturnal, if present you will find them moving around lazily during the day. Get rid of them immediately. As with all nocturnal insects, it is almost impossible to find them during the day and some time will have to be spent in the greenhouse after dark to locate them. Too much emphasis cannot be placed on cleanliness to cut down all insect problems and infestation.

Cutworms. The cutworm is one of the most annoying of all insects that attack young seedlings. The destructive forms of moths, they lay eggs and are barely visible to the naked eye when they hatch. Some reach a length of 1" to 2" when fully grown.

Some species of cutworms are a solid color; some are striped lengthwise or crosswide and others are mottled. Shades of green or brown are common, but various combinations of brown, red, yellow, green, gray, and black are also found. Some are covered with dense hair. They are difficult to find because they hide in the soil or deep in the flowers during the day. Cutworms damage leaves, buds, or flowers that are entirely or partially eaten. Some worms cut off young plants near the soil level or the branches of flowers of larger plants. Dark pellets of excrement might be left on the plant.

Handpicking is often adequate, but if it appears not to be practical. Diazinon or Dylox is effective. Cutworms climb up the plant and feed on buds and leaves. Typically they stay in the soil during the day and feed at night at the base of the tender plants.

Aphids. Also known as plant lice, aphids are small, soft-bellied and 1/16" to ⅛" long. They are green/pink, red, or black with soft rounded or pear-shaped bodies with long legs and antennae (Fig. 3-7). In each species, there are both winged and wingless forms. The wingless form is generally more numerous. They cluster on the underside of leaves or on young, tender leaves and stems or flower buds.

Some feed on the roots. Aphids feed by sucking out the plant juices. Therefore, they cause poor growth, stunted plants, or curled and distorted leaves. Aphids excrete a sweetish, sticky liquid called honeydew. Honeydew of most species is attractive to ants; it imparts a shiny appearance to the foliage and provides a base for the growth of sooty mold.

Obtain a commercially prepared pressurized pesticide pushbutton spray mixture. Make sure that it lists both "house-plants" and "aphids" on the label and use the following guidelines.

☐ When one or a few plants are infested, handpicking, washing, or using alcohol might be practical to control aphids.

☐ Dimethoate, Malathion, Diazinon, Metasystox-R, oil emulsion and Orthene are recommended for control. Apply a second application 10 to 14 days after the initial application.

Scale Insects. Scale insects are the most serious pests. Most ornamentals are susceptible to one or more species of scales. Scales cause damage by sucking the juices from the plants. Heavily infested plants appear unhealthy and produce little new growth. Scales feeding on the underside of the leaves can cause yellow spots that become progressively larger as the scales continue to feed. If the scales are not controlled, the leaves will drop prematurely. Sometimes this will kill portions of twigs and branches.

Scales can be divided into armored scales, soft scales and mealybugs. The armored scales secrete a waxy covering over their bodies. This covering is not an integral part of the insect's body, but the scale lives and feeds under it. Varying in size from 1/16″ to ⅛″ in diameter, they can be almost any color (depending on the species). The soft scales also secrete a waxy covering, but it is attached to their bodies. Soft scales vary widely in color, size and shape. They range from ⅛″ to ½″ in diameter and they are nearly flat to almost spherical in shape.

The eggs of these insects are laid underneath the waxy coating and hatch in one to three weeks. The newly hatched scales (crawlers) move about over the plant until they locate succulent new growth. They insert their piercing-sucking mouthparts into the plant. In the case of the female, it remains there the rest of its life.

In some armored scales, the adult stage is reached in six weeks and there are several generations per year. Some soft scales require one to two years to reach maturity. Mealybugs reach maturity in eight to 10 weeks. Unlike armored and soft scales, they are able to move about throughout their lives.

Whiteflies and mealy bugs are the most common scale insects and they are difficult to control as they grow larger. For scale control in general, apply one of the suggested insecticides (See Table 3-3) as soon as the new growth hardens. Follow with an additional application two or three weeks later.

Slugs and Snails. Several species can be troublesome in the greenhouse. Both snails and slugs (Fig. 3-9) have fleshy, soft, slimy, legless bodies that range in color from whitish yellow to

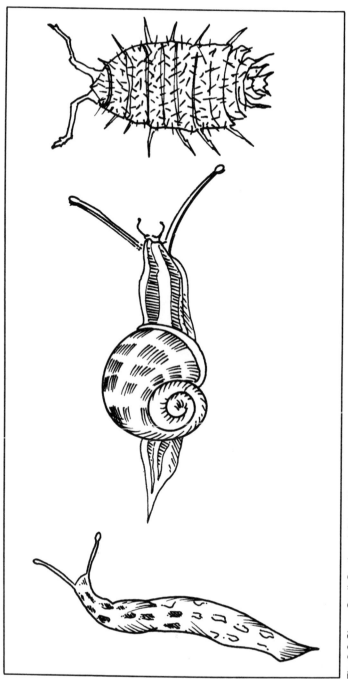

Fig. 3-9. Slugs, Snail, Sowbug, left to right.

Table 3-3. Scale Control Methods.

INSECTICIDE	AMOUNT PER GALLON OF WATER
*Acephate (orthene). *Diazinon. *Dimethoate. *Malathion. *Meta-Systox-R. Ethion plus oil emulsion. Malathion plus oil emulsion.	Apply the suggested pesticide in strict accordance with the container label. Be sure the pest and plant are listed on the label.
**Di-Syston granules.	Available as 2% granules or 1% Di-Systom in fertilizer. Apply according to directions on the container label.

*Recommended for scale crawlers and mealybugs or mature scales.

**Dimenthoate, Meta-Systox-R and Di-Syston are systemic. The insecticides are absorbed by the plant and translocated throughout its tissues making the plant toxic to certain insect pests. Systemic insecticides have been effective primarily against small sucking insects and spider mites. Generally, they have not given satisfactory control of chewing insect pests.

black; most are mottled with shades of gray. They are slow moving and grow to lengths of one-half inch to 4 inches.

Snails have a hard spiral shell on the back. Shells range from about ¼″ to 1″ in diameter and they are off-white to brown or black in color.

Slugs and snails normally hit during the day under pieces of wood or pottery, fallen leaves, or mulches. They are active at night, but they might be active on damp, dark days. They feed on the leaves of flowers, stems or roots of plants by scraping off the tissue or eating holes in the leaves of flowers. They leave a glistening trail of slime wherever they crawl. Eliminating hiding places and placing pieces of shingles or boards for traps is helpful.

Spider Mites. These are among the most common pests that attack ornamental plants. They are not insects. They are more closely related to spiders and ticks. They have needle-like, piercing mouthparts with which they puncture the leaf and suck the plant juices.

Damage from light infestation appears as yellow or gray stippled patterns on the leaves. The undersides of infested leaves usually have fine silken webbing spun across them. Heavy infestation causes the leaves to turn yellow, gray or brownish and eventually drop off. Webbing might be spun over the entire plant.

Chlorobenzilate, Kelthane, Tedion, Malathion plus summer oil emulsion are a means of control. Table 3-4 shows the most common insects which attack orchids and the chemical and dosage required to control these pests.

Diseases

As with insects, diseases attack greenhouse plants. Disease can be recognized by:

☐ Seedlings fail to come up. Seedlings wilt and die shortly after coming up.

☐ Plants wilt or turn yellow and die before maturity.

☐ Old established plants turn yellow and show other signs of weakness and problems.

Learning about some of the most common diseases in greenhouse cultivation will enable you to treat the problem expeditiously and, therefore, treat and save plants which otherwise might be lost. Diseases prevalent in greenhouse cultivation are as follows.

Table 3-4. Spray Chart for Orchid Insects (courtesy of Florida Extension Service).

INSECT	INSECTICIDE AND FORMULATION	DOSAGE 1 GALLON	100 GALLONS
Armored Scales, Soft Scales and Mealybugs	Diazinon 25% EC	2 tsp.	2 pt.
	*Diemethoate (Cygon) 23-25%	2 tsp.	2 pt.
	Malathion 25% WP	6 tbs.	6 lb.
	Malathion 57% EC	1 tbs.	3 pt.
	Meta-Systox-R 25% EC	2 tsp.	2 pt.
Mites	Chlorobenzilate 25% WP	1 tbs.	1 lb.
	Dimite	1 tsp.	1 pt.
	Ethion 23-25% EC	2 tsp.	2 pt.
	Kelthane 18% EC	2 tsp.	2 pt.
	Kelthane 18% WP	2 tbs.	2 lb.
	Meta-Systox-R 25% EC	2 tsp.	2 pt.
Aphids	Diazinon 25% EC	2 tsp.	2 pt.
	*Dimethoate (Cygon) 23-25% EC	2 tsp.	2 pt.
	Lindane 20% EC	1 tsp.	1 pt.
	Lindane 25% WP	1 tbs.	1 lb.
	Malathion 25% WP	4 lbs.	4 lbs.
	Malathion 57% EC	2 tsp.	2 pt.
	Meta-Systox-R 25% EC	1 tsp.	2 pt.
Springtails and Thripes	DDT 50% WP	2 tbs.	2 lb.
	Diazinon 25% EC	2 tsp.	2 pt.
	*Dimethoate (Cygon) 23-25% EC	2 tsp.	1 pt.
	Lindane 25% WP	1 tbs.	1 lb.
	Malathion 25% WP	4 tbs.	4 lb.
	Malathion 50-57% EC	2 tsp.	2 pt.
Beetles and Weeviles	DDT 50% WP	2 tbs.	2 lb.
	Diaxinon 25% EC	2 tsp.	2 pt.
	Lindane 25% WO	1 tbs.	1 lb.
Ants and Coackroaches	Chlordane 40% WP	2 tbs.	2 lb.
	Chlordane 42-46% EC	1 tsp.	2 pt.
	Diazinon 25% EC	2 tsp.	2 pt.
	(Spray benches, interior and exterior walls)		
Snails and Slugs	Metaldehyde 15% D		
	(Dust in and around pots and benches)		
	Metaldehyde WP or Baits		
	(Follow label as directed)		

Abbreviations: tbs - Tablespoons, tsp = Teaspoons, pt = Pint, lb = pound, EC = Emulsifiable concentrate, WP = Wettable power and D = Dust.

*Dimethoate *(Cygon): This material is reported to cause injury to the following orchid plants: Calante sp., Cycnoches dentricosum Bateman (=C. ventricosum Bateman var. warscewiszil (Reichb. f.) (P.H. Allen) which is erroneously advertised in orchid trade lists in the United States as Cyenoches chlorochilonKlotzsch. Dendrobium moschatum Lindl., D. pulchellum Roxburgh (=D. dalhousicanum Wall.), D. phalenopsis (type) and Neomoorea irrorata Rolfe.

Root Knot. Caused by microscopic worms (nemotodes) that cause the roots to become distorted with large swellings or knots. This is especially detrimental to tomatoes and peppers.

Root Rot/Damping Off. Roots are decayed or dead. Affected roots appear brown and hairy and have fungus on the surface. With another type of root rot, the roots are blackened and have a bad odor. This is caused by excessive water in the soil which kills the roots due to air being excluded.

Leaf Spots. This is caused by fungi or bacteria. There are many diseases that fall into this category. Leaves, stems and fruits appear round, angular or irregular in shape—these areas are dead.

Mildew. A fungus disease, mildew is a grayish-white mold that covers the leaves. If severely affected, the leaves will turn yellow, dry up and fall off. This will cause the plant to become stunted and it will yield poorly. It is particularly common on cucumbers.

Botrytis. This is a fungus that is especially and frequently fatal to African violets. A grayish-white mold appears on the upper leaves of plants. It spreads rapidly. If you find a plant in this condition, destroy the plant and remove the plants surrounding it to an isolation area until you are sure that the disease has been alleviated. A means of avoiding this disease is not to overcrowd your planting pot area.

If you feel that Botrytis has attacked a plant and only a few leaves appear to be infected, remove these leaves and move the plant to a well ventilated unit. Avoid overlapping the foliage of all plants. The new location should be well lit. All plants can be easily infected by other plants you have touched. Your hands should be washed immediately after working with infected plants. The same applies for tools.

Chlorosis. This occurs if the soil is too heavy with alkalinity which prevents the plants from absorbing the necessary nutrients of iron and the many trace elements needed. Leaves turn yellow while the leaf veins remain green and the plant becomes stunted in growth. This problem is remedied by feeding the plant a high concentration of acid or applying a commercial chelated iron fertilizer.

To help alleviate greenhouse disease problems:

☐ Regularly disinfect all greenhouse tools and equipment with a non-toxic detergent. This will greatly help control most insects and diseases.

□ Never put freshly acquired plants into the greenhouse. Place them in "quarantine" and find out if there are any problems before you expose healthy plants to them.

□ Remember that too hot or too cold temperatures, too much or too little plant food or water, or too much or too little humidity makes greenhouse plants more vulnerable to disease.

Chapter 4
Management

There are many factors connected with good management of your greenhouse. Potted ornamentals, vegetables, cut flowers, herbs, bulbs, and seedlings, all require varying degrees of light, temperature, humidity, and watering. All of these factors interplay and become integral parts necessary for a congenial environment that is conductive to each of the many plants you will raise. While it is easier to grow plants that all have the same requirements that is difficult for the home greenhouse enthusiast. By experimenting and using knowledge gained from the past to enhance the present, you can assure success in your future greenhousing. With intuition you can intermix many varieties to encompass a "whole" in your greenhouse world.

TEMPERATURE CONTROL

The key to successful greenhouse management is the regulation, as closely as possible, of the natural rise and fall of the temperature. Keeping the temperature cooler will provide sturdier, healthier plants. A too high temperature reading results in plants growing too quickly and becoming overgrown. This condition means additional fertilizing (feeding). In addition, it makes your plants more susceptible to disease.

Temperature control will largely depend upon what plants you plan to raise. Many orchids, for example, require a constant minimum reading of 75 to 80 F while nasturtians can be raised in as low as 30 F. For seed propagation, temperatures between 55 to 60 F provide best results. An ideal greenhouse is a "cool" temperature house where a large variety of plants can be enjoyed.

A good indoor/outdoor thermometer (Fig. 4-1) should be kept in the greenhouse to provide a visual aid in helping you decide whether any major changes have occurred in the temperature desired (or needed) or whether any change is deemed necessary. When you read the thermometer, consideration should be given as to whether the sun is shining on it and causing it to rise.

A higher temperature reading can be advantageous rather than harmful to many plants. Most plants prefer nighttime temperatures approximately 10 degrees lower than the highest daytime reading. Older plants resist both unduly low and high temperatures. Newly sown seeds require higher readings in order to germinate. This

Fig. 4-1. Indoor/outdoor thermometer (courtesy of Evert Thompson, Advertising Architecture).

makes a hot frame an important asset to alleviate concern over regulating the temperature during seed germination time.

The most important consideration is that a too high temperature will have the same effect as hot sun which can damage plants to the extent of burning. Conversely, too low a temperature could ruin them by freezing. Daily recordings of your temperature readings provide a log that can be used as a guide to what temperatures are best for particular plants.

Nighttime is the most critical period for greenhouse plants. Too high or too low a temperature for the particular species means that they will not thrive and flower. Many plants are satisfied and flower at 60 F night temperatures, yet they do poorly at only 10 degrees less. Others, such as snapdragon, stocks and some varieties of orchids, make their best growth at a nighttime temperature of 50 F even though they might fail to produce (flower) at 60 F.

Daytime temperatures are not any less important. They should be approximately 10 to 15 degrees higher than the night temperatures. For example, if the plants being grown adapt themselves to a nighttime reading of 50 F, ideally the temperature during the day should be 60 to 65 F. If you are raising plants that do best at 60 F nighttime temperatures, keep the daytime reading at 70 to 75 F.

For year around greenhouse operation, these daytime readings are easier to maintain and control during the winter. However, with the longer days of summer plus additional sunshine, plants adapt and benefit from somewhat higher temperatures.

Temperature affects other processes such as growth and flowering, producing food and using food produced. The food produced by plants is not as rapidly used as the temperature rises. Known as *respiration*, this means that the plants' natural food is devoured during the period when the greenhouse temperature is the highest. Because respiration—breathing which goes on day and night—means that the plant's natural food is consumed during the period when the greenhouse temperature is the highest and, because respiration continues at night and the manufacture of food does not, it can readily be seen why one should vie for a nighttime reading approximately 10 degrees lower than the day.

The way you operate and control the temperature in your greenhouse, for the species of plants with which you are involved, you should:

□ Attempt to balance the temperature to offer your plants a day time reading for them to produce and use food.

□ Provide a nighttime temperature for food using and plant growth.

Table 4-1 shows the BTU's needed per hour to maintain a night temperature of 55 F with a wind of 15 miles per hour or less. More wind velocity would boost heat needs about 20 percent for each additional 15 mph. Double layering the inside of your greenhouse with 2-mil polyethelene film will reduce the number of BTU's by 20 percent or more.

As can be seen by Table 4-1, using redwood or other types of wood for framing will cost far less to heat than metal frame, glass covered models of comparable size. The reason for this is:

□ Heat loss of aluminum is 128 BTU's per hour per square foot. Wood is over 1400 times more efficient than aluminum in preventing heat loss.

□ Fiberglass is 75 percent more efficient in preventing heat loss than is regular or double-strength glass.

□ Even the coldest climates, fiberglass greenhouses use little or no heat during the daytime.

□ Most plants do not require nighttime temperature readings of more than 55 F to keep them growing.

It must be noted, however, that aluminum is longer-lived whereas, from time to time, wood framing will need replacement. Also, especially in the case of lean-to greenhouses, one's vision is blurred with fiberglass or any other type covering; glass is clear.

HEATING

If you plan to operate a year around greenhouse, in cold climates it will necessitate some type of heating system. Regardless of the size of your greenhouse, the basic heating needs are the same. Whether you are operating your greenhouse for fun or profit

Table 4-1. BTU Comparisions.

	Normal Low Temperature in Degrees Fahrenheit				
			0 degrees	+10 degrees	+20 degrees
8x8 Free-standing	12000	10500	9000	7500	5500
8x12 Free-standing	15500	13500	11500	9500	7500
8x16 Free-standing	19000	16500	14000	11500	9000
7x8 Lean-to	8000	7000	6000	4500	4000
7x12 Lean-to	9500	8500	7000	6000	4500
7x16 Lean-to	11500	10000	8500	7000	5500
	FOR COMPARISON				
Aluminum and Glass					
8x8 Free-standing	23500	20500	17500	14500	11000
7x8 Lean-to	15500	13500	11500	9500	7500

it has one purpose: to provide and maintain the environment that will result in optimum crop production. This includes an environment for work efficiency as well as for crop growth.

Some Heating Generalities

Many types of heaters and heating systems are satisfactory for greenhouses. You must decide which heating system best suits your greenhouse operation. Consider:

— The initial cost.
— Economy of operation.
— Available fuel.

You can heat your greenhouse efficiently with coal, electricity, gas and oil.

Heating equipment can be a space heater, a forced air heater, a hot water or steam system, or electric heaters. Radiant heat lamps over plants or heating cables under plants can also be used. These are all general heating systems. Any of them can be left to the individual's choice.

The capacity of your heating system will depend on the size of your greenhouse, whether it is covered with a single layer or double layer of plastic or glass, and the maximum difference between inside and outside temperature. Regardless of what type of heater you use, the heater size is determined by the following equation: Heater size (BTU/hr) = (total surface area in square feet) times (night temperature difference between inside and outside, °F) times (a heat loss factor).

The heat loss factor is 0.7 for air-separated double plastic heat and 1.2 for single-layer glass, fiberglass or plastic sheet. These figures should be increased by adding 0.3 for hobby greenhouses or for windy locations.

The following steps will assist you in estimating the size heater you will need.

☐ Find the temperature difference. This is the difference in degrees Fahrenheit between the lowest outside temperature and the temperature you want to maintain inside your greenhouse. For instance, if you want to maintain a minimum inside temperature of 60 F and the coldest nighttime temperature you expect is 0 F, your temperature difference is 70 F.

☐ Find the number of square feet of exposed glass or plastic/fiberglass in your greenhouse. Don't forget to add the areas of the sides or ends to the areas of the roof.

274

☐ Multiply the temperature difference by the number of square feet.

This section will concentrate on equipment and methods used to control or maintain desirable temperature and other environmental conditions in a greenhouse of up to 60 F. Many home greenhouse enthusiasts begin small and, very quickly, find that they have to add on sections or even build additional houses—space permitting—to accommodate their plants. During periods when supplemental heat (other than natural heat) is required, there are many ways that it can be obtained from the standpoint of equipment used, types of fuel used, type of construction and management practices.

Each operation usually has some unusual characteristics such as types of plants produced, level of quality of production strived for, type of house used and management procedures followed. It is important that all of these factors be considered when you select and install a heating system.

Unit Space Heater

Unit space heaters, either floor mounted or supported, are normally fueled with natural or bottled gas or fuel oil and use fans for heat distribution. This system requires a relatively moderate capital investment, is easy to install and provides for easy expansion of facilities. If unit air heaters are used, they should be spaced and directed to blanket the entire area with heated air (Fig. 4-2).

Of prime consideration, often ignored, either purposely or from a lack of understanding of what consequences might occur, is the use of unvented or improperly vented gas or oil-fired units. These units produce CO_2 gas which is necessary for improved plant growth. However, other gases that are harmful to humans (carbon monoxide) and many plants (ethylene, sulphur dioxide and unburned hydrocarbons) are also byproducts of combustion. These can cause serious problems if the unit heater's exhaust is not properly vented to the outside and if adequate intake air is not available for combustion.

Heaters normally operate at night when the plants cannot use the CO_2 produced. Another byproduct of combustion is water vapor. High nighttime concentration of CO_2 and water vapor in a closed house with a lowered oxygen supply (combustion uses oxygen) is generally considered undesirable from the standpoint of disease control. Test kits are available to measure the levels of

CO_2 in a greenhouse. To assure good air movement to the outside through the vent stack—necessary only in larger houses—make sure the vent pipe is of adequate size.

Electric Space Heaters

For small greenhouse, up to 12′ in length in areas where the temperatures do not freeze, the most efficient and safest heating system is the electric space heater. Controlled by a thermostat that is set to turn on if temperatures dip to 32 F, it can be placed on the floor in any location in the greenhouse.

In greenhouses above 12 feet, two or several space heaters can be placed in different areas to provide adequate temperatures throughout the greenhouse. If more than one space heater is used, set thermostats at the same reading to assure uniform temperature flow (Fig. 4-3).

Considerations for Selection

If a more sophisticated heating system is necessary—as outlined in the section on a unit space heater—for areas where it freezes and for larger greenhouses, certain factors need to be considered prior to selecting the right system for your particular needs.

A dependable source of heat is necessary for temperature control. The best type of system will depend on many factors. These factors should be carefully considered before you invest in heating equipment. What is best for one operator might not be best for another.

Before determining the type of system to use, it is necessary to calculate the amount of heat that will be required. This should be based on the most adverse conditions that you will reasonably encounter. For instance, if an outside low temperature is 25 F to 30 F in one area, 15 F to 20 F in another, and around 35 F in another, the minimum inside temperature will depend upon the types of plants being grown. Some tropicals cease to grow at 55 F to 60 F and the plants are killed at about 45 F. Many plants, including tropicals, don't suffer any adverse effects at slightly frosty temperatures.

Decide whether you just want to save the plants from severe injury or if you want normal or near normal growth to continue. Then determine the temperature needed to achieve your objective. Subtract the expected minimum adverse temperature for your

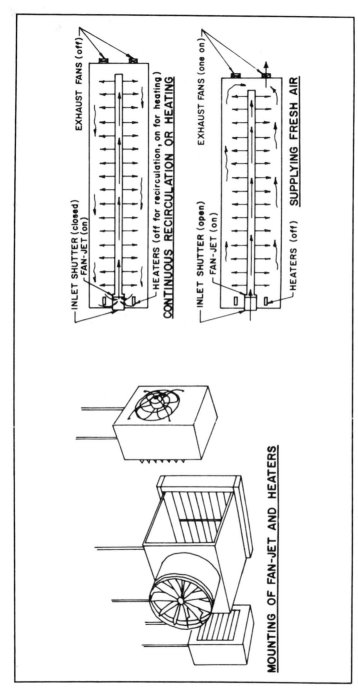

EXHAUST FANS (off)

INLET SHUTTER (closed)
FAN-JET (on)
HEATERS (off for recirculation, on for heating)
CONTINUOUS RECIRCULATION OR HEATING

EXHAUST FANS (one on)

INLET SHUTTER (open)
FAN-JET (on)
HEATERS (off)
SUPPLYING FRESH AIR

MOUNTING OF FAN-JET AND HEATERS

Fig. 4-2. Schematic of a fan-jet polytube system.

Fig. 4-3. A 22-V space heater (courtesy of Evert Thompson Advertising Architecture).

location and obtain the differential in degrees F for which you need to be prepared.

An easy and fairly accurate method for estimating the amount of heat required can be obtained as follows. Multiply the surface area of the greenhouse by the maximum temperature difference to be maintained, and this product, times a heat transmission factor. The transmission factor depends on the coverage of the greenhouse and it is also influenced by the quality of construction.

Check List to Eliminate Problems

☐ Vent all fossil-fueled unit heaters to the outside of any enclosed house. The vent stack should extend a minimum of four feet above the house ridge or any nearby building (Fig. 4-4).

☐ Make sure that you have good air ventilation. Auxiliary fans are sometimes a good investment and especially for larger greenhouses.

☐ Locate thermostats to control the system near plant bed level.

☐ Do not expose the thermostat to a nearby heat source or draft.

☐ Check all burner nozzles, clean fan blades, and oil fan the motor as recommended by the manufacturer prior to initial operation.

☐ Check all flues for leaks.

☐ Do not use unvented fossil-fuel heaters. If, however, you feel this is necessary to save your plants—in freeze zones where house is operated during the winter—from freezing, provide as much ventilation (either natural or mechanical) as practical to reduce damage from the byproducts of combustion. Determine the degree of tolerance of plants prior to the heating season if it is anticipated that unvented heaters might have to be used.

☐ Contact your fuel dealer well in advance to be sure of an adequate fuel supply in the event of a fuel shortage.

☐ Check the accuracy of thermostat calibration. Have all thermostats checked against one that you know is accurate.

☐ Check all equipment at the end of a heating season to be sure that it is in good condition for the next year.

While the cost of electricity is constantly on the rise, the 100 percent efficiency of electric heat, which has no "up the flue" or venting losses, still makes it the most desirable heating method for the home greenhouse.

No matter what style, type or material the greenhouse is made of, the greenhouser can control heating and/or cooling costs with a relatively small amount of time and financial outlay. Almost every plant can withstand from five to 10 degrees less heat without damage.

There are a variety of things that can be done, for those who desire to spend the time and extra finances, to gain as much "heat

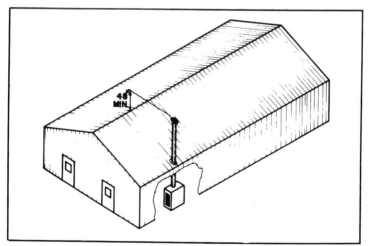

Fig. 4-4. Outside vent set at 48″ above the ridge of the greenhouse.

savings" as possible. The green house can be "double-skinned" with 2-mil or 4-mil polyethelene. This has a claimed heat savings of up to 40 percent. This figure, however, has been derived from laboratory testing and in all probability the 40 percent figure would not be accurate under normal conditions.

Tenting the growing area with polyethelene and directing heat under the tented area will only alleviate heat waste in the balance of the cubic feet of air in the greenhouse. A note of caution is required if this is done. Before the tenting is removed during the day, ascertain that the remainder of the greenhouse is up to the minimum required growing temperature for your plants.

For any greenhouse, attached or free-standing, the cold walls or ends on the north and west can be insulated by using polystyrene panels taped together and held in place with clear poly film. This will cost about 30 cents per square foot or less.

In the most extreme winter climates, the southern exposure wall should be double-skinned with clear material for maximum solar input. When the sun is no longer on this exposure, an insulating blanket can be rolled down to cut heat radiation losses at night.

Although you might lose some growing space by placing rock, brick or water-filled containers under the benches in the greenhouse, these materials will absorb the heat during the day and will radiate it back when temperatures drop. This method can cut heat costs, to a great or lesser degree, depending on the weather and how much storage area is available. Most small home greenhouses do not have indoor watering systems and it is common to have buckets of water for ready use under the benches.

For those who don't plan to use their greenhouse year around, during the coldest periods of the year it can be used to store firewood. The wood will dry up to 35 percent faster than conventional outdoor drying stacks. The wood will burn better and it is more convenient because it is closer to the house.

VENTILATION

The ventilation system must be able to change the air once each minute in a large greenhouse. The system must change the air 1½ times each minute in a small hobby greenhouse. Winter ventilation requirements are about one-fourth of the air changed per minute. Two fans, with one having two speeds, are often used. The low speed of one fan is enough for winter. Motorized intake louvers are placed on the opposite wall.

The volume of a greenhouse is length times width times average height. The total is given in cubic feet. The fan rating will be in cubic feet per minute (cfm).

The ventilation may be natural—caused by wind and temperature forces or mechanical—accomplished by using fans. Ventilation provides control of high temperatures during the summer (caused by the influx of solar radiation), maintenance of relative humidity at acceptable levels during the winter, (providing uniform air flow throughout the entire greenhouse), and maintaining acceptable levels of gas concentration in the greenhouse.

Ventilation prevents too high a rise in temperature and introduces fresh air into the house. The air circulates and keeps the air already in the house dry. This cuts down on the condensation that builds up in all greenhouses. Condensation is especially apparent in greenhouses covered with glass. This can have a good or adverse effect on your plants.

Stagnant air nurtures plant disease. Ideal ventilation lets warm air in through the bottom of the greenhouse. This air is cooled by the shade under the benches. Normally, cold air settles to the ground. In the greenhouse, it is forced to rise by the pressure of the incoming warm air. An exhaust fan accelerates the rise of the cooled air. The air then moves up and over the plants before escaping through the top vents. Figure 4-5 shows details of a manual gear operator for a roof vent sash. Figure 4-6 is an inlet vent that is ideal for a small greenhouse. It can be installed in the bottom of a greenhouse door.

While there are no specific rules for opening or closing the vents, it is well to leave them open at all times other than when a freeze or other inclement conditions are predicted to cause a drastic temperature change.

Fan ventilation systems should be designed and installed so that air moves with prevailing summer winds rather than against them. This procedure will eliminate opposing air forces that can decrease the air flow rate by 10 percent or more. Usually, exhaust fans are installed in the leeward end of the greenhouse and fresh air inlet shutters are installed in the windward end. However, sometimes a sidewall fan location in the leeward side and fresh air inlets on each end are best for certain houses.

Winter Ventilation

To maintain environmental conditions inside the greenhouse conductive for plant growth and development, a heating system

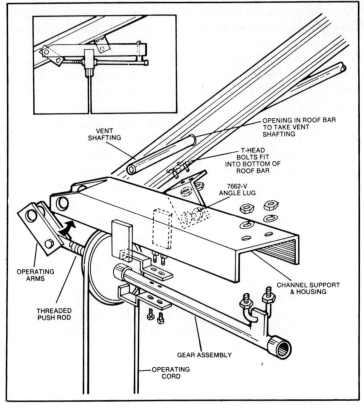

Fig. 4-5. Manual Gear for roof vent sash (courtesy of Lord & Burnham Co.).

with adequate capacity is needed if the greenhouse is to be operated during the coldest months of winter. Even during the coldest part of the winter, when the heating system is running at full capacity, some ventilation is still required in the greenhouse. Fresh outside air must be ventilated into the greenhouse to remove the warm, moisture-laden air from within the greenhouse. If it is not removed, high humidities and excessive condensation will occur. Studies have shown that humidities over 90 percent foster rapid development of leaf mold and fruit and stem rot. Infection of leaf mold on tomatoes actually occurs at humidities above 80 percent. Below 75 percent humidity, problems with infection are slight.

Ventilation requirements of a greenhouse during the winter are generally on the order of two to three air changes per hour. The higher the inside temperature in the greenhouse, the lower the air exchange rate that is required to maintain humidities below the damaging level. However, under no circumstances should a ventilation rate of less than two air changes per hour be used. Besides controlling humidity, this minimum ventilation rate is required to remove any combustible gases that might be present as a result of leaks around the heater and ducting when a direct-fixed heating system is used.

Summer Ventilation

The primary purpose of ventilation in a greenhouse during the summer is to prevent the air temperature inside the greenhouse from rising too high above the outside air temperature. Higher air temperature during the summer prevails due to the large influx of solar radiation through the greenhouse glazing material.

Filtering out a portion of solar radiation can be effective in reducing the inside air temperature of a greenhouse. This can be

Fig. 4-6. Inlet vent (courtesy of Evert Thompson Advertising Architecture).

accomplished by using saran shade fabric stretched eave-to-eave within the greenhouse and sprinkling the roof with a fine mist of water. Filtering solar radiation to decrease heat load on a greenhouse should only be done for those operating a greenhouse solely for plants which do not require "full sun."

COOLING

More difficult than keeping the greenhouse warm in cold weather is cooling it in the summer. The majority of plants enjoy excessive heat if a high humidity is maintained (a humidifier is recommended). Shading provides cooling and it is necessary only if you plan to operate your greenhouse year around.

Shading can be accomplished with moveable slats or lathes, colored netting (muslin) spread above bedding plants, painting the glass (or the fiberglass), or the use of venetian blinds made of light weight, durable plastic. This last item is easy to operate, allows you to adjust the amount of light being let in the greenhouse.

During the summer, it is helpful to use an exhaust vent fan or fans. The number of fans depends upon the size of the greenhouse. The fans assist in moving the air through the greenhouse to regulate temperature and humidity, to provide air around plants and to produce a constant supply of fresh oxygen and carbon dioxide. The fans can be set on the greenhouse floor or mounted securely on the rear wall of the greenhouse (Fig. 4-7).

Both ventilation and evaporative cooling require the introduction of large quantities of outside air during bright warm days. A common method of doing this is to place fans in one sidewall or end and introduce the air through baffles, pads or louvers in the opposite end. When this is done, the air picks up the solar heat in the house as it moves across the house. The result is that the air gradually increases in temperature as it nears the fan. If this temperature rise and air velocity are to be kept within reasonable limits, especially in larger houses, the distance across the house from the fans to the air inlet openings should not be more than 100 to 140 feet. The house length or width in the other direction can be any desired dimension depending on the size of greenhouse range desired.

INSULATION

To keep cold and drafts out of the greenhouse, an easy-to-install insulation is manufactured by the Aircap Corporation. It is distributed by Lord & Burnham, Irvington-on-Hudson, New York. This particular insulation keeps the cold out and lets light in. It is an excellent means of reducing expensive heat loss with a simple method. Studies conducted show that this easy-to-apply, light-transmitting material cuts heat loss in a greenhouse 25 percent to 35 percent while reducing normal visible light by only 12 percent.

This type of material is especially important during cold, windy days when sudden heat loss could mean dangerous icy build-up on the inside of the glass that could threaten your plants and strain your heating system. It helps seal cracks and laps to reduce drafts and air infiltration. If your greenhouse heater is slightly undersized, you will find that by using such a material it will easily make the difference.

If you are operating a greenhouse that requires diffused light, this material can be left on year around. The sun's scorching glare is also reduced. This material, therefore, takes the place of insulation and light diffusing material.

Each roll is 30″ x 150 feet long. One roll will fit a 10 x 16 lean-to. Two rolls fit a 14 x 20 even span. To install:

☐ Measure the length of material required and precut strips long enough to cover each light (glass pane or length required for fiberglass or plastic houses cut either lengthwise or widthwise). See Fig. 4-8.

Fig. 4-7. Vent exhaust fan (courtesy of Evert Thompson Advertising Architecture).

Fig. 4-8. Measuring insulating material (courtesy of Costitch and McConnell, for Lord & Burnham).

☐ If the glass in the greenhouse is dry, thoroughly wet the glass with a garden hose or sponge. If normal condensation is present, evenly distribute the moisture using a wet sponge or water spout (Fig. 4-9).

☐ Apply liquid adhesive evenly to the glass using a paint roller (smooth surfaces type) or paint brush. After use, rinse the brush or roller with water.

☐ Apply Aircap material by simply pressing bubbles onto the glass. *Do not* stretch the material.

☐ For best results, smooth the material with a wallpaper brush to assure firm contact with the glass (Fig. 4-10).

☐ Trim the edges if necessary for a smooth, neat, clean appearance throughout (Fig. 4-11).

☐ After the winter heating season, the material can be removed. Peel the material back, wet the glass to dissolve the adhesive and remove the insulation.

Clean the glass, if necessary, with water and a wet sponge. Note: If the liquid adhesive freezes, fully dissolve it before using. Keep it out of contact with your skin and eyes. If this should occur, wash your skin or flush your eyes with water. If adhesive comes in contact with your eyes, consult a physician. Adhesive is not to be taken internally. (This information is provided courtesy of Lord & Burnham, Distributor for Aircap Window Insulation.)

FANS

Fans are used for drying, ventilating, heating, cooling, aspirating, elevating and conveying. Selection of the right fan for

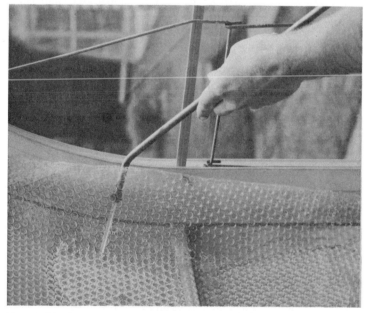

Fig. 4-9. Wet down insulation prior to applying to the glass (courtesy of Costitch and McConnell, for Lord & Burnham).

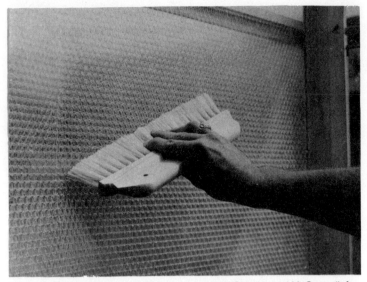

Fig. 4-10. Smooth AirCap with Brush (courtesy of Costitch and McConnell, for Lord & Burnham).

your particular home greenhouse is important. Learning a little about fans will help you make the right decision prior to purchase. This is especially important for the larger home greenhouse.

What is a Fan?

A fan is an air pump. It is a machine that creates a pressure difference and causes air to flow. Depending on the fan type, it provides static and kinetic energy that varies in proportion. The impeller does the work on the air. The propeller fan, essentially an air screw, is used for moving large quantities of air against low static pressures and is the most common fan used for ventilation in a greenhouse.

When selecting a fan, the following information must be known. These factors will govern the type of fan to be selected and its size.

☐ Volume of air to be moved per unit time.

☐ Static pressure: the estimated system resistance and expected variations.

☐ Space available for installing fans.

☐ Efficiency: select a fan that will deliver the required volume at the expected static pressure with the minimum horse-power.

☐ Economic considerations.

Fig. 4-11. Fully insulated greenhouse (courtesy of Costitch and McConnell, for Lord & Burnham).

Fan selection is based on the static pressure for a given volume of air that needs to be moved. Although the volume of air desired can be calculated accurately, the static pressure requirement can only be estimated. For most greenhouse applications, the static pressure resistance will be no higher than 0.10 to 0.15 inches of water. However, when using fans as part of an evaporative or cooling system be sure to obtain the static pressure drop across the cooling pad from the manufacturer. Some of the new types of cooling pads might have higher static pressure requirements than the conventional aspen pad.

If the actual system pressure requirement for a given volume flow is unown, the characteristic curve of a system can be calculated. For most normal systems, this curve is a parabola (as shown in Fig. 4-12) with its origin at zero volume, zero pressure, with the pressure varying as the square of the volume. If the volume flow through a given system is doubled, then the pressure required will be four times greater.

A fan at a given rotational speed has a characteristic pressure/volume curve from wide open volume with no static pressure resistance to block tight with no air movement. Figure 4-13 shows a typical fan characteristic curve.

When the fan characteristic curve is superimposed on the ventilation system characteristic curve, as shown in Fig. 4-12, the intersection of these two curves is the point of operation and is the only point on the system curve at which the fan can operate. Selecting a drive that will allow fan speed to be easily changed within recommended limits is important because system pressure requirements are never exactly known.

Manufacturers supply fan rating tables that supply the static pressure-volume relationships to the right of the peak pressure. Table 4-2 is a fan rating table for three common size fans that are capable of supplying approximately 10,000 cfm (cubic feet per minute) of air.

Fan No. 1 delivers 10,200 cfm at conditions of free air. Free air means there is no static pressure. However, at ⅛" static pressure, the air flow rate drops to 9200 cfm and finally to 4300 cfm at ⅜" static pressure.

Fan No. 2 supplies 10,200 cfm at ⅛" static pressure and drops to 7560 cfm at ⅜" static pressure.

Fan No. 3 delivers much more than 10,000 cfm at all static pressures below three-eighths of an inch. Only at ⅜" static pressure does Fan No. 3 deliver 10,400 cfm.

If you are selecting a fan to deliver 10,000 cfm for greenhouse ventilation and the expected static pressure in the greenhouse is ⅛" of water, then the proper choice would be Fan No. 2. Fan No. 1 could not deliver enough at ⅛" static pressure and Fan No. 3 would deliver too much air.

Fan No. 2 would be much more efficient because it operated close to its peak pressure. Fan No. 1 would be operating far to the right of its peak pressure. Consequently, too, Fan No. 2 would be quieter than Fan No. 1. Furthermore, Fan No. 1 would be more expensive than Fan No. 2 because of its inherent capabilities that are not being utilized in this application.

Whenever selecting a specific brand of fans, make sure the fan manufacturer tests and rates the fan according to AMCA standards. Otherwise the performance characteristics supplied with a fan might not be dependable. All reputable fan manufacturers rate their fans in accordance with AMCA standards.

Maintenance of Fans

☐ Be sure the fan blades, fan housing, and shutters are clean. The accumulation of only several ounces of dust on fan blades can create enough imbalance in the blade to reduce operating efficiency by 30 percent. Clean fans and components as often as necessary to prevent dust accumulations.

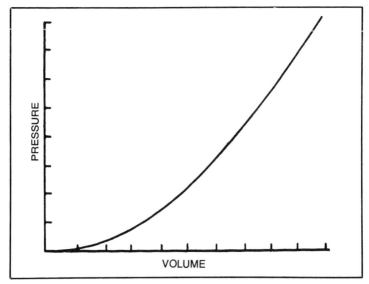

Fig. 4-12. Ventilation system characteristic curve.

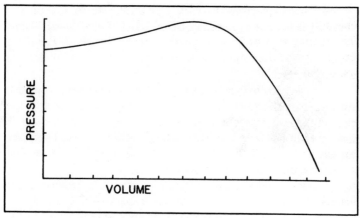

Fig. 4-13. Representative fan characteristic curve.

☐ Whenever you clean the fans, lubricate the fan bearings, motor, and shutters. Any parts that do not move freely should be replaced.

☐ Check the fan belts for proper tension to prevent slippage. If the belts are cracking, splitting, or fraying, replace them immediately. Otherwise, the belt might fail when no one is available to install a new belt.

☐ Inspect the electrical supply cords to the fan from the receptacle and from the thermostat. Whenever the insulation begins to crack or split, replace them with UL-approved insulated wire.

☐ Check the fan wheel for proper rotation. Fan rotation is sometimes reversed when fans are installed, repaired, or when wiring circuits or starters are alternated. Fans move a fraction of their rated capacity when running backwards. Reversed direction often goes unnoticed in spite of much less efficient performance. Proper direction of rotation is generally marked on the fan housing.

☐ Remove weeds and shrubs growing outside the greenhouse within close proximity of the fan. Nothing should obstruct the flow of air from the fan within a distance of two blade diameters of the fan. Any weeds or shrubs would make it harder for the fan to exhaust the air. Therefore, the fan would operate with lower efficiency.

☐ Never allow any obstructions that would limit the flow of air into a fan within a distance of one blade diameter of a fan. Any obstructions to the flow of air would also make the fan operate with less efficiency.

☐ When it is necessary to replace the fan motor, always replace it with a totally enclosed motor having sealed bearings. This type motor is required to protect the motor windings from the corrosive effects of the high humidities and dust accumulations that would otherwise shorten the service life of the motor.

☐ Check for openings around fan housings that permit air flow to bypass the desired air inlet pattern. Close all openings in the house where outside air enters the house at locations other than the desired inlets. Heating and cooling efficiencies are important.

☐ Calibrate thermostats and humidistats to insure that fans operate according to the prescribed environmental conditions. Be sure to carefully wipe any accumulated dust from the sensing elements of the controls before calibrating. Aspirated sensing units are preferred because of increased time response rates to change in greenhouse environments. Thermostats and humidistats should be placed at or near crop level, rather than human level, to insure most accurate environmental control for the plants.

HUMIDITY

Proper relative humidity, the moisture content of the air, is a tremendously important key to success and good greenhouse management. The small initial cost of installing an automatic humidifier (Fig. 4-14) will be returned countless times in more luxuriant plant growth year around.

AIR DISTRIBUTION WITHIN THE GREENHOUSE

Air movement is important to plant growth. Continuous positive air movement is highly desirable because it equalizes temperature, carbon dioxide, and humidity levels. By constantly working to improve environmental conditions within the greenhouse, healthier plant growth can be obtained and problems with disease, associated with high humidity of "stale air," are lessened.

WATERING

Watering is an important aspect that depends on the types of plants being raised, size and whether or not you are operating the

Table 4-2. Fan Comparisons.

	Blade Diameter	Free Air	⅛" SP	¼" SP	⅜" SP	Fan RPM	Motor HP
Fan 1	30"	10200	9200	7400	4300	640	¾
Fan 2	36"	11700	10220	8690	7560	650	1
Fan 3	54"	29100	22300	14100	14100	385	2

Fig. 4-14. Humidifer (courtesy of Evert Thompson, Advertising Architecture).

house occasionally or all year long. Plants putting on faster growth—new and young plants—require more water. This also applies to plants kept in the house all year around.

Some plants, such as cinerarias and hydrangeas, require an abundance of water. Other plants such as certain species of orchids, cyclamen and many cacti require less water. Plants raised in a soil mixture containing more sand must be watered more frequently. Plants and seeds in larger pots remain moist longer than those in smaller pots.

Watering should be done early in the morning to allow excess moisture to evaporate before nightfall. If you are unable to water early in the morning, wait until the sun goes down. Keep in mind that it is, on the whole, better to underwater than overwater. The plants should never be soggy. The soil should be damp to the touch; not dry, not soggy, not dripping wet—but moist to where the soil is friable and slips through the fingers easily.

Plants themselves are indicators of their watering needs. If a plant wilts, you have waited too long to water in most cases. Cacti, for instance, prefer to have the soil dry out completely and then thoroughly watered. This brings them into bloom. A rule of thumb is: plants should be watered when the top one-half inch of soil in the pot is dry to the touch.

Watering will also depend to a great extent on the tempera-ture range of the greenhouse, the time of year and the types of plants you are raising. Plants in clay pots require more frequent watering than do those in plastic containers. Plants in semidormancy or bulbous varieties that are "drying off" need only sufficient water to keep the soil from becoming bone dry.

Capillary watering of pot plants is possible by placing them on a bed of sand kept continuously moist. *Overwatering* will slowly kill your plants. If you use a sprinkler can, do not water so late in the evening that the leaves of plants stay wet at night. Wet leaves encourage plant diseases. If your soil becomes waterlogged, the plants will die from lack of oxygen.

Syringing on hot days is beneficial in that it reduces leaf temperature. It is not, however, a substitute for watering. In addition there are some plants that don't enjoy syringing. Learning the individual plant's needs is the key to successful greenhousing. The safe rule of thumb is water in the morning *before* the sun is high.

As plants grow to maturity, they require less water and many go through a dormant period when little or no water is needed. Plants maintained in pots and other containers require more frequent watering than those in ground beds.

If you are raising plants all year long, the heated greenhouse must be kept humid. This can be obtained by wetting (watering) down the walls and benches. Additional dampening should be done on days when it is very sunny rather than on dull cloudy days and it will be required more often when ventilators are left open than when they are closed.

If you are specializing in tropicals that need high humidity, the plants themselves should be syringed lightly so as to prevent wilting. Water early in the morning in order that the foliage is dry by nightfall.

After you have thoroughly watered the potted plants, seedlings and ground beds, soak the benches thoroughly. When they are dry, it is your indicator that it is time to water again. This takes the guesswork out of whether or not each individual pot needs moisture.

Another indication of watering needs, with clay pots, is the "feel of the pot." If you hear a "thud" upon tapping the pot then the soil is moist. If a "pinging" sound emanates—water. Also, a lighter weight pot means dryer soil than a heavier one.

Another rule of thumb is that a good soaking is preferable rather than superficial sprinkling. This applies throughout the greenhouse.

CONDENSATION

Condensation occurs when warm, moist air in a greenhouse comes in contact with a cold surface such as fiberglass, plastic, glass or structural members. The air in contact with the cold surface is cooled to the temperature of the surface. If the surface temperature is below the dew point temperature of the air, the water vapor in the air will condense onto the surface. For example, condensation will occur if air in a greenhouse at 70 F and 70 percent relative humidity comes in contact with a surface that is 60 F or colder.

Most of the condensation problems in a greenhouse occur when the minimum outside temperature drops below 50 F. In most areas, this occurs between November and March. Condensation will form the heaviest in greenhouses during the period from sundown to several hours after sunrise. During the daylight hours, there is sufficient heating in the greenhouse from solar radiation (the sun) to minimize or eliminate condensation from occurring except on very cold, cloudy days. The time when greenhouses are most likely to experience heavy condensation is sunrise or shortly before. At that time, the outside air temperature is usually at a minimum.

Condensation Control. Condensation forming on the inside surface of greenhouses is of considerable economic significance. Economic problems associated with condensation in greenhouses are fungus diseases, difficulty in maintaining a clean greenhouse, more rapid deterioration of structural components, and damp, uncomfortable environmental conditions in which to work.

Four general methods exist for controlling condensation:

☐ Exhaust moist air and replacing it with heated outside air.

☐ Provide continuous air movement. This is not so necessary in smaller houses.

☐ Apply double layer coverings.

☐ Use a wetting agent.

Of the four methods, only exhausting moist air and replacing it with heated outside air is really effective in eliminating condensation.

LIGHT EXPOSURE

The small home greenhouse requires many environmental conditions and situations and one very important aspect is light. You have constructed your home greenhouse with the most up-to-date materials designed and required. Why then the need for so many considerations—ventilation, aeration, heat, etc.? Because logically "all things are connected."

Some plants enjoy the sun's fullest rays while others do best in shade. The common denominator is that all plants need carbon dioxide, water, plus additional chemical values supplied by photosynthesis (Fig. 4-15).

Because the intensity of light on sunny, summer days might be excessive, plants might do better if they are partially shaded. This is accomplished with little difficulty by placing muslin or any type of netting or screening above the plants. Plants grown in excessive sunlight appear short with heavy stems with small pale leaves and the flowers often are bleached. With the correct amount of light—or shade—the stems will grow longer, the leaves larger and the color of the leaves and flowers brighter.

A plant's stems will turn toward a light source. This is caused by the greater enlargement of the cells in the plant on the shaded side of its stem.

Chlorophyll—the pigment in the plant—is also affected by light. If it appears yellow this can be corrected by moving the plant into an area with more light if it is too shaded. However, with too much light, both leaves and flowers will not be as bright in color. Photosynthesis stops at night, the plants absorb oxygen and give off carbon dioxide.

Regardless of the species, all plants absorb carbon dioxide, water and other inorganic minerals. Prior to a plant being able to reproduce, plants need to grow to a certain stage. According to reports, a prominent factor in the timing of plant maturity is the length of days and nights in the particular area on earth in which a plant is planted. It has to grow to a developmental stage. Therefore, timing/light plays a decisive role in its growth. The length of days and nights vary from, for example, the Gulf Coast states to the Northern zones. The time (hours) of less or more light is important to blossom production.

Growth characteristics are determined by light factors. Examples are bulb formation and the color and shape of leaves. Scientifically it is known as *photoperiodism* and is commonly known as the rhythm of light.

Light and dark hours vary in the greenhouse, but a togetherness can be achieved—again by learning what you want to enjoy and raise—be it specialization of one species or many.

For example, carnations and snapdragaons grow far better and are more prolific in their flowering with full sun, while others—African violets, philodendron, begonias, and gloxinias—prefer shade. Sun loving plants produce more food at high light intensity

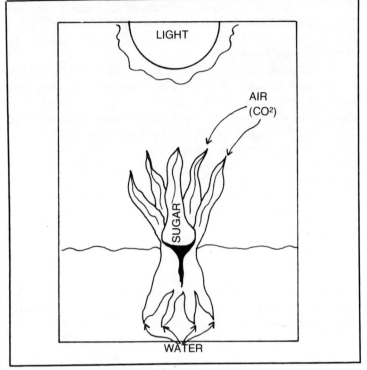

Fig. 4-15. Photosynthesis process.

than in the shade. All plants, however, must have some light even though higher lit intensity does not increase the amount of food produced to the rate of growth. Often, too much light has an adverse affect and causes burning of leaves. Therefore, shade loving plants in the greenhouse must be placed in a position or provided some additional attention in order to reduce the intensity of light.

Both sun and shade loving plants can be raised successfully in the same greenhouse with the use of area shading. The shaded area is ideal for freshly sown seeds, tender seedlings and root cuttings.

For larger greenhouses where a great variety of plants are grown, fluorescent lights can be used to great advantage. With fluorescent light, the amount of illumination is the same all the time. If you have a double light, 40 inches long (standard measurement) you will get the results shown in Table 4-3. Most of the light is emitted from the center of the tube with less at the ends. This is advantageous because a light loving plant, such as a geranium, can be set directly beneath the center while clippings and other plants requiring less light can be placed at the lamp's ends. Fluorescent lights are cool. This eliminates any danger of light burn (Fig. 4-16).

By watching your plants under fluorescent lights, you will quickly learn the best distance at which to place them. If the leaves turn brown or lose their color, and if the plant clings to the pot, it is too much light. If they begin to get leggy and willowy with sparse bloom, the light is insufficient. Usually, non-blooming plants require less light than those that bloom.

There are many flowering plants that are particularly conducive to being raised under fluorescent lights. African violets bloom profusely when set 12″ under fluorescent lights and their foliage appears glossy and velvety. Gloxinias just need to clear the lights. At 750-foot-candles distance—3″ from the pot—begonias do extremely well. At 400-foot-candles, 5″ to 6″ from the pot, caladiums require a minumum of care. Orchids, miniature roses and geraniums are perfectly at home under the lights.

Incandescent Lights. Incandescent lights can be used in the fall and winter on long days. Install one reflector with a 60-watt incandescent bulb every 4 to 5 feet of bench space. Plug this into an automatic timer set to turn the lights on at 5 p.m. and off at 10 p.m. daily. Generally, this supplmentary light is provided from the time seedlings or young plants are making vigorous active growth until the flower buds are beginning to open (Fig. 4-17).

FLOORS

A plain dirt floor is best covered with gravel or crushed rock; it won't dehumidify the air and dry out your plants. The washed gravel is not only attractive it is functional. Besides helping retention of moisture throughout the gravel—which seeps into the

Inches from Light	**Foot Candles**
1″	1,000
2″	950
3″	750
4″	650
5″	560
6″	460
7″	430
8″	370
9″	360
10″	350

Table 4-3. Fluorescent Light Illumination.

Fig. 4-16. Plants grown under fluorescent lights (courtesy of Kathleen Bourke, Lord & Burnham Co.).

plants through the pots set under the benches—the floor does not get muddy from watering. Aisles of slate brick or building blocks are also attractive.

Black plastic that is 4 to 6 mils thick makes an excellent floor covering because it keeps weeds from growing up into the house. Therefore, it aids in pest and insect control.

If your greenhouse is to be built other than *on-grade* (on the roof of a building), a waterproof floor is necessary.

Ground Beds

In free-standing greenhouses, the use of ground beds allows more bench space. When plants are to be raised in the soil, select a site in the greenhouse where deep, good draining soil is available. Avoid top soil below which a tight hardpan is present. Although organic matter and artificial types of conditioners can be added, problems are reduced if a site with good natural soil is selected. If this is not possible, then the soil presently in the site should be completely removed—insofar as possible—and fresh soil added. Grading often produces uneven soil conditions within the greenhouse. Careful soil analysis and preparation are necessary if even plant growth is to be achieved.

Avoid areas where chemical residues would injure greenhouse crops. This includes places heavily sprayed with damaging weed killers and herbicides. This is another reason to use some type of ground covering. If you question the degree of danger—if indeed it exists at all—grow selected plants in samples of the soil to determine if any detrimental injury occurs. If your samples show any signs of nonsalubrious condition, then the soil should be thoroughly tested (even removed and new soil placed in the bed) to determine what the prevailing conditions existing in the soil are and the soil either treated or removed and replaced with a fresh supply of good sterilized soil. Noxious weeds can also be a problem, but generally proper sterilization methods will kill most weed seeds.

Cleanliness

Hygiene is a must in the greenhouse regardless of its size. Although it is difficult to keep from overcrowding in the smaller size home greenhouse, overcrowding is a major cause of uncleanliness. It is, therefore, important that a regular program be initiated from the onset and adhered to in order to minimize the likelihood of susceptibility to insects and other organic diseases.

Keep the house free of debris insofar as possible. Old pots, stakes, leaf residues, unhealthy or diseased plants—any material if allowed to accumulate—provides a breeding ground for organisms that cause diseases and provide a bedding for insects and other pests.

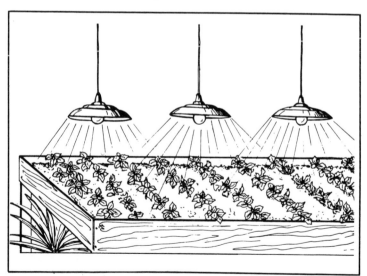

Fig. 4-17. Incandescent lights (courtesy of Kathleen Bourke, Lord & Burnham Co.).

If wood shelves or benches are used, they should be painted at least every third year. An annual scrubbing of the entire greenhouse, including benches, should be carried out with strong soap, disinfectant and hot water. Spraying the greenhouse with an organic pesticide is advisable at least once yearly. Any plants not in a salubric condition should be discarded immediately before other plants become infected if there is any sign of disease.

Algae quickly adheres to pots and should be washed off as soon as time permits. The outside of the greenhouse also requires yearly maintenance because algae and other substances cling to the structure and cut down light emission.

Excessive crowding is prevalent in the small home greenhouse because the tendency is to crowd as many plants as possible into limited space. Fewer, but healthier plants, will produce more pleasure than an overabundance of plants which will produce excessive problems. For good greenhouse maintenance:

☐ Keep only healthy plants.
☐ Keep benches and pots as clean as possible.
☐ Clear all debris.
☐ Wash tools regularly in disinfectant.

SOIL

Plants confined to pots or flats—and space in a home greenhouse being limited—should be kept only if healthy and productive. Sterilized soil is advantageous because it kills off any bacteria that might be in the soil. Potting soil should consist of equal parts compost, peat and sand with perlite added. Sifting compost is viable to mix with the peat and you can never use too much.

Keep in mind the particular plant you are working with because it will have its own soil requirements such as less or higher nitrogen or higher or lower pH. In all cases, soil should be kept looser than in the garden in order that good drainage and moisture retention is assured.

Soil for a hot frame and or seed flats should be light and porous because young seedlings cannot grow into healthy plants in too rich a mixture under greenhouse conditions.

Buckets containing fresh soil, sphagnum and peat should be stored under the benches to provide a ready supply of good, fresh soil for adding to pots and potting new plants. All soils are either acid or alkaline and this has an affect on the life of your plant. Learn just what type of soil each plant requires and then act accordingly.

In this regard, the term *pH* is important to understand because it could mean success or failure for your plant life. The term is used to express the amounts of acidity or alkalinity in the soil and literally means "hydrogen-ion." With an incorrect pH, you acquire such conditions as stunted growth and sparse production.

The initials pH were derived from the German H which means hydrogen and the p is the term used for the negative logarithmic mix value; pH value runs from 0 to 14 and soil factors between 4 and 9. The art of good greenhouse soil cultivation management is to bring the pH factor of the soil up to a reading which will be close to pH 7. This level is considered "neutral." This will provide for near perfect soil conditions regardless of the variety of plants you are growing.

In other words, if your soil checks out to a pH factor of 5:00 it is 10 times as acidic. This will, of course, be fine for plants needing an extra acidic soil condition. Learning the specific soil needs will be necessary for each plant.

Most plants prefer a neutral soil. If any particular variety of plant, ornamental or otherwise, require a more acidic soil condition, it can be corrected by the addition of fertilizers. The same applies to those plants which require a higher alkalinity. Keeping the soil at a neutralized reading pH of 7:00 will provide you with conditions which are more favorable for useful soil bacteria (Fig. 4-18).

FERTILIZERS

Plants kept and raised in the greenhouse require constant, but not over fertilizing. Fertilizing your plants is another way of saying that you are "feeding" them. Along with other elements already discussed—light, air, water, temperature—plants must be well fed and correctly fed to insure healthy plants with abundant fruit or flowers.

There are many commercial fertilizers available. Used alone, however, any one particular fertilizer would not adequately supply the necessary ingredients for all the plants raised in a home greenhouse. Some of the plants your raise will require less or more nitrogen, more or less acidity, alkalinity, phosphorus and other trace elements for the individual variety. All, however, need to begin with a basic mixture.

Organically speaking there are 20 kinds of fertilizers such as: wood ashes, basic slag, leaves, sawdust, blood meal, rock phosphate, greensand, bone meal, peat moss, cottonseed meal,

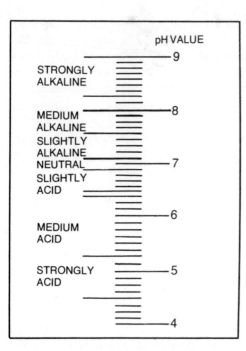

pH VALUE

STRONGLY ALKALINE

MEDIUM ALKALINE

SLIGHTLY ALKALINE

NEUTRAL

SLIGHTLY ACID

MEDIUM ACID

STRONGLY ACID

9

8

7

6

5

4

Fig. 4-18. pH scale.

seaweed, dried manure, peanut shells, leaf mold, wood chips and grass clippings. Besides these organic fertilizers, the soil also needs other foods; these are known as *trace* elements. Magnesium, iron, sulphur, and calcium are just a few elements that—although required in small amounts—are important to the correct growth of healthy plants. Some of these elements have been known to be used as substitutes for other nutrients in addition to increasing resistance to disease.

While you could use each element to provide individual species with their special need, that is not practical. Therefore, by keeping a good supply of well-rounded potting soil, made up of peat moss, leaf mold, compost, manure, sand, perlite and vermiculite, any other element can be added to cater to a specific variety. Make a habit of mixing your fertilizers with water. They are easier to use in liquid form, it provides a uniform feeding and it lessens the chance of burning foliage. Mix fresh animal manure with wood chips, sawdust or peat moss if you plan to use them prior to aging. Compost is the number one soil enricher/constructor/rejuvenator. Best of all, you can never use too much. And it won't burn either. Three major elements are essential to soil: N=Nitrogen, P=Phosphorus, K=Potassium (potash).

General Information on Fertilizers

Blood Meal. This is high in nitrogen (15:00) and a little goes a long way. Use approximately six tablespoons to a bucket of compost filled with water. Put 6 tablespoons of blood meal to every 12 inches of the compost pile.

Bone Meal. This is high in phosophorus (21:00). This fertilizer also carries a goodly nitrogen content making it an ideal combination. It reduces the acidity in soil.

Cottonseed Meal. Acid loving plants need this fertilizer.

Fish Meal. High in phosphorus, this provides a *general* balance to *all* fertilizers.

Lime. This is a very necessary element for most vegetables.

Sludge. Although not as popular, this is an excellent soil builder and it is one of the best sources of natural fertilizers. For the home greenhouseman, it makes a superior additive. The processing method used depends upon its value.

Activated sludge is produced by air bubbling rapidly through it. Usually heat treated prior to being made available, its fertilizer content ranges from 5 percent nitrogen and 3 to 5 percent phosphorus. Its plant food value is similar to cottonseed meal.

Digested sludge is formed when the sewage is left to settle itself without air agitation. Anaerobic (without air) digestion takes about 14 days from the time the sewage reaches the sedimentation tank until the digested solids are pumped into filter beds. The final step is the removal of the dry materials. Digested sludge is lower in nitrogen and phosphorous and, although being odorous when fresh, by the time it is made available it has been sufficiently exposed to the natural elements to eliminate the odor.

Good for lawns, vegetable gardens, flower beds outside, it is certainly a fertilizer to take its place in the "potting mixture" for the greenhouse cultivation. It provides much needed humus along with a moderate but long yielding nitrogen content.

Granite Dust. This is a valuable source of potash and it also has many other trace elements.

Rock Phosphate. An excellent source of phosphorus, it contains many valuable trace elements including calcium, iodine, iron, sodium, magnesium, boron. It is slow acting.

It can be seen from the preceding that plants depend mostly on the soil structure and suitable distribution of necessary mineral particles to keep the soil porous, to permit water to drain away and to permit air to enter.

Values

The first major nutrient is nitrogen. When there is too much or too little of it in the soil, production declines. Nitrogen is responsible for the vegetative growth of plants. Plants with good nitrogen content are sturdy, they mature rapidly and they have a rich, dark green foliage. Lack of sufficient nitrogen is indicated by a lightening of the green color and, with considerable lack of nitrogen, they turn yellow.

Conversely, too much nitrogen can result in as much harm. Commonly, the results are excessive foliage and little or no flowering or fruiting and the decline of flavor and color of both flowers and vegetables.

Phosphorus is the second element of major importance to plants' health. It is essential for growth and strong root systems, fruit development and greater resistance to disease.

The third major nutrient, potassium (potash), is important to the strength of the plant. It is purported to improve preserving quality and the color fruit, helps produce oils, sugar and starch and decrease water requirement and makes the plant more disease resistent. Carrying carbohydrates, through the plant system, it aids in the formation of strong stems. If a plant shows signs of slow growth, becomes stunted, the leaves turn brown and fruits do not mature, there is probably a potassium deficiency.

Trace Elements

Although used in small amounts, trace elements are needed by all plants. Although they constitute only 1 percent of the dry matter of a plant, they are often the major factor that determines the vitality of a plant. A mixture of leaf mold, mulch, compost, lime and rock fertilizers provide a balanced diet of both major and minor trace nutrients.

What Do the Numbers Mean?

The major nutrients are designated: N=Nitrogen, P=Phosphorus, and K=Potassium (potash). Keep in mind that fertilizing feeds the soil first—then the plant. Portions are set out in general terms of 8-8-8; 5-10-5; 4-8-4, etc. The numbers simply indicate the amounts of (1) nitrogen, (2) phosphorus and (3) potassium (potash). For example, 8-8-8 equals 8 percent nitrogen, 8 percent phosphorus and 8 percent potassium; or 5-10-5 equals, 5 percent nitrogen, 10 percent phosphorus and 5 percent potassium.

Whether you use fully organic fertilizers or prepared chemical fertilizers, the numbers all equal NPK. Fully organic fertilizers range from a mixture of 2-4-2 to 3-4-5.

Nitrogen is the major element required by all plants to promote sturdy growth. It lengthens the growing time and provides time for added fruit and flower production. Nitrogen deficient plants have yellow leaves and stunted growth. However, too much nitrogen delays and even stops fruiting. Such nitrogen deficient plants are easily brought back to a salubric condition with additional feedings of nutrients high in nitrogen. Too much, or too little nitrogen, can be corrected by adding low-nitrogen elements to your soil or elements which will lessen the nitrogen content.

When to Feed

Over fertilizing is as bad as under fertilizing. All too often, young seedlings and newly rooted clippings are damaged and even lost. Old established plants also suffer if they are allowed to remain in the same soil and are "forgotten" during fertilizing time. How then can you prevent problems inherent to plant cultivation?

Newly planted seedlings, transplanted cuttings and young plants should not be fertilized until they are placed in their permanent containers. In this case, permanent means until the normal life for the growth of any plant is lived. If soils test to a deficiency of either nitrogen, phosphurus or potassium, additives should be added for correction. If all three are lacking, a highly concentrated mixture needs to be used.

Water soluble fertilizers are preferred over dry because they are easier to use and, for most people, solve the problem of using too much, too close and too soon (which in many instances causes burning). Because a liquid mixture seeps quickly through the plant soil, therefore taking with it some of the fertilization already fed into the plants, feedings are safe and needed every three to four weeks. Nutri-sol is a commercial fertilizer in dry form. It is high in nitrogen and it is an excellent, safe fertilizer when mixed with water. It is highly beneficial for the home greenhouse. Because it can be safely and effectively used on all species, there is no need to worry. It literally takes the guesswork out of feeding.

For larger greenhouses, a piped water system is advantageous because it "sprays" the Nutri-Sol or any other fertilizer of your choice uniformly over the benches. For the owner of a small greenhouse, water soluble fertilizing can be accomplished by mixing the fertilizer, dissolved in a bucket of water, and pouring it over the plants with a long-nosed can or through a syphon hose.

Whether you use dry or wet fertilizers, wetting the pot or bench prior to application is recommended. In this manner, you will be fertilizing and watering simultaneously.

The basic plan to be established for fertilizing with accuracy—as near as possible—is a minimal amount of time and effort. The basic rules are:

☐ Learn the needs of the individual plant.

☐ It is better to under fertilize than over fertilize.

☐ Take regular samplings of new soils mixed, established potted plants' soil, bench/seed bed soil nutrients, and stay abreast of change.

STARTING SEEDS

Perhaps one of the most rewarding greenhouse experiences is the magic of watching those "little brown seeds" turn into flowers and vegetables to provide the home greenhouser the joy of experiencing the full life cycle plants. It is not a difficult task and even the newcomer to greenhousing can be successful without becoming overburdened with the need of additional materials or knowledge. Everything you need is already being used in the greenhouse. By following some easy steps, you will be able to raise all the seedlings you want with complete ease and success.

☐ For seeds to germinate, a bottom temperature of between 70 F and 75 F is desirable. The soil heating cable in your hot frame is the most reliable means of bottom heat. However, most seedlings do well in flats or individual containers kept in a warm area or placed on the soil in the hot frame.

☐ Use screened spaghnum moss mixed with vermiculite for the top half inch of the starting medium. These sterile materials assist in the prevention of damping off of seeds and seedlings.

☐ Many seeds, such as carrots, radishes, and nasturtians, are so fine that it is difficult to separate each one and plant them individually as it would be, for instance, to plant a petunia seed. Therefore, sow seeds as sparingly as possible.

If they are too thick, they will grow bunched together and require more handling, separating and transplanting. When they are bunched together, their air supply is more readily cut off and this causes additional damping-off problems.

You do not have to sow all the seeds in a packet at the same time. The seeds left over should be kept in a dark, dry place, such as a drawer. They can be kept for the following year. On the whole, however, it is best to use fresh seed yearly.

☐ Seeds that are very small—dust-like or powdery—do not need to be covered with soil at the time of planting. They are sown "on top" of the soil medium. For larger seeds, the rule of thumb is—cover them to the depth of their size.

☐ Label each sowing with the name of the variety and the date sown. With flowers label the color and size at maturity.

☐ Water your seedlings (seeds newly sown) daily and in the morning if possible. Never allow the soil to dry out. If for some reason the medium becomes dripping wet, leave off the cover until the excess evaporates. With care, however, this should not be necessary. If you set up a regular watering time—preferably in the morning, or in the evening after the sun goes down—you will find that the time is sufficient to allow just the right amount of time in between daily waterings. When the seedlings have put on sufficient growth—two full sets of leaves—water between the lanes to avoid "drowning" the young seedlings.

HANDLING TRANSPLANTS

Young seedlings are very tender and care should be taken when they are handled. Unless you have planted each seed individually—most unlikely and with most vegetables and flowers virtually impossible—the seeds naturally come up in "clusters." A few basic rules and tools are all that is needed for success.

☐ Separate seedlings into small clumps with a dull knife or thin piece of wood such as an ice cream stick.

☐ Using your left thumb and index finger, *gently* remove the seedling from the dirt.

☐ Drill a hole in your transplant soil container soil, a pencil is the perfect dimension for this phase, set the seedling in and *gently but firmly* press down around the root.

☐ Water the newly transplated seedlings immediately, but take care to water *between* the rows *slowly* so as not to drown them. Use a spray type container if possible.

Transplants grow rapidly and have a tendency to become spindly. This is especially true in unusual climatic conditions such as an extra warm winter. This is of little concern, however, because you will be planting them deeper in the garden or, if you are raising an ornamental for the greenhouse, in the container.

TOOLS FOR GREENHOUSE USE

There are only a few tools that are essential for efficiency in the greenhouse. They include a trowel, hand shears or pruners, gloves, stakes, plant-tie materials, labels and a waterproof marking-pencil. In addition, for pest control you will need a small hand-operated mister or hose-end sprayer. A hose with a pistol-type spray attachment is also useful (Fig. 4-19).

POTS FOR THE GREENHOUSE

Plastic pots are durable; but for the best pot, the old fashioned clay pot is hard to beat. If you purchase pots by mail, the cost of shipping will make the plastic pots the logical choice. For a standard sized greenhouse, approximately 7 x 12 with about 30 feet of bench space, plus shelves, you will need approximately the number of pots suggested in Table 4-4. Allow for dormant types kept underneath the benches or in cold frames and for varieties raised in flats (Fig. 4-20).

HOT FRAME

Easily built from scraps of plywood, even the smallest hot frame is a must for the greenhouse (Fig. 4-21). The heating tape is of the variety used to wrap water pipes to keep them from freezing. It is not necessary to provide a thermostat because they generally turn on at 35 degrees and that is too low to provide adequate plant production.

Line the heating frame with tin foil and cover it with an inch of sand. After spreading the tape, as shown in Fig. 4-21, make sure that the tape does not overlap or crimp because it would overheat and burn out at that point. Press the tape down firmly and fill the frame with a mixture of sand, vermiculite and potting soil.

Besides being an excellent propagating box for slips from your favorite ornamentals, freshly sown seeds in containers can be set on the warm, moist soil, to speed germination. Because the dirt dries out rapidly, place pieces of burlap over the freshly sown seeds and water thoroughly through the burlap. This will help keep the seeds moist and warm and speed up germination time (Fig. 2-22). Slips taken from your favorite cuttings will root quickly in the hot frame with strong roots (Fig. 2-23).

COLD FRAME

A cold frame can nestle against the south side of any structure and even against the greenhouse itself. It is a welcome accessory to the hot frame and greenhouse and it provides flexibility and certainty to your ornamental and vegetable growing programs. As

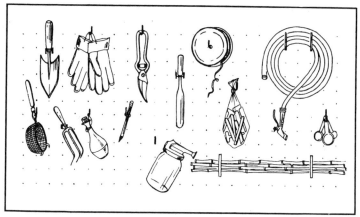

Fig. 4-19. Tools for greenhouse culture (courtesy of Kathleen Bourke, Lord & Burnham Co.).

with all structures, the size depends upon your needs. A 2′ x 3′ x 8′ wide cold frame is used for the "hardening off" period. In the spring, after your plants have been transferred to market packs, they can be placed into the cold frame along with any flats and containers of young seedlings that have been started in the hot frame and transplanted in the greenhouse. This will provide additional space in the greenhouse for new batches of seedlings to be raised in the greenhouse proper and the hot frame.

The plants must be watered generously each morning and the roof must be kept open during the day, but *closed* at night. You will find that a cold frame with a storage shed will save your hours of laborious transplanting first to flats then to a cold frame and finally to the garden. It also alleviates disturbing the young seedlings from the shock of several transplantings. The plants are only disturbed once prior to being planted into the garden proper or greenhouse pot. A 3 x 8 cold frame will accommodate approximately 10,000 plants (Fig. 4-24).

Table 4-4. Pot Size and Quantity.

Size of Pot	Suggested Quantity
2½″	200
3″	100
4″	100
5″	100
6″	100
8″	50
10″	12

311

Fig. 4-20. Clay pots (courtesy of John Wahlfeldt).

CLOCHE (MINIGREENHOUSE) GARDENING

Cloche gardening is another form, only a lesser degree, of greenhousing. It has been used for many years by those who did not have space or money for either a lean-to or free-standing greenhouse. There are people today who can make good use of this simple means of minigreenhousing. The initial idea of the cloche gardening system was to take the glass to a growing crop for protection instead of growing the crop inside a large structure.

Constructed completely from glass, a cloche can be built any size you desire by using four pieces of glass fastened with galvanized wire (Fig. 4-25). Put in rows to form a tunnel, the ends are then fastened with additional pieces of glass.

Each individual 2-foot long section can be used and placed over one or two plants by themselves and closed, as outlined above, or they can be placed in rows to cover a full "garden row" of seedlings. In this manner, the cloche acts as a portable greenhouse

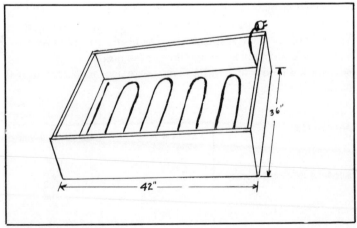

Fig. 4-21. Hot frame detail.

Fig. 4-22. Burlap covering seedlings in a container set in a hot frame (courtesy of John Wahlfeldt).

and can be placed over your already raised sown seedlings, flowers and vegetables until they have grown to the height of the top of the cloche. The height is determined by your individual needs. At this time, the plants are as sturdy as those you have raised in the greenhouse. When they have reached the roof of the cloche, the cloche can be packed away and stored for the next crop's use.

It is important to pay attention to the width of the cloche because one of the most important factors is watering. The surface soil (where the seeds are) is never wetted as it would be in a greenhouse. The rain of daily watering runs down the glass roof and sides. It seeps into the soil and to the roots of the plants. This results in checked caking of the soil under the cloche and it makes hoeing for aeration around the structure unnecessary.

Fig. 4-23. Well-rooted slip from a hot frame (courtesy of John Wahlfeldt).

313

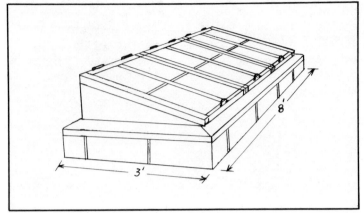

Fig. 4-24. Cold frame detail.

Cloches are find protection against early and late frosts and other inclimate weather conditions even though they are lightweight. If set over your plants correctly and sturdily in place, they will not easily be moved unless by hand. They are made almost completely from glass except for the lightweight frame construction. Depending on your geographic location, you will find that your cloche can be used several times throughout the year. Because they are lightweight and easy to move about, you have a choice of moving them from one crop to another and from place to place in order to achieve success throughout your entire growing season wherever you live.

GREENHOUSE FLAT

Greenhouse flats can be built any size, filled with a mixture of sand and potting soil and used as a storage for new seedlings or to start seeds that you did not want to place in your hot frame. A standard size is 16 x 22 with smaller plastic and fiberboard types in many sizes available (Fig. 4-26).

SEED STARTER CONTAINERS

Very popular today are the highly compressed pellets of a sterile planting mix impregnated with fertilizer. Pellets are approximately one-fourth inch thick until placed in a plastic tray of water. They quickly expand to approximately seven times their original height. They form a "pot" of sphagnum peat enclosed in a plastic mesh. Ideal for sowing seeds or for transplants, they encourage vigorous plant growth. When ready for "planting out," the entire plant and "pellet pot" are set into the garden. Roots continue right through the mesh into the soil to avoid any shock or setback to seedlings. Fine seeds are sprinkled on top of expanded pellets. The center can be lifted out easily with a plant tag or utility tool for larger seeds that must be covered, for small plants from a misting bed, or for cuttings to be rooted (Fig. 4-27).

Also very popular are the peat pots that come in individual pots or market pack varieties. They are sectioned off to take six seedlings. The individual pots, as with the pellets, can be planted directly into the ground. With the sectioned off market packs, the young seedlings can be first removed and then the section can be cut away. Then the clump—seedling and peat—are planted directly into the ground (Fig. 4-28).

These same methods can, of course, be used in greenhouse planting for raising new varieties of plants. The wood fiber,

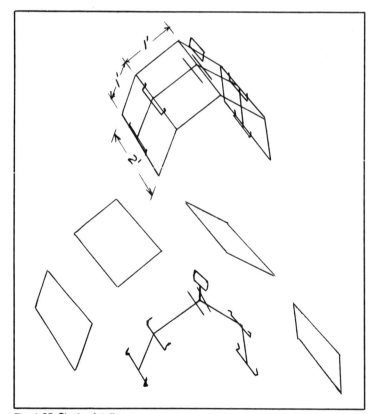

Fig. 4-25. Cloche detail.

315

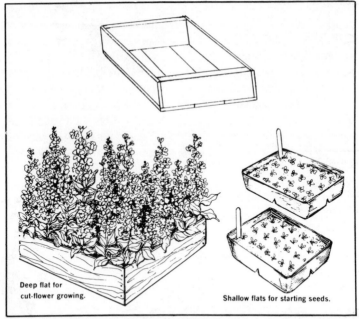

Fig. 4-26. Greenhouse flat details bottom sections (courtesy of Kathleen Bourke, Lord & Burnham Co.).

decay-resistant materials are nontoxic and are ready to use with starting nutrients already added. Molded by heat and pressure into cakes scored into 1½″ blocks, they are easily separated at planting time. Individual blocks provide tapered, fluted holes in three different sizes to accommodate various size seeds or cuttings. They readily absorb and hold water. The color block fibers indicate moisture content and provide an accurate check for additional watering.

HARDENING

Plants should be gradually "hardened" (toughened) for two to three weeks before being moved to the garden site. If you don't

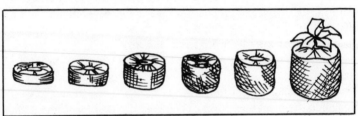

Fig. 4-27. Compressed pellets (courtesy of Kathleen Bourke, Lord & Burnham).

Fig. 4-28. Peat pots (courtesy of Kathleen Bourke, Lord & Burnham).

have a cold frame, this is done by withholding water and lowering the temperature. Hardening slows down the plant's rate of growth to prepare them to withstand such conditions as chilling, drying winds or high temperatures.

Lettuce, cabbage, and many other plants can be toughened to withstand frost; others, such as tomatoes and peppers, cannot be hardened.

PINCHING BACK

To avoid growing plants that are tall and spindly, use your thumb and forefinger—on soft-stemmed varieties—to pinch back the growth of a stem you want to branch out. On woody varieties, use a sharp knife to cut the top out of the plant on a slant. Most woody varieties ooze white or clear liquid. Have ready a small amount of soil. Take a sharp knife and below a leaf, at a slant, make a clean cut. Immediately spread some moistened soil on the cut and then dip the cutting into the soil because the sap must be contained in the plant and the cutting. Dip the cutting into Rootone and place it in a fresh container to root (Fig. 4-29).

TIEING MATERIALS

Strips of vinyl plastic or cotton from your rag bag make excellent plant tie materials for the greenhouse. Do not use a material such as wire that could cut into the plant and thereby cut off the life of the plant. Although covered wire surrounded by plastic, such as the type used to close freezer bags, is in common use, they are often tied to tightly and they severely damage the plants.

When using a plant tie, first cut a piece of wood and place it alongside the plant as a stake. Then loop the tie around the plant stem and tie it securely to the plant stake.

PROPER PRUNING ANGLE

A   B   C   D

RIGHT   WRONG

When possible, cut back to a side
bud and make the cut at a slant. A
is cut correctly. B is too slanting. C
is too far from the bud. D is too
close to the bud.

Fig. 4-29. Pruning woody plants.

REPOTTING

Prepare your fresh soil to suit the needs of the individual plant. For instance, use porous soil for begonnias, a heavier soil for ficuses (rubber plants) and an extra amount of peat moss to hold the moisture in for ferns.

Place one hand across the top of the soil and then turn the plant upside down. Tap the pot rim on the edge of the bench to jar the rootball free.

After removing the pot-bound plant with the root system entangled, take a sharp knife and make four diagonal cuts through the exposed matted roots. This gets your plants off to a fresh start by allowing the root system to expand and bring new life (air) to the inside of the plant. Now, repot in a fresh container at least one size larger; preferably it would be two sizes larger so that you won't have to repot too often. Place the plant in the pot and add new soil beneath and around the plant until it is held firmly in place (Fig. 4-30).

TAKING SLIPS

All plants, regardless of whether they are woody-stemmed or soft, can be propagated. Taking cuttings from existing plants and rooting them in your hot frame is an economical and pleasant way to increase your greenhouse supply. But, all too often promising slips are lost because of poor technique or after-treatment (Fig. 4-31).

318

Most sand-rooters are herbaceous plants (plants bearing soft stems). Unlike the woody stems of trees, cuttings can be taken anytime. Make the cutting 3 to 4″ long. It should preferably having at least two nodes (knot, knob or joint). Remove any flower buds or fruit, in the case of vegetables such as tomatoes, or full blooms. Remove stipules, winglets and beginning leaves, that might have begun growing along the stem. These are susceptible to rotting. Place the cutting in the hot frame.

DIVIDING PLANTS

A plant can be divided when it developes more than one stem from the soil line. Division of plants is done when a many crowned plant is not doing well or when you want more plants from a specific variety. When dividing a plant, remove the plant from the pot and gently remove the soil from the roots. When the roots are exposed, you will be able to separate the crowns or stems and repot the new division (Fig. 4-32).

TERMINOLOGY

Suckers. These are offshoots that grow from the stems of the plants such as Amaryllis. After being rooted in moist sand—in the hot frame or flat—they are transplanted to a separate pot.

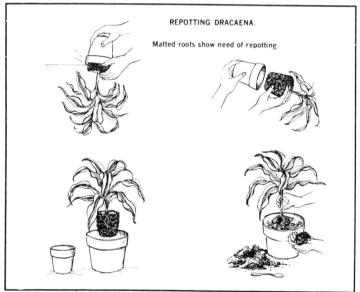

REPOTTING DRACAENA.

Matted roots show need of repotting.

Fig. 4-30. Repotting technique (courtesy of Kathleen Bourke, Lord & Burnham).

PROPAGATING GERANIUMS FROM CUTTINGS

Strip away the lower leaves.

Remove vigorous tip growth.

Insert in flat of moist sand.

Fig. 4-31. Taking cuttings for rooting (courtesy of Kathleen Bourne, Lord & Burnham).

Dormancy. Drying off is the term used to describe the procedures used to put a plant into dormancy. Fertilization and watering is gradually withheld and then finally stopped completely. The foliage becomes yellow and ripe and the growing medium becomes nearly bone dry. The corms are dried off and ready for dormancy.

Forcing Bulbs. This is "coaxing" plants into bloom out of season. Tulips, daffodil, crocus, and hyacinths are especially popular in warm winter climates where the show place is the greenhouse (Fig. 4-33).

To force bulbs in your greenhouse, put the bulbs in a mixture of equal parts loam, peat moss and sand. Plant large bulbs one to a pot. Smaller varieties such as crocus can be planted three or four to a 4″ pot. Six tulips do nicely in a 6 to 10″ pot. Cover the bulbs with one-half inch of soil. For daffodils, cover only the thick portion of the bulb. Place pots in a cool place for the roots to form. A cold frame is ideal for this. Bulbs require from 35 to 55 degrees for the roots to form. You can use your refrigerator.

During the rooting period, the soil should be kept moist. When the leaves begin to push through the soil, the pots can be taken into the greenhouse. To lengthen the time of enjoyment, bring pots inside intermittently during December through March.

Forsythia and pussy willow are popular spring bloomers. They can be forced simply by cutting 8 to 14″ sections from the bush and placing them in clear jars of water. Water should be changed frequently to avoid souring.

Peat Moss. Peat moss is the remains of plants decomposed over the centuries and is almost indispensible as a soil builder. The most common types sold are German and Canadian. It is dark brown in color.

Perlite. Excellent as a substitute for sand, this gritty, white substance is used in potting and propagating mixtures.

Spaghnum Moss. As with peat moss, sphagnum moss is almost indispensible for the greenhouse. Sphagnum is a gray or tan bog moss dried and used as a planting medium for many kinds of plants, especially hanging baskets, and used during the air layering process. Sphagnum moss swells and is therefore ideal for any plant that needs to be extremely well held together.

Vermiculite. Used for rooting cuttings and starting seeds, vermiculite is a sterile planting medium that should also be added to most potting soil. Its course texture provides an excellent substitute for well-rooted leaf mold. It is a good additive.

Cool Greenhouse. This term applies to a greenhouse in which the average nighttime temperatures range between 35 to 50 F in which a great variety of plants may be raised at the same

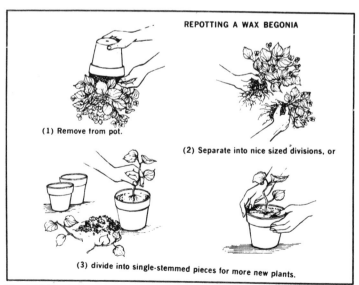

REPOTTING A WAX BEGONIA

(1) Remove from pot.

(2) Separate into nice sized divisions, or

(3) divide into single-stemmed pieces for more new plants.

Fig. 4-32. Dividing plants (courtesy of Kathleen Bourke, Lord & Burnham).

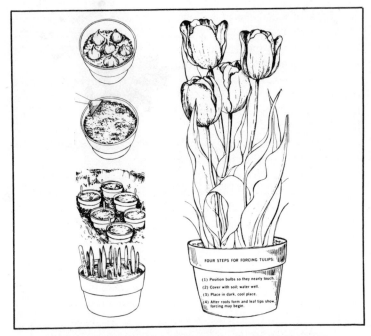

Fig. 4-33. Forcing bulbs (courtesy of Kathleen Bourke, Lord & Burnham).

time. Camellias do especially well with nighttime temperatures of 40 F.

Moderate Greenhouse. This term is used for a greenhouse in which winter nighttime minimum temperatures range from 55 to 60 F. It is excellent for those who want to grow a wide variety of plants requiring consideration variance in nighttime minimum temperatures.

Warm Greenhouse. This is a greenhouse with a nighttime minimum temperature during the winter of 65 F and up. It is used mainly for those who want to specialize in raising one or two types of plants such as "hot loving" orchids that require specific temperature control.

Vacation Time. While the easiest means of greenhouse care during the time when the family plans a vacation is to "vacate the greenhouse of all plants," this is not always possible. There are many people who operate their greenhouse year around. In that case, it is well to have a gardening friend check the greenhouse daily for watering. If your vacation is planned during the winter months, be sure that the heating system is functioning properly so that if a frost or freeze is forecast the thermostat is set to come on.

Chapter 5
Patios

An extension of the greenhouse, especially with a lean-to, is the patio area where both become an intregal part of the home itself. The size of a patio depends on the space you have and the needs of your family. For the most part, patios are used as areas in which to relax and they should be constructed with tranquility of design. They can be made of brick, block, flagstone, aggregate, or poured concrete and they can be left natural or colored, rough or smooth textured, sculptored or plain (Fig. 5-1).

A patio can be one large expanse that is open to the natural elements. It can be sectioned into cubicles to provide intimacy and privacy for family members. An ideal patio is attached to the outside dimensions of the room it surrounds (Fig. 5-2).

PREPARING THE SITE

Good drainage is essential. This is especially true if you are using poured concrete. In that case, drainage tiles should be laid end to end in a trench dug approximately 1 foot deeper along the center of the area being poured. This tile will drain off excessive moisture that collects beneath the solid paving. After the patio is completed pack gravel around the tile and fill in with sand. Let the site "sit" for several days before continuing to the next step.

GRADING

Whether grading is necessary will depend upon the material being used. Grading is accomplished by digging out or adding soil. Section off areas with wooden stakes, string lines between the stakes and use a level to determine the high and low points. Where

Fig. 5-1. Block patio surrounding a lean-to.

areas are low, add dirt and where areas are high dig out excess dirt. Soak the ground and tamp it down well.

FLAGSTONES

Made from slate or sandstone, flagstones are available in a variety of shapes, sizes and colors. When they are intermixed, they produce a pleasing and effective design. In addition, they are durable. Approximately 2″ thick, they can be laid on soil or sand with mortar or gravel set between each slab. The following are guidelines for laying flagstones.

Sand. Rake a bed of sand 2 to 3″ deep. Place the slabs firmly into the bed and fill with gravel or soil.

Soil. Dig soil slightly deeper than the thickness of the slab and place. Fill joints with gravel or soil.

CONCRETE SLABS AND BRICKS

Available in round, oblong and square shapes and in many colors, the use of concrete slabs or masonry bricks provide a quick and easy means of laying a patio floor. After the initial site preparation, the slabs can be laid in a variety of designs. Firm each slab into place and fill the open spaces with dirt, gravel or soil. The finished area will be as solid as if layed in concrete. Wash down the area immediately after filling the cracks with soil or sand and pour additional sand into the cracks until the sand remains level with the set slabs. This can be done over a period of days until the finished slabs are smooth, firm and solid (Fig. 5-1).

Stepping Stones

To provide a colorful yet simply-made walkway connecting the patio area to the greenhouse, lay colored slabs of poured concrete. Stepping stones can be cast to any shape desired by removing sod, and then carving the earth to the shape you want. Concrete is then poured into the hole and finished.

Bricks

The two basic types of bricks most commonly used for laying patio floors are slick surface face brick and rough textured common brick. Rough textured common brick is the most popular because it is readily equated to old-fashioned paving. It is irregular in size and color and it is less expensive (Fig. 5-3).

Bricks are colors of red/reddish, browns/oranges/pinks and other assorted colors that range even to multicolored. Dyes change from batch to batch and, therefore, it is recommended that you purchase sufficient bricks to finish the job. If you are laying the patio floor in a particular pattern, discoloration of a new batch would show.

Shop around to get the best price. Take into account that there are added-on expenses such as delivery charges and the cost of delivering bricks on a pallet. This is well worth the minimum additional cost because it prevents breakage in unloading rather than having the bricks arbitrarily dumped around the site where you are working.

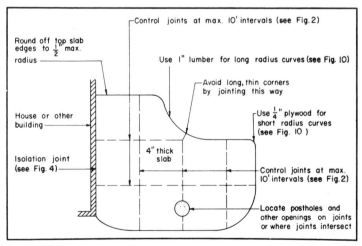

Fig. 5-2. Details for a suggested patio design, metric conversion.

Fig. 5-3. Common brick (left) and modular brick.

There are some basic and very pleasing bricklaying designs. The most popular are the running bond (Fig. 5-4), the basketweave (Fig. 5-5) and the diagonal herringbone (Fig. 5-6). All of these designs can be used separately or together and they can be laid with or without mortar (bonded-concrete), open joint or closed joint.

Running Bond. This design can be made with either regular 4 x 8 common or modular size brick and can be laid on masonry or sand. Tap them down with a rubber hammer. *Don't* use a metal hammer; it will cause the brick to crack. Make sure that the bricks are level. Once the area is "laid," dump the sand onto the area of brick laid, sweep it off, and then wet it down to allow the sand to pack tightly into the cracks. Repeat this until all of the cracks are tightly packed with sand. All of the openings should be completely filled.

Basketweave. If you want to use regular 4 x 8 paving bricks for this design, you will have to set them in mortar because the space caused by the length of the bricks being twice its width produces an opening (Fig. 5-7). A modular size brick, therefore, is recommended for this pattern if you want only to lay them in sand.

Fig. 5-4. Running bond design.

Fig. 5-5. Basketweave design using modular brick, horizontal and vertical pattern.

Herringbone. The herringbone zigzag is most attractive and not difficult to lay. The hammer and chisel come into play using this design because when the area is completed you will have protruding edges. The professional mason uses his trowel to cut off the extension of the brick. However, it is suggested that the beginner use the hammer and chisel. This provides an easier means for the layman to get a better cut. Score it lightly all the way around, go over the same line and the brick will break easily.

Edging. Edging the area adds a finished look to the patio. Dig a trench along the edge and turn the brick on its side (Fig. 5-8). Sink the brick in until it is level with the edge of the brick laid. Do not allow it to stick up because it would form a ditch that would hold water. Another means of edging is to use a piece of 2 x 4 or 2 x 6 redwood or other treated wood to make a stable border.

The procedures described above can be used for either brick or concrete slabs. They will not move and the permanency is more

Fig. 5-6. Herringbone design.

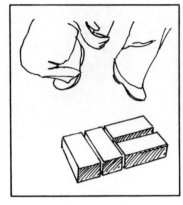

Fig. 5-7. Paving brick 4 x 8 can be used with mortar joint for basket-weave.

than adequate. In freeze zones, the ground will move and when it does, bricks laid in mortar will be susceptible to cracking. In that case, should you use sand or mortar? If there is any cracking after a freeze, then all or sections of the brick-laid patio on concrete would have to be redone, the concrete slab relaid and then the brick reset. Even though the brick laid in sand will move, if suffering from a deep-freezing, it would mean that the brick and the sand would only become unlevel. That would be easy to repair. The choice, regardless, is up to the individual.

Sand. Laying bricks on sand is the simplest way to lay bricks for the do-it-yourself brick mason. Bricks can be set in sand in areas where the ground does not freeze. Set bricks in the design of

Fig. 5-8. Upturned bricks provide edging.

your choice. If they are not butted (closed joints), fill open joints with sand, dirt or gravel. This will be as solid as if layed in masonry concrete.

Mortar. In freeze zones, bricks should be set in mortar. First pour a concrete foundation. Spread a layer of mortar one-half inch deep and leave a one-half inch joint between each brick and each row (course) of bricks. Let things set until you are able to "joint" with trowel. Using the edge of the trowel, push mortar into the joints. See Table 5-1.

SOLID CONCRETE

Although most expensive, a poured concrete slab is the most permanent patio form. A major portion of the cost can be cut down if you do the initial preparation and the finishing yourself. Unlike laying blocks or bricks, the pouring of a slab is a nonstop operation. Therefore, some careful planning is required so that the actual pouring of the slab can be carried out efficiently. Colored concrete is obtained by mixing colored pigment in with the cement.

When planning the job, first calculate roughly the amount of concrete you will need. Calculate the volume by multiplying length by width by thickness. All of this can be expressed in feet:

V (cu. Ft.) = L (ft.) X W (ft.) X T (ft.).

Divide cubic feet by 27 to secure cubic yards. For flatwork, such as patio slabs, a simple rule of thumb for estimating the amount of concrete needed is that one cubic yard of concrete will cover approximately 300 square feet, 1 inch thick, allowing for some waste (usually about 10 percent).

Table 5-1. Bricks and Mortar.

Mortar Mix 4 Parts Plastering Sand 1 Part Cement			
Bricks Laid in Mortar per 100 square Feet			
	Amount of Bricks	**Sand Cubic Feet**	**Sacrete (Bags)**
Laid in 2" sand ½" closed joints	450	17	1
Bricks Laid in Sand per 100 Square Feet			
	Amount of Bricks	**Amount of Bricks Amount of Sand (cubic feet)**	
Laid in 1" sand Closed Joints ½" open joints	500 450	9 13	

Hand mixing in a wheelbarrow or mortar box works well for small jobs. Anything larger is well worth renting a small mixer that will save back-breaking labor and provide better efficiency and end results. To mix one cubic yard of concrete you will need:

Six bags of Portland cement.
1250 pounds of concrete sand.
1000 pounds of gravel or crushed stone.
Approximately 30 gallons of water.

Because sand and gravel vary, you will need to "reach" the desired consistency. For a starter, 1 part cement, 2¼ parts sand, and 3 parts gravel or crushed stone should be mixed. The key to good quality is the proportion of water to cement. Use about 5 gallons of water for each bag of cement and keep this proportion consistent. The amount of sand and gravel can be adjusted in order to attain the workability desired (Fig. 5-9).

The stress of concrete can cause cracks. Divide the area into sections; preferably the sections should be nearly square. Cut dummy groove joints in the fresh concrete to about one-fourth the concrete thickness.

For smaller jobs, such as the pouring of concrete stepping stones, bagged dry mixed concrete is ideal. Dry mixed concrete (Sacrete) need only be mixed with water because the ingredients have been accurately proportioned at the factory.

For a really professional job, it is important not to overwork the concrete. Overworking draws fine material to the surface and results in less durability. Strike the surface off to the desired level. Move the strike-off board across the surface as many times as needed. When the sheen has left the surface, it is ready for final finishing.

The first step is to use a wood or light metal float. For smooth surfaces, use a steel trowel (Fig. 5-12) after the float. However, this does tend to leave a slightly slippery surface that is not conducive to outdoors. Therefore, the first step could also be the final step because it leaves a slightly gritty slip resistant finish. You will also find that if you use a gritty wood float finish, it will hide irregularities better than a smooth surface. The beginner will be better pleased with the finished product if left gritty.

Concrete should be kept moist for several days after it has set. To cure, cover the new concrete with a waterproof material such as a sheet of polyethelene.

Forms

Used as edgings, concrete forms must be sturdy enough to withstand the pressure that the wet concrete exerts. Forms are made by placing 2 x 4's or 2 x 6's completely around the proposed site. For rounded corners or cutout sections in the paving, bend plywood into the desired length or diameter (Fig. 5-10). Drive wooden stakes at 4-foot intervals and slightly below the top of the form to keep it in place. For extra reinforcement, lay concrete reinforcement wire.

Pouring

For large jobs, it is a good idea to have extra help on hand to spread the concrete as it is poured from the truck or from the small machine if you are mixing it yourself. In either case, once the concrete arrives speed is of the essence and a continuous flow of spreading the concrete must be maintained. Using shovels or rakes, spread concrete to the form's edge. Do not overwork the mixture. This will bring moisture to the top and "silt" to the surface.

Design

After the concrete has been smoothed and allowed to sit until workable, artistic designs can be produced with a plastic broom by sweeping in different directions or making swirls. A jointer can be

Fig. 5-9. Workable mortar on a mortar board.

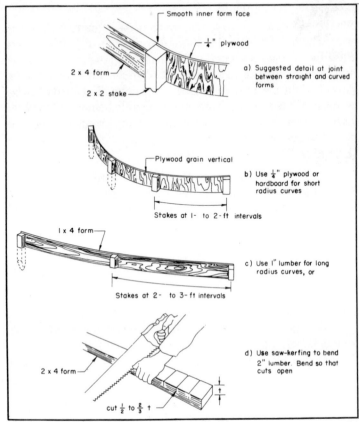

Fig. 5-10. Forms for horizontal curves, metric conversion (courtesy Portland Cement Company).

used to press the edge down into the concrete and pull the mixture into a pattern.

Patterns on Flat Work

Geometric designs make nice decorative patterns in concrete surfaces. Random patterns can be made in concrete by the use of a bent piece of three-fourth inch copper pipe about 18″ long. Circles, squares, ovals, and other designs can be made with household cans of various sizes by imprinting the can surface in the semihardened concrete.

Leaf impressions result in interesting and decorative patterns. Press the leaves' step side down into freshly troweled concrete. Embed the leaf completely but do not allow the concrete to cover the top of the leaf. Carefully remove the leaf after the concrete sets.

Finishing

After the mortar has set—at least overnight—wear rubber gloves and use a wire brush to clean any spilled mortar from bricks or concrete. Use a mixture of 1 part muriatic acid to 9 parts water. Remove the stakes and the edging and hose the area down.

TERMINOLOGY

Mortar Board. A mortar board is a wooden board on which mortar is placed for ease in handling.

Bed Joint. As you lay each row of brick, the one below is "the bed."

Closures. The last brick. It is the brick that "closes" the row in the center of the row if the wall is being built from two directions. The last brick/block of each row (whether laying a patio floor, flat surface, wall or upright structure).

Fig. 5-11. Bullfloating to finish slab (courtesy of Portland Cement Company).

Head Joint. The blocks at each end of the wall or patio.

Striking. Leveling the concrete is accomplished by pulling the flat edge of a 2 x 4 across the freshly poured cement.

Joint Finishing. Each brick laid requires *jointing*. This is done by raking the jointer—a piece of pipe—along the mortar, horizontally and vertically. Attempt to hold the jointer as straight as possible to attain a clean, sharp finish with no jagged edges. By cleaning off this excess mortar between the brick, you are causing a depression. This is what makes the bricks appear as though they are coming forward while the mortar recedes. This provides the finished structure with the "wall" look.

Bonding. The word technically applies to the mortar that "ties" bricks or blocks together. The process of laying them and spreading the mortar (concrete) between them. When dried (set), mortar "bonds" them together.

Course. Masons refer to each row of blocks or bricks as "courses" or "runs." Laying up of brick/block by rows.

Sprinkle Test. Determine at the time of purchase whether bricks are "dry." If they are dry, then you should sprinkle them with water the night prior to beginning the project. In this way you

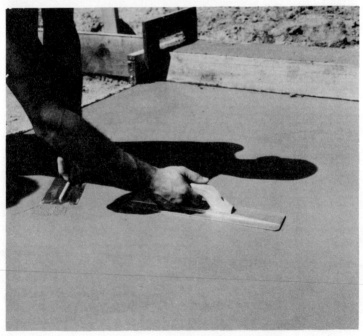

Fig. 5-12. Handling a steel trowel (courtesy of Portland Cement).

Table 5-2. Metric Conversion Chart.

10 millimeters (nm)	⅜ inch
25 mm	1 inch
100 mm	4 inches
300 mm	1 foot
1 meter (10000 mm)	3 to 4 inches
1 square meter (m)	1¾ square feet or 1.2 square feet
1 cubic meter (m)	35 cubic feet
1 liter	1.06 quart
4¼ liters	1 gallon
1 kilogram (kg)	2.2 pounds
45½ (kg)	100 pounds

will be putting sufficient water into them and the moisture will not be absorbed from the mortar when you are laying them up.

Waiting Period. The time allowed for the mortar to set—from 6 to 24 hours—depends on climatic conditions and the type brick used.

Striking or Raking. There are various ways to clean the wall. The simplest method is to use muriatic acid mixed with water. Wearing rubber gloves and using a plastic broom, dip the broom into the bucket, sweep the wall and hose it down with clean water. Do *not* use a straw broom. A wet straw broom will smear the mortar; plastic brooms stay stiff.

Bullfloating. A bullfloat is used immediately after striking off concrete slabs. Work the bullfloat back and forth across the slab to smooth it and remove irregularities. Work a slight amount of cement paste to the surface. Do *not* overwork concrete. It will result in a less durable surface (Fig. 5-11).

Steel Trowel. If a very smooth surface is desired, use a hand trowel (Fig. 5-12).

Metrics. Most of the world is now on the metric system. It is a good idea to learn the metric system because it will figure prominently in determining how much of what to purchase. This is especially true when it comes to figuring building supplies and materials. Table 5-2 is a helpful metric conversion chart.

Chapter 6
Garden and
Screen Walls

Outdoor living areas are greatly enhanced by well engineered, tastefully designed garden walls. Attractive walls can be built in many designs. They are limited only by your imagination (Fig. 6-1).

Concrete and concrete masonry walls offer a new dimension in wall design. From the simple 8 x 8 x 16" concrete block to the newest screen wall unit and grill, block concrete gives the beauty, the appeal and the pleasing backdrop for a beautiful garden setting. A screen or garden wall will afford privacy yet it will not obstruct the flow of air or sunlight. Screen walls, garden walls and entryways can add to the aesthetic value of the home greenhouse. There are many new and unusual units available (Fig. 6-2). As a beginner mason, the important thing is to lay the materials so that they ultimately appear as though they had been laid by a professional. At first, be patient and be consistent in your work. With a little practice, you will find that you will gain speed.

SIZES, SHAPES AND PATTERNS

The versatility of concrete masonry as a building material is demonstrated by the new sizes, shapes, patterns and textures available. Blocks are readily available for structural purposes as well as for decorative uses. Some of the most common shapes and sizes are shown in Fig. 6-3. Other units are available with smooth surfaces, rounded corners, raised patterns and in various colors. Standard masonry is 8 x 8 x 16 inches. There are many other specially sized units for every need.

Fig. 6-1. One of many decorative concrete block designs (courtesy of Portland Cement Company).

FOOTINGS

A substantial garden wall needs a good foundation. The first step is to make a footing of cast-in-place concrete. The bottom of the footing should be on firm soil at least 18″ below ground level; in colder areas it should extend below the frost line. The footing should be twice the wall width and half as thick (deep) as it is wide. Thus, for an 8″ thick wall the footing would be 16″ wide and 8″ deep.

The below-grade portion of the wall can be built of the same block as the wall above grade. The first course (row) of block is placed in a full bed of mortar on the footing (Fig. 6-4).

Fig. 6-2. A concrete block wall set on an oblong block patio. It did not require any footings.

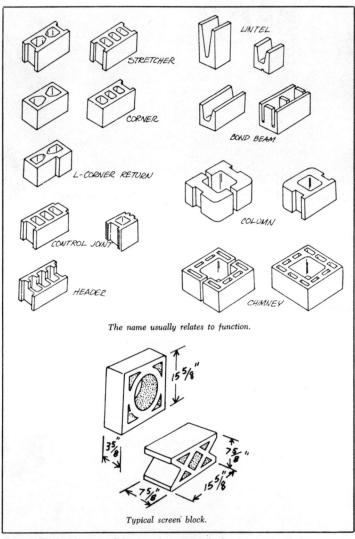

The name usually relates to function.

Typical screen block.

Fig. 6-3. Typical sizes and shapes of concrete block.

REINFORCEMENT

Walls less than 4' high need no reinforcement. For walls 4 to 6' high, reinforcing bars one-half inch in diameter should be used. These bars are set in the footing at 4' centers and extend into the block cores. The core spaces around the bars are then filled with concrete. The bars should be long enough to extend at least 2' above ground level for a 6' high garden wall (Fig. 6-5).

Fig. 6-4. Below grade block (courtesy of John Wahlfeldt).

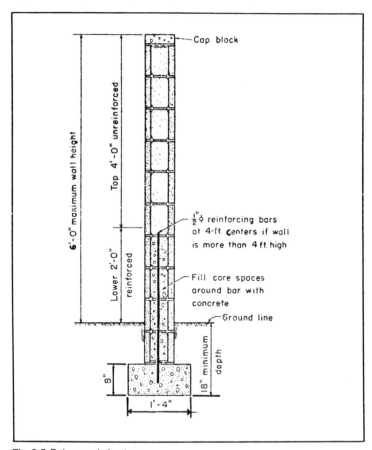

Fig. 6-5. Below grade footing.

CONCRETE AND CEMENT

The layman often confuses the words *cement* and *concrete*. What is Cement? Concrete? Mortar? Before beginning, you should know some basic facts and terminology you will be confronted with in building walls and patios.

Concrete is a building material widely used around the home for foundations, walls, patios, sidewalks, steps, fireplaces, etc. Concrete has several desirable properties that make it a versatile and popular building material. Freshly mixed concrete can be formed into practically any shape. Hardened concrete is strong and durable.

Although ready-mixed concrete is widely used for large construction jobs, it is not always practical to use ready-mixed concrete on small jobs. In some cases the amount of concrete you require might be less than 1 cubic yard. That is less than the most ready-mix producers will supply.

Quality concrete costs no more to make than poor concrete and it is far more economical in the long run because of its greater durability. The rules for making good concrete are simple:

☐ Use proper ingredients.
☐ Proportion the ingredients correctly.
☐ Measure the ingredients accurately.
☐ Mix the ingredients thoroughly.

Portland cement is an extremely fine powder that is manufactured in a cement plant. Portland cement, when mixed with water, forms a paste. This paste binds materials such as sand and gravel or crushed stone (aggregate) into concrete.

The quality of the paste determines the strength and durability of the finished concrete. Too much mixing water makes the paste thin and weak. Water for mixing should be clean and free of oil, acid, and other injurious substances.

Fine aggregate consists of sand; coarse aggregate consists of gravel, crushed stone or air-cooled slag. Good, sound aggregate is necessary for making quality concrete. Loam, clay, dirt, and vegetable matter are detrimental to concrete. Aggregate containing these materials should not be used.

Mortar is a mixture of mortar sand, masonry cement, and water. Mortar is used for laying concrete block, brick, and stones. Various types of cements are manufactured for every use. Normally portland cement is gray. If white concrete is needed, or desired, use white portland cement.

Table 6-1 gives the approximate amount of materials needed for various size batches of concrete. It might be necessary to vary the amounts of aggregates slightly; it depends upon their characteristics.

The amount of concrete needed can be quickly found for any square or rectangular areas by using this formula: Width in ft. x length in ft. x thickness in ft. $= \dfrac{\text{cubic ft.}}{27} = \text{cubic yards.}$

Choosing the Ingredient

Portland cement is not a brand name of cement; it is a type of cement. Most portland cement is gray in color. However, white portland cement is manufactured from special raw materials that produce a pure white color. White portland cement is more expensive and for that reason the regular portland cement is more widely used.

Cement suitable for use in concrete should be free-flowing. The presence of lumps that cannot be pulverized readily between your thumb and finger indicates that the cement has absorbed moisture. Such cement should never be used for important work. When the lumps have been screened out through an ordinary house screen, it can be used for certain minor jobs.

Water for making concrete can be almost any natural water that is drinkable and has no pronounced taste or odor. Some waters that are not suitable for drinking will make satisfactory concrete. To be on the safe side, use only water fit to drink.

Air is also an important ingredient for making good concrete. In the late 1930s it was discovered that air, in the form of

Table 6-1. Concrete Batch Sizes.

A 1:2¼: 3 mix = 1 part cement to 2¼ parts sand to 3 parts 1-inch maximum aggregate				
Concrete Required Cubic Feet	Cement 1 lb.	Maximum Amount of Water to use gallon	Sand 1 pound	Coarse Aggregate 1 pound
1	24	1¼	52	78
3	71	3-¾	156	233
5	118	6¼	260	389
6-¾ (¼ cu. yd)	165	88	350	525
13½ (½ cu. yd)	294	16	700	1050
27 (1 cu. yd)	588	32	1040	2100

microscopic bubbles evenly disbursed throughout the concrete, improved concrete durability. This virtually eliminated scaling due to freeze-thaw and de-icer salt action. Concrete containing such air bubbles is called *air-entrained concrete.*

Hardened concrete usually contains some water. When this water freezes, it expands and causes pressure that can rupture (scale) the concrete surface. The tiny air bubbles act as reservoirs or relief valves for the expanding water. They relieve pressure and prevent damage to the concrete.

Air entrainment is also important for concrete exposed to alternate cycles of freezing and thawing or use of deicers. In cold climates, and even in mild climates that have several cycles of freezing and thawing each year, it should be used for all exterior concrete work—including patios.

Air entraining also has other advantages. For example, the tiny air bubbles act like ball bearings in the mix, increasing its workability, with the result that less mixing water is required.

Aggregates are divided into two sizes—fine and course. Fine aggregate is always sand and coarse aggregate is usually gravel or crushed stone. Natural sand is the most commonly used fine aggregate. Manufactured sand, made by crushing gravel or stone, is also available in some areas. Sand should have particles ranging in sizes from one-third of an inch down to dust-size particles small enough to pass through a No. 100 mesh sieve (10,000 openings to the square inch). Mortar sand should not be used for making concrete because it contains only small particles.

Gravel or crushed stone are the most commonly used coarse aggregates. They should consist of particles that are sound, hard, and durable—not soft or flaky—with a minimum of long, silver-like pieces. Particles should range in size from one-fourth inch up to the maximum size used for the job. The common maximum sizes are ⅛, ½, ¾, 1, or 1½ inches. Generally, the most economical mix is obtained by using the largest size course aggregate that is practical or available. Coarse aggregate up to 1½" in size, for example, can be used in a thick foundation wall or heavy footing. In walls, the largest pieces should never be more than one-fifth the thickness of the finished wall section. For slabs, the maximum size should not exceed one-third the thickness of the slab.

All sizes of aggregates might not be available locally, but within the above limitations try to use the largest size aggregate readily available. Both fine and course aggregates for making concrete must be clean and free of excessive dirt, clay, silt, coal, or other organic matter such as leaves, roots, etc. These foreign materials will prevent the cement from properly binding the aggregate particles that would result in porous concrete with low strength and durability.

If you suspect that the sand contains too much extremely fine material, such as clay and silt, check its suitability for use in making concrete by the so-called *silt test*. Fill an ordinary quart canning jar or milk bottle to a depth of 2" with a representative sample of the sand in question. The sample should be taken from at least five different locations in the sand pile and thoroughly mixed together. Add clean water to the sand in the jar or bottle until it is about three-quarters full.

Shake the container vigorously for about a minute. Use the last few shakes to level off the sand. Allow the container to stand for an hour. Any clay or silt present will settle out in a layer above the sand. If the layer is more than one-sixteenth inch thick, the sand is not satisfactory unless the clay and silt are removed by washing (Fig. 6-6).

Estimating Quantities

Before getting down to the job of measuring and mixing, you will need to know just how much cement, sand, and coarse aggregate to buy for your project. To do this, you will first have to estimate the amount of concrete your project will require. Use the following simple formula. It works for any square or other rectangular-shaped areas.

$$\frac{\text{Width (ft.) x Length (ft.) x Thickness (in)}}{12} = \text{Cubic Ft.}$$

For example: A 4" thick patio slab, 12' wide and 15' long, would require: $\frac{12 \times 15 \times 4}{12} = 60$ cubic feet of concrete. A wall 3' high x 10' long and 8' thick would require: $\frac{3 \times 10 \times 8}{12} = 20$ Cu. ft.

The amount of concrete determined by the above formula does not allow for losses due to uneven subgrade, spillage, etc., so add 5 to 10 percent for such contingencies. In the case of the wall, the total amount of concrete required would be $20 + (0.10 \times 20) = 22$ cubic feet.

The quantities of material to buy can be calculated by multiplying the number of cubic feet of concrete (22 in this example) by the weights of materials needed for 1 cubic foot given in Table 6-2.

343

Assuming the wall will require air-entrained concrete and the maximum size of available aggregate is three-fourth of an inch, the quantities of material needed would be:

22 x 25 = 550 pounds of cement.

22 x 42 = 924 pounds of sand.

22 x 65 = 1430 pounds of gravel.

Plus a 10 percent allowance to cover normal waste.

Mixing the Ingredients

Proper mixing is an essential step in making good concrete. It is not sufficient merely to intermingle the ingredients. They must be thoroughly mixed so that cement paste coats every particle of fine and course aggregate in the mix. Concrete can be machine mixed or hand mixed.

Mixing the Concrete

Make a trial mix using the amounts of material shown in Table 6-1. If this mix does not give satisfactory workability, vary the amounts of aggregate used. Do *not* vary the amounts of cement and water.

All concrete should be mixed thoroughly until uniform in appearance. Add some of the mixing water, then the gravel and cement, then sand and the balance of the mixing water. Each piece of aggregate should be completely coated with cement paste.

Concrete for small improvements can be mixed in a mortar box or wheelbarrow (Fig. 6-7). A bag of cement weighs 94 pounds and is 1 cubic foot in volume.

The following mix (expressed in parts by volume) is recommended for the improvements that will only require small batches of mortar:

1 part portland cement.

2¼ parts sand.

3 parts gravel or crushed stone (1″ maximum size).

Two-thirds parts water (5 gallons of water per sack of cement).

The proportions suggested are based on experience with typical aggregates. The key to quality concrete is the amount of cement and water used. Therefore, the proportions of cement and water recommended should not be changed. If, after mixing the first batch the concrete is too stiff, use less sand and coarse aggregate in subsequent batches. When the mix is too soupy, add more sand and coarse aggregate until the desired consistency is obtained. To make 1 cubic yard of concrete you will need:

6¼ bags of portland cement.

14 cubic feet of sand (1260 pounds).

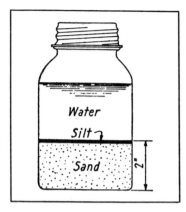

Fig. 6-6. Jar/silt test.

19 cubic feet of gravel or crushed stone (1900 pounds).

31½ gallons of water.

It is wise to order 10 percent extra for waste.

Ready Mixed Concrete

For larger jobs consider using ready mixed concrete. This eliminates the work of mixing and proportioning. Ready mixed concrete is sold by the cubic yard (27 cubic feet). When ordering remember the numbers 6-6-6. These stand for 6 bags of cement per cubic yard, 6 gallons of water per bag of cement, and 6 percent entrained air. Air-entraining portland cement contains an agent that forms billions of microscopic air bubbles in concrete. When hardened, air-entrained concrete virtually eliminates scaling due to freezing and thawing. It also resists scaling due to deicing salts.

Table 6-2. Proportions by Weight to Make
1 Cubic Foot of Concrete (courtesy of Florida Extension Service).

Maximum size Coarse Aggregate in.	Air-entrained Concrete							
	Cement lb.	Sand lb.	Course Agg. lb.	Water lb.	Cement lb.	Sand lb.	Agg. lb.	Water lb.
⅜	29	53	45	10	29	59	45	11
½	27	46	55	10	27	53	55	11
¾	26	42	65	10	25	47	65	10
1	24	39	70	9	24	45	70	10
1-½	23	38	75	9	23	43	75	9

*If crushed stone is used, decrease coarse aggregate by 3 lb, and increase sand by 3 pounds.

Fig. 6-7. Mixing concrete in a wheel barrow (courtesy of John Wahlfeldt).

All concrete exposed to freezing and thawing or deicing salts should be air-entrained concrete.

Machine Mixing

The best way to mix concrete is with a concrete mixer. It ensures thorough mixing of the ingredients and is the only way to produce air-entrained concrete. For best results, load the ingredients into the mixer in the following sequence.

☐ With the mixer stopped, add all the course aggregate and half of the mixing water. If an air-entraining agent is used, mix it with this part of the mixing water.

☐ Start the mixer and then add the sand, cement, and remaining water with the mixer running.

After all ingredients are in the mixer, continue mixing for at least three minutes or until all materials are thoroughly mixed and the concrete has a uniform color. A workable mix should look like Fig. 6-8. The concrete should be just wet enough to stick together without crumbling. It should "slide" down—not run off—a shovel. In a workable mix, there is sufficient cement paste to bind the pieces of aggregate so that they will not separate.

Hand Mixing

For very small jobs, where the volume of concrete required is less than a few cubic feet, it is sometimes more convenient, though less efficient, to mix by hand. Hand mixing is not vigorous enough to make air-entrained concrete regardless of whether air-entraining cement or air-entraining agent is used.

Prepackaged Mixes

Jobs small enough for hand mixing usually can be done with convenient prepackaged concrete mixes carried by building materials suppliers and hardware stores. All of the necessary ingredients—portland cement, dry sand, and dry coarse aggregate—are combined in the bag in the correct premeasured proportions. Packages are available in different weights, but the most common sizes are 45-pound and 90-pound bags. A 90-pound package makes two-thirds of a cubic foot of concrete. All you have to do is add the water and mix. Directions for mixing and the correct amount of water to add are given on the bag—*read carefully*.

To ensure that you get good quality from prepackaged concrete mixes, the American Society for Testing and Materials has adopted specifications for packaged, dry, combined materials for mortar and concrete (ASTM C-387). This specification covers the quality of the ingredients, the strength of the concrete obtained with the ingredients, and the type of bag in which the ingredients are packaged.

CONCRETE BLOCK

The size of a concrete masonry unit is usually described by listing its thickness, or width first, followed by its height and then its length. Therefore, a 4 x 8 x 16 block has a nominal width of 4 inches, a height of 8 inches and a length of 16 inches.

The nominal dimension includes three-eights of an inch allowed for the thickness of a standard mortar joint. The actual dimensions of the well-known 8 x 8 x 16" unit are manufactured as 7⅝ths x 7⅝ths x 15⅝ths.

Concrete masonry units offer a vast array of choices of natural faces and finishes for walls. These range from the wide variety that come at no extra cost to highly unusual, more expensive block for developing luxurious effects.

Customized or *architectural facing* concrete masonry units are designed and manufactured to provide the finished surface of a wall without the addition of opaque coatings or treatments which would appreciably change its appearance.

Using these units, a wall can be built as an exterior and nonloadbearing wall. It can be designed of "through-wall" units where only one masonry unit comprises the wall section. The wall section might consist of architectural facing concrete masonry units as a veneer that is backed up with concrete masonry or other

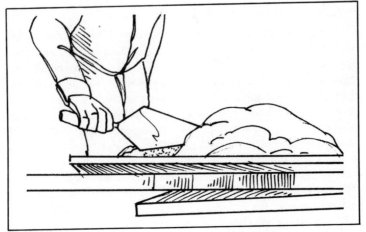

Fig. 6-8. Correct concrete texture (courtesy of John Wahlfeldt).

materials. Or the units might be the facing portion of the structural composite or cavity wall.

Fluted and scored, or ribbed, units provide the architectural design with raised striations that can be developed into many kinds of patterns. The accuracy that is achieved in machine production of these units makes it possible to produce the effect of long, continuous vertical straight lines even when the blocks are laid in running bond.

Shadowall block, developed and introduced by the National Concrete Masonry Association, are units with recessed corners that can be put together in such limitless variety of patterns that this product has been called the "block of 1000 faces." Hi-Lite block, another type of raised pattern, can be used similarly. Interesting changing shadow effects can be obtained with such units when they are used on exteriors.

Open-faced block of many patterns is available for decorative uses or for partially screening walls or yards from either the sun or outside views. Block with colorful, hard, glossy, mar-resistant surfaces that resemble ceramic tile in appearance, durability and ease of cleaning are produced by some manufacturers. Surfaces might be made of epoxy or polyester resins and might contain fine sand or other fillers. Ceramic or porcelanized glazes, mineral glazes and cement-like finishes have also been used.

A number of rapid assembly systems have come into use in the past 20 years. These are systems designed for assembly by the unskilled or partially skilled. They include:

Fig. 6-9. Laying block beginning at a corner (courtesy of Portland Cement Company).

☐ Tongue-and-groove interlocking systems that are assembled dry and then bonded together by grout that flows through horizontal and vertical channels.

☐ Wedge shaped blocks that interlock and are self-aligning and self-plumbing.

☐ Surface bonding application. This involves stacking the block up without mortar and then troweling both sides with a plaster containing strands of fiberglass to provide a waterproof wall with good lateral strength.

Fig. 6-10. Line stretched as guide (courtesy of Portland Cement Company).

Estimating

Before any work is started, the amount of materials should be estimated. Block and mortar materials are estimated as follows.

Block. First, determine the number of courses (rows) by multiplying the height of the wall in feet by 1½ for an 8″ high block. Multiply the wall height by three for a 4″ high block. Find the number of blocks in each course by multiplying the length of the wall in feet by ¾ inches. The total number of blocks is the number of blocks in each course multiplied by the number of courses. Each end of the wall requires a half block for every other course. To determine the number of corner block, multiply the number of corners by the number of courses in the wall.

Mortar. For each 100 of the 8 x 8 x 16″ blocks use 2½ sacks of masonry cement—Type II—and 667 pounds of sand. *Example*: For a 6′ high garden wall that is 50′ long on each of three sides you would need:

6 (height in feet) x 1½ = 9 courses.

150 (length in feet) x ¾ = 112½ blocks for each course.

Each course requires 110 stretcher blocks, 2 corner blocks and 1 half block. The entire wall requires 990 stretcher blocks, 18 corner blocks and 9 half blocks. The mortar necessary for laying up this number of block will require:

26 sacks of masonry cement—Type II—and 6800 pounds of sand.

How to Lay Concrete Block

Concrete block of various shapes and sizes are available for home improvements, but for most around-the-house jobs,

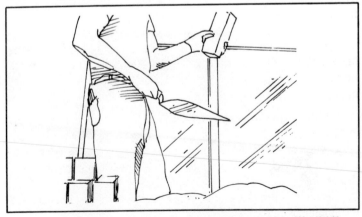

Fig. 6-11. The proper way to hold brick for laying (courtesy of John Wahlfeldt).

Table 6-3. Bricks and Mortar.

Brick Sizes (inches)	Number per 100 Square Feet	Wall	Cubic Feet of Mortar Per 100 Square Feet of Wall		
			Joint Thickness		
		1/4″	3/8″	1/2″	
2 ⅔ x 4 x 8	742	40	58	73	
2 x 4 x 12	660		67	86	
2 ⅔ x 4 x 12	495	37	54	68	
3 1/5 x 4 x 8	618	35	50	64	
4 x 4 x 8	495		43	55	
4 x 4 x 12	330	27	39	49	
2 ⅔ x 6 x 12	495		82	106	
2 ¼ x 3 ¾ x 8	715	4.2	6.0	7.6	

stretcher, corner and half-block are needed. Common sizes are 8 x 8 x 16, 8 x 4 x 16, and 6 x 8 x 16 inches.

The mortar for block work consists of 1 part masonry cement and 2¼ to 3 parts clean sand. Enough mixing water is added to obtain a workable mortar.

Always lay block from the corners first (Fig. 6-9). Each block is carefully leveled and plumbed because the corners are the guides for the rest of the wall. A line stretched between the corners serves as a guide for the intermediate block. If the wall is long and the line sags at the center, lay block near the center to hold up the line (Fig. 6-10).

Many techniques are used to place mortar for the joints. One way is to spread a strip of mortar along the face shells of the block. The only mortar placed on the block being laid is put along the end face shells.

A mason's rule of thumb is to use approximately one-half inch of mortar between the bricks—horizontally and vertically. This is known as *buttering* a thin layer, one-fourth inch, of mortar on the brick.

Holding Brick for Laying

With a trowel in your right hand and a brick in your left hand, layer the brick with mortar and set it into the bed. As the mortar oozes out from the pressure of the brick being set, cut it away with the trowel. Place the excess mortar on the next brick in your hand (Fig. 6-11).

Table 6-3 provides information on the number of bricks and the amount of mortar required for laying up a 4″ brick wall.

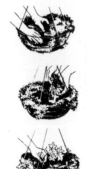

Chapter 7
Greenhouse
Gardening Calendar

As with the outside gardening plot, there are some specific monthly duties required inside the greenhouse. The following sections will help you get started on a "log keeping" program. Undoubtedly, there will be many individual programs added.

JANUARY THROUGH DECEMBER

January. Even for those operating a year around greenhouse, this is probably the slowest month for work. It is also pre-seed sowing month. It provides the opportunity to get your maintenance work completed. Prepare seed flats for the forthcoming seed-sowing season which, in certain areas, is this month.

If you have potted bulbs—tulips, narcissi, daffodil, hyacinths, crocus—in pots outside, bring them into the greenhouse about the third week of this month. Slip geranium, chrysanthemum, and coleus plants.

February. The sun is getting higher now as days grow longer. Take cuttings from mature plants and place them in a hot frame. Schizanthus should be cut back to get a second blooming. However, they won't produce as large blooms.

All annual seeds can be sown. Additional chrysanthemum cuttings can be taken. Check hanging baskets and all pot plants that you plan to take outside during the summer. Add additional soil if it is needed. Make new hanging baskets from rooted clippings.

In frost/freeze zones, transplant vegetable and flower seedlings for planting outside in March and April.

March. With longer, warmer days and more light, plants are making extensive growth this month. Clip back varieties you want to "bush" out and place the slips in the hot frame.

In colder zones, sow vegetable and annual flower seeds. Start begonias and gloxinias sowing by placing them in flats of peat moss.

If you are raising citrus and other fruiting specimens, most are blooming now and will require pollination.

Pot the chrysanthemum, coleus and geranium clippings taken in February.

If you are raising strawberries in pots, deflower and allow no more than 11 to 12 blossoms on each plant to assure large luscious fruit—excessive blossoms drop off anyway. The same applies to citrus and other fruiting plants.

April. This is a busy month. Most plants are rapidly putting on new growth. In many areas, seedlings have already been transplanted to the garden plot. In cold areas, seedlings can be moved outside to a cold frame to "harden off." This makes space to divide ornamentals such as diffenbachia, philodendron, etc.

For those who don't plan an outside garden, sow tomato, cucumbers, melon and any other vegetable you plan to raise for garden greenhouse cultivation.

Repot flowering plants that have become pot-bound. Cut back most ferns, divide and repot. Save some for hanging baskets.

May. It is not too late to plant tomatoes and all other vegetables if you haven't already done so. Again, in freeze zones, most of your seedlings are now ready for transplanting to the garden. Most flowering plants can be sown now for profuse summer blooming if you are operating a year around greenhouse.

With all of the activity, don't overlook spraying and fumigating to keep down diseases and control pests.

June. This is the last call to pot chrysanthemum and cyclamen. It's time to fertilize all other plants except newly potted clippings. Plants that have become top-heavy should be staked.

Don't forget to open ventilators and doors and shade the plants that don't require an overabundance of sunshine.

With the vegetable garden in, the work load outside is lessened. It's a good time to "scrub" down the greenhouse inside and out.

July. The new growth put on your plants since February will require staking. This is especially true for older plants. Pinch back chrysanthemums and other "fall blooming" varieties to insure large blooms.

Again, if you are raising your summer garden inside, fertilize tomatoes and peppers. Keep them well watered and aid pollination by spraying with water on bright sunny days. Use fruit set too!

August. Don't forget that hanging baskets, especially, *must* be watered daily. All plants should be "sprayed" with Nutri-Sol or some other favorite every 10 to 14 days.

If you haven't scrubbed inside and out, this is the last call—busy time is coming up. The house needs to be spotless for the new plants and mature plants you will bring back into the greenhouse if they have had a "change of pace" outside during the summer.

September. All vegetable seeds in all zones should be sown by now. Move the market packs, flats, pots—whatever you have sown them in—inside to a freshly prepared area on your benches.

Many bulbs can be planted and cuttings can be taken. Hot frames should be replenished with seed and fresh soil. Be sure to check the "coil" and replace the tin foil.

Pot chrysanthemums as soon as the buds appear. After potting remove the buds. Azaleas, cyclamen, primulus and others should be brought inside along with other tender plants susceptible to the quick frosts of autumn.

Dig up from the garden pepper plants and even some tomato plants that still have fruit on them. Pot them in good potting soil and you are ahead of the game. All other vegetables, lettuce, carrots, etc., should be sown this month in individual flats to insure continuous vegetable eating all winter long.

October. Indian summer is from warm to frosty. The greenhouse is full with many old potted plants, newly potted plants and winter vegetables, flowers and seedlings.

Temperature control is critical because frosts can occur unexpectedly and just severe enough to hurt the really tender vegetables and other varieties. If frosts are forecast, turn on heaters. Heaters probably can be turned off during the day.

To bring a little "spring" to this time of year, pot daffodil and tulips to flower before Christmas. Poinsettia are especially popular during the upcoming holiday season. Pay extra attention to watering to avoid Botrytis.

November. All flower seeds for a colorful showing, especially in cold climates, should be sown this month. In freeze zone *all* potted plants now return to the greenhouse if a few have been allowed to stay outside. Even in warm zones, it's time to return the newly potted ornamentals. Transplant the vegetables and flower seedlings that have been kept in a "shaded spot." Take clippings from existing shrubs for rooting in the hot frame in a mixture of sand/peat/compost on flats.

December. Slip tomato plants that are now gangly. Pinch back all other tall-growing flowers and vegetables and put slips into hot frame for rooting. If you plan flowering bulbs by Christmas, they must be inside now. Cut back perennials such as chrysanthemum, etc. Plant slips in market packs or pots—several to a container to save space for transplanting—to flower in January and February.

Double check all heating systems—large to individual space heaters—to make sure the thermostats are working and the systems are in good shape for the upcoming cold weather.

OVERVIEW OF SEASONS

Spring. By mid-February (in warm winter climates, January), the first warm, sunny days that spell the beginning of spring arrive. It is the signal to start seeds in the greenhouse that will yield sturdy, bedding plants to be used later in the garden.

For the flower garden make preparations for Ageratum, Aster, Carnation, Coleus, and Dahlia. Make preparations for dwarf varieties such as Dianthus, Lobelia, Marigold, Nierembergia, Periwinkle, Petunia, Phlox, Salpiglosis, Salvia, Snapdragon, Stock, Sweet Alyssum, Torenia, and Verbena. For the vegetable garden, make preparations for Tomatoes, Peppers, Eggplant, Cucumbers, Cauliflower, Cabbage, etc.

More watering will be required as the dark, short days of winter turn to longer more sunlit days of early spring. Plants will show a spurt of new growth that indicates the need for more feeding of diluted liquid fertilizers.

Space is at a premium during this period. The major problem during this time is that as plants multiply most gardeners do not want to throw away the excess. Now is the time to have that plant sale or to give spring gifts to friends. For successful greenhousing, you will have to conquer the desire to keep all plants grown. You will have to devise your own inventory control. But always remember to only keep plants that are healthy and to keep only the amount you can raise without it becoming an excessive chore. Don't let too many plants of any one variety take up valuable space for new varieties to be tried.

Summer. Summer means the period after a late frost in your area until the beginning of autumn (usually after Labor Day). If you plan to operate a year around greenhouse, the following are some varieties which will provide color yet will not hinder your cleaning up and preparing the greenhouse for the "fill-up" time of winter.

Some suggestion varieties and when to start them are: Achimenes—late winter/early spring; Begonnia—seeds or cuttings in winter; Beloperone—cuttings any time; Caladium—tubers in early spring; Gloxinia—tubers in winter or spring and seeds in January; Impatiens—seeds or cuttings in winter; Kaepferis—spring.

Fall. This is a many colored time. The following indicates a good variety and how to start them. Azalea—miniature—buy from nursery. Boston Daisy—bring in from the outside and put in pots to continue blooming. Ageratum—dig plants and pot; trim back or pot cuttings or sow seeds in compact plants from the outside or take cuttings of favorite colors to root in the greenhouse.

Bachelor's button (Centaurea cyanus)—sow a few seeds in several pots. Later, thin to one or two in each pot. Cyclamen—they will provide a long blooming season and may be purchased from your local nursery. Chrysanthemums—dig clumps of low-growing varieties in various stages of growth, bud and flower from the garden. Pot up. Buy plants at this stage from your local nursery.

Coleus—take clippings from those in your flower beds, pot or sow fresh seed. Dwarf marigolds—dig and pot plants from outdoors. Remove the long straggle growth, but don't cut off too much or sow seeds. Dwarf stock—sow seeds in flats and transplant to individual pots or thin to about 4″ apart.

Freesias—plant corms in flats or individual pots. Keep in the coolest part of the greenhouse. Under the bench is an ideal location for at least 6 to 8 weeks and then begin forcing, preferably one flat or a few pots at a time, every two weeks.

Godetia—sow seeds in the flat where they are to mature. After germination, thin to 3″ between seedlings. Geraniums—dig, cut back and pot up plants from the garden or take slips and place in hot frame for rooting and repotting later.

Impatiens—dig plants from outdoors or slip them or sow seeds. Ivy geranium—use at least nine cuttings from plants outdoors. They make excellent hanging baskets. Lobelia—dig, pot up and trim back from the garden or sow seeds in one pot to be transplanted later. Miniature roses—buy plants from a nursery or mailorder house or dig several from your rose garden; cut back to 6 inches.

Nasturtians—plant two or three seeds to a 4-inch pot; thin to one plant in each. Larkspur—sow seeds in 6″ flats. Thin to about 4″

apart. Sweet alyssum—sow seeds in 4" pots and place to border the benches. Schizanthus (poor man's orchid)—sow seeds in pots or in flats to mature where they should be thinned to 4" apart.

Snapdragon—dig clumps from the garden. After they have bloomed, cut back and new growth will give winter/spring flowers, or sow seeds. Place in individual pots beginning with 3 to 4" pots up to 8" pots through spring. Sweet peas—plant 3 seeds in from 6 to 8" pots. Thin and leave the strongest plant in each pot.

QUICK REFERENCE GUIDES

The best plants are grown when optimum nighttime temperatures are provided. However, almost all plants cultivated in home greenhouses are tolerant of considerable variation. For example; many plants that can be grown at 55 F can also be grown at 50 F. They will be firmer in growth, they might mature later and flowers will tend to last longer. The same plants might also be grown at 60 F, but these will be softer, probably taller, and the flower petals will fade more rapidly.

After the heat is on in autumn, place several thermostats in various parts of the greenhouse to determine actual temperatures at different locations at different times of the day and night. This will enable you to properly locate your "cool" "moderate" and "warm" plants to take advantage of the varied temperatures at night that are present in most greenhouse. Check temperatures occasionally because they will vary when you relocate plants and when you grow different crops.

Appendix J provides the names of many plants that can be raised under greenhouse temperatures varying from 40 F to 65 F.

Table 7-1. Palm Plants.

Common Name	Botanical Name	Foliage Color and Notes
Parlor Palm	Chamaedorea elegans	Green, a good dwarf
Madagascar Palm	Chrysalidocarpus lutescens	Green, a good clump-forming palm, will eventually grow too large for pot or tub
Licuala Palm	Licula grandis	Green, attractive small palm when young Eventually grows too large for pot or tub
Seaforthia Palm	Plychosperma elegans	Green. Small, larger only with age
McArthur Cluster Palm	Ptychosperma macarthuri	Green dwarf clump
Lady Palm	Rhapis excelsa	Green, slender dwarf clump growing

Table 7-2. Trees for the Greenhouse.

Common Name	Botanical Name	Foliage Color and Notes
Norfolk Island	Araucaria excelsa	Green, attractive tree.
Schefflera	Brassaia actiniphy-lla	Green. Will outgrow garden room if not cut back. Easy to take cuttings and keep to pot or tub size.
Rubber Plants	Ficus elastica	Variable - grow large but adapt beautifully to cuttings.
Fiddle-leaf Fig	Ficus lyrata	Green, grows large but easy to root.
Kumquat	Fortunella spp.	Green. Many varieties; fruit production lowered by light inside, but worth the effort.

Appendix K provides the names of many plants that can be raised in the greenhouse during the spring, summer, fall and winter. Appendix L provides a suggested plant materials list for a 10 x 16 greenhouse.

PALMS FOR POTS AND TUBS

The very nature of a greenhouse spells "palms." This is especially true for those people greenhousing in cold, frosty zones. Table 7-1 is an easy guide for getting you started in the palm business. Palms are easy to raise in pots and they require little attention. They will last for years in a greenhouse and they will need repotting only occasionally.

TREES FOR POTS

People do forget that trees can also be grown in the greenhouse. Many times, greenhouse trees are dubbed "plants" when they are really trees. Table 7-2 is a quick, handy guide to trees for the greenhouse.

All of the examples are excellent for any size greenhouse and *all*, palms and trees can be kept dwarfed by cutting them back when they become too large. New trees can be started from the clippings.

Plan 1
Sash Greenhouse

This plan is provided by the courtesy of the Cooperative Extension Unit, University of Florida.

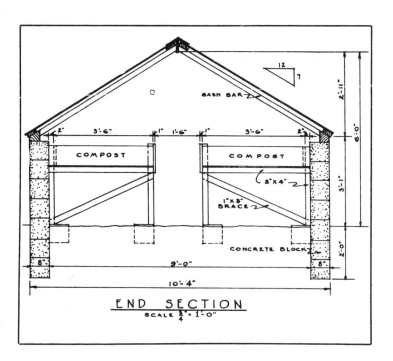

END SECTION
SCALE ¾" = 1'-0"

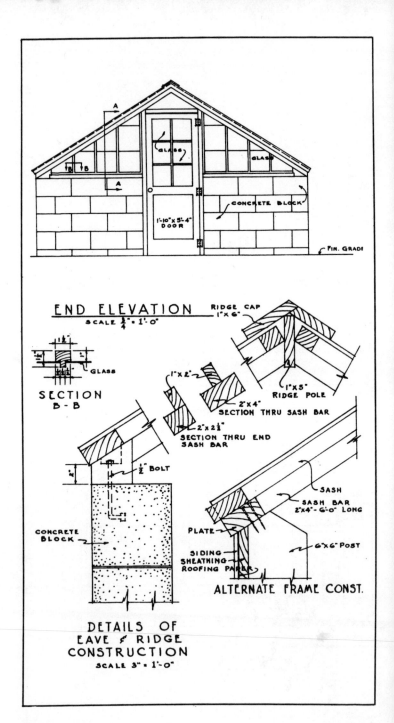

END ELEVATION
SCALE ¼" = 1'-0"

GLASS

SECTION
B-B

RIDGE CAP
1"x 6"

1"x 2"

2"x 4"
SECTION THRU SASH BAR

1"x 5"
RIDGE POLE

2"x 2½"
SECTION THRU END
SASH BAR

½ BOLT

2"

CONCRETE
BLOCK

SASH

SASH BAR
2"x4"-6'-0" LONG

PLATE

SIDING
SHEATHING
ROOFING PAPER

6"x 6" POST

ALTERNATE FRAME CONST.

DETAILS OF
EAVE & RIDGE
CONSTRUCTION
SCALE 3" = 1'-0"

A

B B

A

GLASS

GLASS

CONCRETE BLOCK

FIN. GRADE

1'-10" x 5'-4"
DOOR

360

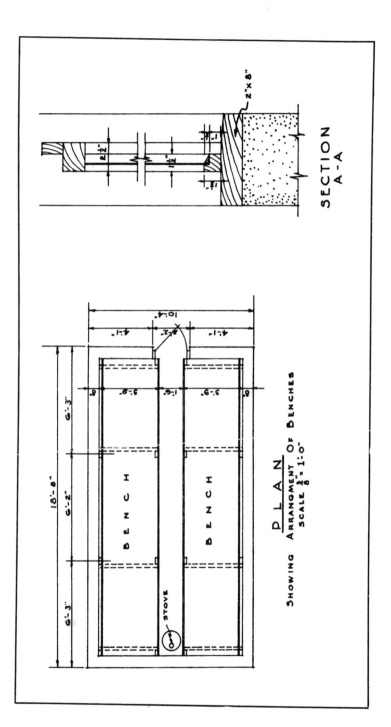

2" x 8"

$2\frac{1}{2}$"

$1\frac{1}{2}$"

1"

1"

SECTION
A-A

10'-4"

4'-1"

2'-2"

4'-1"

18'-6"

6'-3"

6'-2"

6'-3"

3'-6"

1'-6"

3'-6"

6"

6"

BENCH

BENCH

STOVE

PLAN

SHOWING ARRANGEMENT OF BENCHES
SCALE $\frac{1}{8}$" = 1'-0"

361

Plan 2

Flue-Heated Greenhouse

This plan is provided by the courtesy of the Cooperative Extension Unit, University of Florida.

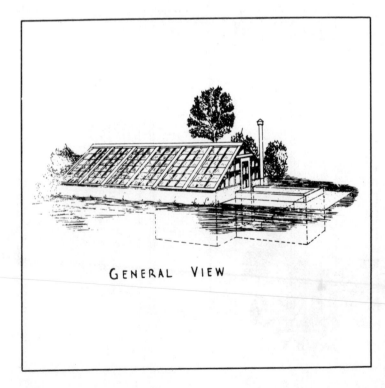

GENERAL VIEW

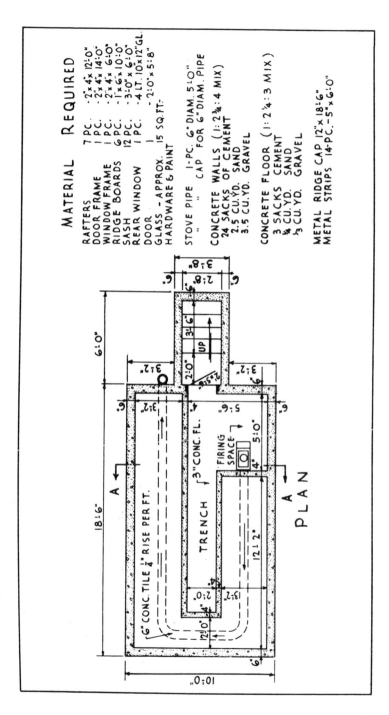

MATERIAL REQUIRED

RAFTERS	7 PC.	— 2″×4″× 12′-0″
DOOR FRAME	1 PC.	— 2″×4″× 14′-0″
WINDOW FRAME	1 PC.	— 2″×4″× 6′-0″
RIDGE BOARDS	6 PC.	— 1″×6″× 10′-0″
SASH	12 PC.	— 3′-0″ × 6′-0″
REAR WINDOW	1 PC.	— 4 LT. 10″×12″ GL.
DOOR	1	— 2′-0″ × 5′-8″
GLASS — APPROX. 15 SQ.FT.		
HARDWARE & PAINT		

STOVE PIPE 1-PC. 6″ DIAM. 5′-0″
      ″   ″ CAP FOR 6″ DIAM. PIPE

CONCRETE WALLS (1:2¾:4 MIX)
24 SACKS OF CEMENT
2.5 CU.YD. SAND
3.5 CU.YD. GRAVEL

CONCRETE FLOOR (1:2¼:3 MIX)
3 SACKS CEMENT
¼ CU.YD. SAND
⅓ CU.YD. GRAVEL

METAL RIDGE CAP 12″×18′-6″
METAL STRIPS 14-PC. — 5″× 6′-0″

PLAN

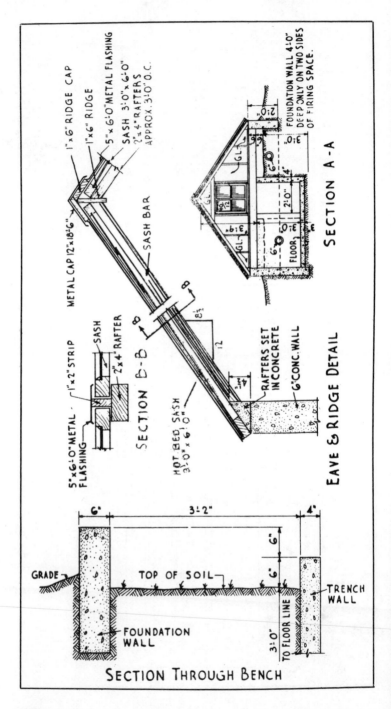

1"x6" RIDGE CAP

1"x6" RIDGE

5"x 6'O" METAL FLASHING

SASH 3'-0"x 6'-0"

2"x 4" RAFTERS
APPROX. 3'-0" O.C.

METAL CAP 12"x18"x6"

SASH BAR

FOUNDATION WALL 4'-0"
DEEP ONLY ON TWO SIDES
OF FIRING SPACE.

2'-0"

3'-0"

G.L.

6"

2'-0"

G.L.

3'-0"

G.L.

6"

FLOOR

3'-0"

SECTION A-A

1"x 2" STRIP

SASH

2"x 4" RAFTER

5"x 6'O" METAL
FLASHING

SECTION B-B

B

8½

12

3½
4

RAFTERS SET
IN CONCRETE

6" CONC. WALL

HOT BED SASH
3'-0"x 6'-0"

EAVE & RIDGE DETAIL

6"

3'-2"

4"

6"

6"

GRADE

TOP OF SOIL

TRENCH
WALL

FOUNDATION
WALL

3'-0"

TO FLOOR LINE

SECTION THROUGH BENCH

Plan 3
Portable Plastic
Greenhouse

This plan is provided by the courtesy of the Cooperative Extension Unit, University of Florida.

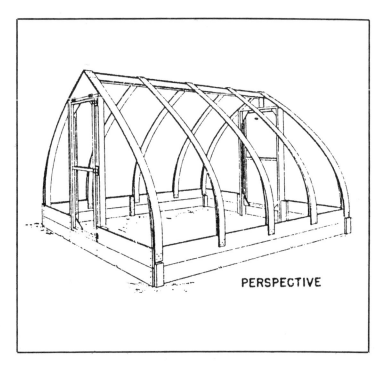

PERSPECTIVE

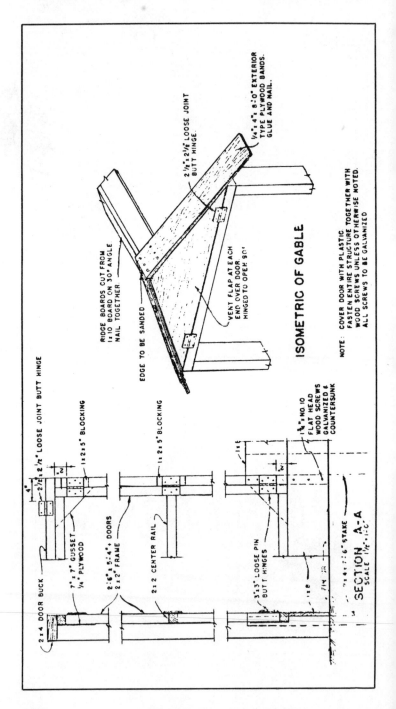

2 1/2" x 2 1/2" LOOSE JOINT BUTT HINGE

2" x 2" x 5" BLOCKING

2 x 4 DOOR BUCK

7" x 7" GUSSET 1/4" PLYWOOD

2'-6" x 5'-4" DOORS 2 x 2 FRAME

1 x 2 x 5" BLOCKING

2 x 2 CENTER RAIL

3" x 3" LOOSE PIN BUTT HINGES

1 1/2" NO 10 FLAT HEAD WOOD SCREWS GALVANIZED & COUNTERSUNK

SECTION A-A
SCALE 1 1/2" = 1'-0"

2" x 4" x 7'-6" STAKE

RIDGE BOARDS CUT FROM 1 x 10 BOARD ON 30° ANGLE NAIL TOGETHER.

2 1/2" x 2 1/2" LOOSE JOINT BUTT HINGE.

EDGE TO BE SANDED

1/4" x 4" x 8'-0" EXTERIOR TYPE PLYWOOD BANDS. GLUE AND NAIL.

VENT FLAP AT EACH END OVER DOOR HINGED TO OPEN 90°.

ISOMETRIC OF GABLE

NOTE: COVER DOOR WITH PLASTIC FASTEN ENTIRE STRUCTURE TOGETHER WITH WOOD SCREWS UNLESS OTHERWISE NOTED. ALL SCREWS TO BE GALVANIZED.

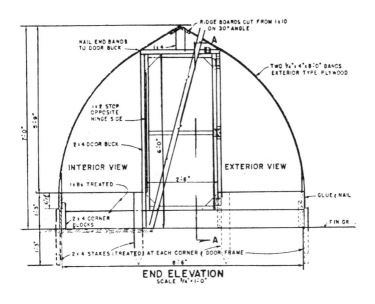

 RIDGE BOARDS CUT FROM 1x10
ON 30° ANGLE

NAIL END BANDS
TO DOOR BUCK

1x4

A

TWO 1/4"x4"x8'0" BANDS
EXTERIOR TYPE PLYWOOD

1x2 STOP
OPPOSITE
HINGE SIDE

2x4 DOOR BUCK

6'0"

INTERIOR VIEW

EXTERIOR VIEW

1x8s TREATED

2'6"

GLUE & NAIL

FIN. GR.

2x4 CORNER
BLOCKS

7'0"

5'9"

1'3"

6"

1'3"

2x4 STAKES (TREATED) AT EACH CORNER & DOOR FRAME

A

8'6"

END ELEVATION
SCALE 3/4"=1'-0"

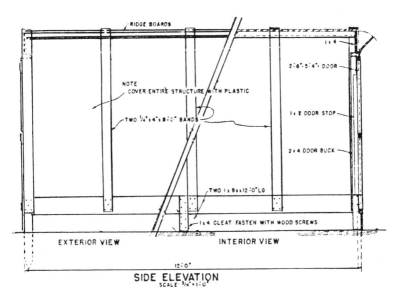

RIDGE BOARDS

1x4

2'6"x5'4" DOOR

NOTE
COVER ENTIRE STRUCTURE WITH PLASTIC

1x2 DOOR STOP

TWO 1/4"x4"x8'0" BANDS

2x4 DOOR BUCK

TWO 1x8x12'0"LG

1x4 CLEAT FASTEN WITH WOOD SCREWS

EXTERIOR VIEW

INTERIOR VIEW

12'0"

SIDE ELEVATION
SCALE 3/4"=1'-0"

367

Plan 4
Cold Frame
Greenhouse

This plan is provided by the courtesy of the Cooperative Extension Unit, University of Florida.

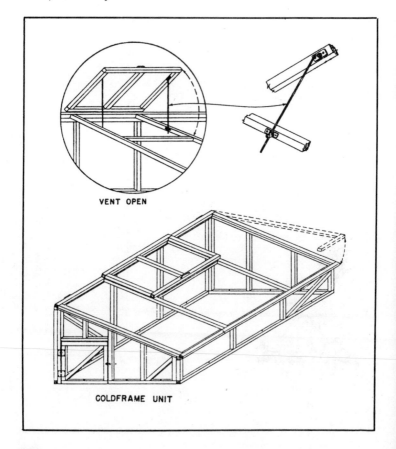

VENT OPEN

COLDFRAME UNIT

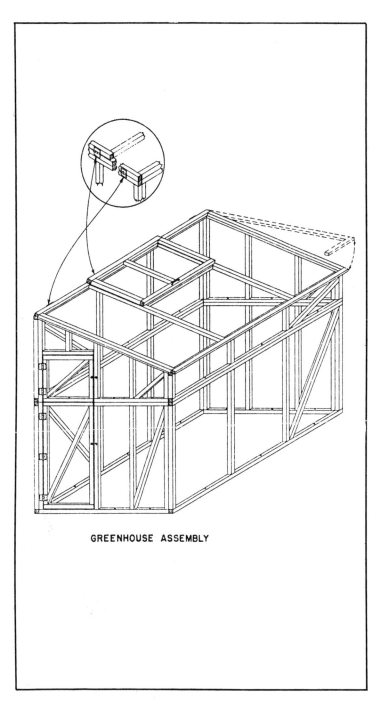

GREENHOUSE ASSEMBLY

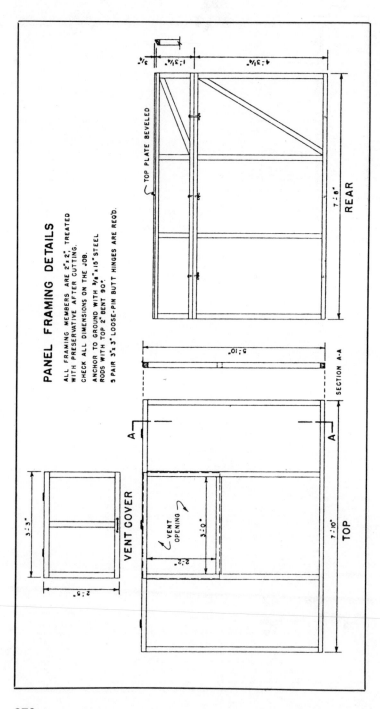

PANEL FRAMING DETAILS

ALL FRAMING MEMBERS ARE 2"x2", TREATED
WITH PRESERVATIVE AFTER CUTTING.

CHECK ALL DIMENSIONS ON THE JOB.

ANCHOR TO GROUND WITH 3/8"x15" STEEL
RODS WITH TOP 2" BENT 90°.

5 PAIR 3"x 3" LOOSE-PIN BUTT HINGES ARE REQD.

TOP PLATE BEVELED

REAR

7'-6"

4'-3¾"   1'-3¾"   ¾"

SECTION A-A

5'-10"

VENT COVER

3'-3"

2'-5"

TOP

7'-10"

VENT OPENING

3'-0"

2'-2"

A   A

370

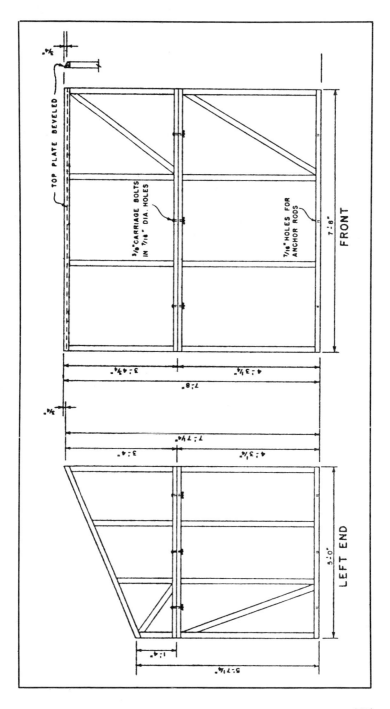

TOP PLATE BEVELED

3/8" CARRIAGE BOLTS IN 7/16" DIA. HOLES

7/16" HOLES FOR ANCHOR RODS

FRONT

7'-8"

3/4"

3'-4¾"

4'-3¼"

7'-8"

3/4"

7'-7¼"

3'-4"

4'-3¼"

LEFT END

5'-0"

1'-8"

1'-4"

5'-7¼"

371

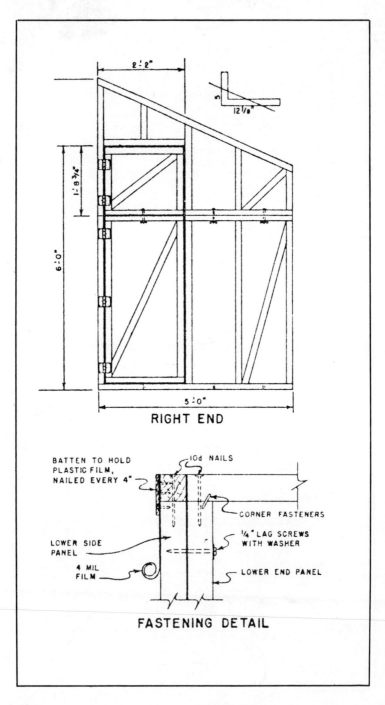

RIGHT END

BATTEN TO HOLD
PLASTIC FILM,
NAILED EVERY 4"

10d NAILS

CORNER FASTENERS

LOWER SIDE
PANEL

¼" LAG SCREWS
WITH WASHER

4 MIL
FILM

LOWER END PANEL

FASTENING DETAIL

Plan 5
Saran Shadehouse

This plan is provided by the courtesy of the Cooperative Extension Unit, University of Florida.

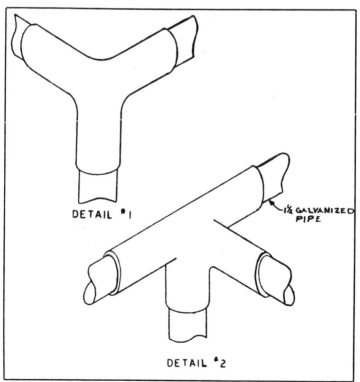

DETAIL #1

1½ GALVANIZED PIPE

DETAIL #2

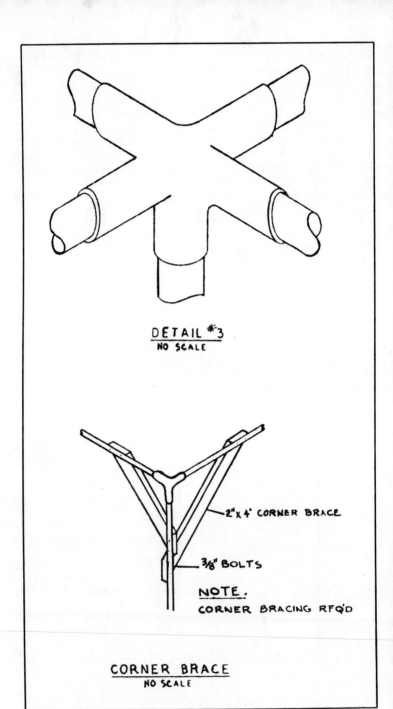

DETAIL #3
NO SCALE

2" x 4' CORNER BRACE

3/8" BOLTS

NOTE.
CORNER BRACING RFQ'D

CORNER BRACE
NO SCALE

374

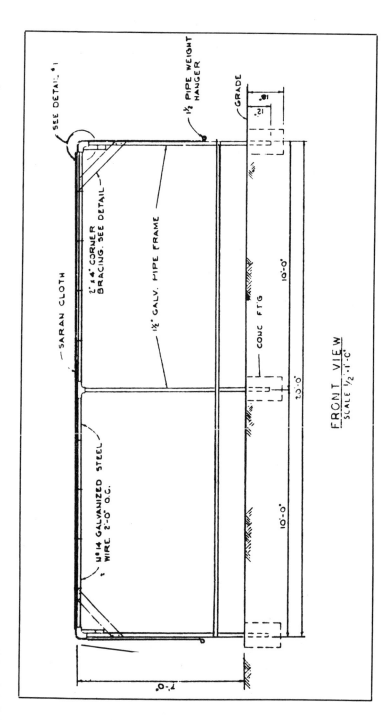

FRONT VIEW
SCALE ½"·1'-0"

SEE DETAIL #1

1½" PIPE WEIGHT HANGER

GRADE

SARAN CLOTH

2"×4" CORNER BRACING. SEE DETAIL

1½" GALV. PIPE FRAME

N°14 GALVANIZED STEEL WIRE 2'-0" O.C.

CONC FTG

10'-0"

20'-0"

10'-0"

7'-0"

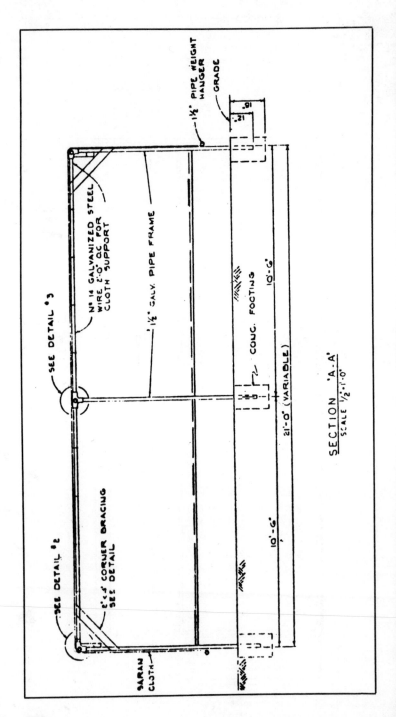

SECTION 'A-A'
SCALE ½"=1'-0"

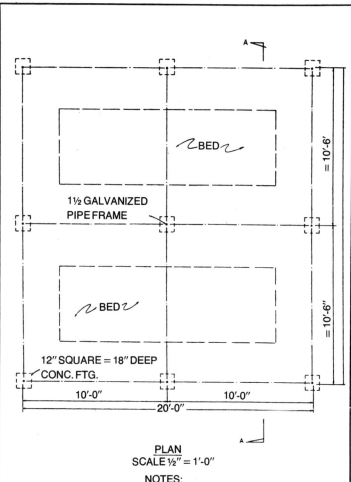

A

= 10'-6'

BED

1½ GALVANIZED
PIPE FRAME

= 10'-6"

BED

12" SQUARE = 18" DEEP
CONC. FTG.

10'-0"   10'-0"

20'-0"

A

PLAN
SCALE ½" = 1'-0"

NOTES:

FRAME IS COVERED W/ UNITS OF 20' WIDE
SECTIONS OF SARAN CLOTH SEWN TOGETHER
TO FORM A SINGLE SECTION FROM GROUND
ON ONE SIDE TO GROUND ON OPPOSITE SIDE.
END FLAPS MAY BE ATTACHED TO MAIN SECTION
W/ METAL GROMMETS & SNAPS.
PIPE WEIGHT HANGER ALSO SERVES AS A
SPINDLE TO ROLL SARAN ON IN THE EVENT
OF REMOVAL FOR PERIODS OF HIGH WIND, ETC.

Plan 6

Orlyt Lean-To Model

This plan is provided by the courtesy of the Cooperative Extension Unit, University of Florida.

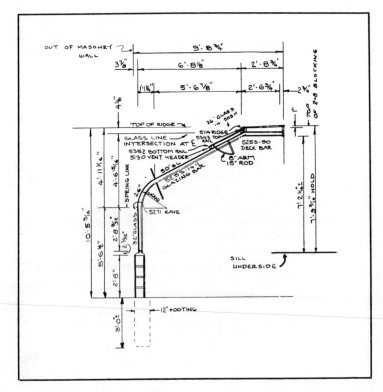

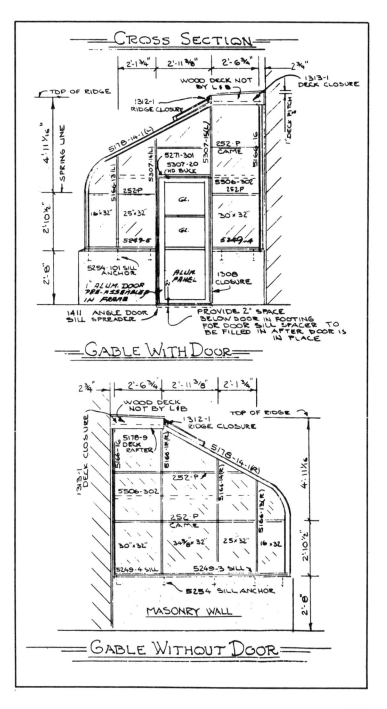

CROSS SECTION

GABLE WITH DOOR

GABLE WITHOUT DOOR

379

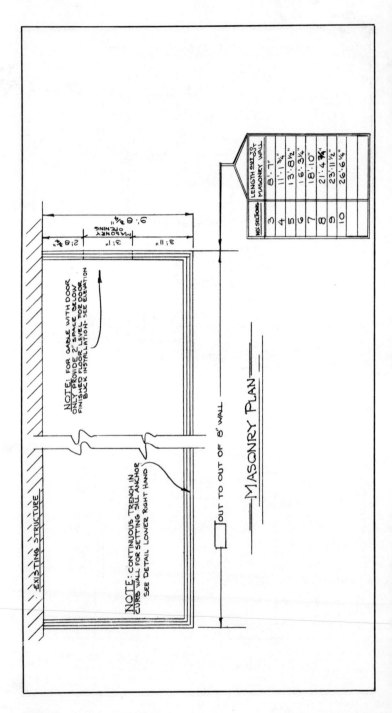

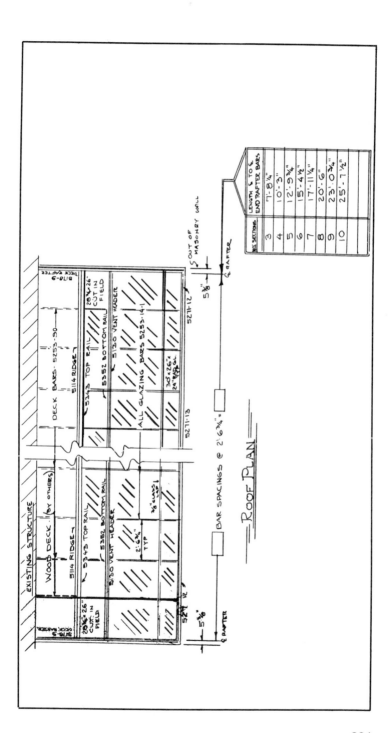

Roof Plan

No. Sections	Length ⅊ to ⅊ END RAFTER BARS
3	7'-8¼"
4	10'-3"
5	12'-9¾"
6	15'-4½"
7	17'-11¼"
8	20'-6"
9	23'-0¾"
10	25'-7½"

EXISTING STRUCTURE

WOOD DECK (BY OTHERS)

5114 RIDGE

DECK RAFTER
5116-9

20¾×26 CUT IN FIELD

5343 TOP RAIL

5352 BOTTOM RAIL

5130 VENT HEADER

⅊ RAFTER

⅊ RAFTER

DECK BARS 5253-90

5211-13

5211-12

5130 VENT HEADER

ALL GLAZING BARS 5253-14-1

2½×26× 24"RAD. O.L.

⅊ OUT OF MASONRY WALL

5%"

5%"

5%"

⅜"GLASS
LAP

2'-6¾"
TYP

BAR SPACINGS @ 2'-6¾" =

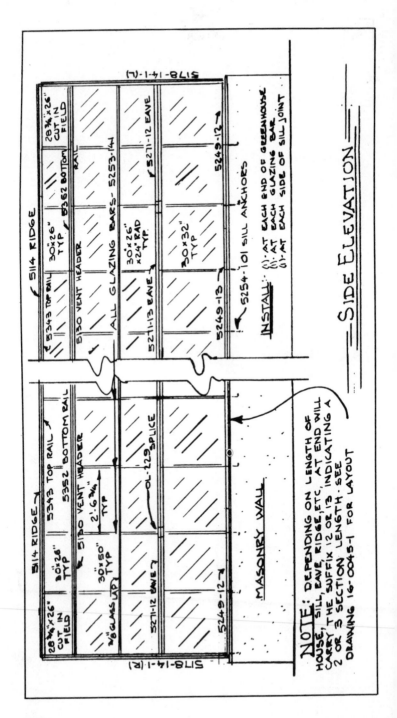

SIDE ELEVATION

S118-14-1(L)

5114 RIDGE

28¾"×26" CUT IN FIELD

30"×26" TYP

5343 TOP RAIL

5150 VENT HEADER

¾" GLASS (UP) TYP

30"×50" TYP

5271-12 EAVE?

5352 BOTTOM RAIL

2'.6¾" TYP

OL-229 SPLICE

5249-12-7

MASONRY WALL

NOTE: DEPENDING ON LENGTH OF HOUSE, SILL, EAVE, RIDGE, ETC., AT END WILL CARRY THE SUFFIX 12 OR 13 INDICATING A 2 OR 3 SECTION LENGTH. SEE DRAWING 16-0045-1 FOR LAYOUT

5114 RIDGE

28¾"×26" CUT IN FIELD

30"×26" TYP 5362 BOTTOM RAIL

5343 TOP RAIL

5150 VENT HEADER

ALL GLAZING BARS- 5253-14

30"×26" ×24" RAD TYP.

5271-13 EAVE

5249-13

30"×32" TYP

5271-12 EAVE

5249-12

5254-101 SILL ANCHORS

INSTALL: (1) AT EACH END OF GREENHOUSE
(1) AT EACH GLAZING BAR
(1) AT EACH SIDE OF SILL JOINT

S118-14-1(R)

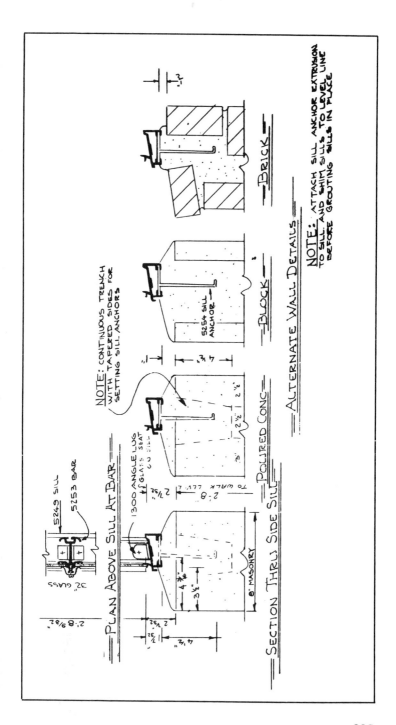

PLAN ABOVE SILL AT BAR

5249 SILL
5253 BAR
3¢ GLASS
2'-8 9/32"

NOTE: CONTINUOUS TRENCH WITH TAPERED SIDES FOR SETTING SILL ANCHORS

BRICK

BLOCK

5254 SILL ANCHOR

POURED CONC.

ALTERNATE WALL DETAILS

NOTE: ATTACH SILL ANCHOR EXTRUSION TO SILL AND SHIM SILLS TO LEVEL LINE BEFORE GROUTING SILLS IN PLACE

1300 ANGLE LUG & GLASS SEAT CO SIDE

TO WALK LEV.
2'-8"

8" MASONRY

SECTION THRU SIDE SILL

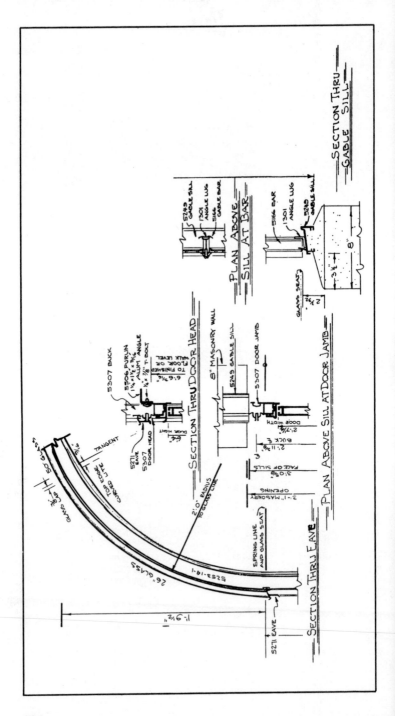

SECTION THRU GABLE SILL

PLAN ABOVE SILL AT BAR

5249 GABLE SILL
1301 ANGLE LUG
5166 GABLE BAR

5166 BAR
1301 ANGLE LUG
5249 GABLE SILL

GLASS SEAT

8"
3¾"
2⁵⁄₁₆"

SECTION THRU DOOR HEAD

5307 BUCK
5506 PURLIN
1¼" x 1½" x ³⁄₁₆"
ALUM ANGLE
⅜" Ø BOLT
TO FINISHED
FLOOR OR
WALK LEVEL
5271 EAVE
5307 DOOR HEAD
DOOR HIGHT
6'-9 ⁵⁄₁₆"

PLAN ABOVE SILL AT DOOR JAMB

8" MASONRY WALL
5249 GABLE SILL
5307 DOOR JAMB
DOOR WIDTH
2'-7½"
BUCK E
2'-11⅛"
FACE OF SILLS
3'-0⅜"
MASONRY OPENING
3'-1"

SECTION THRU EAVE

50 GLASS
TANGENT
TOP EDGE
CURVED LITE
GLASS ⁷⁄₁₆"
2'-0 RADIUS
TO GLASS LINE
26" GLASS
5253-19-1
SPRING LINE
AND GLASS SEAT
5271 EAVE
1'-9½"

384

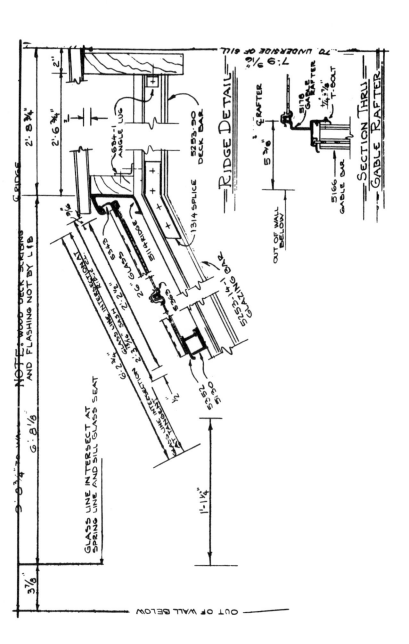

NOTE: WOOD DECK SCREENS
AND FLASHING NOT BY L+B

℄ RIDGE

2'-8¾"

2'-6¾"

2"

2"

684-1
ANGLE LUG

5253-50
DECK BAR

1314 SPLICE

5114 RIDGE

5343

2'6' GLASS

5253-14-1 BAR

5252
5130

5342

½

5261

2'3⅛ GLASS SASH

GLASS LINE INTERSECTION 2'-3⅛"

GLASS LINE INTERSECTION

GLASS LINE INTERSECTION AT SPRING LINE

GLASS LINE INTERSECT AT
SPRING LINE AND SILL GLASS SEAT

6'-2¾"

6'-8⅛"

9'-0¾" TO WALL

3⅛"

OUT OF WALL BELOW

1'-1¼"

═ RIDGE DETAIL ═

TO UNDERSIDE OF SILL 7: 9 9/16"

5253 GLAZING BAR

5118
GABLE
RAFTER

¼x 1⅞
T. BOLT

684
GABLE
RAFTER

5166
GABLE BAR

5'×6' ℄ RAFTER

OUT OF WALL
BELOW

═ SECTION THRU ═
GABLE RAFTER.

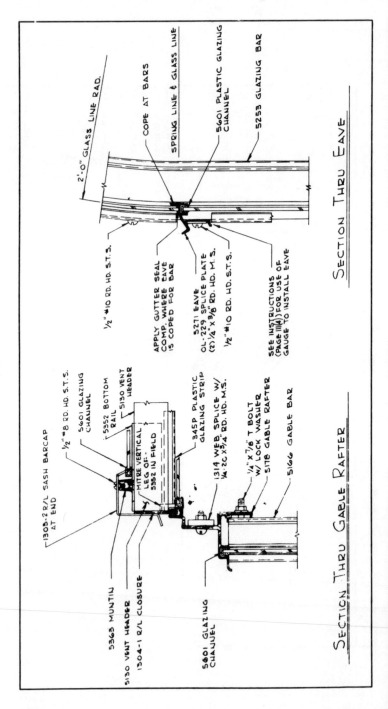

SECTION THRU EAVE

2'-0" GLASS LINE RAD.

GLASS LINE RAD.

COPE AT BARS

SPRING LINE & GLASS LINE

5601 PLASTIC GLAZING CHANNEL

5253 GLAZING BAR

½" #10 RD. HD. S.T.S.

APPLY GUTTER SEAL COMP. WHERE EAVE IS COPED FOR BAR

5271 EAVE
OL-229 SPLICE PLATE
(2) ¼" x ⅜" RD. HD. M.S.

½" #10 RD. HD. S.T.S.

SEE INSTRUCTIONS (PAGE III(4)) FOR USE OF GAUGE TO INSTALL EAVE

SECTION THRU GABLE RAFTER

1305-2 R/L SASH BARCAP AT END

½" #8 RD. HD. S.T.S.

5601 GLAZING CHANNEL

5130 BOTTOM VENT HEADER

5352 BOTTOM RAIL

MITRE VERTICAL LEG OF 5352 IN FIELD

345P PLASTIC GLAZING STRIP

1314 WEB SPLICE W/ ¼-20 x ¾ RD. HD. M.S.

¼" x ⅞" T BOLT W/ LOCK WASHER

5178 GABLE RAFTER

5166 GABLE BAR

5363 MUNTIN

5130 VENT HEADER

1304-1 R/L CLOSURE

5601 GLAZING CHANNEL

386

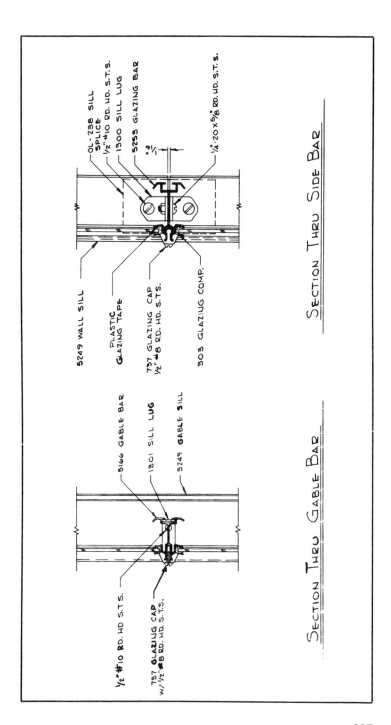

OL-238 SILL SPLICE

½"#10 RD. HD. S.T.S.

1300 SILL LUG

5255 GLAZING BAR

¼-20 x ⅝ RD. HD. S.T.S.

5249 WALL SILL

PLASTIC GLAZING TAPE

757 GLAZING CAP
½"#8 RD. HD. S.T.S.

303 GLAZING COMP.

SECTION THRU SIDE BAR

5166 GABLE BAR

1301 SILL LUG

5249 GABLE SILL

½"#10 RD. HD S.T.S.

757 GLAZING CAP
W/½"#8 RD. HD. S.T.S.

SECTION THRU GABLE BAR

387

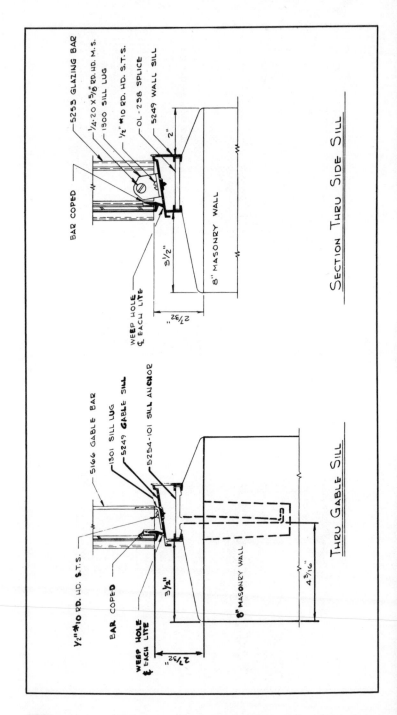

SECTION THRU SIDE SILL

THRU GABLE SILL

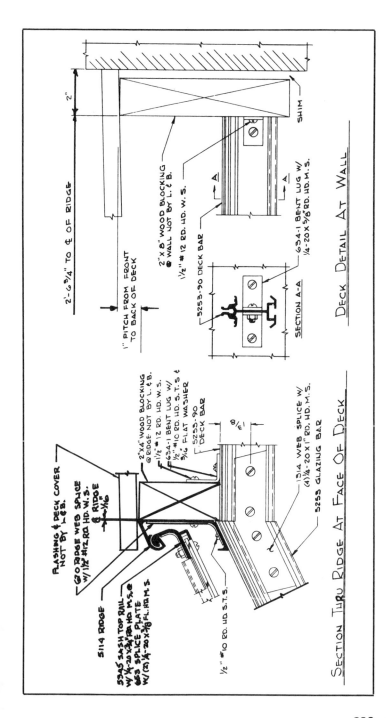

DECK DETAIL AT WALL

2'-6 3/4" TO ℄ OF RIDGE

2"

SHIM

2"X 8" WOOD BLOCKING @ WALL NOT BY L. & B.

1/2" #12 RD. HD. W.S.

634-1 BENT LUG W/ 1/4-20x5/8 RD. HD. M.S.

5255-90 DECK BAR

SECTION A-A

A

1" PITCH FROM FRONT TO BACK OF DECK

SECTION THRU RIDGE AT FACE OF DECK

FLASHING & DECK COVER NOT BY L. & B.

(2) O RIDGE WEB SPLICE W/ 1/2" #12 RD. HD. W.S.

@ RIDGE 9/16"

2'X 4" WOOD BLOCKING @ RIDGE NOT BY L. & B.

1/2" #12 RD. HD. W.S.

634-1 BENT LUG W/ 1/2" #10 RD. HD. S.T.S & 5/16 FLAT WASHER

5255-90 DECK BAR

1" 5/16

5114 RIDGE

5345 SASH TOP RAIL W/ 1/4-20x3/4 PAN HD M.S. @ 653 SPLICE PLATE W/ (2) 1/4-20 x 7/8 FL. HD. M.S.

1/2" #10 RD. S.T.S.

1514 WEB SPLICE W/ (4) 1/4-20 x 1" RD. HD. M.S.

5255 GLAZING BAR

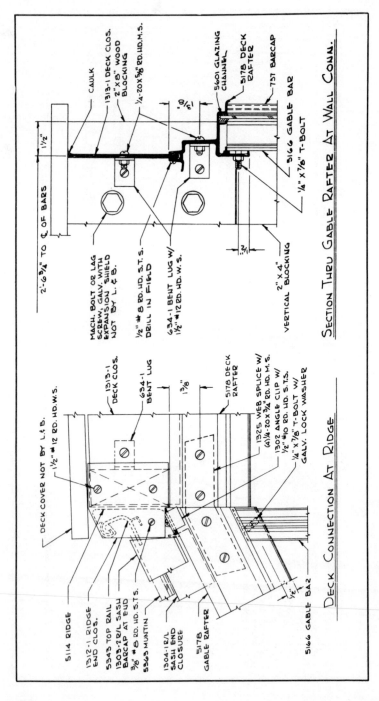

SECTION THRU GABLE RAFTER AT WALL CONN.

CAULK
1313-1 DECK CLOS.
2"x8" WOOD BLOCKING
½"-20x⅝" RD. HD. M.S.
5601 GLAZING CHANNEL
5178 DECK RAFTER
757 BARCAP

1½"

13'-0"

1½"

2'-6¾" TO C/L OF BARS

MACH. BOLT OR LAG SCREW, GALV. WITH EXPANSION SHIELD NOT BY L.& B.

½"#8 RD. HD. S.T.S. DRILL IN FIELD

634-1 BENT LUG W/ 1½"#12 RD. HD. W.S.

5166 GABLE BAR
¼" x ⅞" T-BOLT

¾"

2"x 4" VERTICAL BLOCKING

DECK CONNECTION AT RIDGE

DECK COVER NOT BY L.& B.
½" #12 RD. HD. W.S.

5114 RIDGE
1312-1 RIDGE END CLOS.
5343 TOP RAIL
1303-2/R/L SASH BARCAP AT END
⅜" #8 RD. HD. S.T.S.
5363 MUNTIN

1313-1 DECK CLOS.
634-1 BENT LUG

1⅜"

5178 DECK RAFTER

1325 WEB SPLICE W/ (4)¼"-20x¾" RD. HD. M.S.
1302 ANGLE CLIP W/ ½"#10 RD. HD. S.T.S.
¼"x⅞" T-BOLT W/ GALV. LOCK WASHER

½"

1304-12/L SASH END CLOSURE
5178 GABLE RAFTER

5166 GABLE BAR

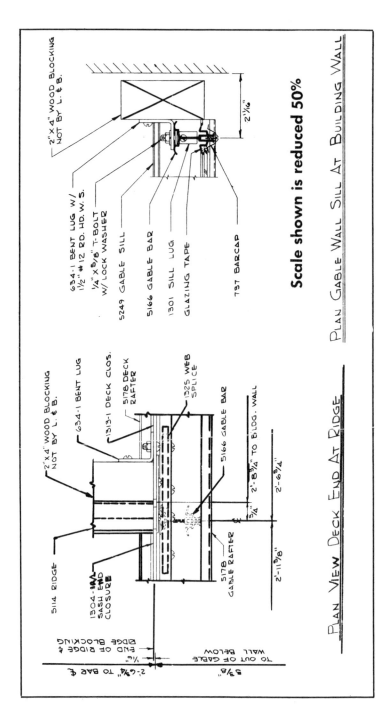

2"X4" WOOD BLOCKING
NOT BY L. & B.

634-1 BENT LUG W/
1½" #12 RD. HD. W.S.
¼" x ⅝" T-BOLT
W/ LOCK WASHER

5249 GABLE SILL

5166 GABLE BAR

1301 SILL LUG

GLAZING TAPE

737 BARCAP

Scale shown is reduced 50%

PLAN GABLE WALL SILL AT BUILDING WALL

2"X4" WOOD BLOCKING
NOT BY L. & B.

634-1 BENT LUG

1313-1 DECK CLOS.

5178 DECK RAFTER

1325 WEB SPLICE

5166 GABLE BAR

2'-8¾" TO BLDG. WALL

2'-6¾"

5114 RIDGE

1304-1A
SASH END
CLOSURE

5178 GABLE RAFTER

2'-11⅝"

END OF RIDGE &
RIDGE BLOCKING

¹⁄₁₆"

TO OUT OF GABLE
WALL BELOW

5⅝"

2'-6¾" TO BAR &

PLAN VIEW DECK END AT RIDGE

391

Plan 7
Orlyt Lean-To Model

This plan is provided by the courtesy of the Cooperative Extension Unit, University of Florida.

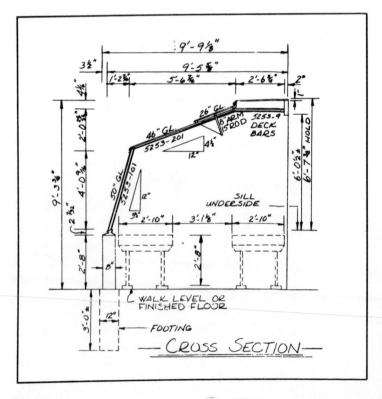

— CROSS SECTION —

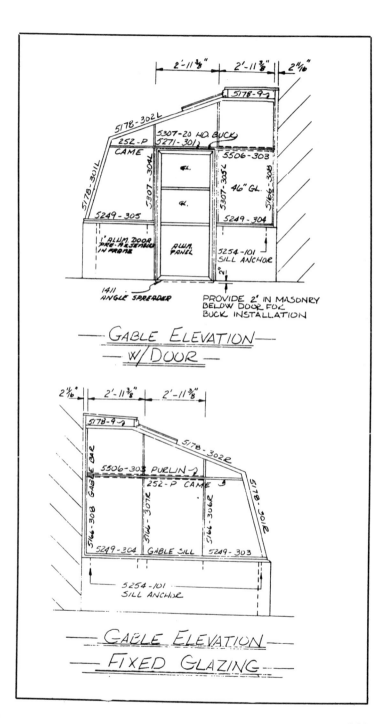

2'-11⅜" 2'-11⅜" 2 ⁱⁱ⁄₁₆"

5178-9

5178-302L

5307-20 HD. BUCK
252-P 5271-301
CAME

5178-301L

5506-303

GL.

5307-304L

GL.

5307-305L

46" GL.

5166-308

5249-305

5249-304

1' ALUM DOOR
PRE-ASSEMBLED
IN FRAME

ALUM.
PANEL

5254-101
SILL ANCHOR

2"

1411
ANGLE SPREADER

PROVIDE 2' IN MASONRY
BELOW DOOR FOR
BUCK INSTALLATION

— GABLE ELEVATION—
— w/DOOR —

2 ⁱⁱ⁄₁₆" 2'-11⅜" 2'-11⅜"

5178-9

5178-302R

GABLE BAR

5506-303 PURLIN

252-P CAME

5166-308

5144-307R

5166-306R

5178-301R

5249-304 GABLE SILL 5249-303

5254-101
SILL ANCHOR

— GABLE ELEVATION—
— FIXED GLAZING—

393

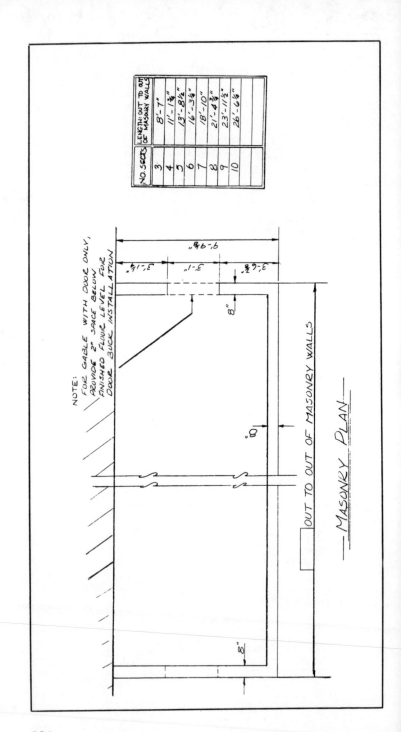

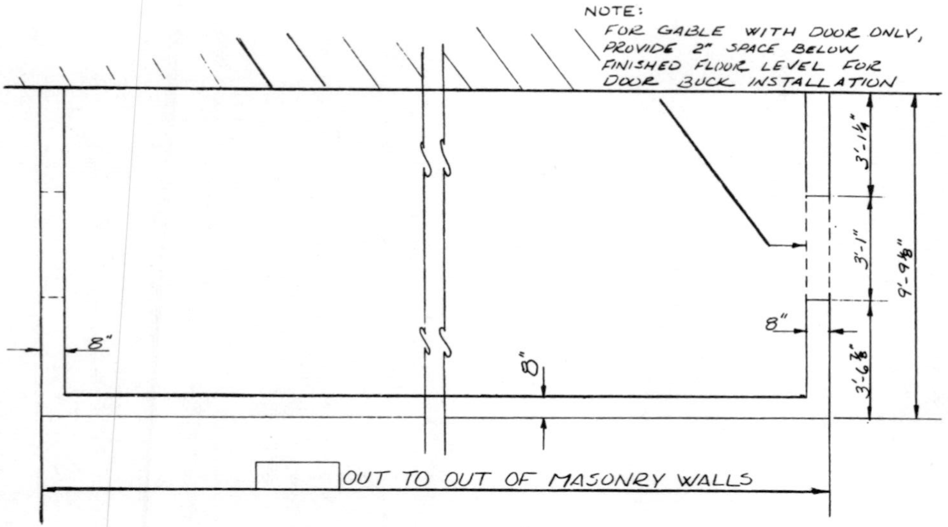
NOTE:
FOR GABLE WITH DOOR ONLY, PROVIDE 2" SPACE BELOW FINISHED FLOOR LEVEL FOR DOOR BUCK INSTALLATION
3'-1¼"
3'-1"
3'-6⅜"
9'-9⅝"
8"
8"
8"
OUT TO OUT OF MASONRY WALLS

NO. SECTS.	LENGTH: OUT TO OUT OF MASONRY WALLS
3	8'-7"
4	11'-1¾"
5	13'-8½"
6	16'-3¼"
7	18'-10"
8	21'-4¾"
9	23'-11½"
10	26'-6¼"

MASONRY PLAN

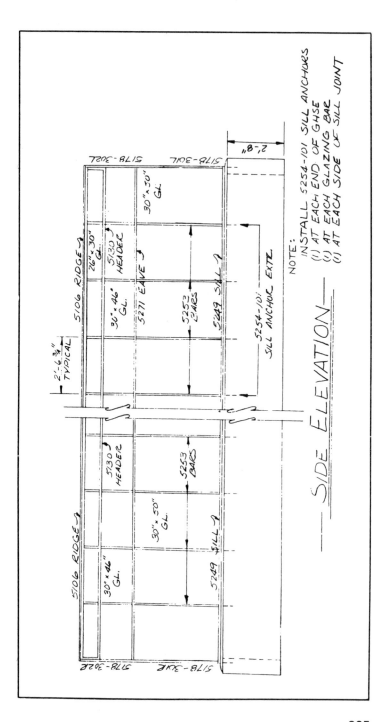

— SIDE ELEVATION —

NOTE:
INSTALL 5254-101 SILL ANCHORS
(1) AT EACH END OF GHSE
(1) AT EACH GLAZING BAR
(1) AT EACH SIDE OF SILL JOINT

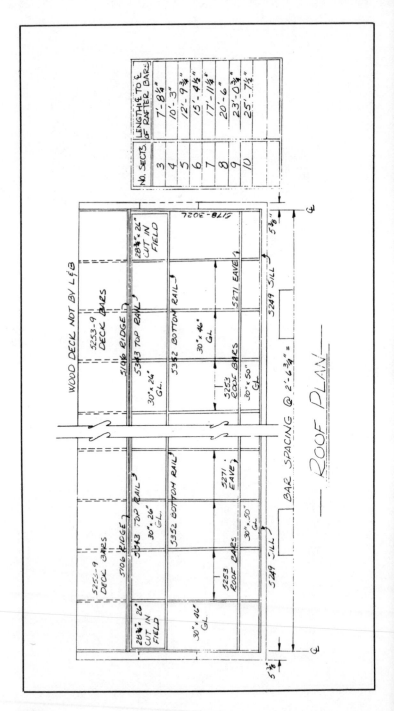

ROOF PLAN

NO. SECTS.	LENGTH'E TO ℄ OF RAFTER BARS
3	7'-8¼"
4	10'-3"
5	12'-9¾"
6	15'-4½"
7	17'-11¼"
8	20'-6"
9	23'-0¾"
10	25'-7½"

WOOD DECK NOT BY L&B

5253-9 DECK BARS

5106 RIDGE

5343 TOP RAIL

28¾"× 22" CUT IN FIELD

30"× 24" G.L.

5352 BOTTOM RAIL

30"× 46" G.L.

5253 ROOF BARS

30"× 50" G.L.

5271 EAVE)

5178-3032L

5249 SILL

BAR SPACING @ 2'-6¾" =

5253-9 DECK BARS

5106 RIDGE)

5343 TOP RAIL

30"× 26" G.L.

5352 BOTTOM RAIL

5271 EAVE)

30"× 50" G.L.

5253 ROOF BARS

28¾"× 26" CUT IN FIELD

30"× 46" G.L.

5249 SILL

5⅜"

5⅜"

℄

℄

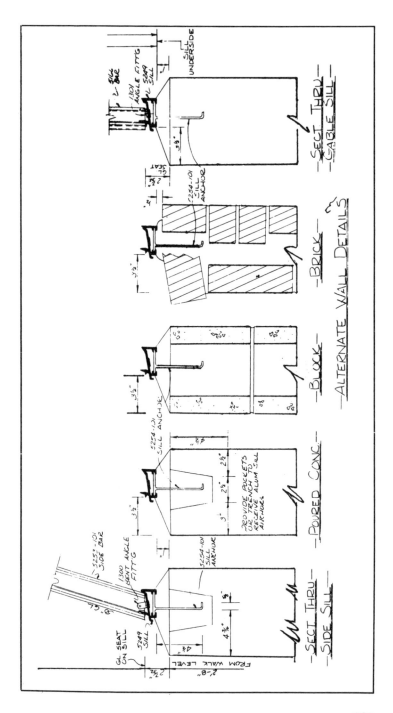

—ALTERNATE WALL DETAILS—

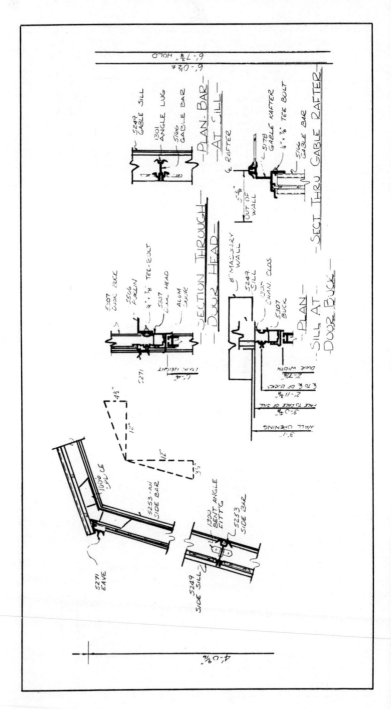

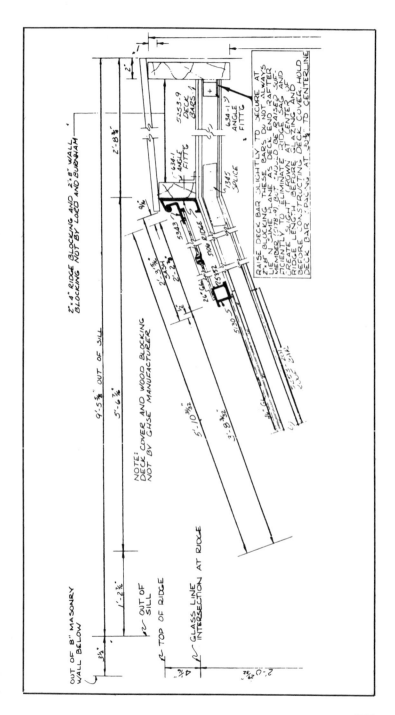

RAISE DECK BAR SLIGHTLY TO SECURE AT 2"x8" BLOCKING. THESE BARS DO NOT ALWAYS LIE IN SAME PLANE AS DECK END RAFTER MEMBER (2"x8"). ALLOW ALSO RAISES SUF-FICIENTLY TO ELIMINATE RIDGE SAG AND CREATE SLIGHT CROWN AT CENTER OF RIDGE LENGTH BEFORE GLAZING AND BEFORE CONSTRUCTING DECK COVER. HOLD DECK BAR SPLICING AT 30¼" TO CENTERLINE

2"x4" RIDGE BLOCKING AND 2"x8" WALL BLOCKING NOT BY LORD AND BURNHAM

NOTE:
DECK COVER AND WOOD BLOCKING
NOT BY GHSE MANUFACTURER

OUT OF 8" MASONRY
WALL BELOW

OUT OF SILL

OUT OF RIDGE

TOP OF RIDGE

GLASS LINE
INTERSECTION AT RIDGE

Plan 8

A 4 x 8 Lean-To

This plan is provided by the courtesy of Lord & Burnham, Irvington, New York.

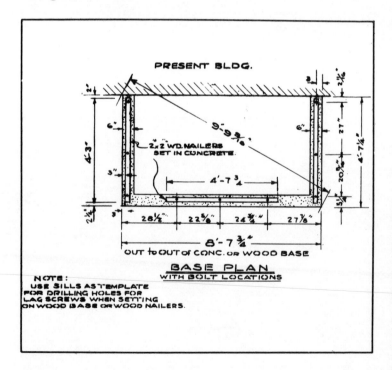

PRESENT BLDG.

2 x 2 WD. NAILERS
SET IN CONCRETE.

9'-9¾"

4'-7¾"

4'-3"

OUT to OUT of CONC. or WOOD BASE

8'-7¾"

28½" 22⅝" 24¾" 27⅞"

BASE PLAN
WITH BOLT LOCATIONS

NOTE:
USE SILLS AS TEMPLATE
FOR DRILLING HOLES FOR
LAG SCREWS WHEN SETTING
ON WOOD BASE OR WOOD NAILERS.

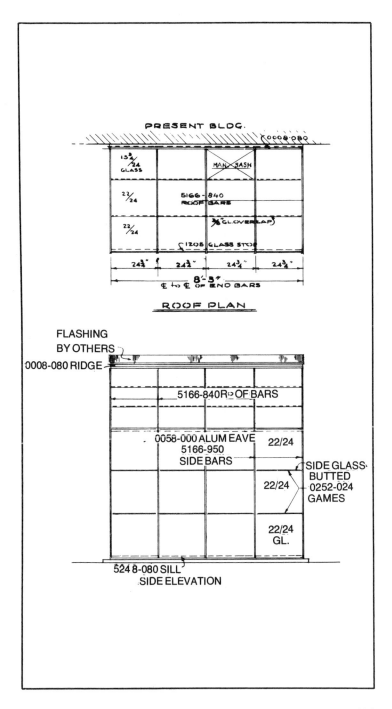

PRESENT BLDG.

0008-080

15¾/24 GLASS

MAN SASH

22/24

5166-840 ROOF BARS

22/24

(GLOVERLAP)

1208 GLASS STOP

24¾"   24¾"   24¾"   24¾"

8'-3"
₵ to ₵ OF END BARS

ROOF PLAN

FLASHING
BY OTHERS

0008-080 RIDGE

5166-840 R⊃ OF BARS

0058-000 ALUM EAVE
5166-950
SIDE BARS

22/24

22/24

SIDE GLASS
BUTTED
0252-024
GAMES

22/24
GL.

524 8-080 SILL

SIDE ELEVATION

401

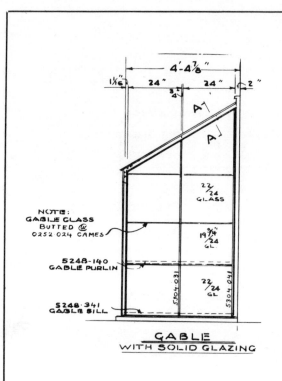

4'-4⅞"

1¹⁄₁₆" 24" 24" 2"
3¾"

A

A

2²⁄₂₄ GLASS

19¾⁄₂₄ GL

22⁄₂₄ GL

NOTE:
GABLE GLASS
BUTTED @
0252 024 CAMES

5248-140
GABLE PURLIN

5304 031

5304 041

5248-341
GABLE SILL

GABLE
WITH SOLID GLAZING

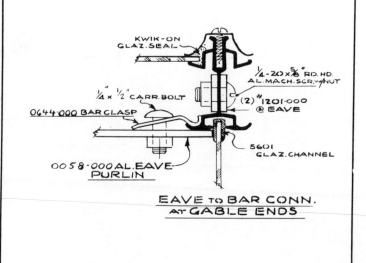

KWIK-ON
GLAZ.SEAL

¼-20 X ⅝" RD. HD.
AL. MACH. SCR. W/NUT

(2) #1201-000
@ EAVE

¼" X ½" CARR. BOLT

0644-000 BAR CLASP

0058-000 AL. EAVE
PURLIN

5601
GLAZ. CHANNEL

EAVE TO BAR CONN.
AT GABLE ENDS

402

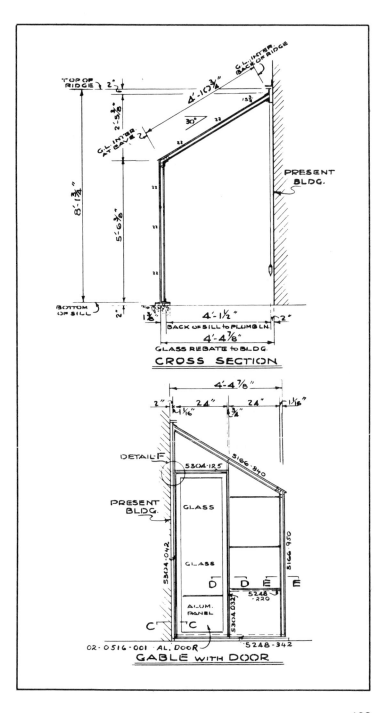

CROSS SECTION

GABLE WITH DOOR

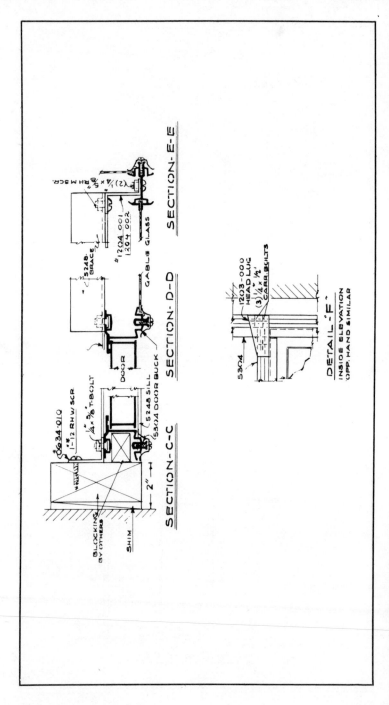

SECTION-C-C

SECTION-D-D

SECTION-E-E

DETAIL "F"
INSIDE ELEVATION
OPP. HAND SIMILAR

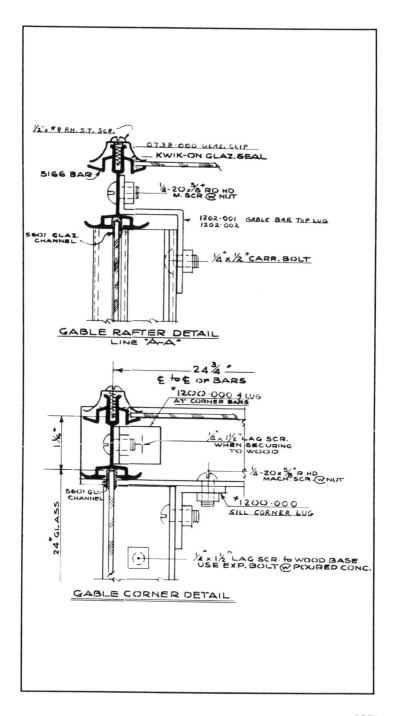

½"x #8 R.H. S.T. SCR.

0738-000 GLAZ. CLIP

KWIK-ON GLAZ. SEAL

5166 BAR

¼-20 x ⅝" RD HD M. SCR. W/ NUT

1202-001 GABLE BAR TOP LUG
1202-002

5601 GLAZ. CHANNEL

¼" x ½" CARR. BOLT

GABLE RAFTER DETAIL
LINE "A-A"

24¾"
℄ to ℄ OF BARS

*1200-000 ℄ LUG
AT CORNER BARS

¼" x 1½" LAG SCR. WHEN SECURING TO WOOD

1⅛"

¼-20 x ⅝" R. HD MACH. SCR. W/ NUT

5601 GL. CHANNEL

*1200-000
SILL CORNER LUG

24" GLASS

¼" x 1½" LAG SCR. to WOOD BASE
USE EXP. BOLT W/ POURED CONC.

GABLE CORNER DETAIL

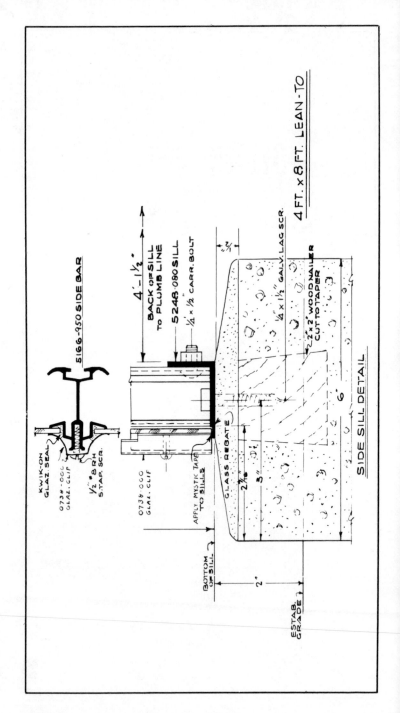

5166-950 SIDE BAR

KWIK-ON GLAZ. SEAL.

0738-000 GLAZ. CLIP

½" x 8 RH S.TAP. SCR.

0738-000 GLAZ. CLIP

APPLY MYSTIC TAPE TO SILLS

BACK OF SILL TO PLUMB LINE

4'-1½"

5248-080 SILL

¼ x ½ CARR. BOLT

GLASS REBATE

¼" x 1½" GALV. LAG SCR.

2 x 2" WOOD NAILER CUT TO TAPER

SIDE SILL DETAIL

2⅛"

3"

6"

¾"

BOTTOM OF SILL

2"

ESTAB. GRADE

4 FT. x 8 FT. LEAN-TO

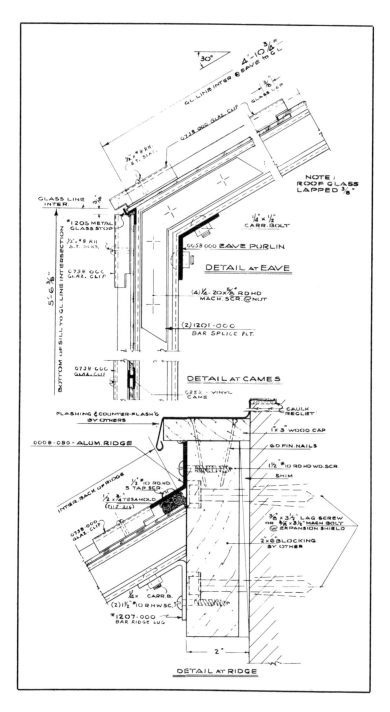

30°

4'-10³/₄" EAVE to C.L.

GL. LINE INTER. EAVE to C.L.

³/₈" GLASS LAP

0738-000 GLAZ. CLIP

¹/₂"-#8 R.H. S.T. SCR.

NOTE:
ROOF GLASS
LAPPED ³/₈"

GLASS LINE INTER.

³/₁₆"

#1205 METAL GLASS STOP

¹/₂"-#8 R.H. S.T. SCRS.

0738-000 GLAZ. CLIP

¹/₄" × ¹/₂" CARR. BOLT

0058-000 EAVE PURLIN

DETAIL at EAVE

(4) ¹/₄-20×⁵/₈" RD HD MACH. SCR. @ NUT

(2) 1201-000 BAR SPLICE PLT.

BOTTOM OF SILL TO GL. LINE INTERSECTION

5'-6³/₈"

0738-000 GLAZ. CLIP

DETAIL at CAMES

0252-VINYL CAME

FLASHING & COUNTER-FLASH'G BY OTHERS

CAULK REGLET

1×3 WOOD CAP

0008-080-ALUM. RIDGE

6D FIN. NAILS

1¹/₂"#10 RD HD WD. SCR.

SHIM

INTER. BACK OF RIDGE

¹/₂"#10 RD. HD. 5 TAP SCR.

¹/₂"×³/₄" TESAMOLD (F113-216)

0738-000 GLAZ. CLIP

³/₈"×3¹/₂" LAG SCREW OR ³/₈"×3¹/₂" MACH BOLT @ EXPANSION SHIELD

2×6 BLOCKING BY OTHER

¹/₄"× CARR. B.

(2) 1¹/₂"#10 R.H W.SC.

#1207-000 BAR RIDGE LUG

2"

DETAIL at RIDGE

407

Plan 9

A 4 x 12 Lean-To

This plan is provided by the courtesy of Lord & Burnham, Irvington, New York.

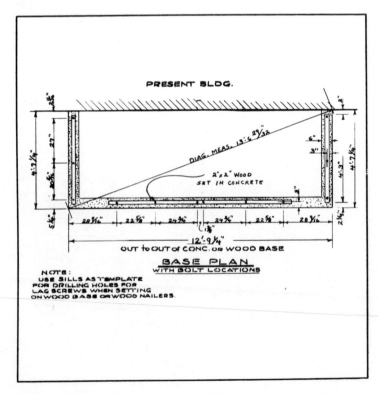

PRESENT BLDG.

DIAG. MEAS. 13'-6 29/32"

2"x2" WOOD
SET IN CONCRETE

12'-9¼"

OUT to OUT of CONC. or WOOD BASE

BASE PLAN
WITH BOLT LOCATIONS

NOTE:
USE SILLS AS TEMPLATE
FOR DRILLING HOLES FOR
LAG SCREWS WHEN SETTING
ON WOOD BASE OR WOOD NAILERS.

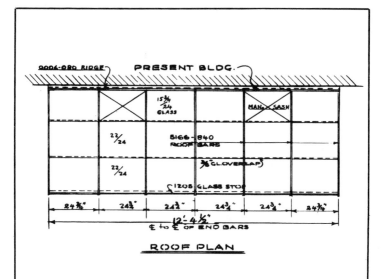

ROOF PLAN

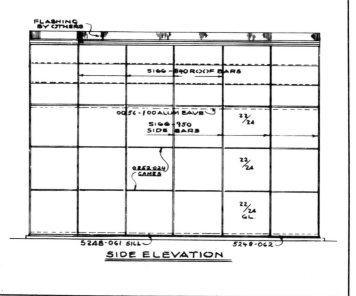

SIDE ELEVATION

409

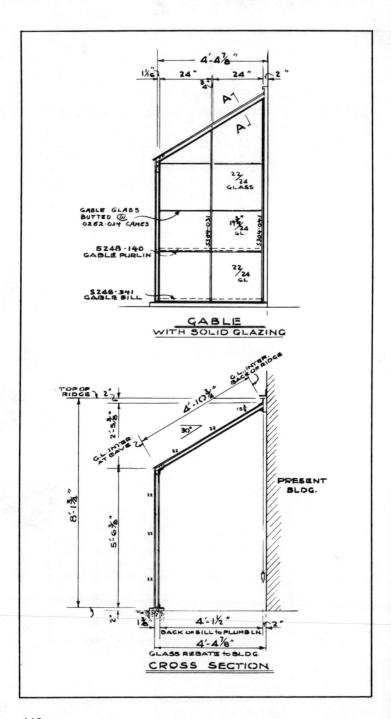

GABLE
WITH SOLID GLAZING

GABLE GLASS
BUTTED @
0252-024 CAMES

5248-140
GABLE PURLIN

5248-341
GABLE SILL

4'-4⅞"

1⅙" 24" 24" 2"

¾"

²²⁄₂₄ GLASS

19¾⁄₂₄ GL.

²²⁄₂₄ GL.

CROSS SECTION

TOP OF RIDGE

PRESENT BLDG.

G.L. INTER. BACK OF RIDGE

G.L. INTER. AT EAVE

4'-10¾"

30°

8'-1¾"

5'-6⅜"

2'-5⅝"

2"

4'-1½"
BACK OF SILL to PLUMB LN.

4'-4⅞"
GLASS REBATE to BLDG.

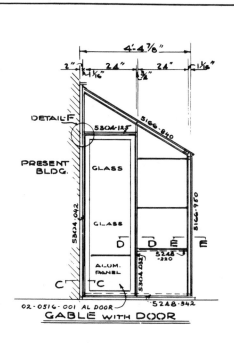

DETAIL·F

PRESENT BLDG.

4'-4⅞"

2" · 2 ¼" · 2 ¼" · 1 1/16"

5304·125

5166·840

GLASS

GLASS

D   D   E   E

5248·220

5304·042

5166·950

ALUM. PANEL

C   C

5304·032

02·0516·001 AL DOOR

5248·342

GABLE WITH DOOR

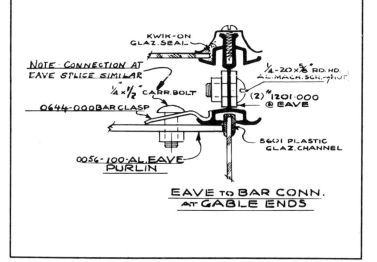

KWIK·ON GLAZ·SEAL

NOTE·CONNECTION AT EAVE·SPLICE SIMILAR

¼·20 X ⅝" RD·HD. AL·MACH·SCR·&NUT

¼"×½" CARR·BOLT

(2) #1201·000 @ EAVE

0644·000 BAR CLASP

5601 PLASTIC GLAZ·CHANNEL

0056·100·AL·EAVE PURLIN

EAVE TO BAR CONN. AT GABLE ENDS

411

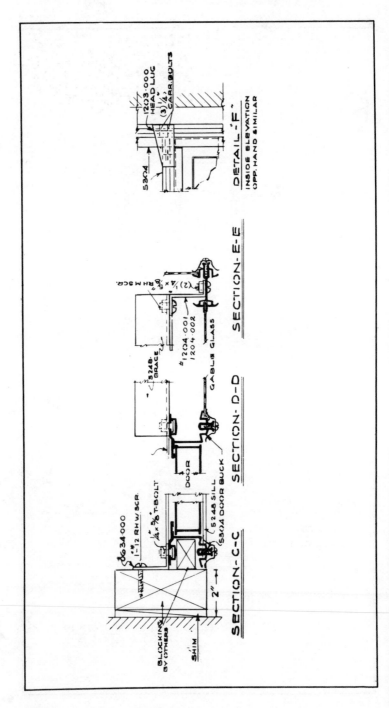

DETAIL·'F'
INSIDE ELEVATION
OPP. HAND SIMILAR

1203·000 HEAD LUG
(3) ¾" CARR. BOLTS

5304

SECTION·E·E

(2) ¼ × ¾" RH M SCR.

#1204·001
1204·002

GABLE GLASS

SECTION·D·D

5248 BRACE

DOOR

SECTION·C·C

#634·000
1-12 RH W SCR

¼ × ⅝ T-BOLT

5248 SILL
(5304 DOOR BUCK)

2"

BLOCKING BY OTHERS

SHIM

412

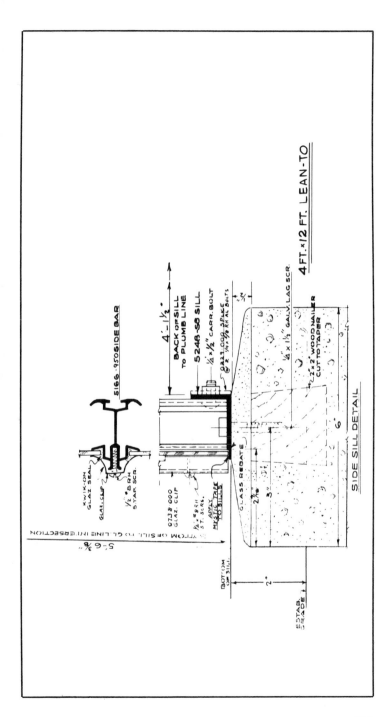

5166 - 950 SIDE BAR

KWIK-ON
GLAZ. SEAL.

GLAZ. CLIP

½" 8 R.H.
STAP. SCR.

BACK OF SILL
TO PLUMB LINE

4' - 1½"

5248 - S6 SILL

½" × ½" CARR. BOLT

@ #39.000 SPIKE
@ 2 ½" × ½" R.H. AL BOLTS

Q738.000
GLAZ. CLIP

½" 8 R.H.
ST. SCR.

APPLY
MASTIC TAPE
TO SILL

GLASS REBATE

BOTTOM OF SILL TO GL. LINE INTERSECTION

5' - 6 ⅜"

BOTTOM
OF SILL

2"

2⅝"

3"

¾"

¼" × 1½" GALV. LAG SCR.

2" × 2" WOOD NAILER
CUT TO TAPER

ESTAB.
GRADE

SIDE SILL DETAIL

4 FT. × 12 FT. LEAN-TO

DETAIL AT RIDGE

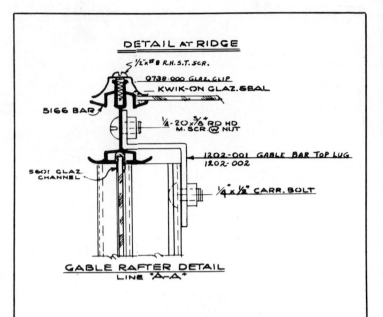

½"x #8 R.H.S.T. SCR.

0738-000 GLAZ CLIP

KWIK-ON GLAZ. SEAL

5166 BAR

¼-20x⅝" RD HD
M. SCR. @ NUT

1202-001 GABLE BAR TOP LUG
1202-002

5601 GLAZ.
CHANNEL

¼"x½" CARR. BOLT

GABLE RAFTER DETAIL
LINE "A-A"

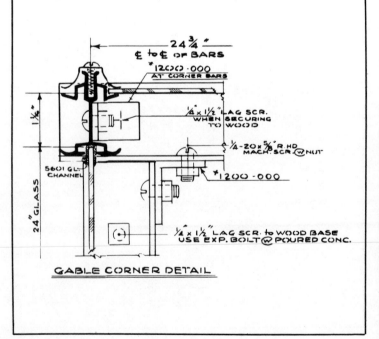

24¾"
ℓ to ℓ OF BARS

*1200-000
AT CORNER BARS

1⅛"

¼"x1½" LAG SCR.
WHEN SECURING
TO WOOD

¼-20x⅝" R HD
MACH. SCR. @ NUT

5601 GL.
CHANNEL

*1200-000

24" GLASS

¼"x1½" LAG SCR. to WOOD BASE
USE EXP. BOLT @ POURED CONC.

GABLE CORNER DETAIL

414

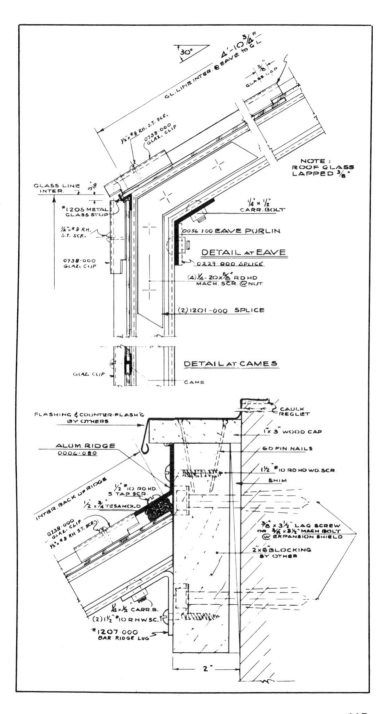

30°

4'-10 3/4" EAVE to C.L.

G.L. LINE INTER. 8 EAVE to C.L.

3/8" GLASS LAP

1/2" × #8 RH. S.T. SCR.
0738-000 GLAZ. CLIP

NOTE:
ROOF GLASS
LAPPED 3/8"

GLASS LINE INTER.

2 3/16"

#1205 METAL GLASS STOP

1/8" × #8 RH. S.T. SCR.

0738-000 GLAZ. CLIP

1/4" × 1/2" CARR. BOLT

0056-100 EAVE PURLIN

DETAIL at EAVE

0229-000 SPLICE

(4) 1/4-20 × 5/8" RD HD MACH. SCR. @ NUT

(2) 1201-000 SPLICE

DETAIL at CAMES

GLAZ. CLIP

CAME

FLASHING & COUNTER-FLASH'G BY OTHERS

CAULK REGLET

ALUM. RIDGE 0006-080

1" × 3" WOOD CAP

6D FIN. NAILS

1 1/2" #10 RD HD WD. SCR.

INTER. BACK OF RIDGE

1/2" #10 RD HD. 5 TAP SCR.

1/2 × 3/4 TESAMOLD

SHIM

0738-000 GLAZ. CLIP

1/2" × #8 RH S.T. SCR.

3/8 × 3 1/2" LAG SCREW OR 3/8 × 3 1/2" MACH. BOLT @ EXPANSION SHIELD

2" × 6" BLOCKING BY OTHER

1/4 × 1/2 CARR. B.

(2) 1 1/2" #10 RH WS C.

#1207-000 BAR RIDGE LUG

2"

415

Plan 10
A 7 x 12 Lean-To

This plan is provided by the courtesy of Lord & Burnham, Irvington, New York.

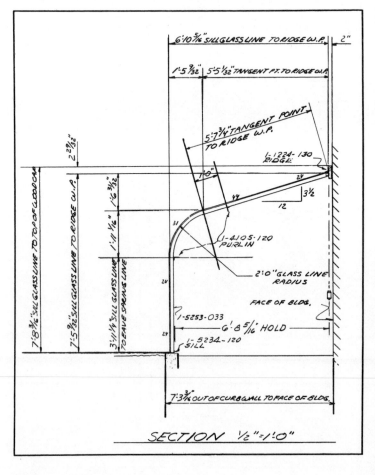

SECTION ½"=1'.0"

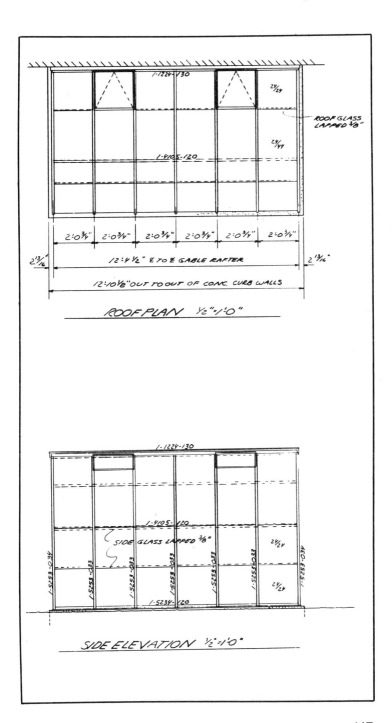

ROOF PLAN ½"=1'0"

SIDE ELEVATION ½"=1'0"

417

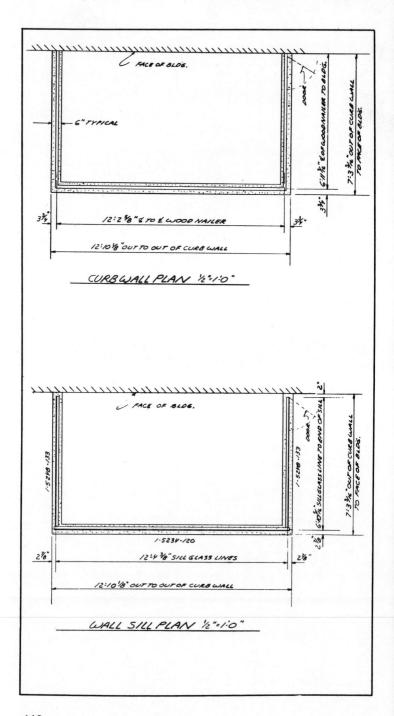

FACE OF BLDG.

6" TYPICAL

DOOR

6'11 ³⁄₁₆" EXP WOOD NAILER TO BLDG.

7'-3 ³⁄₁₆" OUT OF CURB WALL TO FACE OF BLDG.

3 ³⁄₄"

3 ³⁄₄"   3 ³⁄₄"

12'-2 ⁵⁄₈" Ḡ TO Ḡ WOOD NAILER

12'-10 ¹⁄₈" OUT TO OUT OF CURB WALL

CURB WALL PLAN ½"=1'-0"

FACE OF BLDG.

1-5246-.133   1-5246-.133

DOOR

6'-10 ⁵⁄₁₆" SILL GLASS LINE TO END OF SILL

2"

7'-3 ³⁄₁₆" OUT OF CURB WALL TO FACE OF BLDG.

1-523V-120

2 ³⁄₈"

2 ³⁄₈"   2 ³⁄₈"

12'-4 ³⁄₈" SILL GLASS LINES

12'-10 ¹⁄₈" OUT TO OUT OF CURB WALL

WALL SILL PLAN ½"=1'-0"

418

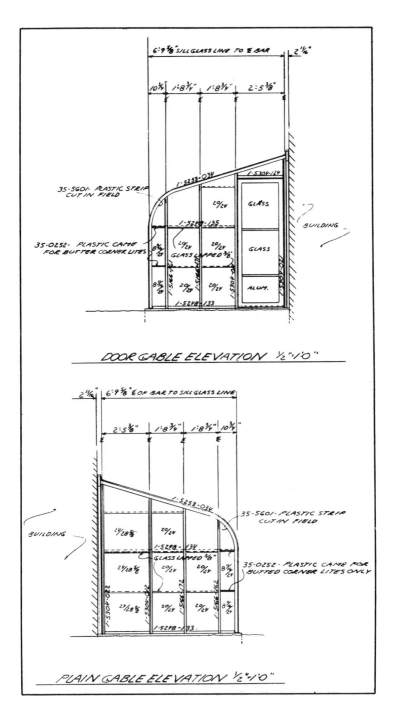

DOOR GABLE ELEVATION ½"=1'0"

PLAIN GABLE ELEVATION ½"=1'0"

419

Plan 11
Aluminum Evenspan

This plan is provided by the courtesy of Lord & Burnham, Irvington, New York.

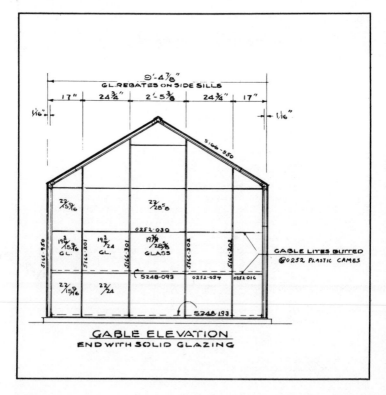

GABLE ELEVATION
END WITH SOLID GLAZING

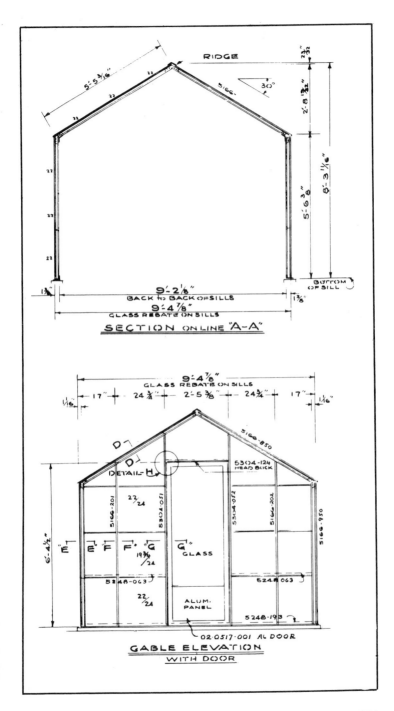

SECTION ON LINE "A-A"

GABLE ELEVATION
WITH DOOR

421

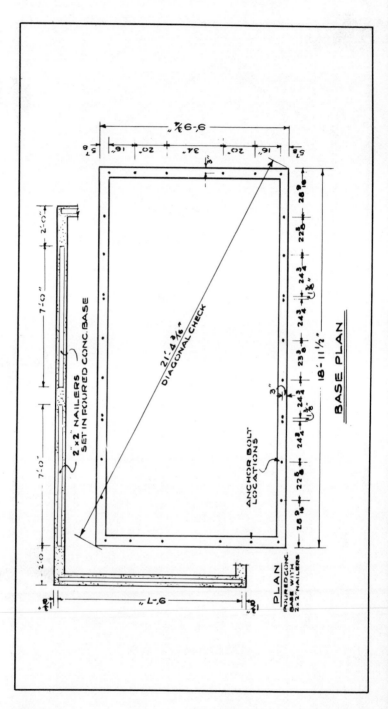

BASE PLAN

PLAN
POURED CONC.
BASE WITH
2"x 2" NAILERS

9'-9⅜"

18'-11½"

21'-4⅝"
DIAGONAL CHECK

ANCHOR BOLT
LOCATIONS

2"x 2" NAILERS
SET IN POURED CONC. BASE

9'-7"

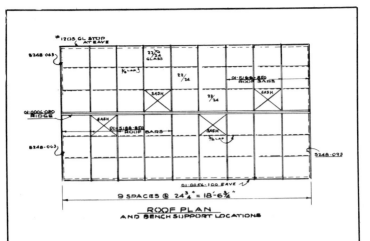

9 SPACES @ 24¾" = 18'-6¾"

ROOF PLAN
AND BENCH SUPPORT LOCATIONS

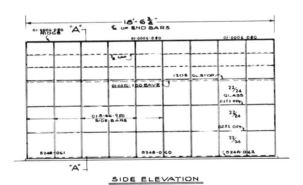

18'-6¾"
C OF END BARS

SIDE ELEVATION

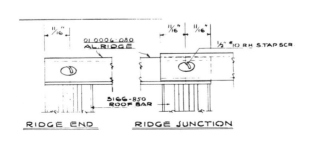

01·0006·080
AL. RIDGE

½" #10 RH S.TAP SCR

5166·850
ROOF BAR

RIDGE END   RIDGE JUNCTION

423

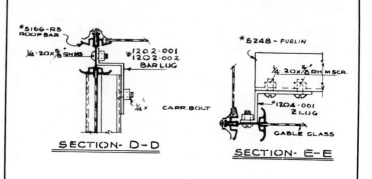

#166-RB
ROOF BAR

1/4-20 x 5/8 RHMS

#1202-001
#1202-002
BARLUG

1/4" CARR.BOLT

SECTION-D-D

#5248 - PURLIN

1/4-20 x 5/8 RH M SCR.

#1204-001
Z LUG

GABLE GLASS

SECTION-E-E

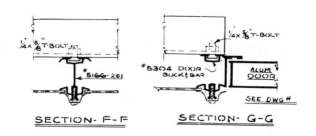

1/4 x 5/8 T-BOLT

#5166-201

SECTION-F-F

1/4 x 5/8 T-BOLT

#5304 DOOR
BUCK & BAR

ALUM
DOOR

SEE DWG #

SECTION-G-G

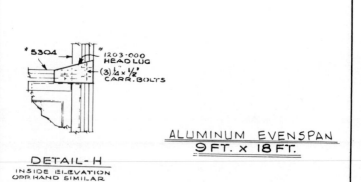

#5304

#1203-000
HEAD LUG

(3) 1/4 x 1/2"
CARR.BOLTS

DETAIL-H

INSIDE ELEVATION
OPP. HAND SIMILAR

ALUMINUM EVENSPAN
9 FT. x 18 FT.

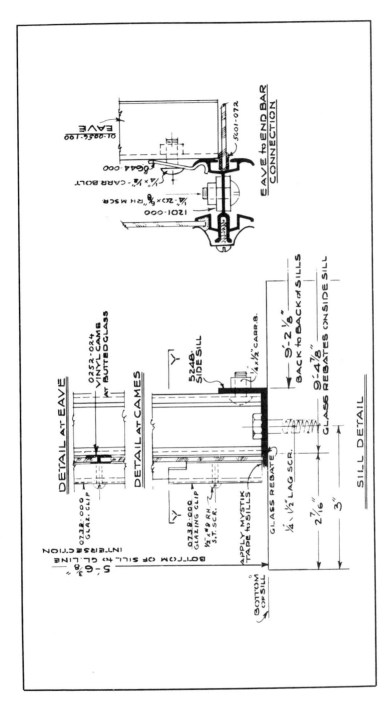

EAVE to END BAR CONNECTION

EAVE
01-0455-100

5601-072

0644-000

1/4" x 1/2" CARR. BOLT

1/4"-20 x 5/8" RH MSCR.

1201-000

DETAIL AT EAVE

0252-024
VINYL CAME
AT BUTTED GLASS

0738-000
GLAZ. CLIP

DETAIL AT CAMES

0738-000
GLAZING CLIP

1/2" #9 RH
S.T. SCR.

APPLY MYSTIK
TAPE to SILLS

BOTTOM OF SILL to GL. LINE
INTERSECTION

5-6 3/8"

BOTTOM
OF SILL

SILL DETAIL

5248-
SIDE SILL

1/4 x 1/2 CARR. B.

GLASS REBATE

1/4 x 1/2" LAG SCR.

9'-2 1/8"
BACK to BACK of SILLS

9'-4 7/8"
GLASS REBATES ON SIDE SILL

2 7/16"

3"

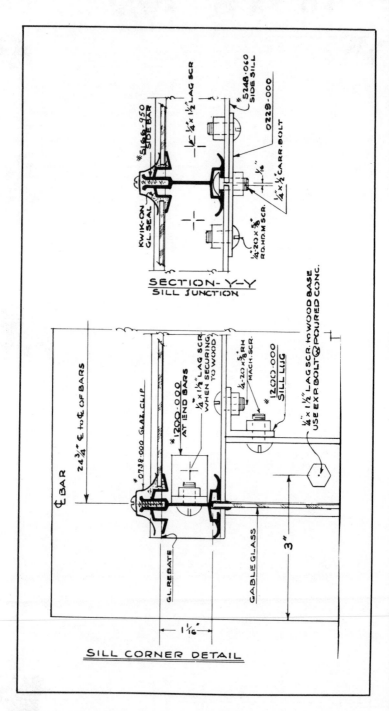

SECTION-Y-Y
SILL JUNCTION

#5188-950 SIDE BAR

KWIK-ON GL. SEAL

1/4-20 x 5/8" RD. HD. M. SCR.

1/4" x 1 1/2" LAG SCR.

#5248-060 SIDE SILL

0229-000

1/4" x 1 1/2" CARR. BOLT

1/16"

SILL CORNER DETAIL

℄ BAR

24 3/4" ℄ to ℄ OF BARS

#0738-000 GLAZ. CLIP

#1200-000 AT END BARS

1/4" x 1 1/2" LAG SCR. WHEN SECURING TO WOOD

1/4-20 x 5/8" RH MACH. SCR.

1200-000 SILL LUG

1/4" x 1 1/2" LAG SCR. to WOOD BASE USE EXP. BOLT @ POURED CONC.

GL. REBATE

GABLE GLASS

3"

1 1/16"

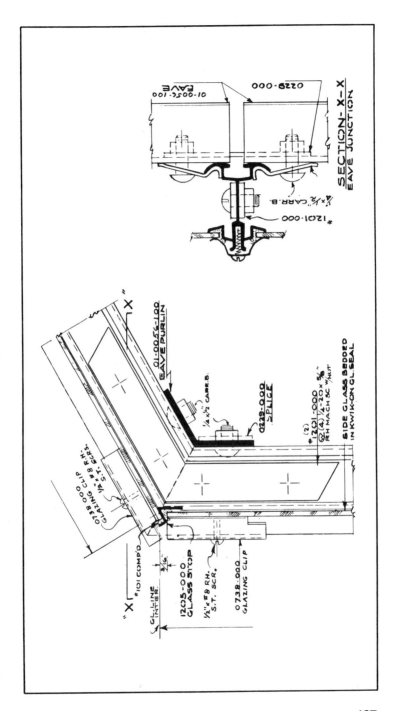

SECTION-X-X
EAVE JUNCTION

EAVE
01-0056-100
0229-000

¾"x½" CARR.B.
#1201-000

01-0056-100
EAVE PURLIN

¼x½ CARR. B.

0229-000
SPLICE

#1201-000
(2) ¼-20x ⅝"
RH MACH SC W/NUT

SIDE GLASS BEDDED
IN KWIK-ON GL SEAL

0138-000 CLIP
GLAZING ½"x#8 RH.
S.T. SCRS.

#101 COMPD

GL-LINE
INTER.

"X"

1205-000
GLASS STOP

½"x#8 RH.
S.T. SCR.

0738-000
GLAZING CLIP

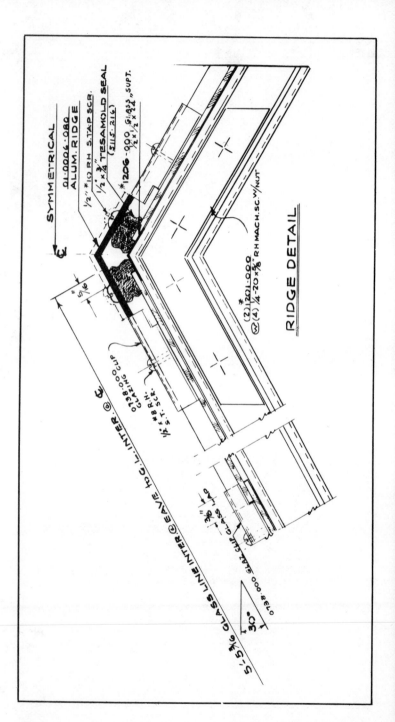

RIDGE DETAIL

Plan 12
A Sunlyt Lean-To

This plan is provided courtesy of Lord & Burnham, Irvington, New York.

**NORMAL SEQUENCE OF
SUNLYT INSTALLATION**

1. FOUNDATION
2. SILL (LEVEL & SQUARE)
3. RIDGE
4. GLAZING BARS
5. ROOF & SIDE PURLINS
6. ROOF VENT SASH
7. VERTICAL GABLE BARS
8. GABLE PURLINS AND DOOR
9. GLASS
10. FLASHING

THIS 3-DIMENSIONAL VIEW OF A
TYPICAL SUNLYT IS INTENDED TO
GIVE YOU A GENERAL "FEEL" FOR
THE ASSEMBLY OF THE STRUCTURE,
THE NAMES OF THE VARIOUS PARTS
AND WHERE THEY ARE LOCATED.
FOR SPECIFIC DETAILS OF ASSEMBLY
CONSULT THE INSTRUCTIONS,
PLANS AND DRAWINGS FURNISHED
WITH YOUR SUNLYT.

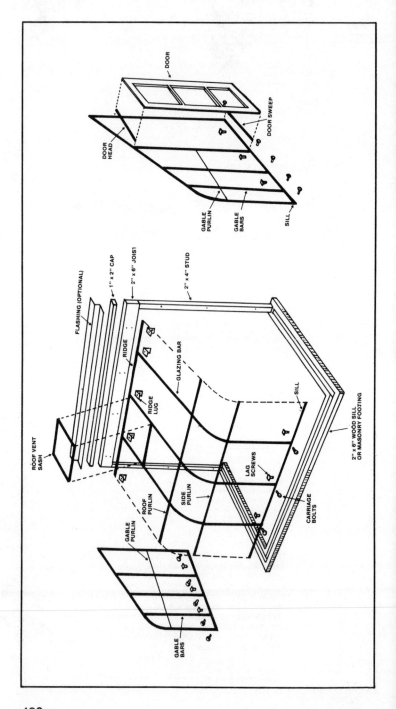

DOOR

DOOR SWEEP

DOOR HEAD

GABLE PURLIN

GABLE BARS

SILL

FLASHING (OPTIONAL)

1" x 2" CAP

2" x 6" JOIST

2" x 4" STUD

RIDGE

GLAZING BAR

RIDGE LUG

ROOF VENT SASH

SILL

2" x 6" WOOD SILL OR MASONRY FOOTING

LAG SCREWS

SIDE PURLIN

ROOF PURLIN

CARRIAGE BOLTS

GABLE PURLIN

GABLE BARS

TIPS WHICH MAY HELP YOU INSTALL YOUR GREENHOUSE

USE A NEARBY WEATHER-PROTECTED PLACE TO KEEP THE GREENHOUSE MATERIALS DURING INSTALLATION (GARAGE, COVERED PATIO).

USE SMALL CONTAINERS, CANS, BOTTLES, OR WHATEVER TO KEEP LIKE BOLTS, SCREWS, ETC., TO-GETHER, (SEPARATE ALL SELF-TAPPING SCREWS, MACHINE SCREWS, MACHINE BOLTS, WOOD SCREWS, T-BOLTS, ETC.)

PUT SIMILAR FASTENERS TOGETHER ....CLIPS, LUGS, SPLICES, ETC.

FAMILIARIZE YOURSELF WITH THE PLANS AND INSTRUCTIONS SO YOU HAVE A GENERAL IDEA OF WHAT EACH PART LOOKS LIKE AND WHERE IT GOES IN THE GREENHOUSE.

ORGANIZE THE LARGER STRUC-TURAL MEMBERS SO THAT ALL LIKE PIECES....SILLS, GLAZING BARS, PURLINS, AND RIDGES ARE GROUPED FOR EASY IDENTIFICATION AND USE.

FOLLOW THE INSTALLATION SE-QUENCE SUGGESTED. IT'S THE RESULT OF OUR MANY YEARS' EXPE-RIENCE BUILDING HOME GREENHOUSES.

THE GREENHOUSE FRAMEWORK SHOULD NOT BE ANCHORED TO THE FOUNDATION UNTIL THE STRUCTURE IS COMPLETELY GLAZED. THE GLASS WILL "SQUARE UP" THE STRUCTURE AND CORRECT ANY MISALIGNMENT OF MEMBERS.

WHERE FASTENERS ARE USED TO CONNECT TWO OR MORE STRUC-TURAL MEMBERS, ASSEMBLY IS SIMPLIFIED BY FIRST ATTACHING THE FASTENER TO ONE OF THE MEM-BERS, SO IT AND THE FASTENER CAN BE MOVED AS ONE INTO POSITION.

INSTALL GLASS IN THE FOLLOWING ORDER:

GREENHOUSES WITH STRAIGHT EAVES-ROOF VENTS, ROOF, SIDE(S), GABLES.

GREENHOUSES WITH CURVED EAVES-

ROOF VENTS, CURVED LITES, ROOF LITES, SIDE(S), GABLE(S), STARTING AT OUTSIDE CORNERS, BOTTOM LITES FIRST, AND WORKING TOWARDS CENTER.

LUMBER & FLASHING (IF REQUIRED) FURNISHED BY OWNER

Plan 13

A Typical Evenspan

This plan is provided courtesy of Lord & Burnham, Irvington, New York.

**NORMAL SEQUENCE OF
GREENHOUSE INSTALLATION:**

1. FOUNDATION WALL
2. SILL (FINAL — LEVEL AND SQUARE)
3. GLAZING BARS AND GABLE
   RAFTER AT ONE END ONLY
4. EAVE
5. RIDGE
6. VENT HEADER AND END
   CLOSURES
7 VENT SHAFTING
8. VENT APPARATUS
9. GABLE RAFTER (IF TWO-ENDED
   HOUSE)
10. ROOF VENT SASH
11. VERTICAL GABLE MEMBERS
12. GABLE PURLIN AND DOOR
13. GLASS
14. SCRIBING AND FLASHING
15. END CLOSURES

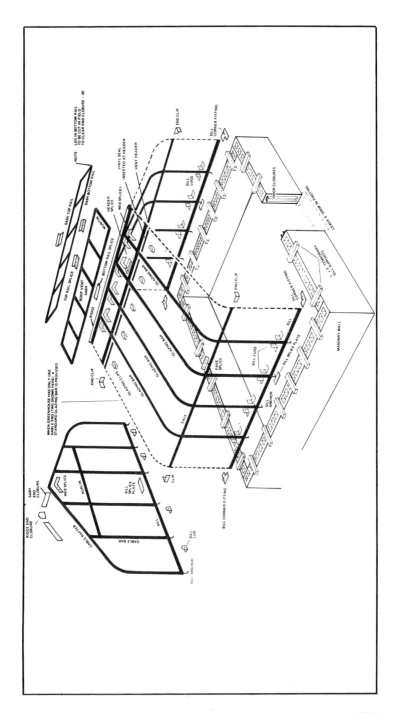

NOTE:
LEG IN BOTTOM RAIL
TO BE CUT IN FIELD
TO CLEAR END CLOSURE – 45

SASH TOP RAIL

SASH BOTTOM RAIL

TOP RAIL SPLICE

MUNTIN

ROOF VENT SASH

BOTTOM RAIL SPLICE

RIDGE

VINYL SEAL INSERTED AT HEADER

VENT HEADER

HEADER SPLICE

END CLIP

SILL CORNER FITTING

SILL LUGS

SILL SPLICES

WEB SPLICES

GLAZING BAR

DOOR CLOSURES

(MAX. 3 BAYS)

END CLIP

GLAZING CLIPS

GLAZING BAR

END CLIP

GLAZING BAR

EAVE SPLICE

SILL CORNER FITTING

SILL

SILL SPLICE PLATE

SILL LUGS

SILL ANCHOR

CORNER SUPPORT (MAX. 3 BAYS)

MASONRY WALL

EAVE

WEB SPLICES

WHEN GREENHOUSE HAS ONLY ONE GABLE END (TWO SHOWN HERE) A STANDARD GLAZING BAR IS PROVIDED

END CLIP

CLIP

SILL CORNER FITTING

RIDGE END CLOSURE

SASH END CLOSURE

WEB SPLICE

PURLIN

SILL SPLICE PLATE

SILL

SILL LUG

GABLE RAFTER

GABLE BAR

SILL ANCHOR

433

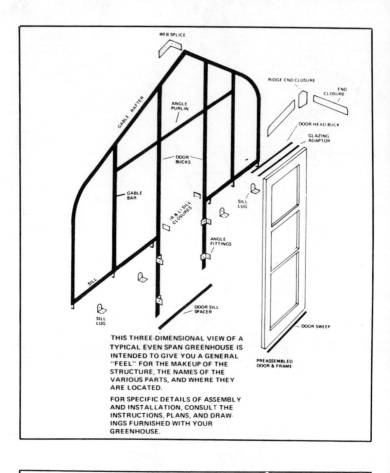

THIS THREE-DIMENSIONAL VIEW OF A TYPICAL EVEN SPAN GREENHOUSE IS INTENDED TO GIVE YOU A GENERAL "FEEL" FOR THE MAKEUP OF THE STRUCTURE, THE NAMES OF THE VARIOUS PARTS, AND WHERE THEY ARE LOCATED.

FOR SPECIFIC DETAILS OF ASSEMBLY AND INSTALLATION, CONSULT THE INSTRUCTIONS, PLANS, AND DRAWINGS FURNISHED WITH YOUR GREENHOUSE.

TIPS WHICH MAY HELP YOU INSTALL YOUR GREENHOUSE

FAMILIARIZE YOURSELF WITH THE PLANS AND INSTRUCTIONS SO YOU HAVE A GENERAL IDEA OF WHAT EACH PART LOOKS LIKE AND WHERE IT GOES IN THE GREENHOUSE.

ORGANIZE THE LARGER STRUCTURAL MEMBERS SO THAT ALL LIKE PIECES....SILLS, GLAZING BARS, EAVE PLATES, RIDGES, AND HEADERS ARE GROUPED FOR EASY IDENTIFICATION AND USE.

FOLLOW THE INSTALLATION SEQUENCE SUGGESTED. IT'S THE RESULT OF OUR MANY YEARS' EXPERIENCE BUILDING HOME GREENHOUSES.

WHEN YOU'RE READY TO INSTALL THE SILLS, BE SURE YOU FIRST LOCATE ANCHOR BOLTS, SPLICE PLATES, AND SILL CORNER FITTINGS WHERE THEY BELONG. THE SILL LUGS TO RECEIVE THE GLAZING MEMBERS CAN ALSO BE ATTACHED.

THE GREENHOUSE FRAMEWORK SHOULD NOT BE ANCHORED TO THE FOUNDATION UNTIL THE STRUCTURE IS COMPLETELY GLAZED. THE GLASS WILL "SQUARE UP" THE STRUCTURE AND CORRECT ANY MISALIGNMENT OF MEMBERS.

CERTAIN ASSEMBLIES, LIKE ROOF AND SIDE GLAZING BARS ARE MORE EASILY COMPLETED ON THE GROUND FIRST, THEN LIFTED INTO POSITION.

WHERE FASTENERS ARE USED TO CONNECT TWO OR MORE STRUCTURAL MEMBERS, ASSEMBLY IS SIMPLIFIED BY FIRST ATTACHING THE FASTENER TO ONE OF THE MEMBERS, SO IT AND THE FASTENER CAN BE MOVED AS ONE INTO POSITION.

INSTALL GLASS IN THE FOLLOWING ORDER:

GREENHOUSES WITH ANGLE EAVES –
ROOF VENTS, ROOF, SIDE(S), GABLES.

GREENHOUSES WITH CURVED EAVES –
ROOF VENTS, CURVED LITES, ROOF LITES, SIDE(S),

GABLE(S), STARTING AT OUTSIDE CORNERS, BOTTOM LITES FIRST, AND WORKING TOWARDS CENTER.

Plan 14
A Typical Lean-To

This plan is provided courtesy of Lord & Burnham, Irvington, New York.

NORMAL SEQUENCE OF GREENHOUSE INSTALLATION:

1. FOUNDATION WALL
2. SILL (PRELIMINARY FOR LEVEL)
3. 2" x 8" JOIST AND 2" x 4" BLOCK-ING AGAINST BUILDING
4. SILL (FINAL — LEVEL AND SQUARE)
5. GLAZING BARS AND GABLE RAFTER AT ONE END ONLY
6. EAVE
7. RIDGE AND 2" x 4" RIDGE BLOCKING
8. VENT HEADER AND END CLOSURES
9. VENT SHAFTING
10. VENT APPARATUS
11. GABLE RAFTER (IF TWO-ENDED HOUSE)
12. ROOF VENT SASH
13. VERTICAL GABLE MEMBERS
14. GABLE PURLIN AND DOOR
15. GLASS
16. SCRIBING AND FLASHING
17. DECK (IF APPLICABLE) AND END CLOSURES

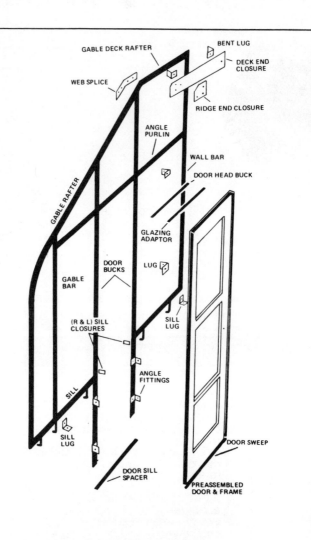

THIS THREE-DIMENSIONAL VIEW OF A
TYPICAL LEAN-TO GREENHOUSE IS
INTENDED TO GIVE YOU A GENERAL
"FEEL" FOR THE MAKEUP OF THE
STRUCTURE, THE NAMES OF THE
VARIOUS PARTS, AND WHERE THEY
ARE LOCATED.

FOR SPECIFIC DETAILS OF ASSEMBLY
AND INSTALLATION, CONSULT THE
INSTRUCTIONS, PLANS, AND DRAW-
INGS FURNISHED WITH YOUR
GREENHOUSE.

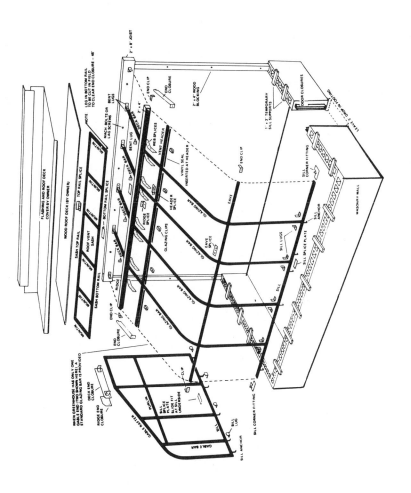

FLASHING AND ROOF DECK COVER BY OWNER

WOOD ROOF DECK (BY OWNER)

NOTE: LEG IN BOTTOM RAIL TO BE CUT IN FIELD TO CLEAR END CLOSURE - 45°

2" x 8" JOIST

END CLIP

END CLOSURE

2" x 4" WOOD BLOCKING

DOOR CLOSURES

MACH BOLTS OR LAG SCREWS

BENT LUGS

1" x 2" TEMPORARY SILL SUPPORTS

SASH TOP RAIL

TOP RAIL SPLICE

MUNTIN

ROOF VENT SASH

MUNTIN

BENT LUG

WEB SPLICES

VENT HEADER

2" x 4"

END CLIP

MUNTIN

BOTTOM RAIL SPLICE

MUNTIN

VINYL SEAL INSERTED AT HEADER

SASH BOTTOM RAIL

MUNTIN

RIDGE SPLICE

HEADER SPLICE

GLAZING BAR

EAVE

SILL CLIP

EAVE

END CLIP

RIDGE

GLAZING CLIPS

GLAZING BAR

SILL ANCHOR

SILL LUGS

GLAZING BAR

SILL SPLICE PLATE

END CLOSURE

SILL

MASONRY WALL

WHEN GREENHOUSE HAS ONLY ONE GABLE END (TWO SHOWN HERE) A STANDARD GLAZING BAR IS PROVIDED

DECK END CLOSURE

RIDGE END CLOSURE

GABLE RAFTER

MUNTIN

SILL SPLICE PLATE SLIDE FIT AT SILL UNDERSIDE

SILL

CLIP

SILL LUG

CABLE BAR

SILL CORNER FITTING

SILL ANCHOR

437

Plan 15
A Typical
Sunlyt Evenspan

This plan is provided courtesy of Lord & Burnham, Irvington, New York.

NORMAL SEQUENCE OF SUNLYT INSTALLATION

1. FOUNDATION
2. SILL (LEVEL & SQUARE)
3. GLAZING BARS
4. RIDGE
5. ROOF & SIDE PURLINS
6. ROOF VENT SASH
7. VERTICAL GABLE BARS
8. GABLE PURLINS AND DOOR
9. GLASS
10. FLASHING (IF ATTACHED TO ANOTHER BLDG.)

THIS 3-DIMENSIONAL VIEW OF A TYPICAL SUNLYT IS INTENDED TO GIVE YOU A GENERAL "FEEL" FOR THE ASSEMBLY OF THE STRUCTURE, THE NAMES OF THE VARIOUS PARTS AND WHERE THEY ARE LOCATED. FOR SPECIFIC DETAILS OF ASSEMBLY CONSULT THE INSTRUCTIONS, PLANS, AND DRAWINGS FURNISHED WITH YOUR SUNLYT.

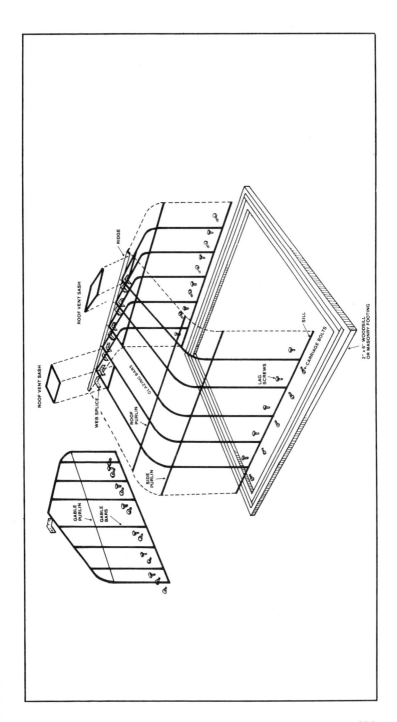

ROOF VENT SASH

ROOF VENT SASH

RIDGE

WEB SPLICE

GLAZING BARS

ROOF PURLIN

SIDE PURLIN

GABLE PURLIN

GABLE BARS

SILL

LAG SCREWS

CARRIAGE BOLTS

2" x 6" WOODSILL OR MASONRY FOOTING

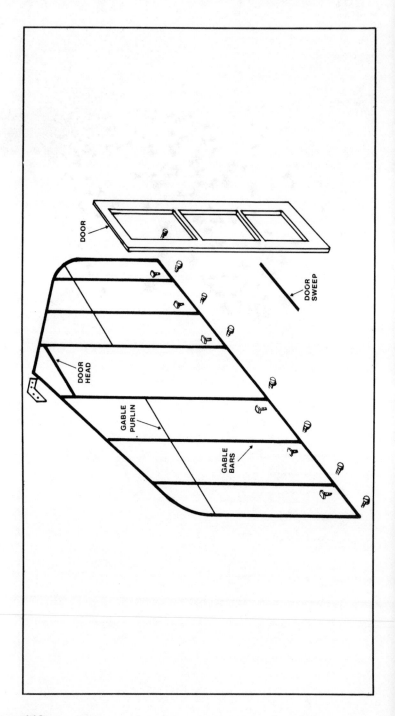

DOOR

DOOR
SWEEP

DOOR HEAD

GABLE
PURLIN

GABLE
BARS

Appendix A
Parts Inventory List

No.	Name of Part	Quan.	Nominal Size	Length
0	Latch Blocks	4	1" x 2"	3¾"
1	Backing Blocks	6	1" x 3"	3¾"
2	Roof Braces	2	1" x 3"	8"
3	Rafter Supports	4	1" x 3"	11"
4	Rear Vent Support	1	1" x 3"	28"
5	Rafter Tie Assemblies	3	1" x 3"	28"
6	Rafters	4	1" x 3"	38½"
7	Roof Supports	4	1½" x 1½"	45"
8	End Posts	4	1" x 3"	72"
9	Side Plate Cross Tie	1	1" x 3"	73¼"
10	End Corner Studs	4	1" x 3"	73¼"
11	End Plate Assemblies	2	1" x 3"	74"
12	Side Studs	6	1" x 3"	78"
13	End Sills	2	1" x 3"	96"
14	Side Sills and Plates	4	1" x 3"	96"
15	Ridge Assembly	1	1" x 3"	96"
19	Inside Rafters	2	1" x 3"	37¼"
	Pre-fabricated Dutch Door (two sections)			

ADDITIONAL LUMBER FOR BENCHES

No.	Name of Part	Quan.	Nominal Size	Length
14	Rear Bench Rails	2	1" x 3"	96"
16	Legs	4	1" x 3"	29"
17	Front Bench Rails	2	1" x 3"	96"
18	Bench Top Boards	48	1" x 3"	30"
	(or)	38	1" x 4"	30"

Size	Item	No. of Pieces
1¼" x ¼"	Carriage Bolts	18
2" x ¼"	Carriage Bolts.	47
3½" x ¼"	Carriage Bolts	8
¼"	Washers	75
¼"	Nuts	76
6d	Galvanized Nails	20
⅜"	Metal Fasteners	25
⅝"	Aluminum Screw Nails	650
	Door Handle	1
	Hinges	4
2" x 4"	Flat Brackets	8
2" x 4"	Corner Angle Brackets	11
1" x 80"	Closure Foam	18
5½" x 15"	Angular Flat Corner Panels	4
6¾" x 15"	Flat Vent Panels	4
10¾" x 15"	Flat Vent Panels	4
21" x 26"	Corrugated Door Panel	1
26" x 34"	Corrugated Door Panel	1
30¾" x 63"	Corrugated Rear Center Panel	1
32" x 76"	Corrugated End Corner Panels	4
40" x 52½"	Corrugated Roof Panels	4
47¼" x 78"	Corrugated Side Panels	4

ADDITIONAL HARDWARE FOR BENCHES

Size	Item	No. of Pieces
1¼" x ¼"	Carriage Bolts	8
2" x ¼"	Carriage Bolts	10
¼"	Washers	18
¼"	Nuts	18
6d	Galvanized Nails	100
2" x 4"	Corner Angle Brackets	4

Appendix B
Parts Inventory List

No.	Name of Part	Quan.	Nominal Size	Length
0	Latch Blocks	4	1" x 2"	3¾"
1	Backing Blocks	6	1" x 3"	3¾"
2	Roof Braces	4	1" x 3"	8"
3	Rafter Supports	4	1" x 3"	11"
4	Rear Vent Support	1	1" x 3"	28"
5	Rafter Tie Assemblies	4	1" x 3"	28"
6	Rafters	4	1" x 3"	38½"
7	Roof Supports	6	1½" x 1½"	45"
8	End Posts	4	1" x 3"	72"
9	Side Plate Cross Tie	2	1" x 3"	73¼"
10	End Corner Studs	4	1" x 3"	73¼"
11	End Plate Assemblies	2	1" x 3"	74"
12	Side Studs	8	1" x 3"	78"
13	End Sills	2	1" x 3"	96"
14	Side Sills and Plates	4	1" x 3"	144"
15	Ridge Assembly	1	1" x 3"	144"
19	Inside Rafters	4	1" x 3"	37¼"
	Pre-fabricated Dutch Door (two sections)			

ADDITIONAL LUMBER FOR BENCHES

No.	Name of Part	Quan.	Nominal Size	Length
14	Rear Bench Rails	2	1" x 3"	144"
16	Legs	4	1" x 3"	29"
17	Front Bench Rails	2	1" x 3"	144"
18	Bench Top Boards	74	1" x 3"	30"
		or) 58	1" x 4"	30"

Size	Item	No. of Pieces
1¼" x ¼"	Carriage Bolts	22
2" x ¼"	Carriage Bolts	59
3½" x ¼"	Carriage Bolts	11
¼"	Washers	93
¼"	Nuts	94
6d	Galvanized Nails	20
⅜"	Metal Fasteners	25
⅝"	Aluminum Screw Nails	908
	Door Handle	1
	Hinges	4
2" x 4"	Flat Brackets	8
2" x 4"	Corner Angle Brackets	14
1" x 80"	Closure Foam	24
5½" x 15"	Angular Flat Corner Panels	4
6¾" x 15"	Flat Vent Panels	4
10¾" x 15"	Flat Vent Panels	4
21" x 26"	Corrugated Door Panel	1
26" x 34"	Corrugated Door Panel	1
30¾" x 63"	Corrugated Rear Center Panel	1
32" x 76"	Corrugated End Corner Panels	4
40" x 52½"	Corrugated Roof Panels	6
47¼" x 78"	Corrugated Side Panels	6

ADDITIONAL HARDWARE FOR BENCHES

Size	Item	No. of Pieces
1¼" x ¼"	Carriage Bolts	8
2" x ¼"	Carriage Bolts	12
¼"	Washers	20
¼"	Nuts	20
6d	Galvanized Nails	150
2" x 4"	Corner Angle Brackets	4

Appendix C
Parts Inventory List

No.	Name of Part	Quan.	Nominal Size	Length
0	Latch Blocks	4	1" x 2"	3¾"
1	Backing Blocks	7	1" x 3"	3¾"
2	Roof Braces	6	1" x 3"	8"
3	Rafter Supports	4	1" x 3"	11"
4	Rear Vent Support	1	1" x 3"	28"
5	Rafter Tie Assemblies	5	1" x 3"	28"
6	Rafters	4	1" x 3"	38½"
7	Roof Supports	6	1½" x 1½"	45"
70	Roof Supports	2	1½" x 1½"	41½"
8	End Posts	4	1" x 3"	72"
9	Side Plate Cross Tie	3	1" x 3"	73¼"
10	End Corner Studs	4	1" x 3"	73¼"
11	End Plate Assemblies	2	1" x 3"	74"
12	Side Studs	10	1" x 3"	78"
13	End Sills	2	1" x 3"	96"
14	Side Sills and Plates	4	1" x 3"	96"
15	Ridge Assembly (two sections) . . .	1	1" x 3"	96"
140	Side Sill & Plate Extensions	4	1" x 3"	94¾"
19	Inside Rafters	6	1" x 3"	37¼"
	Pre-fabricated Dutch Door (two sections)			

ADDITIONAL LUMBER FOR BENCHES

14	Rear Bench Rails	2	1" x 3"	96"
140	Rear Bench Rail Extensions	2	1" x 3"	94¾"
16	Legs	6	1" x 3"	29"
17	Front Bench Rails	2	1" x 3"	96"
170	Front Bench Rail Extensions	2	1" x 3"	94¾"
18	Bench Top Boards	98	1" x 3"	30"
		(or) 78	1" x 4"	30"

Size	Item	No. of Pieces
1¼" x ¼"	Carriage Bolts	26
2" x ¼"	Carriage Bolts	72
3½" x ¼"	Carriage Bolts	14
¼"	Washers	106
¼"	Nuts	107
6d	Galvanized Nails	30
⅜"	Metal Fasteners	30
⅝"	Aluminum Screw Nails	1064
	Door Handle	1
	Hinges	4
2" x 4"	Flat Brackets	13
2" x 4"	Corner Angle Brackets	14
1" x 80"	Closure Foam	30
5½" x 15"	Angular Flat Corner Panels	4
6¾" x 15"	Flat Vent Panels	4
10¾" x 15"	Flat Vent Panels	4
21" x 26"	Corrugated Door Panel	1
26" x 34"	Corrugated Door Panel	1
30¾" x 63"	Corrugated Rear Center Panel	1
32" x 76"	Corrugated End Corner Panels	4
40" x 52½"	Corrugated Roof Panels	8
47¼" x 78"	Corrugated Side Panels	8

ADDITIONAL HARDWARE FOR BENCHES

1¼" x ¼"	Carriage Bolts	8
2" x ¼"	Carriage Bolts	10
¼"	Washers	18
¼"	Nuts	18
6d	Galvanized Nails	100
2" x 4"	Corner Angle Brackets	4
2" x 4"	Flat Brackets	4

Appendix D
Parts Inventory List

No.	Name of Part	Quan.	Nominal Size	Length
0	Latch Blocks	4	1" x 2"	3¾"
1	Backing Blocks	6	1" x 3"	3¾"
4	Rear Vent Support	1	1" x 3"	28"
8	End Posts	6	1" x 3"	72"
10	End Corner Studs	2	1" x 3"	73¼"
12	Side Studs	5	1" x 3"	78"
14	Side Sill, Plate, and Rear Bench Rail	5	1" x 3"	144"
17	Cross Ties and Bench Rails	5	1" x 3"	144"
20	End Plates	2	1" x 3"	74"
21	Rafter Supports	2	1" x 3"	9-1/8"
22	Rafter Supports	2	1" x 3"	14-7/8"
23	Rafter Supports	2	1" x 3"	18¾"
24	Roof Supports	5	1" x 3"	81"
25	Roof Supports	5	1" x 3"	86"
26	Rafters	2	1" x 3"	75-3/8"
27	End Sills	2	1" x 3"	85"
	Stakes	7		
	Pre-Fabricated Dutch Door (two sections)			
140	Sill, Plate and Bench Rail Extensions	5	1" x 3"	94¾"
170	Sill, Plate and Bench Rail Extensions	5	1" x 3"	94¾"

ADDITIONAL LUMBER FOR ONE BENCH

No.	Name of Part	Quan.	Nominal Size	Length
18	Bench Tops	49	1" x 3"	30"

ADDITIONAL LUMBER FOR TWO BENCHES

No.	Name of Part	Quan.	Nominal Size	Length
19	Bench Tops	49	1" x 3"	23"

Size	Item	No. of Pieces
1¼" x ¼"	Carriage Bolts	40
2" x ¼"	Carriage Bolts	65
3" x ¼"	Carriage Bolts	2
¼"	Washers	107
¼"	Nuts	109
6d	Galvanized Nails	20
3/8"	Corrugated Fasteners	30
5/8"	Aluminum Screw Nails	500
3/4"	Aluminum Screw Nails	240
	Door Handle	1
	Hinges	4
2" x 4"	Flat Brackets	16
2" x 4"	Corner Brackets	18
1" x ¾" x 78"	Closure Foam	28
10¾" x 15"	Flat Vent Panels	4
71-1/8" x 14¼"	Flat Angular Panels	2
21" x 26"	Corrugated Door Panel	1
34" x 26"	Corrugated Door Panel	1
30¾" x 63"	Corrugated Rear Center Panel	1
32" x 76"	Corrugated End Corner Panels	2
21" x 76"	Corrugated End Panels	2
78" x 52½"	Corrugated Roof Panels	4
47¼" x 78"	Corrugated Side Panels	4

ADDITIONAL HARDWARE FOR BENCHES

Size	Item	No. of Pieces
6d	Galvanized Nails	200

Appendix E
Parts Inventory List

No.	Name of Part	Quan.	Nominal Size	Length
0	Latch Blocks	4	1" x 2"	3¾"
1	Backing Blocks	8	1" x 3"	3¾"
02	Ridge Supports	2	1" x 3"	11"
03	End Cross Supports	4	1" x 3"	21½"
04	Studs	8	1" x 3"	29"
05	Center Arch Support Cross Members	2	1" x 3"	31½"
06	End Arch Support Cross Members (Headers) .	2	1" x 3"	31½"
07	Lower Vent Support	1	1" x 3"	33"
08	End Posts	4	1" x 3"	76"
010	End Sills	2	1" x 3"	76"
011	Ridge Cap	1	1" x 2"	96"
012	Ridge	1	1" x 3"	96"
013	Arch Supports	2	1" x 3"	96"
014	Side Sills and Plates	4	1" x 3"	96"
	Arches	12	¼" x 2½"	96"
	Pre-fabricated Dutch Door (two sections)			

ADDITIONAL LUMBER FOR BENCHES

No.	Name of Part	Quan.	Nominal Size	Length
015	Legs	4	1" x 3"	29"
016	Bench Rails	2	1" x 3"	96"
017	Bench Top Boards	48	1" x 3"	24"
	(or)	38	1" x 4"	24"

Size	Item	No. of Pieces
1¼" x ¼"	Carriage Bolts	32
2" x ¼"	Carriage Bolts	36
2½" x ¼"	Carriage Bolts	4
3½ x ¼"	Carriage Bolts	2
¼"	Washers for Carriage Bolts	75
¼"	Nuts for Carriage Bolts	75
6d	Galvanized Nails	35
	Door Handle	1
	Hinges	4
2" x 4"	Galvanized Corner Angle Brackets	12
	Masking Tape	1
10½" x 15"	Fiberglass Vent Panels	4
9' x 32½'	Ultra-Violet Inhibited Covering	1
¾"	Tacking Strip	80'
⅝"	Aluminum Screw-Nails	240

ADDITIONAL HARDWARE FOR BENCHES

Size	Item	No. of Pieces
1¼" x ¼"	Carriage Bolts	4
2" x ¼"	Carriage Bolts	4
¼"	Washers for Carriage Bolts	8
¼"	Nuts for Carriage Bolts	8
6d	Galvanized Nails	96
2" x 4"	Galvanized Corner Angle Brackets	4

445

Appendix F
Parts Inventory List

No.	Name of Part	Quan.	Nominal Size	Length
0	Latch Blocks	4	1" x 2"	3¾"
1	Backing Blocks	8	1" x 3"	3¾"
02	Ridge Supports	2	1" x 3"	11"
03	End Cross Supports	4	1" x 3"	21½"
04	Studs	10	1" x 3"	29"
05	Center Arch Support Cross Members	3	1" x 3"	31½"
06	End Arch Support Cross Members (Headers) .	2	1" x 3"	31½"
07	Lower Vent Support	1	1" x 3"	33"
08	End Posts	4	1" x 3"	76"
010	End Sills	2	1" x 3"	76"
011	Ridge Cap	1	1" x 2"	144"
012	Ridge	1	1" x 3"	144"
013	Arch Supports	2	1" x 3"	144"
014	Side Sills and Plates	4	1" x 3"	144"
	Arches	14	¼" x 2½"	96"
	Pre-fabricated Dutch Door (two sections)			

ADDITIONAL LUMBER FOR BENCHES

No.	Name of Part	Quan.	Nominal Size	Length
015	Legs	6	1" x 3"	29"
016	Bench Rails	2	1" x 3"	144"
017	Bench Top Boards	72	1" x 3"	24"
		(or) 58	1" x 4"	24"

Size	Item	No. of Pieces
1¼" x ¼"	Carriage Bolts	34
2" x ¼"	Carriage Bolts	40
2½" x ¼"	Carriage Bolts	4
3½ x ¼"	Carriage Bolts	2
¼"	Washers for Carriage Bolts	81
¼"	Nuts for Carriage Bolts	81
6d	Galvanized Nails	35
	Door Handle	1
	Hinges	4
2" x 4"	Galvanized Corner Angle Brackets	12
	Masking Tape	1
10½" x 15"	Fiberglass Vent Panels	4
13' x 26'	Ultra-Violet Inhibited Covering	1
2' x 4'	Ultra-Violet Inhibited Covering	1
¾"	Tacking Strip	88'
⅝"	Aluminum Screw-Nails	275

ADDITIONAL HARDWARE FOR BENCHES

Size	Item	No. of Pieces
1¼" x ¼"	Carriage Bolts	4
2" x ¼"	Carriage Bolts	6
¼"	Washers for Carriage Bolts	10
¼"	Nuts for Carriage Bolts	10
6d	Galvanized Nails	144
2" x 4"	Galvanized Corner Angle Brackets	4

446

Appendix G

Parts Inventory List

No.	Name of Part	Quan.	Nominal Size	Length
70	Base Segments	10	2" x 4"	57"
71	Base Tie	1	2" x 4"	10"
72	Vent Positioner	1	1" x 1-1/2"	30"
73	Door Jamb	2	1" x 2"	56-3/4"
74	Door Jamb	1	1" x 2"	50-3/16"
75	Door Jamb	1	1" x 2"	50-3/16"
76	Inlet Spacer Block	1	1" x 3"	11"
	Anchoring Stakes	5	1" x 3"	12"

Shape				
A	Triangles	8	50" Tall	
A	Triangles with Accessory Frame	2	50" Tall	
B	Triangles	28	42" Tall	
B	Triangles without Fiberglass	1	42" Tall	
C	Triangles for Door	2	42" Tall	

Size	Item	No. of Pieces
6d	Nails	25
#8-32	Machine Bolts	200
#8-32	Nuts	200
#8	Washers	400
#10 1-1/2"	Wood Screws	40
	Cabinet Hinges with Screws	1 Pr.
	Butt Hinges with Screws	1 Pr.
	Strap Hinges with Screws	1 Pr.
	Hooks and Eyes	3 Sets

447

Appendix H
Parts Inventory List

No.	Name of Part	Quan.	Nominal Size	Length
0	Latch Blocks	4	1" x 2"	3³⁄₄"
1	Backing Blocks	3	1" x 3"	3³⁄₄"
3	Rafter Supports	2	1" x 3"	11"
5	Rafter Tie Assemblies	2	1" x 3"	28"
6	Rafters	4	1" x 3"	38½"
8	Door End Posts	2	1" x 3"	72"
10	End Corner Studs	2	1" x 3"	73¼"
11	End Plate Assemblies	2	1" x 3"	74"
12	Side Studs	4	1" x 3"	78"
13	End Sills	2	1" x 3"	48"
14	Side Sills and Plates	4	1" x 3"	48⅝"
15	Ridge Assembly	1	1" x 3"	48⅝"
20	Rear Rafter Supports	2	1" x 3"	8½"
	Pre-fabricated Dutch Door (two sections)			

ADDITIONAL LUMBER FOR BENCHES

No.	Name of Part	Quan.	Nominal Size	Length
14	Rear Bench Rails	2	1" x 3"	48⅝"
16	Legs	2	1" x 3"	29"
17	Front Bench Rails	2	1" x 3"	48⅝"
18	Bench Top Boards	28	1" x 3"	30"
		(or) 18	1" x 4"	30"
19	Bench End Rails	2	1" x 3"	28¼"

4' HANDI-GRO HARDWARE WITHOUT BENCHES

Size	Item	No. of Pieces
1¼" x ¼"	Carriage Bolts	12
2" x ¼"	Carriage Bolts	28
3" x ¼"	Carriage Bolts	2
¼"	Washers	32
¼"	Nuts	42
6d	Galvanized Nails	10
⅜"	Metal Fasteners	14
⅝"	Aluminum Screw Nails	272
	Door Handle	1
	Hinges	4
2" x 4"	Flat Brackets	4
2" x 4"	Corner Angle Brackets	6
1" x 78"	Closure Foam	12
5½" x 15"	Angular Flat Corner Panels	2
6¾" x 15"	Flat Vent Panels	2
10¾" x 15"	Flat Vent Panels	2
21" x 26"	Corrugated Door Panel	1
26" x 34"	Corrugated Door Panel	1
32" x 76"	Corrugated End Corner Panels	2
40" x 52½"	Corrugated Roof Panels	2
47¼" x 78"	Corrugated Side Panels	2

ADDITIONAL HARDWARE FOR BENCHES

Size	Item	No. of Pieces
1¼" x ¼"	Carriage Bolts	6
2" x ¼"	Carriage Bolts	6
¼"	Washers	8
¼"	Nuts	12
6d	Galvanized Nails	54/84
2" x 4"	Corner Angle Brackets	6

Appendix I
Materials and Tools List For A Solar Greenhouse

This is a list of materials for a 4-feet by 8-feet solar air heater. Several different choices are listed for some of the items. Also by scrounging (using second hand or used materials) you should be able to not only substitute but also cut the cost of the solar air heater considerably. Just keep the purpose of each item in mind and you will easily find all the things you need to build the solar air heater locally.

1 each 4' x 8' x ⅜" CD exterior plywood (this is for the back of the shop-built panel. If you build the panel directly onto the south wall of your home, you can eliminate the backing. Substitute any rigid 4' x 8' panel such as masonite, paneling, etc.).

4 each 1" x 4" x 8' pieces of lumber (these form the frame of the panel including baffle).

5 each 1" x 2" x 8' pieces of lumber (these form the support for the absorber).

1 lb. galvanized nails (4d to 6d to fasten the back to the frame).

Wood glue

2 each 4' x 8' sheet galvanized steel corrugated roofing (absorber plate). Note: Absorber steel is cut and fastened with silicone caulk and pop rivets with corrugations running perpendicular to air flow so 2 each 8' sheets will just fit. Corrugated aluminum (either plain or enameled will work 10% more efficiently than steel. Second hand offset plates available at newspaper printers will work as will 24" aluminum flashing with some support. If smooth metal is used, be sure to fasten air turbulators beneath the absorber to the wall or back of the panel-strips of screen molding will work.

1 small bottle of vinegar (muriatic acid or any metal etcher will work; Weathered or used metal does not need to be etched).

1 pint rustoleum flat black paint (any moderate temperature paint (200 F.) will work.

1 lb. ¾" galvanized roofing nails.

4 tubes black silicone caulk sealant (2 tubes will work if you do neat work, but buy 4 tubes just in case. Geocel will work and can be painted black. Clear silicone caulk will work but cannot be painted).

2 tubes latex caulk.

1 each 3″ x 24″ piece of metal (to support absorber at center bar opening).

1 each 4′ x 8′ piece of flat icy clear filon (kalwall or glass will work. Second-hand window glass is a low cost substitute. Polyethylene or vinyl clear sheets will work for a short period of time).

3 each 8′ long 90 degree angle aluminum for frame edge to hold down glazing. (¾″ by ¾″ aluminum angle is used. Wooden battens can also be used such as screen molding or any ¾″ wide wooden strip. Flat metal can also be used).

1 each 8′ x 3.4″ flat piece of aluminum (substitute with wood as above).

75 each #7 x ¾″ wood screws.

1 each cfm squirrel cage blower (substitute muffin fan of same cfm or fan of 120 to 160cfm size).

1 each thermostat (on between 90 to 115 degrees F. and off under 90 degrees).

1 length 2/12 ug wire (length enough to reach from electric outlet to blower and thermostat.

1 each electric plug.

1 each temp-vent for summer ventilation.

1 qt. exterior latex paint to match house color.

Assorted lumber and duct tape and insulation for ducting cold and hot registers.

1 each 4″ x 12″ floor register (substitute screen for hot air opening).

1 each 4′ x 8′ x 1″ styrofoam insulation board (needed only if wall is thin or uninsulated).

Tools needed for construction of solar air heater

Hammer	2″ to 4″ Paint Brush	Hack Saw
Tape Measure	Rags	Miter Box
Hand or Power Circular Saw	Paint Thinner Knife	Compass Saw or Saber Saw
Calk Gun	Tin Snips	Framing Square
Pencil	Drill	

4 Feet Straight Edge (Straight Piece of Lumber or Rule)

Appendix J
Greenhouse Plants And Minimum Temperatures

GREENHOUSE PLANTS THAT NEED A MINIMUM TEMPERATURE OF 40°

ACACIA
ANEMONE
CALENDULA OFFICINALIS (Pot Marigold)
CAMELLIA
DELPHINIUM AJACIS (Larkspur)
ERICA (Heath or Scotch "Heather")
IRIS, DUTCH (force)
PIQUERIA TRINERVIA (Stevia)

GREENHOUSE PLANTS THAT NEED A MINIMUM TEMPERATURE OF 45°

AGAPANTHUS (Lily-of-the-Nile)
CALCEOLARIA (Pocketbook Plant)
CAMPANULA ISOPHYLLA (Bellflower, Bluebell, Star of Bethlehem)
CHOISYA (Mexican Orange)
CHRYSANTHEMUM CARINATUM (Annual)
CYMBIDIUM ORCHID (some, but not all at this temperature)
CYTISUS (Broom) ("Canariensis Genista" of florists) (force)
FREESIA
LACHENALIA (Cape Cowslip)
LOBELIA
MATHIOLA INCANA (Stock)
NEMESIA
ODONTOGLOSSUM ORCHID (some, but not all at this temperature)
PRIMULA OBCONICA (Primrose)
PRIMULA SINENSIS (Chinese Primrose)
RANUNCULUS (Buttercup, Crowfoot)
SENECIO CRUENTUS (Cineraria)
SPARMANNIA
SWAINSONA (Winter Sweet Pea)
VIOLA TRICOLOR (Pansy or Heart's-ease)

GREENHOUSE PLANTS THAT NEED A MINIMUM TEMPERATURE OF 50°

AGERATUM (Floss Flower)
ANTIRRHINUM (Snapdragon)
ASTILBE JAPONICA (Spirea)
BOSTON DAISY (Chrysanthemum frutescens, Marguerite)
BUDDLEJA or BUDDLEIA (Butterfly Bush)
CALLISTEPHUS CHINENSIS (China Aster)
CAPSICUM (Christmas Pepper)
CHRYSANTHEMUM FRUTESCENS (Marguerite, Paris or Boston Daisy)
CHRYSANTHEMUM PARTHENIUM (Feverfew)
CITRUS (Calamondin, Citron, Lemon, Orange)
CROCUS (force)
CYCLAMEN
DAPHNE CNEORUM
DIANTHUS CARYOPHYLLUS (Carnation)
EXACUM
FELICIA AMELLOIDES (Agathea, Blue Daisy)
GODETIA (Satinflower)
HAEMANTHUS (Blood Lily)
IBERIS AMARA and UMBELLATA (Candytuft)
IMPATIENS (Sultana or Patience Plant)
IXIA
KALANCHOE
LATHYRUS ODORATUS (Sweet Pea)
MILLA BIFLORA (Mexican Star)
MYOSOTIS (Forget-me-not)
NEPHROLEPIS BOSTONIENSIS (Boston Fern)
NERINE
NERIUM OLEANDER
NICOTIANA (Flowering Tobacco)
NIEREMBERGIA FRUTESCENS (Cup-flower)
ONCIDIUM ORCHID (some, but not all at this temperature)
ORNITHOGALUM
OSMANTHUS FRAGRANS (Sweet Olive)
OXALIS
PASSIFLORA (Passion Flower)
PENTAS (Egyptian Star-cluster)
PLUMBAGO (Leadwort)
PRIMULA MALACOIDES (Baby Primrose, Fairy Primrose)
SCHIZANTHUS (Butterfly Flower, Poor Man's Orchid)
TROPAEOLUM (Nasturtium)
VALLOTA (Scarborough Lily)
VELTHEIMIA

GREENHOUSE PLANTS THAT NEED A MINIMUM TEMPERATURE OF 55°

ALYSSUM MARITIMUM (Sweet Alyssum)
AMARCRINUM
APHELANDRA
AZALEA

BELOPERONE (Shrimp Plant)
BOUGAINVILLEA
BRASSAVOLA ORCHID
CATTLEYA ORCHID
CENTAUREA CYANUS (Cornflower or Bachelor's-button)
CLEMATIS
CLIVIA
CROSSANDRA
EPIDENDRUM ORCHIDS (some, but not all at this temperature)
GERANIUM (Pelargonium species and varieties)
GERBERA JAMESONI (Transvaal Daisy)
HYDRANGEA, BLUE and PINK
IXORA
JACOBINIA (King's Crown)
JASMINUM (Jasmine or Jessamine)
LANTANA
NARCISSUS (Daffodil) (force)
PAPHIOPEDILUM ORCHID (some, but not all at this temperature)
PETUNIA
REINWARDTIA
ROSES (pot)
SALPIGLOSSIS (Painted Tongue)
SEDUM
SMITHIANTHA (Naegelia or Temple Bells)
STRELITZIA (Bird of Paradise)
TAGETES ERECTA (African Marigold)
TECOMARIA CAPENSIS (Cape Honeysuckle)
ZANTEDESCHIA (Calla-Lily)
ZYGOCACTUS (Thanksgiving, Christmas or Easter Cactus)

GREENHOUSE PLANTS THAT NEED A MINIMUM TEMPERATURE OF 60°

ABUTILON (Flowering Maple)
ACALYPHA HISPIDA (Red-hot Cat-tail or Chenille Plant)
ACHIMENES (Nut Orchid or Hot-Water Plant)
ALLAMANDA
ARDISIA CRISPA (Coralberry)
ASPARAGUS FERN (A. sprengeri and A. plumosus)
BEGONIA, SEMI-TUBEROUS (Christmas Begonia)
BESSERA ELEGANS (Mexican Coral Drops)
BOUVARDIA
BRUNSVIGIA (Cape Belladonna or Belladonna Lily)
CACTI AND OTHER SUCCULENTS
CALADIUM
CENTROPOGON
CHRYSANTHEMUM MORIFOLIUM (fall)
CLARKIA ELEGANS
CLERODENDRUM
CODIAEUM (Croton)
COLEUS
COLUMNEA
EUPATORIUM (Mist-flower)

EUPHORBIA FULGENS (Scarlet Plume)
EUPHORBIA PULCHERRIMA (Poinsettia)
FUCHSIA
GAZANIA
GYPSOPHILA (Annual Baby's-breath)
HELIOTROPE
HOYA CARNOSA (Wax Plant)
HYACINTH, DUTCH (force)
INCARVILLEA ("Hardy Gloxinia")
KAEMPFERIA
LILIUM (Lily) (force)
RECHSTEINERIA (Gesneria cardinalis)
SOLANUM (Christmas Cherry)
TRACHYMENE CAERULEA (Didiscus, Blue Lace Flower)
TULIP (force)
ZINNIA ELEGANS (Common Zinnia)

GREENHOUSE PLANTS THAT NEED A MINIMUM TEMPERATURE OF 65°

AECHMEA (Bromeliad)
AESCHYNANTHUS (Trichosporum, Lipstick Vine)
AMARYLLIS
ANANAS (Bromeliad)
ANTHURIUM
BEGONIA, FIBROUS-ROOTED (Wax Begonia, B. semperflorens)
BEGONIA, TUBEROUS
BILLBERGIA (Bromeliad)
BROMELIADS
BROWALLIA
CRASSULA (Jade Plant)
CRYPTANTHUS (Bromeliad)
EPISCIA
EUCHARIS GRANDIFLORA (Amazon Lily)
EUCOMIS (Pineapple Flower)
GARDENIA
GLADIOLUS
GLORIOSA (Climbing Lily, Glory Lily)
GUZMANIA (Bromeliad)
HIBISCUS ROSA-SINENSIS (Chinese Hibiscus)
NEOREGELIA (Bromeliad)
PHALAENOPSIS ORCHIDS
PHILODENDRON
SAINTPAULIA (African Violet)
SINNINGIA SPECIOSA (Gloxinia)
SPATHIPHYLLUM
STEPHANOTIS FLORIBUNDA (Madagascar Jasmine)
STREPTOSOLEN JAMESONI (Orange "Browallia")
TILLANDSIA (Bromeliad)
VRIESEA (Bromeliad)
ZEPHYRANTHES (Zephyr-Flower, Fairy or Rain-Lily)

Appendix K

Greenhouse Plants For Summer, Fall, Spring & Winter

GREENHOUSE PLANTS FOR SUMMER FLOWERS

Abutilon
Achimenes
Aeschynanthus (Trichosporum)
Agapanthus
Ageratum
Allamanda
Alyssum maritimum
Amarcrinum
Anthurium
Begonia, fibrous rooted
Begonia, tuberous
Beloperone
Boston Daisy
Cacti, and other Succulents
Caladium
Callistephus chinensis
Campanula isophylla
Centaurea cyanus
Chrysanthemum parthenium
Citrus
Clematis
Clerodendrum
Columnea
Crossandra
Dianthus caryophyllus
Episcia
Eucharis grandiflora
Eucomis
Fuchsia
Gardenia
Gazania
Geranium
Gloriosa
Gloxinia

Gypsophila
Haemanthus
Heliotrope
Hibiscus
Hoya carnosa
Hydrangea, Pink
Impatiens
Incarvillea
Ixora
Jacobinia
Jasminum
Kaempferia
Lantana
Lilium
Lobelia
Nierembergia frutescens
Orchids
Passiflora
Petunia
Plumbago
Saintpaulia
Salpiglossis
Smithiantha
Sinningia speciosa
Sparmannia
Spathiphyllum
Strelitzia
Stephanotis floribunda
Swainsona
Tropaeolum
Zantedeschia
Zephyranthes
Zinnia elegans

GREENHOUSE PLANTS FOR FALL FLOWERS

Abutilon
Acalypha hispida
Achimenes
Aeschynanthus (Trichosporum)
Ageratum
Alyssum maritimum
Amarcrinum
Anthurium
Aphelandra
Begonia, fibrous rooted
Begonia, tuberous
Beloperone
Boston Daisy
Bougainvillea
Bouvardia
Cacti, and other Succulents
Callistephus chinensis
Centaurea cyanus
Chrysanthemum morifolium
Citrus
Columnea
Crossandra
Cyclamen
Dianthus caryophyllus
Episcia
Eucharis grandiflora
Eupatorium
Geranium
Gloxinia

Gypsophila
Haemanthus
Heliotrope
Hibiscus
Impatiens
Ixora
Jacobinia
Kalanchoe
Lantana
Nerine
Nierembergia frutescens
Orchids
Pentas
Petunia
Primula sinensis
Reinwardtia
Saintpaulia
Smithiantha
Sinningia speciosa
Solanum
Spathiphyllum
Strelitzia
Stephanotis floribunda
Swainsona
Tecomaria capensis
Vallota
Zinnia elegans
Zygocactus

GREENHOUSE PLANTS FOR SPRING FLOWERS

Abutilon
Acacia
Acalypha hispida
Achimenes
Aeschynanthus (Trichosporum)
Agapanthus
Ageratum
Alyssum maritimum
Amaryllis
Anthurium
Antirrhinum
Astilbe japonica
Azalea
Begonia, fibrous rooted
Beloperone
Bessera elegans
Boston Daisy
Bougainvillea
Brunsvigia
Cacti, and other Succulents
Calceolaria
Calendula officinalis

Godetia
Haemanthus
Heliotrope
Hibiscus
Hyacinthus
Hydrangea, Blue
Hydrangea, Pink
Iberis
Impatiens
Iris, Dutch
Ixia
Ixora
Jacobinia
Jasminum
Lachenalia
Lantana
Lathyrus odoratus
Lilium
Lobelia
Mathiola incana
Narcissus
Nemesia

Callistephus chinensis
Camellia
Capsicum
Centaurea cyanus
Chrysanthemum carinatum
Citrus
Clarkia elegans
Clematis
Clerodendrum
Clivia
Columnea
Crossandra
Crocus
Cyclamen
Cytisus canariensis
Daphne cneorum
Delphinium ajacis
Dianthus caryophyllus
Episcia
Erica
Eucharis grandiflora
Eucomis
Exacum
Felicia amelloides
Fuchsia
Gardenia
Gazania
Geranium
Gerbera jamesoni
Gladiolus
Gloriosa

Nicotiana
Nierembergia frutescens
Orchids
Ornithogalum
Osmanthus fragrans
Oxalis
Passiflora
Pentas
Petunia
Primula malacoides
Primula obconica
Rechsteineria
Roses
Saintpaulia
Salpiglossis
Schizanthus
Senecio cruentus
Spathiphyllum
Strelitzia
Stephanotis floribunda
Swainsona
Tagetes erecta
Trachymene caerulea
Tropaeolum
Tulip
Veltheimia
Viola tricolor
Zantedeschia
Zinnia elegans
Zygocactus

GREENHOUSE PLANTS FOR WINTER FLOWERS

Acalypha hispida
Ageratum
Alyssum maritimum
Amaryllis
Anemone
Anthurium
Antirrhinum
Azalea
Begonia, fibrous rooted
Begonia, semi-tuberous
Beloperone
Boston Daisy
Bougainvillea
Bouvardia
Browallia
Brunsvigia
Buddleja or Buddleia
Cacti, and other Succulents
Calendula officinalis
Callistephus chinensis
Camellia
Centaurea cyanus
Citrus

Impatiens
Iris, Dutch
Ixia
Ixora
Jacobinia
Kalanchoe
Lachenalia
Lantana
Lathyrus odoratus
Lilium
Mathiola incana
Myosotis
Narcissus
Nemesia
Nerine
Nicotiana
Nierembergia frutescens
Orchids
Osmanthus fragrans
Oxalis
Pentas
Petunia
Piqueria trinervia

Clivia
Columnea
Crossandra
Crocus
Cyclamen
Dianthus caryophyllus
Erica
Eucharis grandiflora
Eupatorium
Euphorbia fulgens
Euphorbia pulcherrima
Exacum
Felicia amelloides
Freesia
Geranium
Gerbera jamesoni
Godetia
Heliotrope
Hibiscus
Hyacinthus

Plumbago
Primula malacoides
Primula sinensis
Ranunculus
Rechsteineria
Reinwardtia
Roses
Saintpaulia
Smithiantha
Senecio cruentus
Solanum
Sparmannia
Swainsona
Tecomaria capensis
Trachymene caerulea
Tropaeolum
Tulip
Viola tricolor
Zantedeschia
Zygocactus

Appendix L

Suggested Plant Materials For A 10×16 Greenhouse

TIME: Labor Day   **MINIMUM NIGHTTIME TEMPERATURE: 55-60 degrees F.**

QUANTITY	NAME	HOW TO START
4 pots	**Salvia splendens** (flowering sage)	Dig compact specimens from the outdoor garden. Pot, and bring inside. Or, take tip cuttings of favorite colors and root in the greenhouse.
3 pots	Boston Daisy	Bring in compact plants from outdoors. Pot in 8-inch containers. OR root tip cuttings.
6 pots	Petunias	Select favorite colors outdoors. Dig, pot up, trim back to 6 inches.
4 pots	Nasturtiums	Plant 2 or 3 seeds in each of 4 pots. Later, thin to 1 in each.
12 pots	Dwarf marigolds	Dig and pot plants from outdoors. Remove long, straggly growth, but don't cut off too much as plants should be flower laden. OR, sow seeds.
1 flat	Larkspur	Sow seeds in 6-inch-deep flat. Thin to stand about 4 inches apart.
24 pots	Coleus	Buy packet of seeds, OR make cuttings of favorite kinds from the outdoor garden.
4 pots	Miniature roses	Buy plants from mail-order specialist OR dig and pot up from outdoor garden; cut back to 6 inches.
2 flats or 12 pots	Freesias	Plant 50 corms in flats, or pots. Keep in coolest part of of greenhouse, probably under the bench for at least 8 weeks. Then begin forcing, preferably one flat at a time, or a few pots, every 2 weeks.
12-16 pots	Impatiens	Make cuttings from plants outdoors. OR dig plants outdoors, pot up and bring inside for immediate color OR sow seeds.

12-16	Wax begonias	Make cuttings of plants outdoors; OR dig plants, pot up and bring inside for instant color.
3 baskets	Ivy geraniums	Use at least 9 cuttings from plants outdoors; OR buy 3 plants planting one to each basket.
3 pots	Cyclamen	Buy 3 well-started plants from florist or greenhouse. These will give a long season of bloom at low cost.
1 pot	Azalea	Buy from florist when buds are just beginning to open, probably Nov.
16 pots	Sweet alyssum	Sow seeds in 4-inch pots to border the bench.
16 pots	Ageratum	Dig plants outdoors; pot up, trim back to compactness. OR root cuttings. OR sow seeds. Use as bench bordering.
2 pots	Nicotiana (flowering tobacco)	Dig plants of compact, white-flowering variety from garden. Pot up. Allow flowering stalks to finish before cutting back to a few inches from soil. When you do cut back, new growth will come that will yield winter-spring flowers.
6 pots	**Centaurea cyanus** (bachelor's-button)	Sow a few seeds in several pots. Later thin to 1 or 2 in each.
1 flat	Godetia	Sow seeds in flat where they are to mature. After germination is complete, thin to 3 inches between seedlings.
2 flats	Schizanthus	Broadcast seeds in flats where they are to grow. Thin out to stand 3 or 4 inches apart.
8 pots	Sweet peas	Plant 3 seeds in each 6- to 8-inch pot, probably using a dwarf, bush type. Thin, leaving strongest plant in each pot.
16 pots	Chrysanthemums	Dig clumps of low-growing types in various stages of growth, bud and flower from garden. Pot up. OR buy plants at this stage from a local grower. OR purchase rooted cuttings from a specialist. (Ideally this should be done in the spring, selecting varieties with natural bloom in times varying from late August to Christmas.)
4 flats	Dwarf stock	Sow seeds in flats. Thin later to stand about 4 inches apart.
12 pots	Snapdragons	Dig clumps of vigorous plants from garden. Those in full bloom with lots of buds will put on quite a show in the greenhouse. Later, cut these back. New growth will give winter-spring flowers. OR, sow seeds now. Transplant first to individual 3-inch pots, then to 5's, finally to 8's. Stake.
9 pots	Geraniums	Dig, cut back and pot up plants from the garden. OR take cuttings of favorites, root now, pot up later. OR buy plants.
16 pots	English ivy	Use rooted cuttings from the garden, or buy selected types with smaller leaves for greenhouse use.
3 pots	Vinca, variegated	This periwinkle is useful for draping the edges of baskets, greenhouse benches, and window boxes.
12 pots	Lobelia	Dig, pot up, and trim back from the garden. OR sow seeds in one pot; transplant later.

Index